A Critical Analysis of the Efficacy of Law as a Tool to Achieve Gender Equality

Natalie Persadie

UNIVERSITY PRESS OF AMERICA, ® INC.
Lanham • Boulder • New York • Toronto • Plymouth, UK

University Press of America,® Inc.
4501 Forbes Boulevard
Suite 200
Lanham, Maryland 20706
UPA Acquisitions Department (301) 459-3366

Estover Road
Plymouth PL6 7PY
United Kingdom

Printed in the United States of America
British Library Cataloging in Publication Information Available

Library of Congress Control Number: 2011943275
ISBN: 978-0-7618-5809-6 (clothbound : alk. paper)
eISBN: 978-0-7618-5810-2

™ The paper used in this publication meets the minimum requirements of American National Standard for Information Sciences—Permanence of Paper for Printed Library Materials, ANSI Z39.48-1992

For

B

Contents

List of Figures

List of Tables

List of Cases

List of Constitutional Provisions

List of Statutory Instruments

Acknowledgments

This book is borne out of my doctoral thesis, a task which can never be accomplished in isolation. For this reason, I wish to acknowledge all those who were instrumental in helping me achieve this undertaking and make specific mention of those who were directly involved in the process.

To all those who were kind enough to share of their time and allow me to interview them:

Kelli Coombs, Natalie O'Brady of the Trinidad and Tobago Coalition Against Domestic Violence; Hazel Brown of the Network of NGOs of Trinidad and Tobago for the Advancement of Women; Jacquie Burgess of Women Working for Social Progress; Sylvia Brathwaite of Lifeline; Ivis Gibson of Families in Action; Cherisse Clarke, Lydia Walcott of the Rape Crisis Society; Prophet Dave Allen of Flaming Word Ministries; Rhonda de Freitas of the Legal Aid Clinic; Dave Berment of Men Against Violence Against Women; Sherla Gordon, Gemma Joseph, Allison Munroe, Anita Joseph of Women Against Abuse and Violent Encounters (Women's Support Group); Joyce Greyson of Goshen House; Sr. Jude-Marie Aird of Vision of Hope Halfway House; Joyce Blenman of Halfway House; Lydia Choate of Madinah House; Jennifer Talma and residents of The Shelter; Dr. Vishnu Jeelal of Hope Shelter for Battered Women and Children; Pundit Bramanand Rambachan of National Home for Family Reconciliation; Barbara Stewart, Sherma Joseph, Shirley Leith of Tobago Women's Enterprise for Empowerment and Rehabilitation Towards Self-Sufficiency; Eulah Marcell, Elaine Douglas, Bernice Butler of Patience Hill Women's Group; Inspector Glen Hackett, Acting Commissioner of Police Winston Cooper (even though we were never able to meet!) of the Trinidad and Tobago Police Service; Natalie Diop of Legal Aid and Advisory Authority.

To all those who assisted me in information gathering:

Various members of staff at the Center for Gender and Development Studies of the University of the West Indies; Geralde of the Caribbean Association for Feminist Research; Jacqueline Sargeant, Clerk of the Court of the Siparia Magistrate's Court; the Office of the Chief Justice, Michelle Austin, Administrative Secretary to the Chief Justice, Arnold Sealy, Area Court Manager, and Karen Nicholas, Deputy Court Statistician and others from the Statistical Unit, all of the Judiciary of Trinidad and Tobago; Rhonda Hogan and Hermian Findlay of the Gender Affairs Division of the Ministry of Community Development, Culture and Gender Affairs; Nafeesa Mohammed of the Ministry of Legal Affairs; Karen Ramlogan, Floris Fraser of the Main Library of the University of the West Indies.

To my supervisors, Jill and Rajendra:

The comments, guidance, and encouragement you provided during this process will never be forgotten. Thank you!

To my family and close friends — and new ones too!

It's been a long, hard road, but I finally made it! You believed in me when I could not do it myself. Your love, support, and encouragement saw me through this sometimes Herculean task. Thank you! ☺

With respect to copyright issues, I would like to note:

Figure 2.1 is reprinted with the permission of Universal Uclick.

Figures 4.1 and 4.2 are reproduced Courtesy of the University Libraries, The University of Texas at Austin.

Any errors are, of course, solely mine.

Abbreviations

BPFA	Beijing Platform for Action
CAFRA	Caribbean Association for Feminist Research and Action
CEDAW	Convention on the Elimination of All Forms of Discrimination against Women
CGDS	Centre for Gender and Development Studies
CIDA	Canadian International Development Agency
CIM	Inter-American Commission of Women
CSO	Civil Society Organisation
CSW	Commission on the Status of Women
DAW	Division for the Advancement of Women
DEDAW	Declaration on the Elimination of All Forms of Discrimination against Women
DEVAW	Declaration on the Elimination of Violence Against Women
DM	Dominica
ECOSOC	Economic and Social Council
GDI	Gender Development Index
GEM	Gender Empowerment Measure
INGO	International Non-Governmental Organisation
JLSC	Judicial and Legal Service Commission
MAVAW	Men Against Violence Against Women
NGO	Non-Governmental Organisation
PSC	Public Service Commission
PSIP	Public Sector Investment Programme
The Coalition	Trinidad and Tobago Coalition Against Domestic Violence

The Committee	Committee on the Elimination of Discrimination Against Women
The Network	The Network of NGOs of Trinidad and Tobago for the Advancement of Women
The Protocol	Optional Protocol to CEDAW
TT	Trinidad and Tobago
TTPS	Trinidad and Tobago Police Service
UN	United Nations
UNDP	United Nations Development Programme
UNICEF	United Nations Children Fund
WEDO	Women's Environment and Development Organization

Chapter One

Gender and the Law

1.1 GENDER AND THE LAW: WOMEN IN THE WEST

Gender issues have made their appearance from as early as the seventh century when women sought to reinterpret the scriptures which deemed women intellectually inferior by nature and given to sin.[1] Women fought for universal suffrage in the early 1900s and have constantly battled for equality and are still struggling even three centuries after the fact. The basis of the struggle for gender equality is firmly rooted in the notion that gender equality is a fundamental human right and also that women's rights are human rights. What exactly does equality on the basis of gender constitute?[2] For the purpose of this book, equality of opportunity (*de jure* or formal or abstract equality) and equality of outcome (*de facto* or substantive equality) are central to an understanding of gender equality.[3] Even where "formal" gender equality is guaranteed in national constitutions or legal systems which provide for *procedural* equality, there is a gap between this and *substantive* equality which takes into account the actual lived experiences, needs and interests of women.[4] An individual's right to equality should not include only notions of abstract equality but also substantive equality where he or she will necessarily have to be treated differently in order to protect his or her right to equality.[5]

Essentially, this book seeks to assess the strengths and weaknesses of both domestic and international law instruments with respect to concrete issues of gender inequality and specific areas of concern to women such as domestic violence. An examination of the scourge of domestic violence and its treatment in law and by governmental (and non-governmental) institutions indicates the importance given at the national level in addressing the problem and provides a somewhat albeit intangible indicator of the distance to be covered in getting to gender equality. Tackling the issue of domestic violence is paramount to the issue of gender equality as the achievement of substantive equality by women requires that the status of women within the private sphere—the primary site of domestic abuses—be addressed. There is no way that women can consider themselves to have attained equality, in practice or in law, if they are still in unequal power relationships at home that end in abuse of any kind.

The efforts of NGOs and other members of civil society are perhaps key in effecting positive legislative and social change. Traditional level of analysis discussions focus on the State and the international system as the main levels of analysis.[6] At the same time, however, the analysis of the State as a level contemplates individuals and institutions, such as NGOs, as having the capacity to inform and influence domestic policy, as well as national positions at international fora. Such power was clearly evidenced at Beijing in 1995. While NGOs are crucial to change, their ability to effect change depends on their degrees of political and financial independence and should, therefore, not be taken as given, as NGOs are generally required to promote the agendas of their sponsors. Achievements may be limited in some cases, but can provide entry into the male stronghold of legislative drafting, for example, by introducing clauses sensitive to women's needs. Enforcement, practical application of the law, and establishment of accompanying social infrastructure are, of course, entirely different issues.

Nations that resist gender equality in domestic practices can hardly be expected to fulfil international obligations seeking to accomplish gender parity. Ultimately, women must assume a greater role in the corridors of power and, perhaps, only then would there be greater effectiveness with respect to the emerging international legal regime for gender equality.[7] Greater female participation in the formulation of international law on gender equality, as well as the introduction of the gender perspective into the general international law making machinery, where appropriate, may just assist in making international law efforts more effective. This must of necessity be combined with the efforts of individuals and non-governmental organisations, as their work in effecting change at all levels should in no way be underestimated.

1.2 LAYING THE THEORETICAL FRAMEWORK: FEMINIST LEGAL THEORY AND FEMINIST CRITICAL THEORY

There are two main theoretical threads from which the fabric of this study is woven. These are feminist legal theory and feminist critical theory. Feminism provides the backdrop against which the issues of gender inequality and inadequate protection of the law for women against violence will be treated. Liberal feminism, in particular, advocates equal rights for women and examines why women are treated as "less than," where men provide the gauge against which they are measured. While liberal feminism addresses the issue of women's formal equality under the law, it has not fully considered issues of social power and women's social, legal and political under-representation in assessing the effectiveness of law as an instrument to advance the status of women or achieve social change more widely. Consequently, a combined theoretical approach is required. Liberal feminist thought, feminist legal theory and feminist critical theory provide the necessary theoretical bases to address not only gender inequality, but also illustrate the ways in which law may be implicated in the subordination of women, as well as empower women out of such positions of inferiority.

This book contemplates a critical assessment of law as an instrument to assist women in their fight for equality and protection of the law against domestic violence. Feminist legal theory, therefore, is necessary to expose the masculine nature of jurisprudential theory and practice which will in itself illustrate the difficulty of achieving gender justice in the absence of legal and institutional reform. This is still, however, not enough. Combining feminist legal theory, which exposes the male bias of law, with feminist critical theory, which offers a space from which women can "emancipate" themselves, allows a comprehensive process of reflection *and* emancipation. This framework illustrates that the very idea of rights, as currently obtains, is fundamentally conceptually flawed, as the concept of rights presupposes "man" as its subject, thereby completely bypassing women and other marginalised groups thereby perpetuating violence, discrimination and subordination of these "others." Feminist critical theory, together with feminist legal theory, is useful in the examination of these issues, as it can be used as a means of critiquing and then "rescuing" the idea of rights in favour of women by exposing its biased normative assumptions and politicised knowledge claims.

This combined theoretical framework, therefore, provides the setting against which legal and institutional structures in place for promoting gender equality and protection for women against domestic violence are examined. Moreover, such an analysis will ultimately reveal that these very structures continue to reinforce problems of gender inequality and inadequate protection against domestic violence.

1.3 GENDER

> One is not born, but rather becomes, a woman.[8]

The key concept in feminist thought is gender. It is, therefore, appropriate to first interrogate this concept. As elucidated by de Beauvoir's ever popu-

statement, feminist theorists understand the term gender not simply as physical, biological differences between males and females, but as "a set of culturally shaped and defined characteristics associated with masculinity and femininity."[9] This is in accordance with the definition set out in the United Nations' Implementation of the Outcome of the Fourth World Conference on Women,

> ...gender refers to the socially constructed roles played by women and men that are ascribed to them on the basis of their sex. Gender analysis is done in order to examine similarities and differences in roles and responsibilities between women and men without direct reference to biology, but rather to the behaviour patterns expected from women and men and their cultural reinforcement. These roles are usually specific to a given area and time, that is, since gender roles are contingent on the social and economic context, they can vary according to the specific context and can change over time. In terms of the use of language, the word "sex" is used to refer to physical and biological characteristics of women and men, while gender is used to refer to the explanations for observed differences between women and men based on socially assigned roles.[10]

Millett correctly reflected that "sex is biological, gender psychological, and therefore cultural."[11] Butler states that the original distinction between sex and gender was conceptualised with a view to disputing Freud's "biology-is-destiny formulation" and that the distinction "serves the argument that whatever biological intractability sex appears to have, gender is culturally constructed…."[12] Socio-cultural constructions of gender are reinforced by both sexes as they tend to deliver what they perceive as expected of them.[13] Critics claim, however, that *gender* is simply synonymous with *women/femininity*,[14] which is a terribly simplistic and uninformed viewpoint, as "gender" examines the social construction of gendered identities which includes both men and women, while "women/femininity" deals with the latter to the exclusion of the former and does not necessarily examine the latter's construction. Gender, then, is the result of a process of cultural socialisation and therefore varies across cultures. It refers to the "asymmetrical social constructs of masculinity and femininity as opposed to ostensibly 'biological' male-female differences."[15]

1.4 FEMINISM

1.4.1 What is Feminism?

> ...the male is by nature superior, and the female inferior; and the one rules, and the other is ruled; this principle, of necessity, extends to all mankind. Where

> there is such a difference as that between soul and body, or between man and animals…, the lower sort are by nature slaves, and it is better for them as for all inferiors that they should be under the rule of a master.[16] Aristotle (350 BCE).

> …there is no pursuit of the administrators of a state that belongs to a woman because she is a woman or to a man because he is a man. But the natural capacities are distributed alike among both creatures, and women naturally have a share in all pursuits and men in all….[17] Plato (427–347 BCE).

Broadly speaking, feminism can be simultaneously understood as theory and social movement, which can be aided by the theoretical component.[18] As theory, feminism may consist of "systems of concepts, propositions and analysis that describe and explain women's situations and experiences and support recommendations about how to improve them."[19] According to Randall, however, the best approach to defining feminism is a historical one. She states that, "[f]eminism emerged as a movement and body of ideas that aimed to enhance women's status and power. It called into question power relations between men and women that were conventionally defended as 'natural.'"[20] The whole nature/nurture debate has persisted for centuries, as illustrated in the above arguments, but it is now accepted (by feminists, at least) that the concept of gender is largely, if not, wholly, a socio-cultural phenomenon.[21] In other words, feminism called for equality between the sexes in economic, social, political, cultural, linguistic and legal spheres which was theorised on a notion of rights.[22]

Feminism should in no way, however, be understood as a monolithic ideology. As Chapman accurately notes, "differences in social and political context produce distinctly different forms of feminism,"[23] such as reflected in Nordic feminism, which is based on notions of social democracy; French feminism, which is rather philosophical (existential) in nature; and liberal and radical forms of feminism popular in the United States. On a micro level, the vast amount of theorising and debate has led feminism in myriad diverse directions,[24] so that even within each feminist school of thought there are conspicuous differences.[25]

1.4.2 The Historical Development of Feminism and Women's Human Rights

The development of feminist thought explicitly questions women's exclusion and marginalisation. The term "feminist" first came into use in English during the 1880s, indicating support for women's equal legal and political rights with men.[26] Feminism, the concept, is widely thought to have its roots in the Age of Enlightenment; however, Lerner has traced the earliest written expression of feminist consciousness all the way back to seventh century Europe, when women sought to reinterpret the scriptures which deemed women intellectually inferior by nature and given to sin.[27] By the beginning of the fifteenth century, feminism took root in liberalist thought. This era witnessed a European-wide public debate led by Christine de Pizan, known as the *Querelle des femmes* and which endured for some 300 years,[28] concerning the misogynistic portrayal of women in literature.

There were many influential writers during this period who believed that both men and women possessed a capacity for reason and true knowledge based on individual experience and self-discovery.[29] Descartes, François Poullain de la Barre, John Stuart Mill, Mary Astell, Catherine Macaulay[30] and Mary Wollstonecraft all believed that women were necessarily capable of reason and could participate equally in all spheres of life—social, economic, political, academic—and that their shortcomings were based entirely on the type of education they received.[31] Astell, however, was politically quite conservative and did not believe in the liberal idea of extending political rights to women, as she strongly believed in patriarchy and that a woman should be subject to the authority of her husband.[32] Mill, too, believed that women could equally partake in professional and political life, but there was one integral caveat: she must be able to successfully juggle her domestic responsibilities with any other she may choose to undertake.[33] While Mill obviously did not problematise the sexual division of labour and believed that only *exceptional* women would choose to compete in the work place,[34] he "implicitly challenge[d] the liberal concept of the public/private divide and the masculinist notions of politics upon which this divide rests."[35]

This period also saw the onset of the Industrial Revolution which brought with it changes in the traditional division of labour, which now became more complex and, according to Bryson, the creation of the distinction between the public and the private. During this change, women of the working class were progressively excluded from trades and professions they previously partook in and aristocratic women became restricted to the domestic sphere as they were no longer needed in the running of their husbands' estates. It was at this point that marriage became an economic necessity, as women became increasingly dependent on their husbands for financial support. Issues of unbalanced demography and religious reformation further complicated the situation and the role of women, now so profoundly altered, came into question.[36] Concurring with the emergence of a clearly delineated public/private realm was the increasing importance of the ancient concept of patriarchy. Historically, the rule of the king over his people was thought to be divinely sanctioned just as a father ruled over his family. Bryson states that patriarchy in the home was used as justification for a parallel power at the state level.[37]

This emergence of the modern secular State embeds, from its very inception, gendered beliefs privileging men, which were accepted as the natural order of things. The subordination of women within this arrangement continues to be of significance today.

1848 was the year of the very first women's rights convention, the Seneca Falls Convention, and was spurred on by the movement for the abolition of slavery across the Atlantic in the United States. A Declaration was issued at the end of the convention and was modelled on the 1776 United States Declaration of Independence. Participants of this convention demanded that the rights of women as bearers of rights in all spheres of life be acknowledged and respected by society. According to Bryson, the declaration laid the foundation for the structured emergence of feminism as a political movement and an ideology.[38]

1.4.2.1 First Wave Feminism

Spurred on by their disadvantaged social, economic and legal position, women formally sought redress. Thus began in the mid-late 19th century what is known as the first wave of feminism with women seeking formal equality in all spheres of life, including education and legal rights. By 1900, ideological differences in the movement (liberal, socialist, maternal) were overpowered by the growing agreement among those in the movement that the "success on key legal, educational and economic issues could not be gained without greater political leverage"[39] and it was at this point that the focus of the movement shifted and coalesced to that of achieving suffrage and political enfranchisement of women. Several achievements were gained when the vote was won in many countries by the 1920s. Educational opportunities expanded for English women, both married and unmarried women gained rights and improved maternity and child welfare in both England and the United States, and, most importantly, winning the vote helped in establishing the legitimacy of women's claim to equal treatment.[40] Notwithstanding these achievements, the patriarchal structures remained largely unchanged and "the ideas and the economic and political realities underpinning them retained their viability."[41] In any event, the energy required to fuel the drive for enfranchisement left the movement drained and the first wave of feminism receded.

1.4.2.2 Second Wave Feminism

Feminism regained its vigour and returned in the 1960s in its second wave.[42] Four main types of feminism emerged here: liberal, psychoanalytic, radical and Marxist/socialist.[43] Second wave liberal feminism, too, saw women questioning their role in society, given the increased production of labour-saving devices for the home and advances in contraceptive technology which bestowed upon women a sense of freedom—sexual, reproductive and otherwise.[44] This new wave was characterised by de Beauvoir's *The Second Sex*, Betty Friedan's *The Feminine Mystique*, Germaine Greer's *The Female Eunuch* and Juliet Mitchell's *Psychoanalysis and Feminism*, three of which focus on the psychological aspects of sex and gender. Women understood female subordination to be more than simply the effect of dominant political forces, but as endemic in all social relations with men.[45] The (initially) radical feminist slogan "the personal is political" was born in this period and brought to the fore the public/private divide, which, as noted earlier, has persisted since the onset of the Industrial Revolution. "The personal is political" "involves a recognition that private and public life interpenetrate in complex ways" and is certainly not immune from the dynamic of power.[46] As Green notes, "[p]ersonal problems are not only private idiosyncratic experiences but part of a social phenomenon amenable to political analysis" and cites the example of both child and spousal abuse which require social and political action for their elimination.[47]

A liberalist notion, the public/private dichotomy refers to both the distinction between State and society, as well as between non-domestic and domestic life. Okin goes on to make the point that, in both dichotomies, the "state is (paradigmatically) public, and the family, domestic, and intimate life are (again paradigmatically) private."[48] The importance of this binary[49] relation to feminist theory is that the notion of privacy has always been bestowed upon *man* as the holder of rights to be free from any State (or church) intervention in the running of his household and in controlling the members of his private sphere.[50] According to MacKinnon, "The liberal state coercively and authoritatively constitutes the social order in the interest of men as a gender—through its legitimating norms... and substantive policies."[51] She also asserts that "[t]he state is jurisprudentially male, meaning that it adopts the standpoint of male power on the relation between law and society...[as] the state, through law, institutionalizes male power over women through institutionalizing the male point of view in law."[52] This point is clearly illustrated in Blackstone's infamous legal interpretation of the status of married women where they were denied legal and civil rights, deemed to be incapable of political activity, and could only be represented by their husband or father.[53] Moreover, the State continues to maintain the distinction between the private and the public, as the legal right to privacy depends on government support.[54] Man's right to privacy, therefore, has justified the State's inaction (deemed to be a reflection of male interests) in the face of abuses that are perpetrated within the home, as it is not the State's place to interfere with what takes place in *his* private realm.[55]

Equality has always been a cornerstone of liberalist thought and it is, therefore, no surprise that liberal feminists also stress the importance of sexual equality, or as it is contemporarily known, gender justice, which is perhaps the single most important goal of women's liberation.[56] But what exactly does sexual equality mean? Since the beginning of liberal feminist discourse, women have advocated equality on the basis that women possess the same capabilities as men but simply need to have similar access to opportunities in order to realise these capabilities. Equality in liberal feminist terms, according to Evans, means equality in the sense of sameness of attainment, and, therefore, treatment, and justifies it via sameness or androgyny.[57] Paradoxically, as Scott correctly notes, "in order to protest women's exclusion, they [feminists] had to act on behalf of women and so invoked the very difference they sought to deny."[58] This issue of equality will be dealt with in greater detail in the section below on feminist legal theory.

1.4.2.3 "Other" Feminisms

Critiques levelled against liberal feminism (as well as the others) were based largely on their exclusionary nature. They were all charged as being inadvertently classist, racist and (hetero)sexist, assuming middle-upper class, college-educated, married, white women to be the only affected groups.[59] While deemed a useful exercise in the study of sex discrimination against one group, it may also be seen as a "case study of narcissism, insensitivity, sentimentality, and self-indulgence."[60] It had the inevitable effect of producing feminist scholarship from the margins to refute the universalising claims made by white feminists who spoke as if for all women,[61] reflecting the divergent historical-political circumstances of each type.[62] While the various criticisms are acknowledged, liberal feminism makes a clarion call for gender equality regardless of individual contexts and provides a useful starting point, together with feminist legal theory and feminist critical theory, to examine law as a potentially valuable, though not unproblematic, instrument to promote gender equality.

While liberal feminists can be criticised for not questioning the male bias in rights discourse and practice, but have merely sought to extend "male rights" to women, this does not invalidate a rights agenda as a tool that can be used to promote the status of women, or even achieve an emancipatory end. Feminist theorists, such as Benhabib, have embraced critical theory because it holds out the possibility of rescuing a universal and emancipatory project for feminism. What is universal, however, is determined not by reference to a posited transcendental subject/subjectivity, as in liberalism, but is inter-subjectively constituted through dialogue. For example, the NGO forum at Beijing can be presented as one such forum for debate and dialogue on women's rights. Here, activists question the meaning and limitation of rights and which rights are women's rights. In this way, the substantive meaning of rights has been transformed to better fit the needs of women. Of course, NGO forums are far from "ideal speech situations," but, nevertheless, represent a "best practice" subject to further improvement vis-à-vis access and inclusion.[63]

Critical (and other) theorists claim that legal scholarship is elitist. For them, the production of knowledge "is in itself a historical process which is conditioned by the socio-political, economic and cultural context in which it is constructed."[64] Critical theorists argue that the production of knowledge is integrally related to power and serves particular interests,[65] where power is associated with the male and masculinity. The power associated with the male and masculinity is underpinned by many factors, one of which is the legal system. It is important, therefore, to develop an understanding of how the law functions to support the power of the male elite and to determine how the assessment of the law can be used to both expose its male bias and posit the gender equality sought by women as part of their fundamental rights. The notion of the relationship between knowledge and power is also a critical component of feminist legal theory.

1.5 FEMINIST LEGAL THEORY: WHERE DO WOMEN FIGURE?

Feminist legal theory, or feminist jurisprudence, came about in the 1980s "out of a political concern for the ways in which law may be implicated in women's subordination."[66] It may be defined very broadly as "the study of the relationship between women and the law"[67] which exposes the male bias of law.[68] West makes the point that

> [j]urisprudence is "masculine" because jurisprudence is about the relationship between human beings and the laws we actually have, and the laws we actually have are "masculine" both in terms of their intended beneficiary and in authorship.[69]

West identifies two main projects of feminist legal theory, the first of which is the "unmasking and critiquing of the patriarchy behind purportedly ungendered law and theory," or uncovering "patriarchal jurisprudence."[70] The second project entails "reconstructive jurisprudence," or feminist law reform in areas such as rape, sexual harassment, discriminatory employment practices and reproductive freedom.

Feminist legal theory is multidisciplinary in its approach and draws upon the lived experiences of women. The critical perspectives developed from the other disciplines help to offer "powerful analyses of the relationship between law and gender and new understandings of the limits of, and opportunities for, legal reform."[71] As such, "[f]eminist legal theory does not constitute a unified body of knowledge or a set of universal concerns or perspectives, but is shaped by different political agendas and institutional frameworks occurring within particular societies."[72]

1.5.1 Feminist Legal Theory: The Early Years

As seen in the above section on the historical development of feminism, women were denied legal subjectivity for centuries, especially when Blackstone conferred "civil and legal death" on (married) women. It is not surprising, therefore, that the feminist critique on legal subjectivity suggests that it "is a site of violent sexual exclusion."[73] In their quest for legal rights, then, recognition as a juridical person was the first step to be taken.[74] In the (in) famous 1873 case of *Jex-blake v Senatus of Edinburgh University*,[75] a group of female medical students was denied the possibility of graduating upon successful completion of their examinations on the basis of "strict legal grounds."[76] Lord Neaves stated in his opinion that the founding of (Scottish) Universities was for the education of young men and that "while males have a right to University education, females have none…."[77] While the University regulations were amended four years earlier to allow admission to women to the study of medicine, the court held that these regulations were "wholly illegal, and palpably beyond the statutory power conferred upon the University Courts."[78] Unfortunately, the Court was of the belief that granting a decision in favour of the pursuers "would incur the risk of lowering the standard"[79] which the medical profession enjoyed at the time. An immediate problem that stems from such a judgement is that not only are women deemed to be physically and intellectually inferior to men, but, as a judicial pronouncement, such stereotyping gains legal authority.[80]

The legal fight for women included their wish to be understood as legal persons, as "persons" or "man" did not include "woman" in its interpretation. In a 1930 Privy Council judgement, the interpretation of "persons" was expanded to include "woman" on the basis of changing legal customs. In Lord Sankey's judgement, he ascribed the prior exclusion of women from the interpretation of "person" to the fact that women were formerly deemed legally incapable at common law of serving in public office. He dismissed this practice as a "relic of days more barbarous than ours."[81] Should any subsequent interpretation of "person" in fact exclude women, it should be stated expressly by Parliament that such is the intention.

Interestingly, the earliest use of the word "person" has been traced to Greek and Roman times in its use in drama. *Persona* originally referred to the mask that actors wore on stage and later meant the part played by a man in life. Later still, the meaning was refined to refer to man himself and, then, to its contemporary use in law, to mean a right-bearing being.[82] It is instructive to note that early Greek and Roman theatre expressly banned women from performing; therefore, only men could have been referred to as "persons" in this context.[83] Perhaps this meaning persisted in denying women legal capacity as the term gained currency in legal jargon.

1.5.2 Feminist Legal Theory: The Public/Private Divide

Overcoming the public/private divide remains of very high importance to women.[84] As mentioned above, this divide holds great implications for women as the private, in this case, the sphere of domesticity, which encompasses the site of the family, reproduction and sexuality, is deemed to be outside the scope of legal regulation and State intervention.[85] This means that the site of the family is a site of tremendous near-unregulated violence against women and children, as the law affords women little, if any, legal protection against such abuses. It is for this reason that "feminism has had to explode the private" and sees the personal as political.[86] While there has been legal reform to accommodate sexual reproductive freedom and violence-free homes, there also needs to be greater understanding and compassion on the part of those in authority in order to help make these reforms effective. Bridgeman and Millns correctly state that "[c]ontraception has to be safe, effective and acceptable; abortion services free [and legalised] and non-judgmental; and violence within the home has to be treated as a serious crime by law enforcement agencies."[87] They also note that an issue may go unregulated if the law does not recognise a particular wrong against women as actual harm, such as certain types of cosmetic surgery,[88] or if it simply privatises the issue, as is common in cases of domestic violence. The enactment of legislation in such areas has caused the line between the public and the private to blur somewhat; although, sadly, such enactment does not necessarily afford women the protection stated in the legislation, as it tends to remain unimplemented for a variety of reasons.

Beveridge and Mullally argue that the exclusion of the private sphere from the application of rights is based on a pre-liberal notion of the "naturalness" of the traditional family.[89] According to these authors, the traditional family is seen as a bastion of civilisation and a precondition for social stability and is thus immune to judicial reform. It would appear that rights has been unable to contemplate the notion of separate spheres of justice and, consequently, only deals with issues stemming from the public sphere. Legal recognition of the right to privacy has only aggravated the situation, as mentioned above. Unfortunately, this dichotomy exists at the international level as well. International human rights law reflects this gendered approach by focusing on direct State violations of individual rights;[90] therefore, the harms suffered by women from private individuals or within the family lie outside of the conceptual framework of international human rights in the same manner as they do within the State apparatus.

1.5.3 Feminist Legal Theory: The Equality Project

> [T]he master's tools will never dismantle the master's house.[91]
>
> —Audre Lorde

Feminist legal theory as a means of improving the status of women is certainly not without its criticisms. The very fact of using law as a means to emancipate women causes concern. Lacey asks: "Is there a certain paradox to finding this apparent germ of emancipation of gender justice in the very body [law] which has been the object of the denigration of women?"[92] The very androcentric nature of law makes it difficult for some to understand the use of law by feminists as the conceptual (legal) framework for promoting women's interests. Smart observes "that law is so deaf to core concerns of feminism that feminists should be extremely cautious of how and whether they resort to law" and that generally we "need to be far more aware of the 'malevolence' of law and the depth of its resistance to women's concerns."[93] This notwithstanding there must be some framework from which to work. To completely reconstruct law to highlight feminist concerns may not be a feasible approach. Given the fact that law in itself has marginalised and penalised women on the basis of their gender and the fact that law's creators are male and seek their own interests, why not begin from there?

There are those who think that diversifying the male character of the judiciary will necessarily improve the quality of justice dispensed, as women will bring different perceptions to the adjudication table. It is also argued that women's absence from the process of decision-making in public bodies undermines the democratic legitimacy of those institutions.[94] The Courts also seem to be of this opinion.[95] There seems to be a misguided presumption that securing a greater presence of female lawyers and judges will help to transform the legal system away from formalism, objectivity, universalism and adversarial methods of conflict resolution towards "the subjective needs of individuals and a greater use of alternative dispute resolution such as mediation."[96] While this may be true in some cases,[97] this will not necessarily hold for all. It has been consistently argued that the legal tradition is masculine in nature.[98] Could it not be true to an extent to say that female lawyers/judges would be socialised to think and behave in a masculine manner and adopt masculine logic as well?[99] This is of course not to say that all women would do so; however, "the type of women who currently succeed in the male-dominated legal world are, by definition, atypical of most women."[100]

Feminist legal theory has also been accused of uncritically accepting the masculine nature of law as the standard by which feminist issues must be measured.[101] Law's masculinity is not problematised, but accepted as universal and transhistorical and applied as is to women. This is particularly the case in the rights debate concerning equal/special treatment. With one foot inside, having been accepted as "persons," the next step for women was a fight for equality. As mentioned above, women's struggle for equality meant that there was some measure against which women were gauging themselves. Difference in the equality debate refers to women's differences from men, "with a clear, implicit acceptance of men as the norm and women as the deviators therefrom."[102] Equality in this sense meant that women were to be treated as identical to men and denied their natural, biological differences and complexities.

This particular sense of equality has led to what can only be referred to as legal absurdities, as the law sought to treat men and women on an equal basis. Nash makes the point that equality is problematic as it reproduces a male norm, both in terms of the content of the law and its form.[103] Sex discrimination legislation uses a "male comparator" test, which, by the very name, affirms Nash's statement.[104] This test requires a woman to prove discrimination by showing that she has been treated less favourably than a man would have been had he been in a comparable situation. Pregnant women have found it necessary to liken female pregnancy, a natural process, to male sickness in order to draw a parallel. How can this be, given that *only* women can possibly become pregnant? Moreover, pregnancy is not a sickness. Pregnancy is specific to women and to describe it in gender-neutral terms is to capitulate to the male norm.[105]

Such occurrences have led to a division in the equality camp, with some feminists advocating equal rights based on the male comparator test to afford them the ability to compete on equal terms with men, which, of course, completely denies their differences; while on the other side are the difference feminists who embrace women's difference and simply want the right to be as *free* as men, yet to be themselves.[106] Nash asks whether the women's movement should focus on rights for women to be treated the same as men or on gender-specific rights, enabling women's differences from men to be valued and taken into account as the means of gaining genuine equality between the sexes.[107] While the latter may appear to be the more desirable option, Sohrab articulates quite clearly the fallacy of having to choose one or the other. She advocates an integrated approach and says,

> The perceived necessity of making a choice between equal or special treatment is a false choice. In some areas equal rights are necessary, while in others it is gender-specific rights that are necessary, for instance in pregnancy. Neither approach is, nor should be, the exclusive 'answer' or strategy or claim, and arguing over substantive equality by opposing equal with special and vice-versa is at best redundant and at worst a costly distraction.[108]

This is complicated by issues of race, nationality and class[109] and is clearly illustrated in the case of *Betty Dukes and ors v Wal-Mart Stores, Inc*. It is interesting to note that sexual equality is still not to be had and worse, complicated by such issues, not even in a country based on a natural rights tradition and that prides itself on the feminist notion of "equality of opportunity" and has anti-discrimination, equal rights and equal pay legislation. In what was described as the "biggest civil rights lawsuit in US history,"[110] Wal-Mart was sued for sexual discrimination despite investing heavily in branding itself "a haven for women."[111] According to the plaintiffs, the discriminatory practices were "the result of an on-going and continuous pattern and practice of intentional sex discrimination in assignments, pay, training and promotions, and reliance on policies and practices that have an adverse impact on female employees that cannot be justified by business necessity…."[112] The fact that the main plaintiff is of African–American descent necessarily adds a racial slant to the case.

Many feminists argue for a politics of difference, as denying differences between the sexes can have perverse effects. Phillips makes the point that, in the absence of sex-specific legislation to deal with pregnancy and maternity leave, women enter the labour market at a disadvantage. "The refusal to recognise difference," she says, "can become a covert way of elevating one group alone as the norm. Men then stand in for humanity, and humanity adopts a masculine form."[113] Palmer concurs on this point and, in her critique on equal rights, adds that, even though women may have a claim to formal rights, the structural inequalities of power are likely to remain unchanged. She raises as a primary concern the possibility that "rights may be appropriated by the powerful and women's concerns will continue to be marginalized."[114] She also states that formal equality for women affect their ability to claim for substantive rights, as gender can no longer be problematised. "Formal equality in the law means that gender as an explicit category of political decision and distribution has been dismantled with the subsequent loss of its critical foothold."[115] Equality in this guise only benefits women who adopt male norms.

Rhode observes that the issue at hand is not difference *per se* "but the difference difference makes,"[116] if it does in fact make one. She states that "analysis should turn on whether legal recognition of gender distinctions is likely to reduce or reinforce gender disparities in power, status, and economic security."[117] Scales observes that "[i]njustice does not flow directly from recognizing differences; injustice results when those differences are transformed into social and economic deprivation."[118] For Littleton, the difference that difference makes should not be such that it adversely affects the unprivileged group. In her "equality as acceptance" model, she proposes that "*[t]he difference between human beings, whether perceived or real, and whether biologically or socially based, should not be permitted to make a difference in the lived-out equality of those persons*."[119] In other words, differences, real or perceived, should not be penalised on any basis.

The South African Courts have adopted an interesting model of equality jurisprudence, which could perhaps serve as a model to be emulated and improved. Based on section 9 of the Constitution of South Africa, which protects an individual's right to equality, the Courts understand this to include not just notions of abstract equality, but also substantive equality.[120] A court will hold that there are instances in which an individual must be treated differently in order to protect his or her right to equality. Van Marle states, "An approach based on substantive equality takes the concrete circumstances of an individual into account in contrast to a formal abstract approach based on sameness."[121] In the case of *President of the Republic of South Africa and another v Hugo*,[122] Hugo was imprisoned when the President at the time, Nelson Mandela, pardoned certain categories of prisoners by the *Presidential Act* 17 of 1994, one of which was all women in prison on 10 May 1994 who were single mothers of children below the age of twelve. Hugo applied for an order to have the act declared unconstitutional on the basis of reverse discrimination on the basis of gender. While the court held that Hugo was in fact discriminated against, said discrimination was not unfair because "he, as a man, was not a member of a group that had previously suffered from discrimination" and that the reality of that time and foreseeable future was that mothers would bear primary child-rearing responsibility. Admittedly, this reinforces certain stereotypes, but simultaneously benefited a particular group in a very material way.[123]

In postmodernist terms, feminist legal theorists, in exposing the androcentrism of law,[124] are accused of seeking simply to substitute their truth claims as preferable and better than other truths,[125] which still fails to deal with the issue of gender bias. The difference, though, is that the masculine truth claims have greater effect as they are deeply embedded in the system as truth and have the advantage of exercising power in a society that values this particular notion of truth. The value placed on certain notions of truth by a society is such that it can deny the possibility of other truth claims[126] and, in this case, it is feminist truth claims that are being denied.

Another postmodern critique is the use by some feminists of universalising, totalising theorising, thereby reducing all aspects of women's oppression to one or two main factors. This is one of the main criticisms laid against MacKinnon's radical offering on feminist legal theory. She claims that "the fatal error of the legal arm of feminism had been its failure to understand that the mainspring of sex inequality is misogyny and the mainspring of misogyny is sexual sadism."[127] Nevertheless, while her theoretical analysis may appear myopic in reducing women's oppression solely to their sexual objectification by men, her legal strategies for fighting pornography and sexual harassment have had the effect of empowering women (and men).[128] Lacey also notes that "MacKinnon's campaign to have sexual harassment recognised as a legal wrong has been an important and in many ways effective feminist strategy."[129]

While closing the gap between formal rights and substantive rights within such a conceptual framework poses a problem, many feminists believe that formal legal equality is no longer much of an issue. These feminists remain concerned that it does not give rise to the substantive equality that women need to reflect the reality of their life experiences. However, Kingdom makes a fourfold argument on the issue of rights for women.[130] Firstly, despite the disenchantment and scepticism born out of equality legislation, equal rights must be sustained. Poor legislative drafting or sexist judiciaries need to be continuously battled against with pressure for legislative reform, better enforcement and public awareness campaigns. Secondly, there are those feminists who believe in putting their efforts into extra-legal strategies which they believe are not tainted by male power, such as the establishment of rape crisis centres. Thirdly, while the gap between formal legal equality and substantive equality is not disputed, law should not be read as gender neutral; however, "it is important to distinguish between the law and the *effects* of law and legal processes in order to identify the contradictions which allow space for change."[131] Fourthly, supporters of special rights see the answer in the redefinition of the moral principle of gender equality in a manner which combines equal rights and special rights and which must be translated into law.

Notwithstanding criticisms of feminist legal theory (and there are more), feminist legal theory offers a glimmer of hope yet. To quote Smart,

> The idea of a feminist jurisprudence is tantalizing in that it appears to hold out the promise of a fully integrated theoretical framework and political practice which will be transformative, unlike the partial or liberal measures of the past which have merely ameliorated or mollified women's oppression (e.g. equal pay legislation). It promises a general theory of law which has practical applications. Because it appears to offer the combination of theory and practice, and because it will be grounded in women's experience, the ideal of a feminist jurisprudence appears to be a way out of the impasse of liberal feminist theories of law reform... While it is the case that law does not hold the key to unlock patriarchy, it provides a forum for articulating alternative visions and accounts.[132]

Having acknowledged that the law is part of the structure that maintains the power of men and restricts women from fully enjoying their fundamental rights, including that of gender equality, it is important for women not only to expose the male bias in the law but also to use that exposure to ensure the reconstruction of the law in a manner that will lead to gender equality. It is important therefore to use a combined theoretical approach, relying on both feminist legal theory and critical theory to uncover inherent biases as a means of offering hope to women in accessing and securing rights. Feminist legal theory is very much aligned with the goal of critical theory, which is to question historically given truths and to expose the inherent biases lying therein as a means for self-advancement; it is for this reason important that the theoretical approach be combined to discuss the possibility of women gaining greater access to the rights that are theirs.

1.6 CRITICAL THEORY AND FEMINISM

The underlying purpose of this study is to critically assess the efficacy of law as a tool to achieve gender equality and to address the problem of domestic violence. This necessarily requires that the male–centred nature of law, with reference to the human rights of women and in particular those just mentioned, be interrogated. Critical theory, together with feminist legal theory, is useful in the examination of these issues, as it can be used as a means of critiquing and then "rescuing" the idea of human rights in favour of women by exposing its biased normative assumptions and politicised knowledge claims.

Figure 1.1. "Knowledge is Paralysing." Musings of a wise-beyond-his-years six year old fictional character, Calvin, to his stuffed toy and constant companion, Hobbes. CALVIN AND HOBBES © 1993 Watterson. Dist. By UNIVERSAL UCLICK. Reprinted with permission. All rights reserved.

Benhabib very nicely states the key role of the feminist critical theorist by acknowledging that,

> the historically known gender-sex systems have contributed to the oppression and exploitation of women. The task of the feminist critical theorist is to uncover this fact, and to develop a theory that is emancipatory and reflective, and which can aid women in their struggles to overcome oppression and exploitation.[133]

Theorising, however, is not enough. Feminist theory must translate into feminist politics/practice/activism for it to positively affect women's lives. Naples cites, as an example, the "development and expansion of battered women's shelters and rape crisis centers" as testimony to the success of feminist political activism.[134] This holds true for Trinidad and Tobago as well, as shelters were established and many groups dedicated to dealing with the problem of domestic violence became operational during the 1980s and 1990s when feminist political activism gained currency. According to Naples, battered women's shelters and rape crisis centres provide a site for organised public advocacy, community education, and crisis intervention on behalf of battered women. They also provide a place where incest survivors, rape victims and children, and other abuse survivors find political allies and support services. Without feminist activism, therefore, these services would not be available to those in need.

In a study on the women's movement in India, Menon makes the point that "there is no alternative to political activism, *equality cannot be legislated into existence*."[135] A case study of Trinidad and Tobago illustrates exactly this point: without feminist intervention, changes cannot be effected. Even with legislative victories, enforcement and implementation require further effort from the ground level. Clauses promoting equality do not always have the intended automatic effect. The struggle, unfortunately, does not end at legislative reform, but must continue on to ensure that such changes are made effective taking into account the situated and lived realities for those whom such changes are meant to benefit. Feminist activism is crucial in this regard to ensure real change at all levels.

Critical theorists emphasise the intimate relationship between theory and practice/praxis. This is appealing to feminists who seek to employ feminist theory in the service of advancing feminist political goals on the ground, so to speak. Theory is more than critique; it serves specific interests in concrete political struggles. Moreover, theory is not merely an abstract activity carried out by ivory tower academics, but is forged in and through practice. Thus, in understanding the emancipatory potential of law, one has to look at what activists have done with it. That is to say, it is necessary to interrogate the way in which activists at the UN, or on the ground in Trinidad and Tobago, have used legal discourse and legal instruments to effect political and social change. There might be emancipatory potential in legal discourses and instruments even if they were indeed originally the "tools of the master."[136]

Linklater identifies what he considers to be the achievements of critical theory. The first, and most important, deals with the political nature of knowledge claims given that "knowledge does not arise from the subject's neutral engagement with an objective reality but reflects pre-existing social purposes and interests."[137] Critical theory further refutes the positivist claim that statements of fact are only valid when grounded in experience; however, the perspective of the researcher contains "blind spots, tacit presuppositions, and prejudgements of which the [researcher] is unaware."[138] "Because cognition is always theoretically mediated," says Hawkesworth, "the world captured in human knowledge and designated "empirical" is itself theoretically constituted."[139] It is within this framework that legal and human rights discourses have been conceptualised, not acknowledging the inherently androcentric claims purporting to be universal.

This critique of knowledge holds great implications for the notion of rights. The traditional representation of rights in the various discourses, most notably liberalism, is identified with rights applicable to men as "citizens," as only "citizens" could be the valid holder of rights. Rights as applied to men then become unproblematically "human" with no regard given to women's specificities or their original exclusion. While there have been Marxist and cultural relativist critiques of the liberal notion of rights, for example, this was still done from the perspectives of men. It was only with feminist intervention that the male biases in knowledge construction, such as the construction of human rights discourses, have been exposed and illustrated women's exclusion. According to Benhabib's definition above, task number one—uncovering biases—is complete.

Critical theory, like other theories, does not present one unified position but has certain common ideological assumptions, among which include the ideas of reflection, societal transformation and emancipation of the individual. It is not simply about reproducing society, but understanding the oppressive nature of social structures and seeking to overcome and transform them. According to Hoffman, critical theory is "not merely an expression of the concrete realities of the historical situation, but also a force for change within those conditions."[140] Given that critical theory is politically and ethically driven by an interest in social and political transformation, critical theory is most certainly not neutral.[141] Devetak asserts that "[i]t criticizes and debunks theories that legitimise the prevailing order and affirms progressive alternatives that promote emancipation."[142] Linklater notes that the concept of emancipation distinguishes Marxist critical theory from postmodernist critical theory.[143]

While knowledge can indeed have a paralytic and overwhelming effect for some, as noted above, critical theorists view knowledge as a means of empowerment and, ultimately, as a means of liberation. Critical theorists believe that knowledge is historically rooted and interest bound but its emancipatory project envisages independent and critical thinking by individuals to understand hegemonic discourses, criticise them and eventually overcome them in their struggle to free themselves from the oppressive and subordinating nature of such discourses. This is important, as emancipation must have the effect of both freeing *and* enfranchising its former prisoners.[144] The goal here reflects the emancipatory intent of feminism. It is not simply about critiquing rights and remaining content with the menu of rights currently available to women (such as the right to vote), but expanding the content of substantive rights to address areas that were previously invisible, such as protection against domestic violence. This is recognised at the international level as well, as evidenced by Recommendation 19 of 1992 on the UN Convention on the Elimination of All Forms of Discrimination Against Women. However, implementation of measures geared towards the expansion of the content of substantive rights, such as dealing with domestic violence, is met with difficulty, particularly in the national environment. Trinidad and Tobago is a case in point, the main issue being deeply culturally entrenched notions of masculinity and the difficulties of overcoming the need to exhibit machismo, one such exhibition being spousal abuse despite laws criminalising such behaviour.

Can rights as an issue then ever be deemed objective? Popper says that "the *objectivity* of scientific statements lies in the fact that they can be *inter-subjectively* tested."[145] The problem with objectivity borne of an intersubjectively achieved consensus is that the "intersubjectivity" is often exclusionary.[146] Take human rights discourses for example. These discourses are espoused by men for men which then parade as "human"; there is no input by those who are most adversely affected, thereby taking away from the truly intersubjective nature of the discourse. Women have historically been excluded on the basis of intellectual inferiority and relegation to the "private" sphere. Their relegation to the private side of the divide has meant that their concerns have had no place in discourses that take place in the public sphere. Women's inability to access spaces where debates take place, such as at the UN, further compounds their exclusion. Even though in Trinidad and Tobago women may have some government representatives in the form of a Prime Minister and Members of Parliament, this does not guarantee that their concerns will be given priority, as economic development is at the top of the government agenda and government is overwhelmingly masculine in number and in the concerns that receive greatest attention. Unsurprisingly, female Ministers of Parliament have been relegated to ministries dealing with what are perceived to be non-economic aspects of development, such as women's affairs, culture, education and the environment.[147] Unfortunately, as long as the majority, or a powerful elite (in this case, men), holds an idea to be true,[148] then it must be so, as the powerless (in this case, women) are generally voiceless and/or lack the intellectual means to know otherwise—this is how hegemonic discourses gain currency and maintain their grip as objective and as "the truth."

A similar position is held concerning legal scholarship. It is said that critical theory, in particular the Frankfurt School, has had little influence on legal scholarship;[149] however, it is agreed that legal discourse, as with all other discourses, is the result of power relationships in society. "Law exists to support the interests of the party or class that forms it and is merely a collection of beliefs and prejudices that legitimise the injustices of society. The wealthy and the powerful use law as an instrument for oppression in order to maintain their place in hierarchy."[150] The exclusionary and biased character of law cannot be denied and is pertinent to both domestic law and international law. This has implications for all minority, voiceless groups and it will be shown later on, with particular reference to women, how human rights legal discourse privileges men as the advocates of said discourse and take into very little consideration the needs of women. For human rights discourses, a critical reflection on the subject of human rights would include women and examine their marginalisation from the discourse as it currently obtains. It can very easily be argued that human rights discourse is an exemplary case of a skewed power relationship—espoused by men, for men. This is not surprising, as discourses are merely "efforts to provide reasons or justifications for any kinds of knowledge claims"[151] and generally tend to be biased.[152]

On a more general level, post-modernists attack critical theory's project of emancipation as being "logocentric[153] and humanist, [they] criticize its emphasis on the societal totality at the expense of *le quotidian* (the local or daily life), and consider the critical theorist's search for truth to be naïve."[154] Critical theorists' immediate rebuttal is that post-modernism's need for deconstruction[155] is *destructive*, as it does not *construct* knowledge, to which post-modernists argue that they never made any pretence to theory building.[156] Nevertheless, it must be borne in mind that theories produced in the social sciences will always be less than perfect compared to theories of the natural sciences which can be tested.[157] In any event, critical theory offers a space to feminists to explore male biases in the law and then rescue the notion of rights to include women as well.

1.7 CONCLUSION

A common link in the different manifestations of feminist theorising is that of gender equality and reasons for women's subordination. Feminist legal theory, one such manifestation, is significant because the law represents a major component of the social fabric and an underlying mechanism for attaining gender equality. Not only is the law important at the national level, but also at the international level, as international law is seen as the primary mechanism for ensuring that States comply with their global pronouncements. The application of feminist legal theory, therefore, to the domestic legal regime of Trinidad and Tobago exposes the gender bias in the law while illustrating how legal principles might be employed towards the attainment of gender equality.

Critical theory provides a space for women to understand and overcome the oppression they face through their own struggles. The difficulties experienced by the international community to forge effective legal instruments that promote gender equality, where such legal instruments are negotiated to have States accept the obligations contained therein and to introduce same in domestic legal systems, continue to resonate in debates at the international level. Even when nations accept certain international instruments that promote gender equality, such States have to be constantly reminded to meet their international legal obligations.

It is within this combined feminist, legal and critical theoretical framework that the information presented in the rest of this study will be couched. The analysis above clearly illustrates the male bias intrinsic to legal discourses generally, as well as specifically, as applied to women in the rights debate. This is further exacerbated by the ability of the powerful to espouse their truth claims as knowledge and Truth, making it difficult for alternative versions to gain currency.

Chapter two will examine the machinations of male bias at the international level, with particular reference to international law, international relations and international human rights discourses and the consequent marginalisation of women. This is important as the effectiveness of the "top-down"[158] approach in dealing with human rights for women must be properly scrutinised. The real issue to be determined is the effectiveness of the international community as an agent of change with respect to gender equality, particularly in the context of developing countries that dominate the international stage from a numerical standpoint and where gender equality is largely subjected to the whims and fancies of the male elite. Power and knowledge reside in the male elite and therefore it is not in its interest to voluntarily subscribe to a view that would promote the interest of the non-elite, women.

NOTES

1. Gerda Lerner, *The Creation of Feminist Consciousness: From the Middle Ages to Eighteen-Seventy* (New York: Oxford University Press, 1993), 13.

2. The Department of Economic and Social Affairs of the United Nations (UN) defines gender equality as "equal opportunities, rights and responsibilities for women and men.... It implies that the interests, needs and priorities of both women and men are taken into consideration." UN, Department of Economic and Social Affairs, *The World's Women 2005: Progress in Statistics* (New York: United Nations, 2006), 1.

3. See Hilary Charlesworth and Christine Chinkin, *The boundaries of international law: A feminist analysis* (Manchester: Manchester University Press, 2000), 217. UNICEF has produced a report that reveals startling global gender inequalities throughout a girl's / woman's life cycle. See UNICEF, *The State of the World's Children. Women and Children: The Double Dividend of Gender Equality* (New York: UNICEF, 2006), 4–5.

4. Charlesworth and Chinkin, *The boundaries of international law*, 10, 32.

5. See Karin Van Marle, "'The Capabilities Approach,' 'The Imaginary Domain,' and 'Asymmetrical Reciprocity': Feminist Perspectives on Equality and Justice," *Feminist Legal Studies* 11 (2003): 266–272. Equal rights will not always be appropriate, as in the case of pregnancy where a gender-specific right would be more suitable.

6. See J. David Singer, "The Level-of-Analysis Problem in International Relations," *World Politics* 14, no. 1 (October 1961): 88.

7. Studies have been conducted at the national level (in the UK) to assess whether the inclusion of women in politics makes a difference. MacKay, for example, makes the point that the political under-representation of women was reframed as a serious problem for democracy and human development which consequently brought into question the issue of distribution of power. It is further argued that women make a dif-

ference by their mere presence. She differentiates between numerical representation and substantive representation, where the latter refers to the theoretical and practical expectations that, once present (in sufficient numbers), women representatives will "act for" women and ensure women's needs, interests and concerns are more fully represented in the policy process with consequent policy outcomes. Such representation will still vary in its degree, form and content according to different political parties, representative sites, issues and political context and is also dependent on the ability of the women not to adopt male standards. See Fiona MacKay, "Gender and Political Representation in the UK: The State of 'Discipline,'" *British Journal of Politics and International Relations* 6 (2004): 99–120. Childs makes the point that women practice politics differently to men—they are less combative and aggressive, more collaborative and speak in a different language (layman's terms). See Sarah Childs, "A Feminised Style of Politics? Women MPs in the House of Commons," *British Journal of Politics and International Relations* 6 (2004): 3–19. Puwar also refers to the "politics of presence," but notes the greater burden placed on women to perform, be heard, and "manage their femininity." Nirmal Puwar, "Thinking About Making a Difference," *British Journal of Politics and International Relations* 6 (2004): 65–80.

8. Simone de Beauvoir, *The Second Sex*, trans. and ed. H. M. Parshley (London: Vintage, 1997), 295.

9. J. Ann Tickner, *Gender in International Relations: Feminist Perspectives on Achieving Global Security* (New York: Columbia University Press, 1992), 7.

10. UN, General Assembly, "Implementation of the Outcome of the Fourth World Conference on Women: Report of the Secretary General," A/51/322, 03 September 1996. Accessed 08 June 2004, http://www.un.org/documents/ga/docs/51/plenary/a51-322.htm. The definition of gender as a purely social construction can present somewhat of problem. Alcoff points out that "[i]f gender is simply a social construct, the need and even the possibility of a feminist politics becomes immediately problematic. What can we demand in the name of women if "women" do not exist and demands in their name simply reinforce the myth that they do? How can we speak out against sexism as detrimental to the interests of women if the category is a fiction? How can we demand legal abortions, adequate child care, or wages based on comparable worth without invoking the concept of "woman"?" Linda Alcoff, "Cultural Feminism versus Post-Structuralism: The Identity Crisis in Feminist Theory," in *Feminist Theory in Practice and Process*, ed. Micheline Malson et al (Chicago: University of Chicago Press, 1989), 310. It should, however, be noted that, while Alcoff accepts the notion of gender as a socio-cultural construct, what she does take issue with is the poststructuralist approach that argues that gendered subjects are produced through discursive practices and so there is no "essence" or "being" that is woman.

11. Kate Millett, *Sexual Politics* (Champaign, IL: First Illinois Paperback, 2000), 30.

12. Judith Butler, *Gender Trouble: Feminism and the Subversion of Identity* (New York: Routledge, 1999), 9.

13. See Anne Phillips, "Introduction," in *Feminism and Politics*, ed. Anne Phillips (Oxford: Oxford University Press, 1998), 12.

14. Adam Jones, "Does 'Gender' Make the World Go Round? Feminist Critiques of International Relations," *Review of International Studies* 22, no. 4 (1996):

406–407. This article has "engendered" an interesting debate between the author and three scholars from the University of Bristol. See *Review of International Studies* 24 (1998): 283–303.

15. Jacqui True, "Feminism," in *Theories of International Relations*, ed. Scott Burchill et al. (Hampshire: Palgrave, 2001), 236.

16. Aristotle, *Politics*, trans. Benjamin Jowett (Whitefish, MT: Kessinger Publishing, 2004), 10.

17. Plato, *Republic*, trans. Paul Shorey (Cambridge, MA: Harvard University Press, 1969), 455.

18. The author has purposely decided against referring here to "a" theory or "a" social movement, as explained in the paragraph that follows.

19. Marilyn Frye, "Feminism," in *Encyclopedia of Feminist Theories*, ed. Lorraine Code (London: Routledge, 2003), 195.

20. Vicky Randall, "Feminism," in *Theory and Methods in Political Science*, ed. David Marsh and Gerry Stoker (Basingstoke: Palgrave MacMillan, 2002), 110.

21. The debate continues, however, as to whether gender is natural and essential or cultural and constructed. See Claire Colebrook, *Gender* (Basingstoke: Palgrave MacMillan, 2004), 9–17.

22. Connell describes "equal rights" as a "wholly logical doctrine that is as effective against the "aristocracy of sex" as the doctrine of the "rights of man" was against the aristocracy of property. Robert Connell, "The State, Gender and Sexual Politics: Theory and Appraisal," *Theory and Society* 19, no. 5 (October 1990): 512.

23. Jenny Chapman, "The Feminist Perspective," in Marsh and Stoker, *Theory and Methods in Political Science*, 95.

24. Ibid., 94.

25. One such example is illustrated in Rosemarie Tong's distinction between radical-libertarian feminists and radical-cultural feminists. While they are both premised on the notion that the sex/gender dichotomy is the fundamental cause of women's oppression, they differ on issues of sexuality and reproduction and how to eliminate women's oppression. See Rosemarie Tong, "Radical Feminism," in Code, *Encyclopedia of Feminist Theories*, 419–421.

26. Valerie Bryson, *Feminist Political Theory: An Introduction* (Basingstoke: Palgrave MacMillan, 2003), 1.

27. Ibid., 5 and Lerner, *The Creation of Feminist Consciousness*, 13.

28. Lerner, *The Creation of Feminist Consciousness*, 144.

29. Feminist critiques of Cartesian philosophy today, however, see this very duality as contributing to a gender dichotomy which supports "an ideology that privileges an autonomous rational masculinity over a relational, emotional, corporeal femininity." Margaret Atherton, "Feminist Critiques of Cartesianism," in Code, *Encyclopedia of Feminist Theories*, 72.

30. Catherine Macaulay's writings, however, were eclipsed by the fame of her close contemporary, Mary Wollstonecraft.

31. François Poullain de la Barre, *De L'Egalité des Deux Sexes: Discours Physique et Moral (Où l'on voit l'importance de se défaire des Préjugez)* (Paris: Jean Du Puis, 1673), vii.

32. Bryson, *Feminist Political Theory*, 9–10.

33. According to Mill, "...the common arrangement, by which the man earns the income and the wife superintends the domestic expenditure, seems to me in general the most suitable division of labour between the two persons. ...If she undertakes any additional portion, it seldom relieves her from this [her domestic/maternal duties], but only prevents her from performing it properly. The care which she is herself disabled from taking of the children and the household, nobody else takes; those of the children who do not die, grow up as they best can, and the management of the household is likely to be so bad, as even in point of economy to be a great drawback from the value of the wife's earnings." John Stuart Mill, *The Subjection of Women* (New York: Prometheus Books, 1986), 53.

34. Kate Nash, "Liberal Feminism," in Code, *Encyclopedia of Feminist Theories*, 303.

35. John Hoffman, "Blind Alley: Defining Feminism," *Politics* 21, no. 3 (2001): 194.

36. See Bryson, *Feminist Political Theory*, 7.

37. Ibid., 8.

38. Ibid., 32.

39. Kathryn McPherson, "First-Wave/Second-Wave Feminism," in Code, *Encyclopedia of Feminist Theories*, 208–209.

40. Vicky Randall, *Women and Politics: An International Perspective* (Basingstoke: MacMillan, 1987), 218.

41. Jean Bethke Elshtain, *Public Man, Private Woman: Women in Social and Political Thought* (Oxford: Princeton University Press, 1981), 238.

42. According to Randall, however, the movement was not fully dormant in the intervening year and the reason for the ebb in the movement was a lot more complex than has otherwise been suggested. See Randall, *Women and Politics*, 218–224.

43. For the purposes of this study, though, the author shall only be looking at liberal feminism, as the feminist issues raised here are the most pertinent to the discussion on law and gender equality. While radical feminism, particularly MacKinnon's offering on radical feminism, explores women's inequality as a product of sexual domination by men, her focus remains too essentialist as she develops "a monolithic, "grand" feminist jurisprudence which seeks to reduce all aspects of women's oppression to one dimension, and which treads dangerously close to biologistic essentialism." Nicola Lacey, "Closure and Critique in Feminist Jurisprudence: Transcending the Dichotomy or a Foot in Both Camps?" in *Unspeakable Subjects: Feminist Essays in Legal and Social Theory* (Oxford: Hart Publishing, 1998), 179. It does not take into account factors such as race or class. Liberal feminism, however, does not regard the legal system itself as contributing to the inferior position of women, while MacKinnon does. See Charlesworth and Chinkin, *The boundaries of international law*, 38–44. This is not to decry MacKinnon's campaign to have sexual harassment recognised as a legal wrong, as it has been an effective feminist strategy in many ways. See Lacey, "Closure and Critique in Feminist Jurisprudence," 180.

44. Randall, *Women and Politics*, 222.

45. Imelda Whelehan, *Modern Feminist Thought: From the Second Wave to 'Post-Feminism'* (Edinburgh: Edinburgh University Press, 1995), 5.

46. Don Slater, "Public/Private," in *Core Sociological Dichotomies*, ed. Chris Jenks (London: Sage Publications, 1998), 149.

47. Joyce Green, "Public/Private," in Code, *Encyclopedia of Feminist Theories*, 412.

48. Susan Moller Okin, "Gender, the Public, and the Private," in Phillips, *Feminism and Politics*, 117.

49. Squires contests the notion of the binary distinction, as she believes that it should be a tripartite division. Public/private refers to state and civil society respectively, where civil society does *not* include domestic or personal life. Civil society is private in the sense that it is not governed by the state. The concept of personal life, however, while indeed private, is private in reference to civil society and not to the state. According to her, "civil society is cast as private when opposed to the state and public when opposed to the personal. This makes any discussion of a single public/private dichotomy either partial or confused, or both." The three spheres of social relations, therefore, are the state, civil society and the personal. Judith Squires, *Gender in Political Theory* (Cambridge: Polity Press, 2000), 25.

50. Okin, "Gender, the Public, and the Private," 118–119.

51. Catharine MacKinnon, "The Liberal State," in *Toward A Feminist Theory of the State* (Cambridge, MA.: Harvard University Press, 1991), 162.

52. Ibid., 163, 169.

53. Blackstone's interpretation: "By marriage, the husband and wife are one person in law: that is, the very being or legal existence of the woman is suspended during the marriage, or at least is incorporated and consolidated into that of the husband: under whose wing, protection, and cover, she performs everything…." Sir William Blackstone, "Commentaries on the Laws of England (1765–1769)," accessed 05 February 2008, http://www.lonang.com/exlibris/blackstone/bla-115.htm. See Terri Collier's study on mid-seventeenth century political activities by women in England, where women are still currently seen as incapable of holding serious political identity. "Women at the Edge of Politics: Past and Present," *Political Studies Association*, Conference Proceedings (University of Nottingham, 1999). See also Teresa Brennan and Carole Pateman, "'Mere Auxiliaries to the Commonwealth': Women and the Origins of Liberalism," in Phillips, *Feminism and Politics*, 109.

54. Annabelle Lever, "Must Privacy and Sexual Equality Conflict? A Philosophical Examination of Some Legal Evidence," *Social Research* 67, no. 4 (Winter 2000): 1144.

55. This holds despite the fact that the State does regulate "private"-sphere issues such as marriage, divorce and child custody. See Nicola Lacey, "Theory into Practice? Pornography and the Public/Private Dichotomy," *Journal of Law and Society* 20, no. 1 (Spring 1993): 95. This will be explored further in a later chapter concerning the State's role as an effective agent and enforcer of legislative change in the protection of women's rights.

56. Rosemarie Tong, *Feminist Thought: A More Comprehensive Introduction* (Boulder, CO: Westview Press, 1998), 32. Participants at a seminar organised by

AAWORD/AFARD agreed that "Feminism is international in defining as its aim the liberation of women from all types of oppression and in providing solidarity among women of all countries; it is national in stating its priorities and strategies in accordance with particular cultural and socioeconomic conditions." AAWORD/AFARD Seminar Participants, "The Dakar Declaration on Another Development with Women," *Development Dialogue* 1–2 (1982), 15.

57. Judith Evans, *Feminist Theory Today: An Introduction to Second-Wave Feminism* (London: Sage Publications, 1995), 13.

58. Joan Wallach Scott, *Only Paradoxes to Offer: French Feminists and the Rights of Man* (Cambridge: Harvard University Press, 1996), x.

59. It is also interesting to note that while feminist discourse defines its problematique as "women," it unwittingly and ironically forgets that it should problematise the subject "man." See Jane Flax, "Postmodernism and Gender Relations in Feminist Theory," in *Feminism/Postmodernism*, ed. Linda Nicholson (New York: Routledge, 1990), 45. She states, though, "The single most important advance in feminist theory is that the existence of gender relations has been problematized," 43–44.

60. bell hooks, "Black Women: Shaping Feminist Theory," in *The Black Feminist Reader*, ed. Joy James and T. Denean Sharpley-Whiting (Malden, MA: Blackwell Publishers Limited, 2000), 132. She refers particularly to Betty Friedan's *The Feminine Mystique.*

61. See for example Reina Lewis and Sara Mills, "Introduction," in *Feminist Postcolonial Theory: A Reader*, ed. Reina Lewis and Sara Mills, (Edinburgh: Edinburgh University Press, 2003), 4.

62. Among these included African Feminism, Asian Feminism, Black Feminism, Chicana Feminism, Latin American Feminism, Lesbian Feminism, Postcolonial Feminism, Postmodern Feminism and Poststructural Feminism. For more on these and others, see generally Code, ed., *Encyclopedia of Feminist Thought.*

63. See Brooke Ackerly, "Women's Human Rights Activists as Cross Cultural Theorists," *International Feminist Journal of Politics* 3, no. 3 (Autumn 2001): 324–325.

64. Jill Krause, "Gender Inequalities and Feminist Politics in a Global Perspective," in *Globalization: Theory and Practice*, ed. Eleonore Kofman and Gillian Youngs, (London: Pinter, 1996), 226.

65. Chris Weedon, "Poststructuralism/Postmodernism," in Code, *Encyclopedia of Feminist Theories*, 398.

66. Reg Graycar, "Feminist Legal Theory," in Code, *Encyclopedia of Feminist Theories*, 198.

67. Gary Lawson, "Feminist Legal Theories," *Harvard Journal of Law and Public Policy* 18, no. 2 (Spring 1995).

68. Patricia A. Cain, "Feminist Jurisprudence: Grounding the Theories," in *Feminist Legal Theory: Readings in Law and Gender*, ed. Katharine Bartlett and Rosanne Kennedy (Boulder: Westview Press, 1991), 264.

69. Robin West, "Jurisprudence and Gender," in Bartlett, *Feminist Legal Theory*, 231. West writes an instructive article on how the different values that men and women identify with affect the character of law (which is inherently masculine)

and its effectiveness (or lack thereof) in affording protection and security of self to individuals.

70. Even if women were able to conquer patriarchy (on one level) and obtain equal pay for equal work, would that make them immune to the effects of patriarchy elsewhere, such as, say, male violence at home? See Mark Cowling's interesting insights on patriarchy and feminism, based on the work of Sylvia Walby who identifies six patriarchal social structures, in his draft paper, "Socialism, Feminism and Patriarchy: Does the Concept of Femininities Provide a Useful Link?" *Political Studies Association*, Conference Proceedings (University of Nottingham, 1999), 1–24.

71. Katharine Bartlett and Rosanne Kennedy, "Introduction," in Bartlett, *Feminist Legal Theory*, 1.

72. Sharyn L. Roach Anleu, "Critiquing the Law: Themes and Dilemmas in Anglo-American Feminist Legal Theory," *Journal of Law and Society* 19 (Winter 1992): 423.

73. Nicola Lacey, "Violence, Ethics and Law: Feminist Reflections in a Familiar Dilemma," in *Visible Women: Essays on Feminist Legal Theory and Political Philosophy*, ed. Susan James and Stephanie Palmer (Oxford: Hart Publishing, 2002), 123.

74. Jo Bridgeman and Susan Millns, *Feminist Perspectives on Law: Law's Engagement with the Female Body* (London: Sweet and Maxwell, 1998), 11.

75. (1873) 11 M. 784.

76. Ibid., 837.

77. Ibid., 832.

78. Ibid., 835.

79. Ibid., 837.

80. See Bridgeman and Millns, *Feminist Perspectives on Law*, 20.

81. Per Lord Sankey L.C. in *Edwards v Att.-Gen. of Canada*, [1930] A.C. 124 at 128. See also p. 134.

82. See Ngaire Naffine, "Can Women be Legal Persons?" in James and Palmer, *Visible Women*, 75.

83. See for example, K. Phillips, "Ancient Greek Theatre," 29 March 2000, accessed 03 November 2004, http://www.richeast.org/htwm/Greeks/theatre/actors.html and Edward R. Merganthal Jr., "Greek & Roman Theatre," 01 December 1998, accessed 03 November 2004, http://www.geocities.com/Broadway/Balcony/7634/greek_and_roman_theatre.htm.

84. This divide has been used historically to justify the exclusion of women from the political/public sphere. See Diemut Bubeck, "Thin, Thick and Feminist Conceptions of Citizenship," *Political Studies Association*, Conference Proceedings (University of York, 1995), 466.

85. Bridgeman and Millns, *Feminist Perspectives on Law*, 24–25.

86. Catharine A. MacKinnon, "Privacy v. Equality: Roe v. Wade," in *Feminism Unmodified: Discourses on Life and Law* (Cambridge: Harvard University Press, 1987), 100.

87. Bridgeman and Millns, *Feminist Perspectives on Law*, 25.

88. There is an argument that this constitutes a form of voluntary mutilation as compared to forced female genital mutilation in certain cultures.

89. Fiona Beveridge and Siobhan Mullally, "International Human Rights and Body Politics," in *Law and Body Politics: Regulating the Female Body*, ed. Jo Bridgeman and Susan Millns (Aldershot: Dartmouth, 1995), 248–251. (Text of which is partially reproduced in Bridgeman and Millns, *Feminist Perspectives on Law*, 31–33.)

90. It has been argued that the State's inaction against harms suffered by women may be construed as a direct State violation as part of its positive obligation to control the behaviour of private individuals. See Stephanie Palmer, "Feminism and the Promise of Human Rights: Possibilities and Paradoxes," in James and Palmer, *Visible Women*, 106 and chapter three below.

91. Quoted in Isabelle R. Gunning, "Uneasy Alliances and Solid Sisterhood: A Response to Professor Obiora's "Bridges and Barricades,"" in *Global Critical Race Feminism: An International Reader*, ed. Adrien Wing (New York: New York University Press, 2000), 276.

92. Lacey, "Violence, Ethics and Law," 128.

93. Carol Smart, *Feminism and the Power of Law* (London: Routledge, 1989), 2.

94. See Kate Malleson, "Justifying Gender Equality on the Bench: Why Difference Won't Do," *Feminist Legal Studies* 11 (2003): 1–2.

95. See for example *R. v S. (R.D.)*, [1997] 118 CCC (3d) para 119.

96. Malleson, "Justifying Gender Equality," 3–4. These presumptions draw largely from Carol Gilligan's "ethic of care," articulated in her *In a Different Voice: Psychological Theory and Women's Development* (Cambridge: Harvard University Press, 1982). See also, for example, 73–74 and West, "Jurisprudence and Gender."

97. A quick look at lawyers who practice family law, viewed perhaps as less formal [masculine] than other areas of law, in Trinidad and Tobago will show that many of them are in fact women.

98. A study on women and tokenism in the legal profession in southern Arizona produced interesting results, reflecting the fact that gender makes a huge difference, regardless of qualifications, and that such bias is recognised by both males and females. See Patricia MacCorquodale and Gary Jensen, "Women in the Law: Partners or Tokens?" *Gender and Society* 7, no. 4 (Dec., 1993): 582–593. Another study undertaken in Florida, on the differential treatment of women and men in the state legal system, shows that "compared with men judges and attorneys, women judges and attorneys are more conscious of gender inequality, observe more gender bias in legal settings, and show a stronger connection between experiences with gender bias and feminist consciousness." Patricia Martin, John Reynolds, and Shelley Keith, "Gender Bias and Feminist Consciousness among Judges and Attorneys: A Standpoint Theory Analysis," *Signs* 27, no. 3 (Spring, 2002): 669.

99. The Martin, Reynolds, Keith study would suggest that this is in fact not so, especially with reference to women judges. See "Gender Bias and Feminist Consciousness," 689.

100. Malleson, "Justifying Gender Equality," 8.

101. See Catharine A. MacKinnon, "Difference and Dominance: On Sex Discrimination," in *Feminism Unmodified*, 43.

102. Diana Majury, "Strategizing in Equality," in *At the Boundaries of Law: Feminism and Legal Theory*, ed. Martha A. Fineman and Nancy S. Thomadsen (London: Routledge, 1991), 321.

103. Kate Nash, "Equality and Difference," in Code, *Encyclopedia of Feminist Theories*, 174.

104. See discussions on *General Electric Company v Gilbert* et al and *Geduldig v Aiello* in chapter two below.

105. Kate Nash, *Contemporary Political Sociology: Globalization, Politics, and Power* (Malden: Blackwell Publishers Limited, 2000), 166.

106. Tong, *Feminist Thought*, 208.

107. Nash, *Contemporary Political Sociology*, 165.

108. Julia A. Sohrab, "Avoiding the 'Exquisite Trap': A Critical look at the Equal Treatment/Special Treatment Debate in Law," *Feminist Legal Studies* 1, no. 2 (1993): 141–162. (Text of which is partially reproduced in Bridgeman and Millns, *Feminist Perspectives on Law*, 51–52.).

109. Smith makes the point that inequality has been consistently justified throughout history based on "relevant difference." As an example, while "the American revolutionaries declared all men to be created equally, their Constitution recognized slavery as a legitimate practice, because blacks were different." See Patricia Smith, "On Equality: Justice, Discrimination, and Equal Treatment," in *Feminist Jurisprudence*, ed. Patricia Smith (Oxford: Oxford University Press, 1993), 17–20. (Text of which is partially reproduced in Bridgeman and Millns, *Feminist Perspectives on Law*, 37–39.)

110. Lawrence Donegan, "The Woman who is taking on Wal-Mart," *The Observer*, 27 June 2004, accessed 28 June 2004, http://observer.guardian.co.uk/international/story/0,6903,1248204,00.html.

111. Sharon Krum, "Store Wars," *The Observer*, 02 July 2001, accessed 28 June 2004, http://www.guardian.co.uk/women/story/0,3604,515455,00.html.

112. *Betty Dukes and ors v. Wal-Mart Stores, Inc*, No. C-01-2252 MJJ (2001), 7. Accessed 28 June 2004, http://news.findlaw.com/hdocs/docs/walmart/dukeswalmart61901.pdf.

113. Anne Phillips, "Feminism and the Politics of Difference. Or, Where Have All the Women Gone?" in James and Palmer, *Visible Women*, 16.

114. Palmer, "Feminism and the Promise of Human Rights," 96–97.

115. Stephanie Palmer, "Critical Perspectives on Women's Rights: The European Convention on Human Rights and Fundamental Freedoms," in *Feminist Perspectives on the Foundational Subjects of Law*, ed. Anne Bottomley (London: Cavendish Publishing Limited, 1996), 228.

116. Deborah L. Rhode, "Feminist Critical Theories," in Bartlett, *Feminist Legal Theory*, 336.

117. Ibid., 336.

118. Ann C. Scales, "The Emergence of Feminist Jurisprudence: An Essay," in *Feminist Jurisprudence*, ed. Patricia Smith (Oxford: Oxford University Press, 1993),

101–104. (Text of which is partially reproduced in Bridgeman and Millns, *Feminist Perspectives on Law*, 80–82.)

119. Christine A. Littleton, "Reconstructing Sexual Equality," *California Law Review* 79 (1987): 1284–1285. Emphasis in the original.

120. See Van Marle, "Feminist Perspectives on Equality and Justice," 266–272.

121. Ibid., 267.

122. 1997(6) B.C.L.R. 708 (C.C.).

123. The court refined its "test" to determine unfair discrimination by the government in law or executive conduct in *Harksen v Lane*, 1997 (11) B.C.L.R. 1489 (C.C.). First, the Court will decide whether there was, in fact, discrimination/differentiation and then decide whether it was unfair. If unfair, it must then decide whether there was a rational connection between the differentiation and a legitimate government purpose. If the purpose is proved rational, then the differentiation will not have amounted to a breach of the guarantee of equality before the law. Where the purpose is proved irrational, then it will amount to a violation of the guarantee. There are several other subsequent permutations to this test: see Van Marle, "Feminist Perspectives on Equality and Justice," 269–270.

124. See Nicola Lacey, "An Introduction to the Essays," in *Unspeakable Subjects*, 7.

125. See Smart, *The Power of Law*, 71. See also Samantha Ashenden, "At the Boundaries of the Political: Feminist Beyond Identity Politics?" *Political Studies Association*, Conference Proceedings (University of Glasgow, 1996): 1856–1857.

126. See Smart, *The Power of Law*, 9, 11 borrowing from Foucault's notion of truth.

127. Catharine A. MacKinnon, "Introduction: The Art of the Impossible," in *Feminism Unmodified*, 5.

128. Lacey, "Closure and Critique in Feminist Jurisprudence," 180.

129. Ibid.

130. See Elizabeth Kingdom, *What's Wrong With Rights? Problems for Feminist Politics of Law* (Edinburgh: Edinburgh University Press, 1991), 120–121.

131. Quoting Smart and Brophy in Kingdom, *What's Wrong With Rights?* 120.

132. Smart, *The Power of Law*, 66, 88.

133. Seyla Benhabib, "The Generalized and the Concrete Other," in *Situating the Self: Gender, Community and Postmodernism in Contemporary Ethics* (Oxford: Polity Press, 1992), 152.

134. Nancy Naples, "The Challenges and Possibilities of Transnational Feminist Praxis," in *Women's Activism and Globalization: Linking Local Struggles and Transnational Politics*, ed. Nancy Naples and Manisha Desai (New York: Routledge, 2002), 274.

135. Nivedita Menon, "Introduction," in *Gender and Politics in India*, ed. Nivedita Menon (New Delhi: Oxford University Press, 1999), 29. Emphasis added.

136. See Ackerly, "Women's Human Rights Activists." The crucial role of feminist practice at both the international and national levels will be further explored later in the study.

137. Andrew Linklater, "The Achievements of Critical Theory," in *International Theory: Positivism and Beyond*, ed. Steve Smith et al (Cambridge: Cambridge University Press, 2002), 279.

138. Mary Hawkesworth, "Knowers, Knowing, Known: Feminist Theory and Claims of Truth," in Malson et al, *Feminist Theory in Practice and Process*, 348.

139. Hawkesworth, "Knowers, Knowing, Known," 343.

140. Mark Hoffman, "Critical Theory and the Inter-Paradigm Debate," *Millennium: Journal of International Studies* 16, no. 2 (1987): 233. Emphasis in the original.

141. Richard Devetak, "Critical Theory," in Burchill et al. *Theories of International Relations*, 161.

142. Ibid., 161–162.

143. Linklater, "The Achievements of Critical Theory," 279.

144. See Christopher Broniak, "What is Emancipation for Habermas?" *Philosophy Today* 32, no. 3 (Fall 1988): 195, 200. According to Broniak, Kant's revolutionary theory frees the self, but leaves it disenfranchised, "deprived of something worthwhile about the previously submissive relationship," therefore falling short of the Habermasian concept of emancipation. See p. 200.

145. Karl Popper, *The Logic of Scientific Discovery* (London: Routledge, 2002), 22. Emphasis in the original. He defines inter-subjective testing as the "idea of mutual rational control by critical discussion."

146. See Nancy Fraser, "What's Critical About Critical Theory? The Case of Habermas and Gender," in *Feminism and Philosophy: Essential Reading in Theory, Reinterpretation, and Application*, ed. Nancy Tuana and Rosemarie Tong (Colorado: Westview Press, 1995), 275.

147. On the issue of structural and cultural impediments to upward mobility in the public service for women in a postcolonial society, see, for example, Ann Marie Bissessar, "Determinants of Gender Mobility in the Public Service of Trinidad and Tobago," *Public Personnel Management* 28, no. 3 (Fall 1999): 409–422.

148. See Michiel Korthals, "The Philosophical Foundation of the Social Sciences in the Theory of Jürgen Habermas," *Philosophy of the Social Sciences* 18, no. 1 (March 1988): 69. Korthals makes the point that, under Habermasian conditions, actors "claim that their propositions about the objective world of things and events are true; ...that their normative statements belonging to the social world of norms are right, and ...that their expressions, which belong to their own subjective world of feelings, are authentic." Couple this with the ability of powerful groups to espouse this as the truth and the difficulties of seeing beyond this become evident.

149. See David Kennedy, "Critical Theory, Structuralism and Contemporary Legal Scholarship," *New England Law Review* 21, no. 2 (1985–1986): 244–248.

150. Legal Information Institute, "Critical Legal Studies: An Overview," accessed 08 February 2005, http://www.law.cornell.edu/topics/critical_theory.html.

151. Fred R. Dallmayr, "Critical Theory Criticized: Habermas's *Knowledge and Human Interests* and its Aftermath," *Philosophy of the Social Sciences* 2, no. 3 (Sept 1972): 212.

152. See Chapter two below on Grotius' contribution to the development of international maritime law and the conditions under which this was born.

153. An adjective used to describe systems of thought that claim legitimacy by reference to external, universally truthful propositions. Pauline Rosenau, *Post-*

Modernism and the Social Sciences: Insights, Inroads and Intrusions (Princeton: Princeton University Press, 1992), xii.

154. Ibid., 14.

155. A post-modern method of analysis. Deconstruction tears apart a text, reveals its contradictions and assumptions but is never meant to provide an alternative. Ibid., xi. Deconstructionism is directed to the interrogation of texts. It involves the attempt to take apart and expose the underlying meanings, biases, and preconceptions that structure the way a text conceptualizes its relation to what it describes. This requires that traditional concepts, theory, and understanding surrounding a text be unraveled... Norman Denzin, "Postmodernism and Deconstructionism," in *Postmodernism and Social Inquiry*, ed. David Dickens and Andrea Fontana (London: University College of London Press, 1994), 185.

156. Rosenau, *Post-Modernism and the Social Sciences*, 123.

157. Although, even Einstein's theory of relatively is under threat of being falsified. A group of Australian scientists have discovered that one of the constants in the ever famous formula $E = mc^2$ is no longer constant and, therefore, affects the accuracy of the formula. They contend that the speed of light—c—is in fact slowing down, which undermines Einstein's theory. Imagine the consequences for the natural sciences should it be falsified... See Reuters, "Einstein's Theory May Be Relatively Wrong," 08 August 2002, accessed 13 September 2004, http://edition.cnn.com/2002/WORLD/asiapcf/auspac/08/07/australia.lightspeed/.

158. The "top-down" approach refers to the method of changing behaviour at the national level through international persuasion either by law, policy or custom.

Chapter Two

The Androcentrism of International Law and Human Rights

Law is a social phenomenon. It has grown into an essential principle of social organisation in Western civilisations as a result of the historicity of those societies.[1] Law functions as the formal machinery for creating and maintaining social order, as seen in the Western world and is often perceived as an instrument to effect change. The plight of women with respect to their fundamental rights is almost universal in nature and, therefore, it is hardly surprising that there are calls for the issue to be addressed at the international level. This "top-down" approach has many supporters, as it is commonly felt that the near global phenomenon of gender inequality can only be resolved by a common approach implemented across state borders. Important, therefore, is an assessment of the effectiveness of international law as an instrument to effect change in the context of women's rights.

An examination of the relationship between international law and gender will provide the basis for the argument that international law, on many occasions, fails to contemplate a gender perspective and, even when this is done, the effectiveness of the legal regime is called into question. This aside, issues of sovereignty would suggest that exclusive reliance on international law to effect change is perhaps ill-advised and would explain why women's issues, in particular, are not universally or fully implemented with alacrity, or even at all. This chapter, therefore, will analyse the development of international law, expose its male nature and discuss the manner in which the international rights discourse has developed in this regard, fundamentally privileging men. The chapter goes on to examine the "reinvention" of international law by feminists in an attempt to carve a place for women's rights as a real issue at this level. Legal initiatives designed specifically for the promotion of gender equality and protection for women against domestic violence at the level of the United Nations are assessed and so too are a couple of non-gender specific conventions with the potential to enhance women's rights. An examination of the feminist work in international relations towards the end of the chapter further points to the heavily gendered nature of international relations and, consequently, international law.

2.1 THE DEVELOPMENT OF INTERNATIONAL LAW

International law seeks to maintain order and facilitate relations between States, as well as non-state actors, in areas, *inter alia*, such as trade, travel and communication. International law may be defined as that body of law which is composed for its greater part of the principles and rules of conduct which States feel themselves bound to observe and, therefore, do commonly observe in their relations with each other and includes international organisations and other non-state actors.[2] Bentham has been attributed with having coined the term "international law" in the 1780s.[3] In the absence of an international legislative body for creating laws, international law is drawn from a variety of sources. Article 38(1) of the Statute of the International Court of Justice states that the sources of international law are:

1. international conventions, whether general or particular, establishing rules expressly recognized by the contesting states;
2. international custom, as evidence of a general practice accepted as law;
3. the general principles of law recognized by civilized nations;
4. subject to the provisions of Article 59, judicial decisions and the teachings of the most highly qualified publicists of the various nations, as subsidiary means for the determination of rules of law.[4]

Other sources include United Nations General Assembly Resolutions, the International Law Commission, other United Nations bodies and "soft law," which consists of non-legally binding instruments.

It follows that, unlike domestic law, international law does not embrace such a formal organisational structure for the regulation of international affairs and it has taken on a largely "soft law" approach,[5] even more so on "softer" issues such as protection of the environment and the promotion of human rights, within which are to be found issues affecting women and children, highlighting their marginalisation and exclusion from issues deemed worthy of regulation. Given the economic, political, social and cultural differences of international society, it is difficult to secure consensus on new rules. What soft law does is to provide a type of half-measure in the law-making process on the international level. It can be described as "law in the process of making. It is nascent, incipient, or potential law."[6] According to Birnie

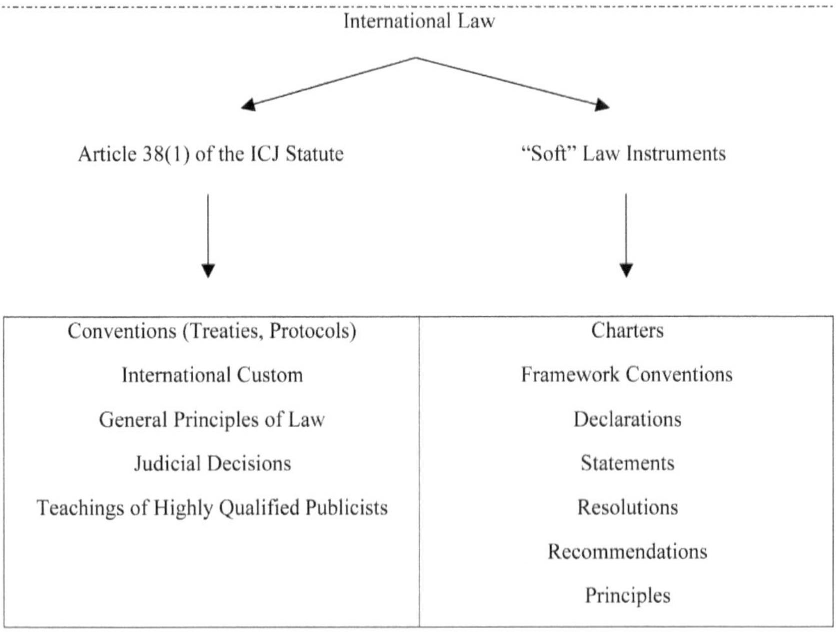

Figure 2.1. Sources of International Law.

and Boyle, it may take the form of "codes of practice, recommendations, guidelines, resolutions, declarations of principles, standards, and so called 'framework' or 'umbrella' treaties which do not fit neatly into the categories of legal sources referred to in Article 38(1)(c) of the ICJ Statute."[7] While critics may argue that the term is inadequate and misleading, its flexibility allows for overcoming deadlocks, thereby facilitating consensus among States pursuing conflicting goals.[8]

The very legality of international law is constantly questioned, as it is near impossible to enforce laws in a realist anarchic framework, and was dubbed a "positive morality" by John Austin.[9] This is compounded by the fact that international law is not structured in the same manner as domestic law as it does not have a legislative body to enact laws, no judges to apply them in particular disputes and limited power to compel obedience.[10] Akashi states that from a Hobbesian theoretical perspective, because there is "no common sovereign, nor legislative body, [that] exists among nations, there is no law in this sense applied to international relations."[11]

Despite these difficulties, and the view of international law as merely "an aesthetic achievement,"[12] international law continues to grow in importance in international relations. The reasons for its importance are threefold, according to Savage.[13] International law has grown in practice through the creation of new agreements and conventions for the prosecution of war criminals; developments in international relations have led to a renewal of interest in normative issues (such as sovereignty, statehood, human rights practices) and international law is regarded as a mechanism for the incorporation of these concerns in the practices of international politics; and, international law is gaining currency as it is linked to wider developments in legal thinking which includes, very broadly, jurisprudence and discussions of law at a national and political level. Its mounting value is also derived from the fact that actors in international law are no longer restricted to the State, but include other actors such as NGOs. A tool for promoting progressive social policies,[14] international law can be used in reliance on the persuasive nature of norms to promote better state practices, such as human rights practices.[15]

Having defined international law and reviewed its growing importance, it is useful to examine the development of international law to illustrate the inherent gender bias contained therein as a subject of international relations.

2.2 THE MALE NATURE OF INTERNATIONAL LAW

International law, as it is known today, was born in the era of Enlightenment, the age of reason, which emphasised positivist philosophy. It highlighted the importance of scientific inquiry, reason, empiricism and value-neutral research, allegedly objective traits associated with men and masculinity.[16] International law, then, was based on observable phenomena of what actually took place between States and their relations with one another. However, in its earliest formulations, international law adopted a somewhat more natural law approach which emphasised the importance of morality, justice and reason.

Modern international law, nevertheless, emerged within the philosophical framework of early Christian principles which would explain the emphasis on morality. The leading thinkers of modern international law were either theologians or Western scholars coming from civilisations dominated by Christian principles. Christianity, as contained in the teachings of Christ and his disciples, contained clear elements of male supremacy. While it is acknowledged that Christ had strong female support from followers such as Mary Magdalene, the traditionalists note that there were no female disciples. Indeed, Paul, who has been associated with the phenomenal growth of the early Christian movement, said "[l]et your women keep silent in the churches, for they are not permitted to speak; but they are to be *submissive*, as the *law* also says."[17]

Hugo Grotius, Dutch theologian and lawyer, is hailed as the father of modern public international law, although this is disputed by some, including those loyal to jurists such as Gentili.[18] His writings in the early seventeenth century on the law of nations, as he understood it, is very heavily reliant on his theosophical beliefs and, consequently, of a highly moral nature. Grotius was committed to the pursuit of peace and felt that this was only attainable through consensus. In order to achieve consensus, Grotius believed that Christian doctrine would have to be reduced to its barest minimum so as to minimise the potential for conflict.[19] Once there is nothing over which Christians could argue about, there would be consensus, which would lead to peace. Despite Grotius' heavy leaning on theology and his belief that high levels of individual morality and reason could function to keep society regulated, (and by extension States, as States are made up of individuals), it is claimed by many writers that he removed the concept of natural law, or divine law,[20] from theology making the idea of international law a purely positivist conception.

Grotius' contribution to the development of international law is best reflected in his first major work, *Mare liberum*, which advocated the freedom of the high seas.[21] He was writing at a time when, according to Shaw, "this theory happened to accord rather nicely with prevailing Dutch ideas as to free trade and the needs of an expanding commercial empire."[22] This immediately brings to mind Cox's famous statement that "theory is always *for* someone and *for* some purpose"[23] and always rooted in socio-political spatial and temporal contexts.[24] In this work, Grotius espouses the complete free use of the high seas for the benefit of mankind; he explains the relationship between natural, divine and international law; he states that natural law forms part of a higher law and that international law was subject to it; and claims that international law applied to all nations, even the nations of the East despite the fact that East Indians were "sunk in grievous sin" because they practised idolatry.[25]

Like many juristic writers of this era, Vattel saw one of the primary functions of the Law of Nations as promoting peace and limiting wartime hostilities without prejudice to a nation's own real interests.[26] An 18th century Swiss lawyer, his work on the law of nations practically combined aspects of both positivism and naturalism.[27] He defined the Law of Nations as "the science which teaches the rights subsisting between nations or states, and the obligations correspondent to those rights."[28] Vattel was able to clearly delineate two integral aspects of international law. These are natural or necessary law and positive or secondary law. It may be said that natural law provides the standard for measuring the moral rightness of positive law.[29] According to Vattel, "the necessary law of nations consists in the application of the law of nature [derived from God and conscience] to states,—which law is immutable, as being founded on the nature of things, and particularly on the nature of man...."[30] Like Grotius, he believed that the "law [of nations] is not less obligatory [to states] than on individuals, since states are composed of men..."[31] Positive law comprised three features: voluntary, conventional, and customary features which have persisted in contemporary international law. According to Vattel, they all stem from the will of nations—the voluntary from their presumed consent; the conventional, or treaty law, from their express consent; and the customary from their tacit consent,[32] important features of current day international law. He also advocated for the equality of nations. "A dwarf is as much a man as a giant; a small republic is no less a sovereign state than the most powerful kingdom."[33]

Having demonstrated the male bias in the emerging field of international law as predicated on Christian dogma, the next section explores the subsequent transformation of international law in the Renaissance period with respect to discussions on the notion of rights. It is, therefore, critical to understand whether the examination of rights as part of the development of international law also contemplated the specific issue of women's rights and, in particular, the right to equality.

2.3 INTERNATIONAL LAW AND RIGHTS

Rights as a concept has existed for millennia. Interestingly, from its inception, the right of the citizen, which assumed a set of universal ideals such as freedom, equality and liberty,[34] has always referred to the rights of man and not of women. The notion of citizenship emerged in the classical Greek era in the time of Aristotle. According to Aristotle, citizenship can only be bestowed on a property-owning individual very active in political life. This necessarily excluded women, children and slaves.[35]

2.3.1 States, Sovereignty and International Law

With the Renaissance movement, law took on a more secular character. Positivist thought coincided with the emergence of the modern nation State, the Bodinian and Hobbesian notion of sovereignty and the Peace of Westphalia of 1648, which is held to be a watershed in the history of State relations. Beaulac states that it is portrayed as a historical fact that Westphalia represented a new diplomatic arrangement—an order created by States, for States and that it consecrated the principle of sovereign equality of States which, since then, has been at the core of international law.[36]

Autonomy of the nation State is the defining characteristic of realist thought and means that the State has supreme authority. In its relations with other States, a sovereign State is said to exist in an anarchic system, meaning simply that there is no common power over and above the State to regulate its behaviour and enforce laws.[37] In this state of affairs, power assumed great importance, and, by extension, issues of security, and was traditionally measured in terms of military capability. Realists described the situation in existence during the nineteenth century as a balance of power which prevented the dominance of any one State in the international system. The primary aim of the balance of power was not to preserve peace but to preserve the security of States, and, if necessary, by means of war.[38] Despite the move towards a more positivistic approach, natural law has re-emerged and plays a very important part of international law, particularly with reference to the idea of natural rights and, by extension, human rights.

Reliance on the realist, reified notion of sovereignty, however, poses great difficulty to the effective implementation and practicality of international human rights law. In this particular regard, Reisman makes a distinction between territorial sovereignty and popular sovereignty, where the former term "is used in the jurisprudentially bizarre sense to mean that inanimate territory has political rights that preempt those of its inhabitants,"[39] while the latter puts the needs of the population first.[40] Sikkink correctly notes that "human rights issues offer particularly potent challenges to the central logic of a [realist] system of sovereign states"[41] and one of the most powerful critiques of sovereignty.

Social constructivists offer a more accommodating, fluid version of sovereignty which is perhaps better suited to explaining the adoption of better human rights practices in some countries and the possibility of promoting change in the more authoritarian states. In emphasising the ideational factors that propel change, this view is also helpful in explaining the influences at the State level from above (United Nations), laterally (other States) and below (NGOs) and how international norms, in particular, human rights, affect domestic politics. Wendt describes sovereignty as "an institution" which "exists only in virtue of certain intersubjective understanding and expectations; there is no sovereignty without an other."[42] Sikkink builds on Wendt's notion of sovereignty and explains it as subject to change according to sociocultural context, a representation of "shared understandings and expectations that are constantly reinforced both through the practices of states and the practices of nonstate actors."[43] The effects of such a fluid perspective of sovereignty mean that, where there is a change in the intersubjective understandings and practices by States, or what Legro refers to as concordance,[44] the notion of sovereignty will be subject to change as well. Reisman notes that these shifting boundaries of sovereignty also "change the cast of characters who can violate that sovereignty,"[45] which is integral to an understanding of human rights issues. This notion of a shifting sovereignty and its implications for international human rights law will be revisited in a later chapter which examines the influences of the UN and NGOs on State practices.[46]

2.3.2 Universal Rights

As noted above, rights discourse has its foundations in natural law concepts which take on a moral, rather than, positivistic character. It is said that the concept of natural rights in the seventeenth century embodies rights to life, liberty and property and is attributed to Locke. According to Locke,

> Man [is] born with a title to perfect freedom and an uncontrolled enjoyment of all the rights and privileges of the law of nature, equally with any other man... [and] hath by nature a power... to preserve his property, that is his life, liberty, and estate, against the injuries and attempts of other men...[47]

It is, of course, significant to note that Locke talks of "man," as he is not using the word generically but to denote that any rights holder can only be white, European, property-owning males, again excluding women, children and non-whites, very similar to the Greek conception of a citizen.

Notions of rights and equality can be found in the Bible. Rights seem to be grounded in the notion of equity such that one could "take life for life, eye for eye, tooth for tooth, hand for hand, foot for foot, burn for burn, wound for wound, bruise for bruise"[48] in the event of having been wronged. Locke reflects this sentiment when he says that man has a right to be "judge of and punish the breaches of that law in others, as he is persuaded the offence deserves, even with death itself, in crimes where the heinousness of the fact, in his opinion, requires it."[49] It would also appear that despite the existence and allowance of slavery, there were notions of equality. "There is neither Jew nor Greek, slave nor free, male nor female...."[50] This implies a universality that, as Vincent notes, applies to the kingdom of God, not in that of man.[51]

Human rights are said to belong to all human beings simply by virtue of their very humanity. Booth makes a very interesting argument on this definition. He argues that this is an essentialist and tautological construction.[52] According to him, we have human rights in order to make the species human and not by virtue of our humanity.[53] The issue of human rights was officially instituted as an area of international concern following the atrocities of the Second World War when Germany had been able to commit acts of genocide against millions of its own people with little interference by other nations. This prompted the formulation of the United Nations Charter and the establishment of the United Nations Commission on Human Rights as part of the United Nations Economic and Social Council in 1946.[54]

The United Nations Declaration of Human Rights was adopted on 10 December 1948 in the form of United Nations General Assembly Resolution 2174 (III), UN Doc A/810.[55] It was drafted by the first Director of the United Nations Human Rights Division, a Canadian, John Peters Humphrey, whose main objective was to make the document universal in its application by drawing on sources from many different legal cultures.[56] According to Article 1 of the Declaration, "All human beings are born free and equal in dignity and rights…."[57] Article 2 goes on to state that everyone is entitled to the rights and freedom as set out in the Declaration without fear or favour. Importantly, article 4 states that everyone has the right to life, liberty and security of person. The work of Eleanor Roosevelt, as Chair of the Commission of Human Rights, was pivotal not only in the formulation of the Declaration but in ensuring that the gains made on the basis of sex equality were not lost.[58] Noteworthy too, with respect to the UN Charter, is the fact that women, again, were the driving force behind the inclusion of the sex equality principle. NGOs working under the umbrella of the Inter-American Commission on the Status of Women,[59] in particular, Latin American activists from Brazil, the Dominican Republic, and Mexico,[60] insisted that the application of human rights and fundamental freedoms be "without distinction as to…sex…."[61] The UN Charter made the first concrete step in moving the issue of rights and human rights into the specific realm of equality of men and women. This is a key moment in history as this represented the first time that women and equality were treated in a gender neutral international legal document.

However, the issue of gender parity creates a problem in dealing with the international law concept of the "subject" of international law. In as much as gender equality is a concern of human rights law, it faces the obstacle posed by the principle that obligations created by international human rights instruments are directed towards the State and it is the State that has obligations towards its nationals and foreign nationals within their territory and under their jurisdiction.[62] The enforcement and application of human rights instruments by the State is like a double-edged sword, as "the modern state has emerged as both the principal threat to the enjoyment of human rights and the essential institution for their effective implementation and enforcement."[63] In some common law countries (like Trinidad and Tobago), international law instruments are not automatically applicable in its domestic law, as they must first be enacted by Parliament and there exists no real mandate to force countries to enact such legislation, in effect removing the State's obligations towards nationals in its territory and under its jurisdiction.[64] As the Honourable Madame Justice Désirée Bernard, Judge of the Caribbean Court of Justice notes, convention implementation and enforceability present difficulties depending on the relationship between a State's international obligations and its domestic laws.[65] She goes on to explain that,

> According to monist theory in international law treaties ratified by a state for the protection of the human person automatically become part of the municipal law of that state. The dualist theory, on the other hand, advocates separation of international law from municipal law, and international obligations of a state are not automatically incorporated into its municipal law which is supreme. For international treaties to be enforceable in the domestic court system of a state they have to be specifically legislated or adopted into the municipal law... In countries where a treaty or convention is not incorporated into the domestic law its enforceability depends in large measure on the integrity and commitment of the particular state in honouring its international obligations and undertakings by enacting the necessary legislation to ensure enforceability in its municipal courts. Most of the countries within the English-speaking Caribbean and which inherited the English common law and systems of government adopted the practice of the United Kingdom which followed the dualist theory; hence in our Region international treaties are not automatically incorporated into domestic law upon ratification, and separate legislation and enactment of statutes are required to ensure enforceability in the municipal courts of the state.[66]

This situation creates obvious difficulties, but nevertheless reflects what actually currently obtains in such countries, Trinidad and Tobago included, and the problems inherent in relying exclusively on international law to effect change in such jurisdictions.

Many say that international law has broadened its scope to capture non-state actors and even individuals as subjects of international law. While human rights abuses that take place within a state's borders are directed towards individuals or groups based on ethnicity, religious beliefs or any other status, international law, in a legal positivist sense, cannot treat with such abuses. The reasons for this are twofold. The first is that positivist public international law holds the State as the subject of international law where "the individual was not a proper subject of international law... public international law went to matters affecting states, while private international law[67] concerned matters between individuals."[68] Vincent puts it quite succinctly, "Individuals and groups other than states have access to this society [the international society] only through the agency of their states; they are objects not subjects of international law."[69] This is compounded by the assurance in the United Nations Charter of non-intervention in the domestic affairs of a state.[70] Dunne and Wheeler, however, believe that in the post-Cold War era, the United Nations Security Council has found a way around this assurance. The United Nation Security Council has revised its definition of human rights abuses and humanitarian concerns which are now viewed "as a threat to 'international peace and security' thereby legitimising coercive intervention under Chapter VII of the UN Charter."[71]

This strict interpretation notwithstanding, optional protocols to some human rights conventions do allow for sub-state agency (individuals, groups). Under the Convention on the Elimination of All Forms of Discrimination Against Women, for example, an optional protocol was adopted by the General Assembly in 1999 to afford individuals, as well as groups and non-governmental organisations, the right to report violations by the State of the main convention directly to the Committee on the Elimination of Discrimination Against Women.[72] This right is, of course, circumscribed by the State's willingness to accede to the protocol. In the absence of accession, it poses particular problems for women as abuses meted out in the home are strictly theoretically outside of the sphere of international law due to the public/private divide and the notion of the sanctity of the family.[73]

The universal applicability of human rights discourses confronts several barriers. As Dunne and Wheeler observe, the authors of human rights documents such as the United Nations Charter and the Universal Declaration of Human Rights, with a view to universal application, assumed that "there was no necessary conflict between the principles of sovereignty and non-intervention and respect for human rights."[74] While there are advocates for conceding sovereignty in the name of promoting human rights, there are those who are against it. A case in point is the establishment of the International Criminal Court. The establishment of this Court has not benefited from the support of one of the most powerful nations of the world simply because it requires the concession of that which realists hold so dear—sovereignty. In a newspaper article, a former President of the Republic of Trinidad and Tobago, who was also instrumental in the establishment of the Court, was quoted as saying that national sovereignty should give way to humanitarian issues with respect to the International Criminal Court.[75] He also stated that "sovereignty will more and more become subordinated to the importance of the individual, to our humanity."[76] This is significant coming from a former President of a fairly new independent republic. In addition to issues presented by sovereignty, the formulation of human rights documents were executed by those influenced by Western, liberal, political thought which means that any claim to universality would imply an imposition of these ideas on societies and cultures with their own conception of rights and morality.

2.3.3 Arguments Against the Notion of Universal Rights

Human rights discourse, as advocated by the United Nations, assumes the individual to be the holder of human rights. Eastern and African cultures have very different notions of human rights in this regard. They privilege communal rights over individual rights. On the African continent, collective rights reign supreme above economic and social rights, and civil and political rights rank third in the hierarchy of importance.[77] In China, the importance of communal rights emphasises hierarchy, deference and interdependence, which, according to Dunne and Wheeler, is completely at odds with the West's understanding of what it is to be human.[78] According to Ames, in China, "an individual can only become a human being in community."[79] Brown observed that restrictions on individual liberties become a necessary pre-requisite for economic development in East Asian authoritarian regimes which also coincides with local custom.[80] He seems to be unable to comprehend human equality premised on a caste system or on social arrangements that privilege family over individual,[81] but then again, he is writing from the Western tradition. Booth may have a point when he says, "The universality of human rights is an ideology which is a cover for the imposition of Western values."[82] While western human rights discourse presumes a certain hegemony and universality, there are indeed positive aspects to it but it needs to be able to accommodate cultural variety.

Cultural relativism, which may be said to have a somewhat postmodernist foundation, provides perhaps one of the most pervasive arguments against a universal conception of international human rights. The doctrine of cultural relativism takes a three-pronged approach. It states firstly that ideas and conceptions of morality differ from place to place and (secondly) that they can only be understood within their particular cultural contexts. In the third place, moral claims are necessarily an integral part of the cultural context which is itself the source of their validity.[83] As a result, any human rights discourse purporting a universal character must take these differences into consideration. This is, of course, easier said than done. There have been writers advocating the use of a range of minimalist to maximalist understandings of universal values. Parekh gives the example that respect for human dignity can be understood in minimalist terms to mean that no human being should be traded as a commodity, subject to torture or genocidal policies and in maximalist terms to mean that all human beings should be ensured all "the desirable conditions of the good life,"[84] which in itself is relative. While it is all well and good to promote harmony in diversity, Booth talks of the "tyranny of cultures" where culturalism reinforces traditionalism which "can have several regressive consequences for the theory and practice of human rights."[85] Traditionalism, it should be noted, is not to be confused with traditions, as these are very important in holding societies together. As with all other practices, traditionalism has both positive and negative aspects. For Booth, the negative aspects can be profoundly threatening as traditionalist practices, for example, invariably translate into masculinist values hostile to women which legitimise domestic violence, the Hindu practice of *sati* and all other practices of patriarchal society[86] which seek to continue to disempower and marginalise women.

One of the problems with the defence of cultural relativism in not adhering to positive human rights practices is that it is generally a claim made by an elite of the group claiming to speak and act on behalf of the group and, therefore, the reality of the situation is mediated through this self appointed group.[87] This elite, therefore, speaks on behalf of culture as its "authentic" voice. Culture, however, is heterogeneous and cultural claims are contested from within as well as without. An example of culture's inherently politically and socially contested terrain is exemplified in Islamic fundamentalist States where the voices of women's activists are suppressed. It is curious that those who completely oppose the universality of human rights law on the basis of its Eurocentricity or Western nature and its inability to accommodate cultural difference gladly retain certain aspects of Western ideologies, in this case, the right to privacy, as it helps maintain their physically and intellectually elitist position in society.

Booth has an inverse understanding of the universalist approach to human rights which may provide a more appropriate means of dealing with the issue. He believes that the only universal aspect to human rights is the universality of human wrongs. This is because they are easier to recognise than human rights, they are ubiquitous and, by inverting the approach, "concentration on wrongs shifts subjectivity to the victims by emphasising a "bottom-up" conception of world politics. This has the crucial effect of humanising the powerless."[88] While human rights discourse as currently proposed in the international arena is quite contentious, the very fact that it exists and continues to play an important role in international relations signifies some hope that perhaps, one day, there will be consensus on the issue. What of women's rights?

2.4 REINVENTING INTERNATIONAL LAW: WOMEN'S RIGHTS AS HUMAN RIGHTS IN THE INTERNATIONAL COMMUNITY[89]

A child of the inherently patriarchal and androcentric structures of both international law and international relations, international human rights law is inevitably a profoundly gendered discourse privileging men. It has been accused of belonging to "the masculine world of rights, masquerading as "human,""[90] as it completely ignores concepts of gender.

Due to the fact that Enlightenment man is both the creator and subject of international law and human rights discourse, issues dealing with human rights abuses of women have been largely ignored or seen to be a natural part of the status quo. The fact that political entities at both the national and international levels are dominated by men "means that issues traditionally of concern to men are seen as *general* human concerns; "women's concerns," by contrast, are regarded as a distinct and limited category."[91] White, western property-owning men, those responsible for creating human rights discourse, were more concerned with protection against violations of their civil and political rights in the public sphere and, as a result, these concerns are privileged in human rights discourse. As noted by Charlesworth, "rights are defined by the criterion of what men fear will happen to them."[92] Violations in the private sphere—the home—were not an issue "because they were the masters of that territory."[93] Power relations and the very political nature of the family unit went ignored for precisely this reason.[94]

"Women's rights are human rights," a phrase that gained increasing currency since the early 1990s, should be tautological and transhistorical, but, unfortunately, this is not the case. According to Charlesworth, this should be but a "distracting redundancy."[95] Unfortunately, abuses against women have become almost naturalised. As Kerr puts it, "So pervasive and systemic are the human rights abuses against women that they are regarded as part of the natural order."[96] For Bell, "the ambiguity of the phrase captures the essence of the feminist claim: an assertion for inclusion in the project of human rights and a radical redefinition of what that project entails."[97] Bunch thinks that because the dominant image of the political actor on the world stage is male that the problem for women is visibility, or lack thereof.[98] In an earlier article, she takes a more gynocentric approach and uses as a starting point the fact that women *do* have inalienable human rights and sees the crux of the matter as understanding "why they were excluded before and how to gain wider implementation of these rights now."[99] Whereas Bunch sees visibility as the problem, Ashworth sees the problem as arising out of the silencing of women. "In the silencing, the fact and acts of silencing also become invisible: without a visible victim, there is no crime, and without a crime there is no perpetrator,"[100] thereby perpetuating the abuses against women.

2.4.1 The Public/Private Divide and Women's Rights

The public/private debate that permeates international law provides fertile ground in international human rights discourse for feminist claims against State (ir)responsibility in incidences of abuses against women in the private sphere. Where has this distinction come from? It is said that the concept of the private sphere (versus the public sphere) is "a distinction that came… with a colonial inheritance of personal laws."[101] Charlesworth makes the point that the imposition of this distinction "replicates the "reforms" imposed by many colonial administrators which often weakened the position of women in colonial societies."[102] Public international law is very heavily premised on this dichotomy; this is not surprising given that this subject area is a western concept, as discussed at the beginning of this chapter. The divide is, therefore, a Western import to developing countries and carries with it heavy burdens for women, particularly in countries where culture and religion are deemed integral to the maintenance of the patriarchal structures that rely on the subordination and oppression of women for their existence.

Like human rights discourse, the public/private dichotomy is profoundly gendered and "an inherently political process that both reflects and reinforces power relations"[103] within society. The public sphere is said to encompass politics, economics, law and the workplace all of which are associated with men and their relationship with government. The private sphere, on the other hand, is where the family is found and, by necessary implication, where women belong. There is a "primal division of labour between the male warrior and the female childbearer" because "[m]an's place is in the public sphere of political government and the market economy, while women's place in the private sphere of domesticity"[104] due to her supposed frailty of body and mind. As one Iranian scholar noted, quoting an ayatollah, "The specific task of women in society is to marry and bear children. They will be discouraged from entering legislative, judicial, or whatever careers may require decision, as women *lack the intellectual ability and discerning required for those careers*."[105] It is this self assumed intellectual arrogance, coupled with the brute force that men may display over women, that continues to oppress women and keep them dependent on men in such societies.

It is often within the home, or private realm, that women are at risk of facing the greatest physical and/or mental abuse and yet, such abuses are "not within the proper scope of national criminal justice systems."[106] At the international level, international human rights law operates largely within the public sphere (optional protocol provisions and inherent complications aside) and the State is encouraged to protect the sanctity of the institution of the family which encompasses the family's right to privacy. This translates into the non-intervention by the State into the realm of family life, because of its allegedly sacrosanct nature and, as Sullivan rightly notes, "the family is the site of many of the most egregious violations of women's physical and mental integrity, [and] any blanket deferment to the institution of the family or privacy rights within the family has disastrous consequences for women."[107] The hypocrisy of the enshrined principle of non-intervention by the State into the affairs of the family is revealed by feminist research. Peterson and Parisi note that "the state intervenes in private sphere dynamics in part to impose centralized authority" over women's sexuality, the transfer of property and certain types of socialisation, such as heterosexuality (by criminalising homosexual behaviour).[108] While the State uses its power to intervene in the private sphere dynamics to suit male-dominated State interests, it uses that same power to promote the public-private divide as protecting the private from State interference.[109] Such targeted intervention "is a vital part of the authority and power the state receives and institutionalizes for men,"[110] thereby marginalizing and excluding women.

The fact that international human rights law operates primarily within the public sphere reflects the fact that the State is the subject of international law and that the transgressions of a State or its officials against individuals are the only offences that can be dealt with at this level. The actions of a private individual against another private individual are, of necessity, not subject to international scrutiny. The irony of the situation is that human rights activists are quick to pressure States to prevent other abuses, such as slavery and racism, which are often performed by private actors as well. Could it be that because slavery and racism are largely ungendered that they receive greater attention, as all of humanity and not just half (and the inferior half at that) is affected?

2.4.2 State Culpability and CEDAW

This is not to say that States cannot be held responsible for the actions of private individuals. Indeed, there are ways by which to infer culpability on the State for violations against women by private actors. With the adoption and ratification of the Convention on the Elimination of All Forms of Discrimination against Women ("CEDAW")[111], despite the myriad reservations and notwithstanding its soft law nature, according to article 2, States Parties have a positive duty towards women

> (b) To adopt appropriate legislative and other measures, including sanctions where appropriate, prohibiting all discrimination against women; and
> (f) To take all appropriate measures, including legislation, to modify or abolish existing laws, regulations, customs and practices which constitute discrimination against women...[112]

Threading the articles of the convention together is the call for the introduction and enforcement of legislation designed to protect and promote the social (as well as economic, political and cultural) advancement of women. Such articles, however, are of absolutely no legal force until the convention is incorporated into the domestic laws of States Parties.[113]

It is at this point that State culpability may be implied. Where a State refuses, actively or passively, to introduce legislative measures to give effect to the convention and prevent abuses against women, it may be said that it gives its tacit approval of such abuse. In the case of countries following the dualist theory of international law, there is even greater onus on the State to act and incorporate international law principles into domestic law. Failure to do so constitutes refusal on the part of the State to honour its commitments. While a State is not directly responsible for the abuses of private actors, the State may be accused of a lack of due diligence with regard to the awareness of human rights violations, as well as its failure to address the situation through sanctions and/or compensation and through denying women equal protection before the law. Women's human rights advocates hold that it is in condoning the acts of these private actors that the State may be held accountable.[114] It may even be said that "such actors are not really private because they could not function without the approval of the state."[115] Concerning the abuses against women, "a state may be considered to have facilitated an international wrong or to be complicit in its commission when the wrong is of a pervasive or persistent character."[116] State complicity in the commission of such abuses generally takes the form of a State's failure to act. Romany makes the point that a State's

> failure to arrest, prosecute, and imprison perpetrators of violence against women can be interpreted as acquiescence in (or ratification of) the private actor's conduct. State failure to prevent crimes against women can also be viewed as a conspiracy between the private actor and the state law enforcement agencies, thus rendering the state complicit.[117]

It must be mentioned that the introduction of legislative measures into the domestic law of a State party, while extremely commendable, is not enough by itself. The judiciary, police and any other State entity responsible for ensuring women's protection must be given the necessary capacity to perform. This includes general sensitisation to the rights of women and the changes in the law, education, training to deal with gender specific issues, and human and financial resources. Perhaps, most importantly, is the need to educate *men* to understand women's issues and get them to recognise the skewed nature of male-oriented "norms." Sadly, these are all dependent on the political will of the State, as without any State directive (through the implementation of laws and all follow up procedures), there is no need to change the status quo.[118] This is further compounded by the fact that the relationship between women and the State is extremely varied from State to State and continues both to evolve and regress in instances.[119] This lack of political will is not particular to women's and human rights law but is also seen in other areas considered to be of "lesser" importance, such as environmental law, particularly in developing economies, where emphasis is placed on the more pressing issues of maximising revenues by whatever means possible.[120] Political will and resource prioritisation always favour economic development in growing economies.

2.4.3 Cultural / Religious Relativism and Women's Rights

As mentioned above, the division of society into two different spheres, where one sphere is completely unregulated by law, creates greater difficulties for women living in societies ostensibly defined by cultural and religious practices. "No social group has suffered greater violation of its human rights in the name of culture than women,"[121] observes one Indian writer. Culture, for women, includes on a broader level, the denial of civil, political, social, economic, sexual and reproductive rights; on a more specific level, it may include female genital mutilation, *sati*, the inability to obtain a divorce, lack of choice in marriage, the imposition of a dress code, discrimination in inheritance and property laws, among myriad other issues. Women, in countries regulated by religious legal systems where religion and, by necessary implication, culture become enshrined into law and legalise patriarchal norms, face the greatest difficulty in abolishing discriminatory practices either through their own agency or with external help. In such instances, demands for equality based on sex are "met with resistance on the grounds that such demands amount to interference with the right to freedom of religion."[122]

Cultural relativists claim that women are the embodiment of a nation's culture and that the current human rights legal regime does not take this into consideration and, as a result, is not universally applicable.[123] This embodiment depends on the subordination of women and the maintenance of male elites. According to Chinkin, "Cultural and religious groups are often identified by the role and behaviour that they *designate* to women,"[124] implying that women have no choice as to what their role might be. Women in such groups are ostensibly held to be "the repository of tradition and old affection and family history,"[125] which provides the justification for their continued and unquestioning oppression. The imposition of the Western notion of the public/private divide only reinforced this conception as Coomaraswamy notes that "private life remained immune and was constructed and reinvented so that women's position [in society] became tied up with the cultural symbolism of the nation or ethnic group."[126] It is in this way that religion, culture and the Western import of the right to privacy have become inextricably linked and even more powerful in terms of keeping women subordinated. As Raday notes, "deference to religious and subculture norms operates to impose patriarchy on women" and is worsened when such ideals are formally institutionalised into law.[127]

Cries of cultural imperialism by non-western countries have allowed many States Parties to CEDAW to enter significant reservations on ratification, accession or succession, despite the fact that these reservations have the effect of nullifying the objective of the convention and are contrary to article 28(2) which states that "[a] reservation incompatible with the object and purpose of the present Convention shall not be permitted,"[128] which is also in keeping with Article 19(c) of the Vienna Convention on the Law of Treaties that says, "A State may...formulate a reservation unless: (c) in cases not falling under sub-paragraphs (a)[129] and (b)[130], the reservation is incompatible with the object and purpose of the treaty."[131] According to the United Nations Division for the Advancement of Women website, there are 188 States Parties as of 13 July 2011.[132] From its update on 18 December 2003 to its current update, this number went up by only eight. CEDAW, not surprisingly, is known as having the highest number of reservations of any human rights convention ever formulated[133] despite the fact that it is in apparent violation of specific articles within CEDAW itself and the Vienna Convention on the Law of Treaties, which governs treaty making. The soft law approach taken in this convention allows for "consensus" (in its *loosest* possible meaning) where it would have otherwise been impossible despite the obvious absurdity the many reservations have resulted in and the fact that the status quo of women worldwide remains largely unchanged.[134]

2.4.4 Gender Equality and the Male Standard

Coming out of the treaty was the obvious and pressing need for gender equality and the means by which to achieve this. Unfortunately, equality for women in the human rights discourse has come to be understood to mean the achievement of rights accorded to men with reluctance to recognise the inherent differences between men and women. Men provide the measure by which equality is measured. The very title of CEDAW "presupposes a male standard...attempting to bring women into the male world through the removal of legal constraints."[135] The search for equality initially led to severe absurdities in the interpretation of the law, particularly in cases of sex discrimination and unfair dismissal due to pregnancy. In the infamous American case, *General Electric Company v Gilbert et al*,[136] a group of women brought an action against the firm on the basis that the firm's disability plan which paid weekly non-occupational sickness and accident benefits precluded "disabilities" arising from pregnancy. In a strange turn of events, the lower courts held that this amounted to discrimination under the Civil Rights Act but the highest Court of Appeal, in a majority decision, reversed the decision. Justice Rehnquist, referring to a decision taken by him and his colleagues in *Geduldig v Aiello*,[137] stated in the decision that the plan "is facially nondiscriminatory in the sense that "[t]here is no risk from which men are protected and women are not. Likewise, there is no risk from which women are protected and men are not."" He also went on to show that the company's plan simply divided "potential recipients into two groups—pregnant women and non-pregnant persons. While the first group is exclusively female, the second includes members of both sexes." Could the first group possibly *be* constituted differently? This was a case of "if men don't need it, women don't get it,"[138] as one author noted rather sardonically.

Kaufman and Lindquist sought to justify this ludicrous decision by emphasising the need for maintaining consistency in the common law tradition.[139] The Court could have equally *overruled* the decision and still adhered to the principles of the common law tradition and not produced such a startlingly gendered (not to mention nonsensical) judgement; although this would have meant overruling one of their own decisions. There are those who believe that the use of gender-neutral language and having more female lawyers and judges can help improve the lot of women. While the latter may deal with issues of female under-representation in a male dominated arena, most women who undertake such professions are socialised by the legal practice to think and behave like men and, while sympathetic, may not always be able to render objective decisions, or even decisions tending towards a female-oriented view of the world. They also tend to be discriminated against on the basis of their female gender.[140] Those who are, in fact, strong enough to maintain a female perspective may not be aggressive enough or be able to gather consensus from fellow colleagues on certain issues.

Equality should recognise the inherently differential roles and contributions of both sexes and should not seek to level the playing field as such, as again men are used as the standard by which to achieve such equality and can result in absurdities as highlighted in the case above. Instead of an androcentric approach, or even a gynocentric approach, a "humanocentric" approach should be applied which neither reduces women by attempting to eliminate their differences or marginalise them *because* of those differences, but one which embraces said differences and treats women with similar regard as men are accorded all at once. The concept of women's rights as human rights, as painted above, does present a picture of gloom; however, the situation would appear to be changing with women of all professions and status taking on a much more aggressive, active and visible role in promoting the rights of women around the world.

2.5 INTERNATIONAL LAW AND WOMEN'S RIGHTS: THE STRUGGLE FOR EQUAL TREATMENT

2.5.1 The Politics of Rights

International law's weaknesses as a tool for the promotion of gender equality and human rights generally have been explored. Inherent gender bias; its soft law character and associated issues of implementation and enforcement at the national level; primacy of the State as actor in the international arena; unwillingness of States to relinquish any degree of sovereignty; and cultural / religious relativist arguments comprise the main obstacles to the effectiveness of international law instruments. These difficulties notwithstanding, international legal instruments have the potential to be used as political tools with positive effect. When States sign up to a convention, this provides a site for activists on the ground to organise and pressure States to act. Activists can now engage in "accountability politics"[141] to remind governments of their obligations and, in the face of inaction, expose the recalcitrant State and bring pressure to bear on the powers that be and even successfully force change. NGOs have been successful at the international level in having provisions dealing with the status of women and their participation included in international legal instruments and subsequently using these documents as leverage to effect change at the national level.[142] Sankey makes the point that international law filters downward

> [d]ue in part to the slow but steady pressure of NGOs… declarations have been replaced by binding conventions, monitoring their implementation has been entrusted to special committees and rapporteurs, and individual governments suddenly find themselves being called to account for cases of torture, detention and 'disappearances.'[143]

The potential for international law to have effect at the national level, therefore, is real and can be effected through the work of activists especially where international law seems to lack the mechanisms to do so in areas not deemed to be vital to State interests, such as the promotion of women's rights.[144]

2.5.2 Women's Rights and the United Nations

The fight by women for equality has taken on a largely legal character,[145] as it is recognised that legal reform, combined with the necessary changes to the education system (to deal with deeply entrenched patriarchal attitudes), has the ability to provide one of the greatest catalysts for societal change. This fight has to be examined at the international level so as to determine the effectiveness of the top-down approach in remedying the repression of women's rights, a problem that has existed throughout much of human history. It should be noted that the term "legal" is used loosely, as the non-binding aspect of declarations, conventions[146] and platforms for action (despite States' ostensible intention to be bound), as well individual legal systems, make domestic application and enforcement rather difficult.[147] While protocols tend to be of greater force, they, too, suffer from similar problems.

The United Nations has formulated eight conventions and two declarations that are committed specifically to promoting women's rights. These include:[148]

- The UN Convention for the Suppression of the Traffic in Persons and of the Exploitation of the Prostitution of Others[149] which calls for the punishment of those procuring others for prostitution;
- The International Labour Organization Convention on Equal Remuneration (1951) which establishes the principle and practice of equal pay for work of equal value as requested and endorsed by ECOSOC;[150]
- The UN Convention on the Political Rights of Women[151] fully supported by the General Assembly as early as 1946[152] which commits Member States to allow women to vote and hold public office on terms with men;[153]
- The UN Convention on the Nationality of Married Women[154] which sought to protect the right of a married woman to retain her nationality;[155]
- The UN Convention on Consent to Marriage, Minimum Age for Marriage and Registration of Marriages[156] which states that marriage can only take place with the consent of both parties;[157]
- The United Nations Educational, Scientific and Cultural Organization Convention against Discrimination in Education (1960) which provides for equal educational opportunities for girls and boys;
- The UN Declaration on the Elimination of Discrimination Against Women[158] which declares women's equal status with men;[159]
- The UN Convention on the Elimination of All Forms of Discrimination against women which prohibits any distinction, exclusion or restriction made on the basis of sex that impairs or nullifies the human rights and fundamental freedoms of women in all areas;[160]
- The UN Declaration on the Elimination of Violence Against Women[161] which condemns any act causing physical, sexual or psychological harm or suffering to women of violence against women by the family, community or state;
- The UN Convention on the Rights of the Child which recognises the right of the child to fundamental human rights and special care.[162]

The question here really is whether international legal instruments can have positive effects in domestic legal regimes,[163] but again this relies on commitment, priority and political will of the State concerned. To determine the effectiveness of the top-down approach, one convention (including its precursor and follow-ups) and two declarations are examined in some detail.

2.5.3 Convention on the Elimination of All Forms of Discrimination Against Women

2.5.3.1 Declaration on the Elimination of Discrimination Against Women

While the UN made moves towards establishing a fair amount of legislative and institutional support for the promotion of women's equal rights, the organisation recognised that women were still largely unprotected by these changes and discrimination continued unabated. In light of this, the General Assembly requested the drafting of a Declaration on the Elimination of Discrimination Against Women ("DEDAW") and this was unanimously approved by the General Assembly on 07 November 1967. It consisted of eleven Articles which declare that discrimination against women is unjust and incompatible with the welfare of the family and society and called on States to implement new laws to end discrimination against women so that women would be afforded full protection under the law.[164] As a declaration, it meant that this was but a statement of intent, moral and political, and was, therefore, of even less contractual force than treaties which have also proved problematic in terms of enforcement at the national level.

2.5.3.2 Convention on the Elimination of Discrimination Against Women

The above mentioned UN Conventions provided a very scattered approach to dealing with the issue of women's human rights; a comprehensive approach was required and there was need to prepare a single, comprehensive and internationally binding legal instrument to eliminate discrimination against women.[165] As a means of "preparing a binding treaty that would give normative force to the provisions of the Declaration,"[166] the Commission on the Status of Women ("CSW") requested the Secretary-General to call upon UN member States to communicate their ideas on such a proposal. This instrument was to be prepared without prejudice to any future recommendations that might be made by the United Nations or its specialised agencies with respect to the preparation of legal instruments to eliminate discrimination in specific fields.[167]

These initiatives led to the adoption by the General Assembly of the Convention on the Elimination of All Forms of Discrimination Against Women

("CEDAW"), which was subsequently dubbed an international bill of rights for women. Article one of the convention defined discrimination against women as

> any distinction, exclusion or restriction made on the basis of sex which has the effect or purpose of impairing or nullifying the recognition, enjoyment or exercise by women irrespective of their marital status, on a basis of equality of men and women, of human rights and fundamental freedoms on the political, economic, social, cultural, civil or any other field.[168]

While it may have been the swiftest entry into force of any human rights instrument at the time,[169] it was also the convention with the largest number of reservations entered, reflecting States Parties' unwillingness to accept the full scope of obligations stated in the instrument.[170]

Noteworthy are the reasons for reservations. The most significant number of reservations, as seen in tables 2.1 [which provides an aggregate of the data provided in table 2.2] and 2.2 [which provides a breakdown by country of the specific reservations and declarations made], concerns articles 2, 9, 11, 15, 16 and 29 and reflect States' unwillingness to be bound by provisions that strike at the root of the convention, especially articles 2 and 16. Several countries which practice Islamic law have clearly stated that the convention will not be given preference over current religious practices which are legislated in those countries; however, it is said practices which negate the effect of the convention.[171]

Other countries have also invoked multiculturalism, custom and tradition [or cultural relativism, which is ordinarily discriminatory towards women[172]] as reasons for not implementing the convention, thereby justifying the continued discriminatory practices against women, representing "nothing more than disguises for the universality of male determination to cling to power and privilege."[173] On the other hand, however, there are countries that have entered reservations on the basis that their constitutions and/or domestic legislation is already more generous than the requirements stated by the convention and will continue to give preference to their own legislation, even though Article 23 provides for such an occurrence.[174]

The reservations incompatible with the purposes and objectives of the convention continue despite the General Assembly's appeal at the fiftieth anniversary of the Universal Declaration of Human Rights to States Parties to honour their obligations under the convention.[175] CEDAW has also called on States Parties to remove or modify reservations, especially those made to articles 2 and 16, as this

> would indicate a State party's determination to remove all barriers to women's full equality and its commitment to ensuring that women are able to participate

Table 2.1. Number of Reservations and Declarations Entered Per Article of the Convention on the Elimination of All Forms of Discrimination Against Women

Convention Article Number	*Number of Reservations*	*Number of Declarations*
1	3	
2	17	1
5	3	5
7	3	1
9	18	3
11	8	1
13	3	
14	1	
15	12	2
16	27	3
29	36	4
TOTAL	131	29

Information for tables 2.1 and 2.2 are derived from United Nations Treaty Collection, "Convention on the Elimination of All Forms of Discrimination against Women: Declarations and Reservations," last updated 13 July 2011, accessed 13 July 2011, http://treaties.un.org/Pages/ViewDetails.aspx?src=TREATY&mtdsg_no=IV-8&chapter=4&lang=en#74.

> fully in all aspects of public and private life without fear of discrimination or recrimination. States which remove reservations would be making a major contribution to achieving the objectives of both formal and de facto or substantive compliance with the Convention.[176]

Despite the myriad obstacles faced in obtaining international consensus on the issue, CEDAW may be seen as a watershed in the development of an international legal instrument for the promotion, protection and recognition of women's human rights as well for the recognition and incorporation of the specificity of the female subject. If nothing else, it has certainly contributed to raising worldwide awareness of women's issues.

2.5.3.3 The Beijing Declaration and the Platform for Action

At the largest UN Conference ever held, the Fourth World Conference on Women, the Beijing Declaration reaffirmed its commitment to continue to promote and protect the rights of women in all spheres and to ensure that they are treated with the same respect as men.[177] The Declaration also called for the implementation of the Platform for Action ("BPFA") and the mainstreaming of a gender perspective into all UN policy and programmes. The objectives of the conference were to review and appraise the advancement of women since 1985 with regard to the Nairobi Forward-Looking Strategies; to mobilise women and men at both the policy-making level and grass-roots level to achieve the objectives; to adopt a Platform for Action which deals with key issues identified as posing grave hindrances to the advancement of

Table 2.2. Reservations and Declarations Entered by States Parties According to Specific Articles of the Convention on the Elimination of All Forms of Discrimination Against Women

*Country**	*Articles of the Convention with Reservations/Declarations*										
	1	2	5	7	9	11	13	14	15	16	29
Algeria		R			R				R	R	R
Argentina											R
Australia						R					
Austria						R					
Bahamas		R			R						R
Bahrain		R			R				R	R	R
Bangladesh		R								R	
Brazil											R
Brunei Darussalem					R						R
China											R
Cuba											R
DPR Korea		R			R						R
Egypt		R								R	R
El Salvador											R
Ethiopia											R
France			D		D			R		R	R
India			D							D	R
Indonesia											R
Iraq		R			R					R	R
Ireland					R	R	R		R	R	
Israel				R						R	D
Jamaica											D
Jordan					D					D	
Kuwait					R					R	R
Lebanon					R					R	D
Lesotho		R									
Libyan Arab Jamahiriya		R								R	
Liechtenstein	R										
Malaysia			D	D	D	D				D	
Maldives				R						R	
Malta						R	R		R	R	
Mauritius											R
Micronesia		R	R			R				R	R
Monaco				R	R					R	R
Morocco		D							D		R
Myanmar											R
New Zealand		R	R								
Niger		R	RD						R	R	R
Oman					R				R	R	R
Pakistan											R
Qatar	D	R	D	R					R	R	R

(continued)

Table 2.2. *Continued*

*Country**	*Articles of the Convention with Reservations/Declarations*							
Rep. of Korea			R				R	
Saudi Arabia			R					R
Singapore		R		R			R	R
Switzerland						R	R	
Syrian Arab Republic		R	R			R	R	R
Thailand							R	R
Trinidad and Tobago								R
Tunisia			R			D	R	R
Turkey								R
United Arab Emirates		R	R			R	R	R
United Kingdom	R		R	R		R	R	
UK on behalf of Isle of Man, BVI, the Falkland Islands, South Georgia and the South Sandwich Islands, the Turks and Caicos Islands	R	R	R	R	R	R	R	
Venezuela								R
Viet Nam								R
Yemen								D

References to articles do not necessarily indicate reservations or declarations with the whole article, as many states entered reservations and declarations to specific sub-articles. It should be noted that this table does not include countries that have entered only general reservations and/or declarations. The following countries have entered general reservations: Italy, Mauritania and Saudi Arabia. The following countries have entered general declarations: Australia, Chile, Germany, Monaco, Mexico, Netherlands, Pakistan, Spain, Thailand and Tunisia. This information is correct as at 13 July 2011.

women; and to determine the priorities for the following five years for implementation of the BPFA.[178] As a tool for the implementation of the Declaration, the BPFA is an agenda for women's empowerment[179] and identifies the following as critical areas of concern for women:[180]

- The persistent and increasing burden of poverty on women
- Inequalities and inadequacies in and unequal access to education and training
- Inequalities and inadequacies in and unequal access to health care and related services
- Violence against women
- The effects of armed or other kinds of conflict on women, including those living under foreign occupation
- Inequality in economic structures and policies, in all forms of productive activities and in access to resources

- Inequality between men and women in the sharing of power and decision-making at all levels
- Insufficient mechanisms at all levels to promote the advancement of women
- Lack of respect for and inadequate promotion and protection of the human rights of women
- Stereotyping of women and inequality in women's access to and participation in all communication systems, especially in the media
- Gender inequalities in the management of natural resources and in the safeguarding of the environment
- Persistent discrimination against and violation of the rights of the girl child.

This document provides the countries of the world with "a comprehensive action plan to enhance the social, economic and political empowerment of women."[181] It draws on the legacies of past UN Conferences that dealt with women's issues, such Nairobi (1985), New York (children 1990), Rio de Janeiro (environment 1992), Vienna (human rights 1993), Cairo (population and development 1994) and Copenhagen (social development 1995) and reviews and assesses progress in implementing the Nairobi Forward-Looking Strategies for the Advancement of Women. Beijing represented a "stock-taking of the progress made in the worldwide advancement of women."[182] Unfortunately, the BPFA had to call for efforts to be made to achieve the goals drawn up at Nairobi ten years earlier.[183]

As with the other conferences dealing with women's issues, it is instructive to note that "[t]he most visible and active forces behind this movement [for gender equality] have been the non-governmental organizations."[184] Some 30,000 NGO representatives gathered at the parallel unofficial NGO Forum held in Houairou, some thirty miles outside of Beijing.[185] At the same time, however, "some NGOs were part of their country's state apparatus, serving as advocates and even watchdogs for their governments, silencing grassroots NGOs and keeping even those from other countries under scrutiny."[186] It was, nevertheless, still quite free and representatives stated their opinions.

There were three main problematic issues which Charlesworth correctly described as being Sisyphean.[187] Just when the feminist movement thought that important advances were made in particular areas at previous conferences, objections were taken at Beijing which could have negated the progress made before. The Holy See objected to the use of the term "gender" as it could lead to dubious interpretations, with the potential to endorse homosexuality and bestiality;[188] Islamic States were able keep the universalist-cultural relativist issue alive by decrying the universality of women's human rights as western feminist imperialism;[189] and this was also applied by Islamic States and the Vatican to their strong opposition "to sections of the BPA that dealt with women's autonomy in relation to sexuality and reproductive function."[190]

These difficulties notwithstanding there were also some limited, but important, gains that are captured in the BPFA. Steans and Ahmady state that efforts towards gender mainstreaming have institutionalised the link between selected NGOs and women's groups and various bodies in the UN system.[191] According to Rao, the BPFA has emphasised women's rights as human rights and believes that there is some, though minimal, acknowledgment of the difference between rights versus needs.[192] There has been, too, some recognition of violence against women as a public issue and not a private one and there have also been some advances in the issue of women's reproductive health.

Unsurprisingly, Beijing +5 (2000) and Beijing +10 (2005) both represent reaffirmations by governments of their commitment to implementing the BPFA, as well as appeals to governments to advocate its implementation.[193] *Beijing Betrayed*, an aptly named report issued in time for Beijing +10, which examines global progress made to date vis-à-vis the implementation of the BPFA, asserts that

> Governments worldwide have displayed a lack of will in turning their commitments to women's rights into decisive action, instead adopting a piecemeal and incremental approach that cannot achieve the economic, social and political transformation underlying the promises of Beijing.[194]

The organisation attributes the non-implementation of the BPFA to a combination of global trends. The lack of practical commitment can be attributed to "the predominance of the neo-liberal economic framework, growing militarization, and rising fundamentalism" in addition to a lack of resources and political will.[195]

Similar to the Vienna Declaration and Programme of Action, the Beijing Declaration and BPFA are not legally binding. Bunch and Fried make the point that such instruments "carry the political and moral weight as policy guidelines" and "must be approached as statements of best intentions and commitments to which organized groups can seek to hold governments and the UN accountable."[196] Given this, it is the responsibility of individual governments to implement the measures suggested in the BPFA for the advancement of women and without the necessary incentives (either positive or negative) domestic changes will be slow in coming. The gap between rhetoric and reality is still alarming. Governments keep pledging their commitment but there is little of substance to reflect this. In the absence of any truly legally binding instrument, hope lies possibly only with the NGO movement and civil society which hold the power to have the Platform effectively implemented by gathering support from those who are truly affected and lobbying governments from below to effect positive change at the national level.

2.5.3.4 The Optional Protocol

Hailed as a landmark decision for women,[197] the Optional Protocol ("the Protocol") to CEDAW was adopted by the General Assembly on 06 October 1999 at its 28th plenary meeting[198] and entered into force on 22 December 2000.[199] It set out the first gender-specific international complaints procedure seeking to reinforce human rights monitoring.[200] It was borne out of initiatives taken by the CSW and supported by the Vienna Declaration and Programme of Action, as well as the Beijing Platform for Action. Optional protocols often follow human rights treaties to provide procedures with regard to the treaty or address a substantive area related to the treaty.[201] They are treaties in their own right and bring specificity to the main treaty. This Protocol was seen as necessary to strengthen CEDAW by giving individuals, groups and NGOs the right to complain to the Committee about violations of the convention and to allow the Committee to conduct enquiries into grave or systematic abuses of women's human rights in countries that have ratified the Protocol.[202] It is meant to:

1. Improve and add to existing enforcement mechanisms for women's human rights
2. Improve States' and individuals' understanding of CEDAW
3. Stimulate States to take steps to implement CEDAW
4. Stimulate changes in discriminatory laws and practices
5. Enhance existing mechanisms for the implementation of human rights within the UN system
6. Create greater public awareness of human rights standards relating to discrimination against women[203]

Nevertheless, there are several problems that are immediately discernable with the Protocol. First of all, like treaties generally, it is *optional*, States need not become a party to it. What is the point of having an optional protocol that provides specificity when States are not legally obligated to join and, further, view the main treaty (CEDAW) as optional in itself and refuse to implement the provisions found therein? Article 17 states that no reservations to the Protocol are permitted but, in the same breath, States may opt out of the of the enquiry clause of the Protocol, Article 10, by refusing to recognise the competence of the Committee to conduct investigations into claims of grave or systematic violations, thereby nullifying the potentially positive effects of Articles 8 and 9. This continues to leave the Committee toothless. Article 19 also allows for a State Party to denounce the Protocol at any time. International law is already especially problematic as concerns the domestic application of international instruments; with these conditions, how is this self-negating Protocol supposed to serve its purpose, besides, perhaps, to temporarily placate interest groups until they recognise the Protocol for what it truly is?

2.5.4 The Vienna Declaration

The World Conference on Human Rights produced the Vienna Declaration and Programme of Action.[204] Section II.A.3 deals specifically with the equal status and human rights of women, emphasising the importance of synchronising the *de jure* and *de facto* human rights of women. The Declaration highlighted the inalienability and universality of women's human rights; the importance of gender mainstreaming;[205] and the elimination of violence and discrimination against women.[206] One author believes that Vienna represented the commencement of the narrowing of the universalist-cultural relativist gulf which plagues the promotion of women's human rights and the beginning of the ability of the international community to achieve practical commitments and enforceable standards for the protection of women's rights.[207] This may be so in light of the steps taken (on paper) at the Conference towards institutional and legal capacity building with a view to rendering the legal human rights regime of women effective.[208] Nevertheless, documents produced as a result of the conference are of no legal effect and it is left to governments to decide whether to act on the suggestions made.

2.5.5 Declaration on the Elimination of Violence Against Women

Not only was discrimination against women a problem, but so too was the issue of violence, as they both continue to be. The right to equality sought by women included the right to equal treatment by the law and to be protected against violence. In recognition of the scourge of violence faced by millions of women and the fact that CEDAW did not expressly deal with violence, the General Assembly requested the CSW to draft a document to deal with the elimination of violence against women.[209] The Declaration on the Elimination of Violence Against Women ("DEVAW") was adopted by the General Assembly on 20 December 1993.[210] It is important to note that it was the NGO movement that spearheaded efforts at the international level to have violence against women recognised as a serious problem.[211] It was the first attempt to define gender—based violence that traversed the private/public divide and recognised individuals, communities and the State, as perpetrators of violence against women. According to Article 1, gender-based violence refers to the "physical, sexual or psychological harm or suffering to women, including threats of such acts, coercion or arbitrary deprivation of liberty, whether occurring in public or in private life." This is explicitly developed in Article 2 which states:

> Violence against women shall be understood to encompass, but not be limited to, the following:
>
> (a) Physical, sexual and psychological violence occurring in the family, including battering, sexual abuse of female children in the household, dowry-related violence, marital rape, female genital mutilation and other traditional practices harmful to women, non-spousal violence and violence related to exploitation;
>
> (b) Physical, sexual and psychological violence occurring within the general community, including rape, sexual abuse, sexual harassment and intimidation at work, in educational institutions and elsewhere, trafficking in women and forced prostitution;
>
> (c) Physical, sexual and psychological violence perpetrated or condoned by the State, wherever it occurs.

Article 4 of DEVAW, which echoes Article 5 of CEDAW, specifically requests that States not "invoke any custom, tradition or religious consideration to avoid their obligations with respect to its elimination." It also declares that "States should pursue by all appropriate means and without delay a policy of eliminating violence against women…"

The Commission on Human Rights appointed a Special Rapporteur[212] to investigate the issue of gender-based violence and make recommendations for its elimination. Her preliminary report revealed that gender-based violence was a result of historically unequal power relations between men and women which became institutionalised over time.[213] She made a very interesting point that "men control the knowledge systems of the world" and that "it is this lack of control over knowledge systems which allows them [women] not only to be victims of violence, but to be part of a discourse which often legitimizes or trivializes violence against women."[214] This ties in very neatly with the arguments made in chapter one above on critical theory and the feminist exposure of male biases in knowledge construction. The Special Rapporteur has taken the first step of recognising the bias and making recommendations for its removal. It is the last step of emancipation that is proving quite challenging.

In her conclusions and recommendations, the Special Rapporteur called on States to:

1. Condemn violence against women and not invoke custom, tradition or religion to avoid their obligations to eliminate such violence
2. Ratify CEDAW without reservation

3. Formulate national plans of action to combat violence against women
4. Initiate strategies to develop legal and administrative mechanisms to ensure effective justice for women victims of violence
5. Train and sensitize judicial and police officials with regard to the issues concerning violence against women
6. Reform educational curricula so as to instil values which prevent violence against women
7. Promote research with regard to the issues concerning violence against women
8. Ensure proper reporting of the problem of violence against women to international human rights mechanism.[215]

She also called for the formulation of an optional protocol to CEDAW to allow for an individual right of petition once local remedies have been exhausted.[216]

Unfortunately, despite these excellent recommendations, should this Declaration be formalised into a convention, it would likely receive a similar response to CEDAW in terms of the number of reservations that are likely to be entered. The duties placed on States to eliminate violence against women would be quite onerous and wide-ranging and will meet with opposition as it will have the effect of "infringing" on custom and tradition and, in some cases, would require a complete socio-cultural and legal overhaul, as is currently the case with CEDAW.

2.6 NON GENDER-SPECIFIC INTERNATIONAL LEGAL INSTRUMENTS

There are other conventions that are non-gender specific but have the potential to enhance women's rights at the international level. Initially, women played an insignificant role in the determination of political, legal and institutional structures both in the USA and in Europe where much of the human rights debate was pursued,[217] largely because women historically have been denied political identity and agency.[218] International law as it pertains to the rights of women (as humans) is biased by the probability that the main international law makers are men and really do not take into account the needs of women. A look at the various conventions dealing with war crimes and crimes committed against humanity would suggest that they still do not take into consideration women's issues. The Convention of the Prevention and Punishment of the Crime of Genocide[219] defines genocide in reference to national, ethnical, racial or religious groups as

> (a) killing members of the group; (b) causing serious bodily or mental harm to members of the group; (c) deliberately inflicting in the group conditions of life calculated to bring about its physical destruction in whole or in part; (d) imposing measures intended to prevent births within the group; (f) forcibly transferring children of the group to another group.

It is prohibited in the Geneva Convention relative to the Protection of Civilian Persons in Time of War[220] to commit any of the following: *"(a) Violence to life and person, in particular murder of all kinds, mutilation, cruel treatment and torture; (b) taking of hostages; (c) outrages upon personal dignity, in particular humiliating and degrading treatment:..."* The former would appear to include women by virtue of section (d), while there are no gender specific references in the latter convention. How does either of these conventions treat with the issue of ethnic cleansing in the form of rape after which these women are forced to bear these children? It is to be inferred in sections (a) and (c) of the Geneva Convention relative to the Protection of Civilian Persons in the Time of War? If not, why has neither of these conventions been amended to consider this fact? Why have there not been any attempts to make new international legal instruments to deal with such grievous crimes?[221]

It would appear from a survey of gender-based treaty law that these types of conventions are discriminatory in the sense that they describe "exclusionary provisions which reflect a societal concept of women as a group which either should or cannot engage in specified activities."[222] In contrast, corrective or non-discriminatory conventions seek to improve treatment meted out to women without making overt comparisons to the treatment of man, such as seen in the Convention for the Suppression of the Traffic in Persons and of the Exploitation of the Prostitution of Others.[223] Hevener goes on to describe the non-discriminatory conventions as those which do not separate women as a different group and which do not assert that biological differences should create the basis for social of political discrimination. This is evidenced in the Universal Declaration of Human Rights of 1948.

These conventions prove that historically there has been a concern with the rights of women in the arena of international law and human rights. International law has proven, however, to be somewhat myopic and the fact of an absence of a forum for international review of these instruments aggravates the situation. These legal instruments have remained rather restrained in their ability to improve, or even affect, the condition of women and are criticised as representing little more than statements of good intentions on behalf of the parties to the international conventions.[224] This is further aggravated by the fact that women generally remain under-represented in decision-making structures,[225] particularly where governance is concerned on both the domestic and international level.

According to Gaer, there are several reasons why women's issues do not rank high in the United Nations human rights mechanisms.[226] Firstly, many delegates to these UN conventions are lawyers and there is a tendency on their part to focus on due process and traditional formal procedures. Further, human rights bodies tend to focus on civil and political rights rather than on socio-economic rights. Even if socio-economic rights are contemplated, it is generally through the lens of development issues. Gaer states that there would appear to be a lack of consciousness of gender discrimination among human rights organisations. Finally, the sentiment that gender discrimination is a private affair justifies keeping it outside the responsibilities of governments. There would also seem to be little communication between the separate UN bodies mandated to examine the legal instruments.

2.7 MANAGING THE RELATIONSHIP BETWEEN STATES: INTERNATIONAL RELATIONS AND THE GENDER BIAS

The above discussions clearly place the State as the central actor in international law and it is, therefore, critical to examine the attitude of States in the management of their relationships with each other as this attitude would certainly enhance the understanding of the place of women's rights issues in the spectrum of international law. Feminist writings illustrate that gender *is* in fact enormously important to the understanding of international relations. Peterson notes that international relations feminists have expanded and transformed international relations theories as they pertain to issues of identity, sexuality, militarism, polity, revolutions, nationalisms, social hierarchies, transnational economics, political movements and international organisations.[227] Sylvester has grouped such issues and identified three main areas of international relations in which gender is interested: critique and reappropriation of stories told about the proper scope of international relations; revisions of war and peace narratives; and reevaluations of women and development in the international system and its parts.[228] It is the very first area which is of concern here, as it forms the subject of study here in illustrating male bias.

The very notion of the principal actor in (realist) international relations, the sovereign State, is gendered. Sovereignty revolves around notions of the exercise of power within State boundaries, the duty of non-intervention in the affairs that fall within the exclusive jurisdiction of other States, and protection of the people and property that form part of that State.[229] In order to fulfil these requirements, the State adopted a certain character and came to personify an idealised concept of masculinity.[230] Certain decidedly masculine characteristics were projected onto the State—strength, power, autonomy, independence and rationality[231]—all necessary in exercising sovereignty and maintaining the integrity of State security.

According to Steans, this personification of the State into a "purposive individual," known as sovereign man or rational political man,[232] is a rational choice-making individual able to legitimise violence. He is placed at the centre of the conceptual universe and therefore becomes the subject of knowledge. Sovereign man is held to embody the "truth" of international relations where international relations refer to the relations between "him, the state… and a series of marginalized and displaced others."[233] Examining international relations critically from a gender perspective allows not only for rendering visible structural gender inequalities but also for "empowering women as subjects of knowledge"[234] and not seeing them solely as passive objects.

Runyan and Peterson posit a very interesting argument concerning women's ostensible unimportance to international relations. According to these authors, women are "both invisible in and yet central to the tenets of realism."[235] They liken woman to all that realist international relations theory has no control over, such as the state of anarchy, war and crises, which states ultimately seek to control. They examine it from the perspective of patriarchal relations of "manstate" seeking to control "women," which it construes as an unreasonable (mad), anarchical "outsider" or "other."[236] This construction of woman as madness, other and outsider is coterminous with realism's definition of international relations and gives rise to the need to "tame" and "domesticate" her, as she must be brought under control due to her inability to ever be capable of reason.[237] This reinforces Enloe's examination of "how the conduct of international politics has *depended* on men's control of women."[238]

As an alternative perspective and part of the "third debate" or "inter-paradigm debate," the introduction of the gender viewpoint problematises the "truths" presented in various paradigms of international relations. It questions the "underlying ontological, epistemological, and axiological premises and assumptions"[239] of these paradigms by highlighting the gendered premises on which international relations is based. Feminist theorising

> critically probes social theories for marks of gender that have gone unnoticed, and reveals distortions, biases, exclusions, inequalities, and denied identity politics in such theories; it traces how it has come to be that gendered theories seem neutral and universal and without gender; it transgresses the boundaries of supposedly true theories by posing gender experiences or narratives that counter or deepen our knowledge, or that reveal another side, a different puzzle, perhaps a different story than gender; it looks in 'strange' places for the people, stories, or even data…to fill out or rewrite, sometimes with unusual linguistic moves, what we think we know.[240]

Whitworth's approach to analysing gender in international relations is to ask whether international relations theory allows for a discussion on the social construction of meaning, historical variability and for the theorisation of power, as gender cannot be understood without reference to these issues.[241] In using these premises, Whitworth deliberates whether there exist any spaces within the various paradigmatic traditions of international relations to facilitate gender discussions.[242] According to her review, realism's ontological commitments to States and states*men* preclude any incorporation of gender into its analysis; neither can it theorise power. Pluralism is equally myopic as it is ahistorical and incapable of understanding the structural features of gender inequality and women's oppression. Critical theory, however, takes into account the three criteria mentioned above as central to theorising about international relations and holds the greatest promise for incorporating gender into international relations theory. Criticisms of critical theory itself notwithstanding, critical international relations theory presents the most appropriate place for treating with feminist concerns.

Whitworth also assesses mainstream feminist theories and identifies important deficiencies.[243] Liberal feminism was concerned mainly with the absence of women from both the study and practice of international relations, erroneously implying that women were not there in the first place. It uncritically accepts the realist "high politics" agenda and fails to comprehend the structural features of socio-political behaviour. Radical feminism suffers from essentialism, as it privileges women over men and perpetuates gender dichotomies. Feminist postmodernism argues for the social construction of meaning but also lacks the ability to identify and change gender inequalities. Again, for Whitworth, only critical feminist theory is able to assess biases, why and how such biases came into being, the effects of such biases and the possibility for change. Concurring with Whitworth, Steans states, "Feminist critical theory attempts a complex analysis of why and how the construction of gender has served to legitimize the subordination of women and of how hegemonic structures are imbued with patriarchal ideology."[244]

Tickner identifies the origin of the dichotomisation of gender roles with the birth of the public/private divide at the onset of the Industrial Revolution as the foundation upon which modern theories of international politics have been constructed.[245] This is coupled with the fact that policy formulations on the core concerns of international relations are conducted by men and international relations, as a discipline that analyses these activities, is "bound to be primarily about men and masculinity."[246] The reverse of this notion may also be true. If international relations, from an orthodox perspective, is comprised mainly of the activities of men, then this may also provide a forum for the production and maintenance of masculinities. According to Hooper, "It is likely that political events and masculine identities are both *simultaneous* products of men's participation in the practices of international relations."[247]

Women are also generally absent from warfare but, according to Steans, this is no historical accident.[248] Women symbolise masculinity subordinated or insufficient. Echoing de Beauvoir's sentiment, a boy is not born a soldier; he becomes a soldier. Many studies on the military reveal the fact that "[w]ar does not come naturally to humans. Men must be trained to fight and kill others."[249] Such training is achieved through misogynistic means by expunging feminine traits and behaviours in men in order to make them "real men."[250] Steans goes on to make a link between war and domestic violence.[251] The cultivation of a particular brand of masculinity for the killing fields, strongly linked to patriotism and violence, unfortunately makes its way into homes where it is completely inappropriate, as the battered are simply not similarly mentally and physically equipped.[252]

Brown's definition of a critical feminist international relations reflects the ideas postulated by both Whitworth and Steans and is quite instructive.

> A feminist international relations that is genuinely emancipatory will take gender difference as its starting point but will not take it as given. Its proper object and purpose must be to explain how gender has been constructed and maintained in international relations and if and how it can be removed."[253]

For Steans, critical feminist international relations has a fourfold purpose. It must point to the exclusions and biases of mainstream international relations; make women visible as social, economic and political subjects in international politics; analyse how gender inequalities have been embedded in the daily practices of international relations; and, importantly, empower women as subjects of knowledge.[254]

These indeed amount to a monumental task and are what this work seeks to achieve with particular reference to law. It is of fundamental importance not to reduce gender relations in international relations to *women* in international relations,[255] as gender is simply *not* synonymous with "woman." Brown recognises that a feminist critical theory of international relations is basically a political act of commitment to see the world through the eyes of the socially subjugated.[256] An immediate problem that arises here is that the socially subjugated speak from a position of marginality (and powerlessness) but lack the resources, access and knowledge to be heard.[257] The difficulty for the critical feminist theorist is to get the socially subjugated to appreciate the implications of what they see and to improve their condition if possible.

2.8 CONCLUSION

Groups are discriminated against on the basis of class, nationality, race, gender and sexual orientation. Human rights conventions have evolved over time and are indeed becoming increasingly inclusive. This is evidenced by the fact that human rights theory has expanded across ethnic and national lines in the context of decolonisation.[258] Interestingly, though, human rights are not necessarily synonymous with women's rights and have not included the notion of gender, where gender may refer to the ideological and material relations which exist between men and women;[259] human rights would seem to be the human rights of men.

Early international law was predicated on Western theological notions and the role of women was accorded little or no significance. The situation did not change perceptibly in the Renaissance period when international law assumed a more secular character. This period emphasised the notion of sovereignty and rights, but rights as applicable to men.

In the post-World War II era with the establishment of the UN Charter, human rights discourses assumed great importance. The UN Charter and the Declaration on Principles of International Law concerning Friendly Relations and Co-operation among States in Accordance with the Charter of the United Nations reflect the priorities of powerful States by firmly emphasising the importance of sovereign equality and the duty of non-intervention, with the UN Charter simultaneously promoting human rights and gender equality. These latter are also reaffirmed in the Universal Declaration of Human Rights but there is obvious tension in reconciling State concerns and individual rights. Continued bias at the level of the State in international law has circumscribed the inclusion of women's rights as part of general human rights discussions. The male bias in the system of governance in most nations has translated into a similar bias in the management of the relationship between States, rendering it hardly surprising that women's rights in international law have been ascribed limited importance.

The picture painted above is admittedly bleak but it is the reality facing the world's women. Does international law provide the means for women to achieve equality? Yes and no. As seen above, while the international community can get together and achieve some degree of consensus on the advancement of women's human rights, obvious problems of resource prioritisation combined with a lack of political will can spell a death sentence for the promotion of women's human rights nationally and internationally. International instruments mean nothing if they are not incorporated into domestic legislation. Even if incorporated, legislation alone cannot change the very real power imbalances that exist between men and women.[260] Important to the process are education to change traditional and (often) discriminatory attitudes; training; legal literacy; adequate gender representation in top policy making positions; and the provision of resources, financial and otherwise, which, if provided, would indicate political will at the level of the State. This political will can be forced through the application of pressure from above and below. The discussions on international law, international relations and the rights of women, particularly with respect to the right to equality, illustrate the limitations of the "top-down" approach. Noteworthy is the fact that DEVAW arose from the pressures being asserted by NGOs concerned with violence against women, exemplifying the strength of the "bottom-up" approach and illustrating the fallacy that international law can exclusively effect change.

In this vein, chapter three examines the role of the United Nations in promoting women's human rights. It will treat with the development of the international machinery dealing with women's human rights in the post-1945 period through the various United Nations bodies.

NOTES

1. Surya Prakash Sinha, *What is Law?: The Differing Theories of Jurisprudence* (New York: Paragon House, 1989), 218.
2. Ian Shearer, *Starke's International Law* (London: Butterworths, 1994), 3.
3. See Malcolm Shaw, *International Law* (Cambridge: Cambridge University Press, 1997), 1.
4. International Court of Justice, "Statute of the International Court of Justice," accessed 18 October 2004, http://www.icj-cij.org/icjwww/ibasicdocuments/Basetext/istatute.htm.
5. For an exposition on the differences of "hard law" and "soft law" in international law, see Kenneth W. Abbott and Duncan Snidal, "Hard and Soft Law in International Governance," *International Organization* 54, no. 3 (Summer 2000): 421–456.
6. Foo Kim Boon, "The Rio Declaration and its Influence on International Environmental Law," *Singapore Journal of Legal Studies* (1992): 350.
7. See Patricia Birnie and Alan Boyle, *International Law and the Environment* (Oxford: Clarendon Press, 1992), 27–30.
8. See David J. Harris, *Cases and Materials on International Law* (London: Sweet & Maxwell, 1998), 65.
9. Shaw, *International Law*, 3.
10. Terry Nardin, "International pluralism and the rule of law," *Review of International Studies* 26 (2000): 103 and see Shaw, *International Law*, 3.
11. Kinji Akashi, "Hobbes' Relevance to the Modern Law of Nations," *Journal of the History of International Law* 2 (2000): 200.
12. Anthony Carty, "Critical International Law: Recent Trends in the Theory of International Law," *European Journal of International Law* 2 (1999): 1.
13. See Michael Savage, "The Juridification of International Law: Sovereignty and International Legal Theory," *Political Studies Association*, Conference Proceedings (University of Nottingham, 1999): 2.

14. Ibid., 4.

15. The work by Thomas Risse, Stephen Ropp and Kathryn Sikkink, ed., *The Power of Human Rights: International Norms and Domestic Change* (Cambridge: Cambridge University Press, 2002) is important in understanding the way in which the power of international norms can alter the domestic behaviour of states, especially when reinforced by NGO activism. See also Thomas Risse and Kathryn Sikkink, "The Socialization of International Human Rights Norms into Domestic Practices: Introduction," in Risse et al, *The Power of Human Rights.*

16. Theorists of this era were concerned with men being able to control and dominate nature, which, not surprisingly, was given female characteristics.

17. 1 Corinthians 14:34. Emphasis added.

18. See Gesina van der Molen, *Alberico Gentili and the Development of International Law: His Life, Work and Times* (Leyden: A. W. Sijthoff Uitgeversmaatschappi, 1968), 197.

19. See Jeremy Thomas, "The Intertwining of Law and Theology in the Writings of Grotius," *Journal of the History of International Law* 1 (1999): 63–64.

20. See Shaw, *International Law*, 20–21.

21. This is also claimed to be based primarily on the work of Gentili. See van der Molen, *Alberico Gentili.*

22. Shaw, *International Law*, 21.

23. Robert Cox, "Social forces, state and world orders: beyond international relations theory," *Millennium: Journal of International Studies* 10, no. 2 (1981): 128.

24. Foucault also makes the point that "Discourse and system produce each other…." Michel Foucault, *The Archaeology of Knowledge* (London: Routledge, 2002), 85. Once the discourse is espoused and accepted as true, it becomes institutionalised and they continue to produce and reinforce each other.

25. See Thomas, "The Intertwining of Law and Theology," 97–98.

26. Emmerich de Vattel, *The Law of Nations or Principles of the Law of Nature, Applied to the Conduct and Affairs of Nations and Sovereigns*, trans. and ed. Joseph Chitty (London: Law Booksellers and Publishers, 1834), lv.

27. Shaw, *International Law*, 23.

28. de Vattel, *The Law of Nations*, lv.

29. Nardin, "International pluralism," 98.

30. de Vattel, *The Law of Nations*, lviii.

31. Ibid., lviii.

32. See ibid., lxii–lxvi.

33. Ibid., lxii.

34. Davina Bhandar, "Citizenship," in Code, *Encyclopedia of Feminist Theories*, 89.

35. See Code, "Introduction," xx.

36. Stéphane Beaulac, "The Westphalian Legal Orthodoxy—Myth or Reality?" *Journal of the History of International Law* 2 (2000): 148–149. He goes on to argue, however, that the Peace of Westphalia simply formally institutionalised that which was taking place for over half a century.

37. Timothy Dunne, "Realism," in *The Globalization of World Politics: An Introduction to International Relations*, ed. John Baylis and Steve Smith (New York: Oxford University Press, 1997), 115.

38. Jill Steans and Lloyd Pettiford, *International Relations: Perspectives and Themes* (London: Longman, 2001), 30–31.

39. W. Michael Reisman, "Sovereignty and Human Rights in Contemporary International Law," *The American Journal of International Law* 84, no. 4 (October 1990): 871.

40. Ibid., 872.

41. Kathryn Sikkink, "Transnational Politics, International Relations Theory, and Human Rights," *Political Science and Politics* 31, no. 3 (Sept. 1998): 517. She refers to the classic work of Hedley Bull who speaks of the subversion of the society of sovereign states by the doctrine of human rights and their duties under international law. See Hedley Bull, *The Anarchical Society: A Study of Order in World Politics* (New York: Columbia University Press, 1977), 146.

42. Alexander Wendt, "Anarchy is What States Make of It: The Social Construction of Power Politics," *International Organization* 46, no. 2 (Spring 1992): 412.

43. Kathryn Sikkink, "Human Rights, Principled Issue-Networks, and Sovereignty in Latin America," *International Organization* 47, no. 3 (Summer 1993): 412.

44. See Jeffrey Legro, "Which Norms Matter? Revisiting the "Failure" of Internationalism," *International Organization* 51, no. 1 (Winter 1997): 35, where he describes "concordance" as how widely accepted the rules are in diplomatic discussions and treaties, or the degree of intersubjective agreement attained.

45. Reisman, "Sovereignty and Human Rights," 869.

46. This still does not deal with the issues of women's exclusion in international relations or human rights issues.

47. John Locke, "Second Treatise on Civil Government: An Essay Concerning the True Original, Extent and End of Civil Government," in *Social Contract: Essays by Locke, Hume and Rousseau*, ed. Ernest Barker (London: Oxford University Press, 1947), 71.

48. Exodus 21: 23–25.

49. Locke, "Second Treatise," 71.

50. Galations 3: 28.

51. R. John Vincent, *Human Rights and International Relations* (Cambridge: Cambridge University Press, 1986), 35.

52. Ken Booth, "Three Tyrannies," in *Human Rights in Global Politics*, ed. Tim Dunne and Nicholas Wheeler (Cambridge: Cambridge University Press, 1999), 51–52.

53. Ibid., 52.

54. Vincent, *Human Rights and International Law*, 93.

55. Peter Cumper, "Human Rights: History, Development and Classification," in *Human Rights: An Agenda for the 21st Century*, ed. Angela Hegarty and Siobhan Leonard (London: Cavendish Publishing Limited, 1999), 5 and footnote 29.

56. Mary Ann Glendon, "John P. Humphrey and the Drafting of the Universal Declaration of Human Rights," *Journal of the History of International Law* 2 (2000): 250. Humphrey's success in making the Declaration a universally applicable document is a source of contention, particularly by non-Western cultures which, *inter alia*, place emphasis on group rights rather than individual rights.

57. UN, "United Nations Declaration of Human Rights," in *Basic Documents on Human Rights*, ed. Ian Brownlie (Oxford: Oxford University Press, 1992), 22.

58. Much of the conceptual groundwork for the Charter's language on women's rights grew out of the pioneering efforts of the Organisation of American States and its Inter-American Commission on the Status of Women. UN, *The United Nations and the Advancement of Women 1945–1996* (New York: Department of Public Information, 1996), 9.

59. Jane Connors, "NGOs and the Human Rights of Women at the United Nations," in *"The Conscience of the World": The Influence of Non-Governmental Organisations in the U.N. System*, ed. Peter Willetts (London: Hurst & Company, 1996), 151.

60. Margaret Galey, "Forerunners in Women's Quest for Partnership," in *Women, Politics and the United Nations*, ed. Anne Winslow (Westport, Connecticut: Greenwood Press, 1995), 7.

61. See Chapter 1, Article 1:3, UN Charter, 26 June 1945, entered into force 24 October 1945.

62. Jack Donnelly, "The Social Construction of International Human Rights," in Dunne and Wheeler, *Human Rights in Global Politics*, 85.

63. Ibid., 86.

64. See discussions on monism and dualism where monists assert that international law automatically becomes part of domestic law, while dualists assert that international law and domestic law are two discrete systems of law. It would appear that dualism is more widespread in countries of the common law tradition. See for example, Alpha Connelly, "Ireland and the European Convention," in *Human Rights and the European Convention: The Effects of the Convention on the United Kingdom and Ireland*, ed. Brice Dickson (London: Sweet and Maxwell, 1997), 196–197; Justice Michael Kirby, "The Growing Rapprochement Between International and National Law," Essays to honour His Excellency Judge C.J. Weeramantry, 1998, accessed 15 January 2005, http://www.hcourt.gov.au/speeches/kirbyj/kirbyj_weeram.htm; Pierre-Marie Dupuy, "Dionisio Anzilotti and the Law of International Responsibility of States," *European Journal of International Law* 3 (1992): 140; Stephen J. Toope, "Inside and Out: The Stories of International Law and Domestic Law," accessed 15 January 2005, http://www.lawsite.ca/IAWJ/CRToope_e.htm. See also summary of the Convener on Article 4 of the Bangalore Principles which deals with the domestic application of human rights norms in common law jurisdictions. "In most countries whose legal systems are based upon common law, international conventions are not directly enforceable in national courts unless their provisions have been incorporated by legislation into domestic law." Accessed 15 January 2005, http://www.nji.ca/cciawj/Bangalore%20Principles.doc.

65. Désirée Bernard, "The Promotion and Enforcement of Women's Human Rights within the Judicial Systems of the Caribbean," paper presented at the University of the West Indies, Cave Hill, Barbados, 18 November 2005, 2. Also available from http://www.caribbeancourtofjustice.org/papers_addresses.html.

66. Ibid., 2–3. Guyana, however, provides a conditional exception to the rule as a 2003 constitutional amendment allows for automatic incorporation of human rights provisions of international legal instruments upon ratification.

67. Private international law deals with controversies between private persons, natural or juridical, arising out of situations having significant relationship to more than one nation. Such issues include international judicial and administrative co-operation; conflict of laws for contracts, torts, maintenance obligations, status and protection of children, relations between spouses, wills and estates or trusts; and jurisdiction and enforcement of foreign judgments. Recently, the line between public and private international law has become increasingly uncertain, as issues of private international law may also implicate issues of public international law, and many matters of private international law have substantial significance for the international community of nations. See Rajendra Ramlogan and Natalie Persadie, *Commonwealth Caribbean Business Law* (London: Cavendish Publishing Limited, 2004), 22–23 and accompanying notes.

68. A. Claire Cutler, "Critical reflections on the Westphalian assumptions of international law and organization: a crisis of legitimacy," *Review of International Studies* 27 (2001): 140. Quoting Mark Janis.

69. Vincent, *Human Rights and International Relations*, 113.

70. See Chapter 1, Article 2:7, UN Charter.

71. Tim Dunne and Nicholas Wheeler, "Introduction: Human Rights and the Fifty Years' Crisis," in Dunne and Wheeler, *Human Rights in Global Politics*, 23.

72. For more on the Protocol, see section 2.5.3.4 below.

73. Nevertheless, it provides fertile ground for activist struggle and political pressure. This is dealt with in greater detail in chapter three.

74. Dunne and Wheeler, "Introduction," in Dunne and Wheeler, *Human Rights in Global Politics*, 1.

75. Richard Lord, "Humanity over sovereignty," *Trinidad Express*, 11 December 2003, accessed 11 December 2003, http://www.trinidadexpress.com/politics.asp?mylink=2003-12-11%2Fpolitics%2FHumanity%20over%20sovereignty.htm&mydate=2003-12-11&mypage=politics.

76. Ibid.

77. See Vincent, *Human Rights and International Relations*, 40.

78. Dunne and Wheeler, "Introduction," 13.

79. Roger T. Ames, "Continuing the Conversation on Chinese Human Rights," *Ethics and International Affairs* 11 (1997): 193.

80. Chris Brown, "Universal Human Rights: A Critique," in Dunne and Wheeler, *Human Rights in Global Politics*, 116.

81. Ibid., 117.

82. Booth, "Three Tyrannies," 52.

83. See Vincent, *Human Rights and International Relations*, 37.

84. Bhikhu Parekh, "Non-Ethnocentric Universalism," in Dunne and Wheeler, *Human Rights in Global Politics*, 151–152.

85. Booth, "Three Tyrannies," 39.

86. Ibid.

87. See Michael Singer, "Relativism, Culture, Religion and Identity," in *Religious Fundamentalisms and the Human Rights of Women*, ed. Courtney Howland (New York: Palgrave, 1999), 46–47.

88. Booth, "Three Tyrannies," 62–63.

89. Heading of a paper written by Radhika Coomaraswamy, *Reinventing International Law: Women's Rights as Human Rights in the International Community* (Massachusetts: Harvard Law School Human Rights Program, 1997).

90. Hilary Charlesworth, "What are "Women's International Human Rights"?" in *Human Rights of Women: National and International Perspectives*, ed. Rebecca Cook (Philadelphia: University of Pennsylvania Press, 1994), 67.

91. Hilary Charlesworth, "Human Rights as Men's Rights," in *Women's Rights, Human Rights: International Feminist Perspectives*, ed. Julie Peters and Andrea Wolper (London: Routledge, 1995), 105. Emphasis in the original.

92. Charlesworth, "What are "Women's International Human Rights"?" 71.

93. Charlotte Bunch, "Transforming Human Rights from a Feminist Perspective," in Peters and Wolper, *Women's Rights, Human Rights*, 13.

94. See Coomaraswamy, *Reinventing International Law*, 8.

95. Charlesworth, "What are "Women's International Human Rights"?" 59.

96. Joanna Kerr, "The Context and the Goal," in *Ours By Right: Women's Right as Human Rights*, ed. Joanna Kerr (London: Zed Books, 1993), 3.

97. Christine Bell, "Women's rights as Human Rights: Old Agenda in New Guises," in Hegarty and Leonard, *Human Rights*, 139.

98. Bunch, "Transforming Human Rights from a Feminist Perspective," 12.

99. Charlotte Bunch, "Organizing for Women's Human Rights Globally," in Kerr, *Ours By Right*, 145–146.

100. Georgina Ashworth, "The Silencing of Women," in Dunne and Wheeler, *Human Rights in Global Politics*, 261.

101. Radhika Coomaraswamy, "To Bellow like a Cow: Women, Ethnicity, and the Discourse of Rights," in Cook, *Human Rights of Women*, 55.

102. Charlesworth, "What are "Women's International Human Rights"?" 70.

103. Donna Sullivan, "The Public/Private Distinction in International Human Rights Law," in Peters and Wolper, *Women's Rights, Human Rights*, 128.

104. Carmel Shalev, "Women in Israel: Fighting Tradition," in Peters and Wolper, *Women's Rights, Human Rights*, 90, 91–92.

105. Akram Mirhosseini, "After the Revolution: Violations of Women's Human Rights in Iran," in Peters and Wolper, *Women's Rights, Human Rights*, 73. Emphasis added.

106. Charlesworth, "Human Rights as Men's Rights," 107.

107. Sullivan, "The Public/Private Distinction in International Human Rights Law," 127.

108. V. Spike Peterson and Laura Parisi, "Are Women Human? It's Not an Academic Question," in *Human Rights Fifty Years On: A Reappraisal*, ed. Tony Evans (Manchester: Manchester University Press, 1998), 140.

109. Ibid., 145.

110. Zillah Eisenstein, *The Radical Future of Liberal Feminism* (New York: Longman, 1981), 25.

111. Adopted by the UN General Assembly on 18 December 1979 and entered into force on 3 September 1981.

112. UN, "Convention on the Elimination of All Forms of Discrimination Against Women," in Brownlie, *Basic Documents*, 171.

113. See section 2.3.2 above. This argument is developed further in section 4.3.2.4 below which deals with the responsibility of the State to protect women within the context of constitutional equality in Trinidad and Tobago.

114. See Elizabeth Friedman, "Women's Human Rights: The Emergence of a Movement," in Peters and Wolper, *Women's Rights, Human Rights*, 20–21.

115. Courtney Howland, "Safeguarding Women's Political Freedoms under the International Covenant on Civil and Political Rights in the Face of Religious Fundamentalism," in Howland, *Religious Fundamentalisms*, 95.

116. Rebecca Cook, "State Accountability Under the Convention on the Elimination of All Forms of Discrimination Against Women," in Cook, *Human Rights of Women*, 237.

117. Celina Romany, "State Responsibility Goes Private: A Feminist Critique of the Public/Private Distinction in International Human Rights Law," in Cook, *Human Rights of Women*, 100–101.

118. One writer believes that the lack of political will exhibited in developing countries is indicative of a deeper problem, namely the (continued) deterioration of morality and moral rectitude. See Kirk Meighoo, "Leadership and Legitimacy," *Sunday Express*, 24 October 2004, accessed 03 November 2004, http://www.trinidadexpress.com/index.pl/article_opinion?id=43442127.

119. See Rebecca Cook, "Women's International Human Rights Law: The Way Forward," in Cook, *Human Rights of Women*, 31 and Marsha Freeman, "Women, Development and Justice: Using the International Convention on Women's Rights," in Kerr, *Ours By Right*, 94.

120. See generally for example, Rajendra Ramlogan and Natalie Persadie, *Developing Environmental Law and Policy in Trinidad and Tobago* (San Juan, Trinidad: Lexicon, 2004), 31–32; 89–95.

121. Arati Rao, "The Politics of Gender and Culture in International Human Rights Discourse," in Peters and Wolper, *Women's Rights, Human Rights*, 169.

122. Indira Jaising, "Violence against Women: The Indian Perspective," in Peters and Wolper, *Women's Rights, Human Rights*, 52.

123. There has always been a problem in "exporting feminism." See Jean Bethke Elshtain, "Exporting Feminism," *Journal of International Affairs* 48, no. 2 (Winter 1995): 541–558, where she explores criticisms directed specifically against American Feminism, which assumes political/cultural superiority.

124. Christine Chinkin, "Cultural Relativism and International Law," in Howland, *Religious Fundamentalisms*, 57. Emphasis added.

125. Vickram Seth, *A Suitable Boy* (London: Phoenix, 1994), 285.

126. Radhika Coomaraswamy, "Different but Free: Cultural Relativism and Women's Rights as Human Rights," in Howland, *Religious Fundamentalisms*, 82.

127. Frances Raday, "Religion and Patriarchal Politics: The Israeli Experience," in Howland, *Religious Fundamentalisms*, 156.

128. UN, "CEDAW," in Brownlie, *Basic Documents*, 181.

129. Where the reservation is prohibited by the treaty.

130. Where the treaty provides that only specified reservations, which do not include the reservation in question, may be made.

131. International Law Commission, *Vienna Convention on the Law of Treaties*. The Convention was adopted on 22 May 1969 and opened for signature on 23 May 1969 by the *United Nations Conference on the Law of Treaties*. Entered into force on 27 January 1980, in accordance with article 84(1). Accessed 23 January 2003, http://www.un.org/law/ilc/texts/treaties.htm.

132. See UN, Division for the Advancement of Women, "States Parties," updated 13 July 2011, accessed 13 July 2011, http://www.un.org/womenwatch/daw/cedaw/states.htm.

133. Bell, "Women's rights as Human Rights," 147–148 and Coomaraswamy, *Reinventing International Law*, 3. Some 60 countries initially entered reservations that range from specific provisions to broad reservations of the convention. Some reservations were subsequently withdrawn, such that the number of countries expressing reservations to the Convention has dropped to about 53. See tables 2.1 and 2.2 below.

134. See more on reservations to the convention in section 2.5.3.2 below.

135. Natalie Hevener Kaufman and Stefanie Lindquist, "Critiquing Gender-Neutral Treaty Language: The Convention on the Elimination of All Forms of Discrimination Against Women," in Peters and Wolper, *Women's Rights, Human Rights*, 121.

136. 429 U.S. 125 (1976).

137. 417 U.S. 484 (1974)

138. Kathleen Mahoney, "Gender and the Judiciary: Confronting Gender Bias," in *Gender Equality and the Judiciary: Using International Human Rights Standards to Promote the Human Rights of Women and the Girl-child at the National Level*, ed. Kirstine Adams and Andrew Byrnes (London: Commonwealth Secretariat, 1999), 97. Quoting Catherine MacKinnon.

139. See Kaufman and Lindquist, "Critiquing Gender-Neutral Treaty Language," 116. For more on the common law tradition, see section 4.2 below.

140. See section 1.5.3 above.

141. See Margaret Keck and Kathryn Sikkink, *Activists Beyond Borders, Advocacy Networks in International Politics* (New York: Cornell University Press, 1998), 24–25. The authors cite information politics, symbolic politics, leverage politics, and accountability politics as the means by which transnational advocacy networks effect change from within the "political spaces" in which they operate. See 16–25.

142. Carolyn Stephenson, "Women's International Nongovernmental Organizations at the United Nations," in Winslow, *Women, Politics*, 151.

143. John Sankey, "Conclusions," in Willetts, *"The Conscience of the World,"* 272–273.

144. This is discussed in greater detail in chapter three.

145. Although this holds true since the era of first wave feminism, it has taken a much more organised and focussed approach since post-1945.

146. Lack of enforceability tends to counteract the binding nature of conventions.

147. See section 2.1 of above on critiques of the soft law approach in international law.

148. This list is taken largely from UN Department of Public Information, "Focus on Women: UN Action for Women," DPI/1796/Rev.1, May 1996.

149. UN Treaty Series, Vol. 96, No. 1342, 271.

150. See UN ECOSOC, "ECOSOC resolution calling on Member States to implement the principle of equal pay for work of equal value for men and women workers, irrespective of nationality, race, language or religion," E/RES/121 (VI), 10 March 1948.

151. UN Treaty Series, Vol. 193, No. 2613, 135.

152. See UN General Assembly, "General Assembly resolution calling on Member States to adopt measures necessary to fulfil the aims of the Charter of the United Nations in granting women the same political rights as men," A/RES/56 (I), 11 December 1946.

153. See also UN Commission on the Status of Women, "Report of the Secretary-General to the CSW on the possibility of proposing a convention on the political rights of women," E/CN.6/143, 28 April 1950.

154. UN Treaty Series, Vol. 309, No. 4468, 65.

155. See UN ECOSOC, "ECOSOC resolution calling for the preparation of a convention on the nationality of a married woman," E/RES/242 C (IX), 1 August 1949.

156. UN Treaty Series, Vol. 521, No. 7525, 231.

157. See UN ECOSOC resolution A/RES/1763 (XVII), 07 November 1962.

158. See A/RES/2263 (XXII), 7 November 1967.

159. See also UN General Assembly, "General Assembly resolution requesting ECOSOC and the CSW to prepare a draft declaration on the elimination of discrimination against women," A/RES/1921 (XVIII), 05 December 1963.

160. See UN General Assembly, "General Assembly resolution calling on the CSW to complete the draft convention on the elimination of discrimination against women," A/RES/3521 (XXX), 15 December 1975.

161. See A/RES/48/104, 20 December 1993.

162. This convention was not part of the list but should be included.

163. See discussion on the incorporation of international law into domestic law above.

164. See UN, *The United Nations and the Advancement of Women*, 79.

165. See UN, Division for the Advancement of Women, "Short History of CEDAW Convention," updated 10 February 2005, accessed 06 April 2005, http://www.un.org/womenwatch/daw/cedaw/history.htm.

166. UN DAW, "Short History."

167. Ibid.

168. Article 1 of CEDAW.

169. It entered into force less than two years after it was adopted by the General Assembly. See UN, *The United Nations and the Advancement of Women*, 42.

170. Some 58 countries initially entered reservations on specific provisions of the convention; although, some have since been withdrawn.

171. This is blatantly contrary to Article 5 of the convention. 14 countries have entered reservations on the basis of the Convention's incompatibility with Islamic *Shari'ah* (Algeria, Bahrain, Bangladesh, Egypt, Iraq, Kuwait, Libyan Arab Jamhiriya, Malaysia, the Maldives, Mauritania, Morocco, Pakistan, Saudi Arabia and Syrian Arab Republic); 2 countries have entered reservations on the basis of incompatibility with their constitution (Lesotho and Tunisia [where Tunisia's

constitution is based on Islamic *Shari'ah*]); 2 countries have entered reservations on the basis of incompatibility with the multicultural nature of their society (India and Singapore); two countries have entered reservations on the basis of incompatibility with customs and traditions (Micronesia and Niger [where Niger's customs are regulated by Islamic *Shari'ah*]); one country has entered reservations on the basis of incompatibility with Judaic *Halakhah* (Israel); and one country has entered reservations on the basis of its finite resources with which to implement the provisions of the Convention (Mexico) which surely applies to many more countries. For more on the religious legal systems, see for *Shari'ah*, Michael Mumisa, *Islamic Law: Theory and Interpretation* (Maryland: Amana Publications, 2002) and Konrad Zweigert and Hein Kötz, *An Introduction to Comparative Law*, trans. Tony Weir (Oxford: Oxford University Press, 1998); for *Halakhah*, see Moshe Zemer, *Evolving Halakhah: A Progressive Approach to Traditional Jewish Law* (Vermont: Jewish Lights Publishing, 1999) and Jeremy Call, "The Halakhah and its Role in Modern Israeli Law," accessed 08 April 2005, http://www.law2.byu.edu/lwb/papers/Call-Halakhah_FINAL.PDF.

172. See section 2.4.3 above on issues of cultural relativism and women.

173. Ann Mayer, "Cultural Particularism as a Bar to Women's Rights: Reflections on the Middle Eastern Experience," in Peters and Wolper, *Women's Rights, Human Rights*, 185.

174. See for example, France, Ireland, Liechtenstein, Luxembourg, and the United Kingdom which reserve the right to give preference to domestic legislation which are more favourable to women than is provided for in the Convention.

175. See UN, General Assembly, "Convention on the Elimination of All Forms of Discrimination Against Women," A/RES/53/118, 05 February 1999 and UN, General Assembly, "Report of the Committee on the Elimination of Discrimination Against Women," A/54/38, 04 May 1999, paragraph 11. See also, Committee on the Elimination of Discrimination Against Women, "General Recommendations," nos. 4, 20 and 21, updated 10 February 2005, accessed 11 April 2005, http://www.un.org/womenwatch/daw/cedaw/recommendations/recomm.htm.

176. UN, Division for the Advancement of Women, "Reservations to CEDAW," updated 10 February 2005. Accessed 08 April 2005, http://www.un.org/womenwatch/daw/cedaw/reservations.htm.

177. See UN, "Report of the Fourth World Conference on Women," A/CONF.177/20, 17 October 1995.

178. UN, Department of Public Information, "Fourth World Conference on Women: Beijing, China, 4–15 September 1995," DPI/1324, February 1993.

179. UN, Fourth World Conference on Women, "Platform for Action: Mission Statement," accessed 28 January 2004, http://www.un.org/womenwatch/daw/beijing/platform/plat1.htm#statement.

180. UN, Fourth World Conference on Women, "Platform for Action: Critical Areas for Concern," accessed 28 January 2004, http://www.un.org/womenwatch/daw/beijing/platform/plat1.htm#concern.

181. UN, Department of Public Information, "From Beijing, a Platform for Action and a clear mandate for women's progress," DPI/1749/WOM, October 1995, 1.

182. Hilkka Pietilä and Jeanne Vickers, *Making Women Matter: The Role of the United Nations* (London: Zed Books, 1994), 160.

183. UN DPI, "Beijing Declaration," para. 22.

184. UN DPI, "From Beijing," p. 5.

185. Judith Howard and Carolyn Allen, "Introduction," *Signs* 22, no. 1 (Autumn 1996): 181. Why was the NGO Forum distanced from the main convention at Beijing? The NGO Forum represented a threat to the political stability [read: state control of power] and the distancing of the Forum expressed "not only the leaders' determination not to let this event disturb China's political status quo but also the state's suspicion and hostility towards women's spontaneous activities." The situation was so severe that Chinese representatives at the NGO Forum had to behave like political puppets, expressing only favourable views of the status of women in China. See Wang Zheng, "A Historic Turning Point for the Women's Movement in China," *Signs* 22, no. 1 (Autumn 1996): 192–199.

186. Esther Chow, "Making Waves, Moving Mountains: Reflections on Beijing '95 and Beyond," *Signs* 22, no. 1 (Autumn 1996): 186.

187. See Hilary Charlesworth, "Women as Sherpas: Are Global Summits Useful for Women?" *Feminist Studies* 22, no. 3 (Autumn, 1996): 542–544. See also Charlotte Bunch and Susana Fried, "Beijing '95: Moving Women's Human Rights from Margin to Center," *Signs* 22, no. 1 (Autumn 1996): 202–203.

188. See "Adoption of the Beijing Declaration and Platform for Action," para. 11 and Charlesworth, "Women as Sherpas," 543.

189. Bunch and Fried, "Beijing '95," 202–203.

190. Jill Steans and Vafa Ahmady, "Negotiating the Politics of Gender and Rights: Some Reflections on the Status of Women's Human Rights at 'Beijing Plus Ten,'" *Global Society* 19, no. 3 (July 2005): 240–241.

191. Ibid., 5.

192. See Aruna Rao, "Engendering Institutional Change," *Signs* 22, no. 1 (Autumn 1996): 219.

193. See for example, UN, Division for the Advancement of Women, "Beijing +5: Process and Beyond," http://www.un.org/womenwatch/daw/followup/bfbeyond.htm; UN, General Assembly, "Political Declaration," A/RES/S-23/2, 16 November 2000; UN, General Assembly, "Further Actions and Initiatives to Implement the Beijing Declaration and Platform for Action," A/RES/S-23/3, 16 November 2000; UN Economic and Social Council, "Declaration adopted by the Commission on the Status of Women as its forty-ninth session as orally amended," E/CN.6/2005/L.1, 03 March 2005; Center for Women's Global Leadership, the NGO Committee on the Status of Women, and the Women's Environment and Development Organization, "2005 CSW Review of the Beijing Platform for Action (Beijing +10)," April 2004, http://www.peacewomen.org/un/Beijing10%20/NGOCSWBeijing10.html; UN, Department of Public Information, "Beijing at Ten: Achieving Gender Equality, Development and Peace," Press Release, DPI/2363F, March 2005.

194. Women's Environment and Development Organization, *Beijing Betrayed: Women Worldwide Report that Governments have failed to turn the Platform into Action* (New York: Women's Environment and Development Organization, 2005), 11.

195. Ibid., 7.

196. Bunch and Fried, "Beijing '95," 201.

197. UN, Division for the Advancement of Women, "Optional Protocol to Women's Convention Comes Into Force," Press Release, WOM/1242, 21 December 2000. Accessed 11 April 2005, http://www.un.org/womenwatch/daw/cedaw/protocol/wom1242.htm.

198. UN, General Assembly, "Optional Protocol to the Convention on the Elimination of All Forms of Discrimination against Women," A/RES/54/4, 15 October 1999.

199. UN, Division for the Advancement of Women, "Optional Protocol to the Convention on the Elimination of All Forms of Discrimination against Women," updated 10 February 2005. Accessed 11 April 2005, http://www.un.org/womenwatch/daw/cedaw/protocol.

200. Janusz Symonides and Vladimir Volodin, *A Guide to Human Rights: Institutions, Standards, Procedures* (Paris: United Nations Educational, Scientific and Cultural Organization, 2003), 328.

201. UN, Division for the Advancement of Women, "What is an Optional Protocol?" updated 10 February 2005, accessed 11 April 2005, http://www.un.org/womenwatch/daw/cedaw/protocol/whatis.htm.

202. Kwong-Leung Tang, "The Leadership Role of International Law in Enforcing Women's Rights," *Gender and Development* 8, no. 3 (November 2000): 68.

203. UN, Division for the Advancement of Women, "Why an Optional Protocol?" updated 10 February 2005, accessed 11 April 2005, http://www.un.org/womenwatch/daw/cedaw/protocol/why.htm.

204. UN, "Vienna Declaration and Programme of Action," A/CONF.157/24, 13 October 1993.

205. Ibid., paragraph 37.

206. Ibid., paragraphs 38 and 39.

207. See generally Manisha Desai, "From Vienna to Beijing: Women's Human Rights Activism and the Human Rights Community," in *Debating Human Rights: Critical Essays from the United States and Asia*, ed. Peter Van Ness (London: Routledge, 1999) and 184–185.

208. See Dorota Gierycz, "Human Rights of Women at the Fiftieth Anniversary of the United Nations," in *Human Rights of Women: International Instruments and African Experiences*, ed. Wolfgang Benedek, Esther Kisaakye and Gerd Oberleitner (London: Zed Books, 2002), 45–46.

209. See UN, General Assembly, "Resolution on Implementation of the Nairobi Forward-Looking Strategies and requesting the CSW to complete work on a declaration on the elimination of violence against women," A/RES/47/95, 16 December 1992. DEVAW builds on the Committee's General Recommendation No. 19. See Committee on the Elimination of Discrimination Against Women, "General Recommendations," updated 10 February 2005, accessed 11 April 2005, http://www.un.org/womenwatch/daw/cedaw/recommendations/recomm.htm.

210. UN, General Assembly, "Declaration on the Elimination of Violence Against Women," A/RES/48/104, 23 February 1994.

211. Christine Brautigam, "International Human Rights Law: The Relevance of Gender," in Benedek et al, *Human Rights of Women*, 12.

212. UN, Commission on Human Rights, "Resolution appointing a Special Rapporteur on violence against women," ESCOR, 1994, Suppl. No. 4.

213. Special Rapporteur on violence, "Preliminary Report to the Commission on Human Rights," E/CN.4/1995/42, 22 November 1994, Part II, B.

214. Ibid., Part II, B, para. 57.

215. Ibid., Part V, para. 315.

216. Ibid., Part V, para. 317.

217. Noreen Burrows, "International Law and Human Rights: the Case of Women's Rights," in *Human Rights: From Rhetoric to Reality*, ed. Tom Campbell, David Goldberg, Sheila Mclean and Tom Mullen (Oxford: Basil Blackwell, 1986).

218. Spike Peterson, "The Politics of Identity in International Relations," *The Fletcher Forum of World Affairs* 17, no. 2 (1993): 7.

219. Entered into force on 12 January 1951.

220. Entered into force on 21 October 1950.

221. This is not to say that international law cannot deal with such issues in a non gender-specific manner. In the unprecedented case of *Prosecutor v Akayesu*, Case No. ICTR-96-4-T (Trial Chamber), 02 September 1998, rape was defined for the first time in international law and the Trial Chamber "underscored the fact that rape and sexual violence also constitute genocide in the same way as any other act, as long as they were committed with intent to destroy a particular group targeted as such." UN, "Rwanda International Criminal Tribunal Pronounces Guilty Verdict in Historic Genocide Trial," Press Release AFR/94 L/2895, 02 September 1998, accessed 16 January 2008, http://www.un.org/News/Press/docs/1998/19980902.afr94.html. See also, "When Rape becomes Genocide," *The New York Times*, 05 September 1998, accessed 16 January 2008, http://query.nytimes.com/gst/fullpage.html?res=990DE3D9163EF936A3575AC0A96E958260 where a very interesting observation was made: "When charges were first brought against Mr. Akayesu, rape was not among them. Despite extensive media reports of rapes, the tribunal's investigators, at the time, virtually all men, could not find evidence to support an indictment. But during the trial a witness brought up rape in the cultural center. Questioned by Navanethem Pillay, a South African who is the tribunal's only female judge, the witness gave details. Other witnesses followed. Largely due to pressure from women's groups, the investigators went back to ask about rape, and those charges were added. *Without female judges and investigators, this cruel aspect of the Rwandan genocide might never have been addressed*." Emphasis added.

222. Natalie Hevener, "An Analysis of Gender Based Treaty Law: Contemporary Developments in Historical Perspective," *Human Rights Quarterly* 8, no. 1 (1986): 71.

223. This was entered into force on 25 July 1951.

224. Laura Reanda, "Human Rights and Women's Rights: The United Nations Approach," *Human Rights Quarterly* 3, no. 2 (1981): 21.

225. Jill Steans, *Gender and International Relations: An Introduction* (New Jersey: Rutgers University Press, 1998), 5.

226. Felice Gaer, "Human Rights at the UN: Women's Rights are Human Rights," *In Brief* No. 14 (November 1999).

227. V. Spike Peterson, "Feminisms and International Relations," *Gender and History* 10, no. 3 (November 1998): 587.

228. Christine Sylvester, "Feminist Theory and Gender Studies in International Relations," *International Studies Notes* 16/17, 3/1 (Fall 1991/Winter 1992): 32–38, http://www.isanet.org/sections/ftgs/femir.html.

229. See Ian Brownlie, *Principles of Public International Law* (Oxford: Clarendon Press, 1996), 287 and Rajendra Ramlogan, *The Developing World and the Environment: Making the Case for the Effective Protection of the Global Environment* (Lanham: University Press of America, 2004), 204. In Bull's classical realist text, he has divided sovereignty into two types: "internal sovereignty"—state supremacy over all other authorities with that territory and population—and "external sovereignty"—not supremacy, but independence of outside authorities. Bull, *The Anarchical Society*, 8.

230. According to Connell's idea of "hegemonic masculinity," which he defines as "the configuration of gender practice which embodies the *currently accepted* answer to the problem of the legitimacy of patriarchy, [and] which guarantees…the dominant position of men and the subordination of women," the concept of masculinity, as accepted by society, varies over time and reflects the need for intermittent change. Rob Connell, *Masculinities* (Cambridge: Polity Press, 1995), 77. Emphasis added. Masculinity, as defined here, does not apply to all men, as men, like women, do not constitute a homogenous group and are also differentiated on the bases of race, class, ethnicity, nationality, culture, age and sexual preference.

231. Tickner, *Gender in International Relations*, 3.

232. Note the parallel to rational economic man, where both are white, rational and male—another uncritical universalisation.

233. Steans, *Gender and International Relations*, 53.

234. Ibid., 31.

235. Anne Sisson Runyan and V. Spike Peterson, "The Radical Future of Realism: Feminist Subversions of IR Theory," *Alternatives* 16 (1991): 68.

236. Ibid., 68.

237. Ibid., 69.

238. Cynthia Enloe, *Bananas, Beaches and Bases: Making Feminist Sense of International Politics* (Berkeley: University of California Press, 2000), 4. Emphasis in the original.

239. Yosef Lapid, "The Third Debate: On the Prospects of International Theory in a Post-Positivist Era," *International Studies Quarterly* 33, no. 3 (Sept. 1989): 241.

240. Christine Sylvester, "The contributions of feminist theory to international relations," in Smith et al, *International Theory*, 257.

241. Sandra Whitworth, *Feminism and International Relations: Towards a Political Economy of Gender in Interstate and Non-Governmental Institutions* (Basingstoke: Palgrave MacMillan, 1997), 42. This is dealt with in chapter one and is an expansion of her discussion in "Gender in the Inter-Paradigm Debate," *Millennium: Journal of International Studies* 18, no. 2 (Summer 1989): 265–272.

242. Ibid., 42–56.

243. See ibid., 12–24, 30–31.

244. Steans, *Gender and International Relations*, 174.

245. Tickner, *Gender in International Relations*, 135–136. See also chapter one above.

246. Tickner, *Gender in International Relations*, 5. See also Fred Halliday, "Hidden from International Relations: Women and the International Arena," *Millennium: Journal of International Studies* 17, no. 3 (Winter 1988): 420.

247. Charlotte Hooper, "Masculinities, IR and the 'Gender Variable': A Cost-Benefit Analysis for (Sympathetic) Gender Sceptics," *Review of International Studies* 25 (1999): 478. Emphasis in the original.

248. See Steans, *Gender and International Relations*, 93.

249. Jane Jaquette, "States Make War," *Foreign Affairs* 78, no. 1 (Jan/Feb 1999): 128. Her article was (one of a few) in response to Fukuyama's claim that males are naturally aggressive and ready for war based on a crude comparison of chimp behaviour in a human controlled environment with the natural aggression of young men and biological tendencies. See Francis Fukuyama, "Women and the Evolution of World Politics," *Foreign Affairs* 77, no. 5 (Sept/Oct 1998): 24–40 and responses, Barbara Ehrenreich, Katha Pollit, R. Brian Ferguson, Lionel Tiger, and Jane Jaquette, "Fukuyama's Follies: So What if Women Ruled the World?" *Foreign Affairs* 78, no. 1 (Jan/Feb 1999): 118–129.

250. See also Marysia Zalewski, "Well, what is the feminist perspective on Bosnia?" *International Affairs* 71, no. 2 (1995): 351–352, 353 and Ehrenreich et al, "Fukuyama's Follies," 118–129.

251. Steans, *Gender and International Relations*, 101.

252. This, however, is *not* to condone the construction of a wartime behaviour.

253. Sarah Brown, "Feminism, International Theory, and International Relations of Gender Inequality," *Millennium: Journal of International Studies* 17, no. 3 (Winter 1988): 473.

254. Jill Steans, "Engaging from the Margins: Feminist Encounters with the 'Mainstream' of International Relations," *British Journal of Politics and International Relations* 5, no. 3 (August 2003): 435.

255. Brown, "Feminism, International Theory," 472.

256. Ibid.

257. See generally Cynthia Enloe's "Margins, Silences and Bottom Rungs: How to Overcome the Underestimation of Power in the Study of International Relations," in Smith et al, *International Theory*.

258. Andrew Deutz, "Gender and International Human Rights," *The Fletcher Forum of World Affairs* 17, no. 2 (1993): 34.

259. Steans, *Gender and International Relations*, 10.

260. See Christine Chinkin, "Violence Against Women: The International Legal Response," *Gender and Development* 3, no. 2 (June 1995): 28.

Chapter Three

The Institutional Framework—The United Nations and Non-Governmental Organisations Post-1945

3.1 WOMEN AND THE UNITED NATIONS

Women have been struggling to have their voices heard for centuries.[1] It was only until the late 1800s, however, that women were truly able to mobilise themselves in the fight against gender discrimination concerning political, economic and social issues. With the establishment of the United Nations in 1945 and the formulation of the Charter of the United Nations came the purposive call for the promotion and encouragement of respect for human rights and for fundamental freedoms for all without distinction as to race, sex, language or religion.[2] The inclusion of this sex equality provision is attributed to the work of feminists working with the Inter-American Commission of Women.[3]

This chapter will review the institutional framework established by the United Nations, including women's groups, for the promotion of women's human rights through an examination of institutions such as the Commission on the Status of Women, the Division for the Advancement of Women and the Committee on the Elimination of Discrimination Against Women. The chapter will also examine the role of NGOs in influencing the international response to the struggle for women's rights. Figure 3.1 illustrates the structure of the UN human rights bodies.

3.2 INSTITUTIONAL

3.2.1 Commission on the Status of Women

The development of women's issues at the level of the United Nations began as early as 1946 with a request from the United States delegation at the

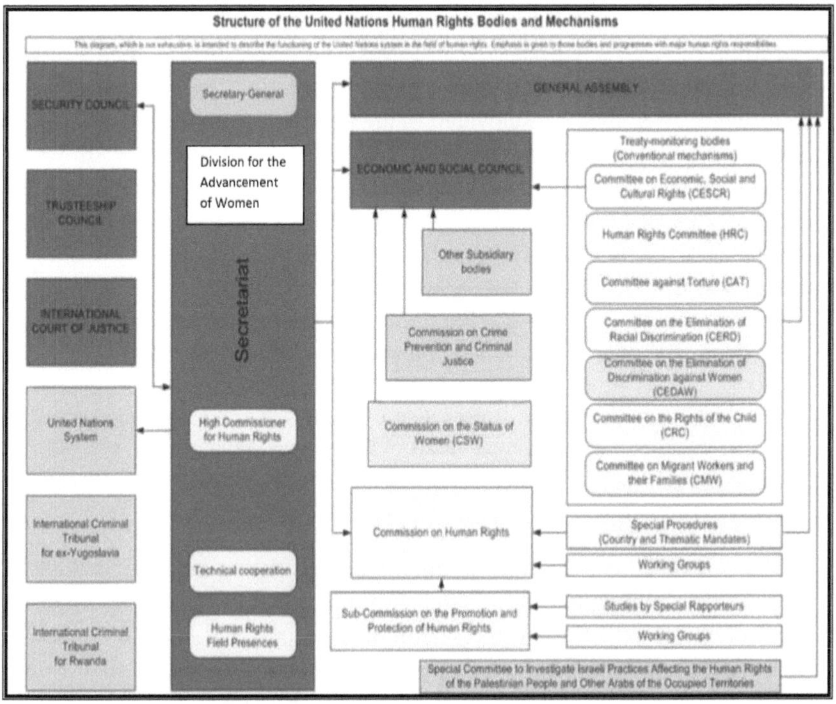

Figure 3.1. Structure of the United Nations Human Rights Bodies and Mechanisms. UN, Office of the United Nations High Commissioner for Human Rights, "Structure of the United Nations Human Rights Bodies and Mechanisms," accessed 23 June 2005, http://www.ohchr.org/english/structure_small.htm. This diagram is not an exhaustive list but shows the Commission on the Status of Women, the Committee on the Elimination of Discrimination Against Women, and the Division for the Advancement of Women and their respective positions in the general UN human rights structure.

inaugural session of the General Assembly to governments of the world "to encourage women everywhere to take a more active part in national and international affairs."[4] This was very quickly followed by the establishment of a Commission on Human Rights and a Subcommission on the Status of Women by the United Nations Economic and Social Council ("ECOSOC") for the purposes of pursuing the objectives stated in Article 1, paragraph 3 of the Charter of the United Nations.[5]

The Subcommission was established "to make proposals about how to raise the status of women to equality with men in all fields of human enterprise,"[6] thereby providing the Commission on Human Rights with special support regarding problems relating to women. Immediately upon its establishment, though, interest groups and non-governmental organisations ("NGOs") recognised that the parent body would not have been able to give due attention to the Subcommission in face of the vast amount of work facing it, including the drafting of an international bill of rights, and feared that women's issues would not be considered with the urgency required.[7] The Subcommission therefore requested that it be elevated to the status of Commission. ECOSOC conferred upon the Subcommission status of full Commission, now known as the Commission on the Status of Women ("CSW"), less than one month after the request.[8] ECOSOC stated the CSW's functions as focussing on the preparation of recommendations and reports to ECOSOC on promoting women's rights in political, economic, social and educations fields.

In its first report to ECOSOC, the CSW recognised the need for legislative change to advance the status of women and stated that it intended

> to raise the status of women, irrespective of nationality, race, language or religion, to equality with men in all fields of human enterprise, and to eliminate all discrimination against women in the provisions of statutory law, in legal maxims or rules, or in interpretations of customary law.[9]

It further went on to state that its aims included the equal participation of women in government and full citizenship; full equality for women to exercise all civil rights; full opportunity for women to take equal part in social life; and equal opportunity for compulsory, free and full education, all very important in empowering women to realise their full potential. In recognition of the importance of strengthening the legal framework to provide women with the means to achieve equality, ECOSOC requested CSW to examine the legal and customary disabilities that women face with regard to political, economic, and social rights and educational opportunities with a view to framing proposals for action.[10]

Despite what appeared to be very positive moves towards advancing the status of women in all spheres of life, there existed a very disturbing restriction on the powers of the CSW. While the CSW, like the Commission on Human Rights, was free to receive communications from individuals, groups and NGOs, neither was given the power to take any action in regard to complaints concerning the status of women.[11] The CSW had neither the power to investigate specific cases of discrimination nor did it have the authority to take measures to ensure compliance with United Nations standards.[12] So, what was its purpose? It was established to be the main policy-making body of the United Nations dealing with women that promoted global sensitisation to women's status and encouraged governments to incorporate international conventions into their domestic laws.

The CSW faced many other problems as a body dealing specifically with women's issues. While it was suggested that the CSW be comprised of experts serving in a personal capacity so as to avoid governmental control, it was decided that its composition should be of States members and meant that it was basically an intergovernmental body representing the official policies of States rather than the concerns of interest groups.[13] At the same time, nevertheless, the CSW's members are largely women, but if they do not have necessary support of their respective governments, and it can be argued that women's issues will not have the same force as economic development, for example, and therefore not be afforded priority, the operations of the CSW will continue to be constrained. This is further compounded by the CSW's lack of institutional weight as evidenced by the budgetary and procedural restrictions imposed on the CSW by ECOSOC.[14]

The mandate of the CSW was expanded in 1987 to include the objectives of the Nairobi Forward-Looking Strategies for the Advancement of Women to deal not only with matters of equality for women, but also to include women as integral agents of change and beneficiaries in issues of development and peace.[15] At the General Assembly's request,[16] after the Fourth World Conference on Women, ECOSOC once again modified the CSW's terms of reference stating that it shall:

(a) Assist the Economic and Social Council in monitoring, reviewing and appraising progress achieved and problems encountered in the implementation of the Beijing Declaration and Platform for Action at all levels, and shall advise the Council thereon;
(b) Continue to ensure support for mainstreaming a gender perspective in United Nations activities and develop further its catalytic role in this regard in other areas;
(c) Identify issues where United Nations system-wide coordination needs to be improved in order to assist the Council in its coordination function;
(d) Identify emerging issues, trends and new approaches to issues affecting the situation of women or equality between women and men that require urgent consideration, and make substantive recommendations thereon;
(e) Maintain and enhance public awareness and support for the implementation of the Platform for Action.[17]

While the CSW was previously emphasising gender-specific machinery and projects, it was now responsible for implementing the Beijing Platform for Action and for mainstreaming a gender perspective into the activities of the United Nations.[18]

Despite the many obstacles faced by CSW, it has still been able to secure recognition in law of women's rights in many countries, notwithstanding the *de jure / de facto* divide, and has raised the problem of discrimination against women politically, economically, socially and institutionally.[19]

3.2.2 Division for the Advancement of Women

The CSW has had the support of a unit within the United Nations Secretariat dealing with the status of women.[20] While the Division for the Advancement of Women ("DAW"), as it is now known, was established in 1946, it was originally established as a Section on the Status of Women within the Human Rights Division of the United Nations Department of Social Affairs. In 1972, it was upgraded to the Branch for the Promotion of Equality of Men and Women and moved to the Centre for Social Development and Humanitarian Affairs established in the same year. It was renamed the Branch for the Advancement of Women in 1978 and was further upgraded to its current status as a Division in 1993 when it was moved to the UN headquarters in New York and is now part of the Department of Economic and Social Affairs which in turn forms part of the UN Secretariat.

DAW is meant to act as a catalyst in mainstreaming gender issues and has four main branches:[21]

1. The Gender Analysis Section conducts research and develops policy options, fosters interaction between governments and civil society and provides substantive servicing for UN intergovernmental and expert bodies;
2. The Women's Rights Unit assists in breaking down the barriers between human rights and development and fosters the attainment of women's human rights as an integral part of development;
3. The Coordination and Outreach Unit raises awareness, promotes international standards and norms and sharing of best practices, and strengthens communication between the international and national policy-making processes and the women of the world; and
4. The Gender Advisory Services Unit provides governments with advisory services and technical support in the activities related to gender in development.

DAW's most important role came about in 1995 when it acted as the substantive secretariat for the Fourth World Conference on Women in Beijing, the largest conference in the history of the United Nations, and was also responsible for the preparations for the three previous World Conferences on Women (Mexico 1975, Copenhagen 1980, Nairobi 1985).[22] In its mission statement, it says:

> …the Division for the Advancement of Women (DAW) advocates the improvement of the status of women of the world and the achievement of their equality with men. Aiming to ensure the participation of women as equal partners with men in all aspects of human endeavour, the Division promotes women as equal

participants and beneficiaries of sustainable development, peace and security, governance and human rights. As part of its mandate, it strives to stimulate the mainstreaming of gender perspectives both within and outside the United Nations system.[23]

DAW's placement in the Department of Economic and Social Affairs was aimed at "ensuring the integration of gender issues in policy formulation and coordination, including the servicing of the intergovernmental machinery."[24] As seen above from the responsibilities of its four main branches, it is meant to foster dialogue, provide advisory services and raise awareness. It is, therefore, very important in the UN's decision to move away from gender specific machinery towards gender mainstreaming in all areas and continues to provide the support required by the CSW.

3.2.3 Committee on the Elimination of Discrimination Against Women

The United Nations Committee on the Elimination of Discrimination against Women ("the Committee") was established in 1982 to monitor compliance with CEDAW and is composed of 23 experts, elected by States Parties but serving in their personal capacity,[25] on women's issues from around the world.[26]

Part V Articles 17–22 of CEDAW outlines the form and functions of the Committee. Article 17 establishes the Committee and its main tasks, as stated in Article 18, is to meet annually (Article 20) to report on the legislative, judicial, administrative or other measures which States Parties have adopted and to indicate the factors and difficulties affecting the degree of States Parties' ability to fulfil their obligations under the convention. This single annual meeting proved inadequate and Article 20 was amended in 1995 where the duration of the meeting of the Committee would be determined by States Parties to CEDAW, subject to the approval of the General Assembly.[27] In addition to communications received from States Parties, the Committee may also request information from other UN agencies and NGOs to assist its members in assessing government reports.[28] While NGOs are accorded no formal involvement in the Committee's work,[29] either as part of the Committee's procedures and practices or through CEDAW, the involvement of NGOs cannot be overstated as they have the ability to get information at the ground level to which other groups may not have access.

According to Article 18 of CEDAW, States Parties are obligated to submit an initial report within one year after the entry into force of the State concerned and thereafter at a four yearly interval or whenever the Committee so requests. The initial report is meant to be comprehensive, establishing a baseline of information against which progress can be measured in the four yearly reports.[30] Due to the lack of enforcement capabilities of the Committee and associated sanctions, many countries have been delinquent in submitting their reports. As at the end of January 2005 at the Committee's thirty-second session, 112 countries have a total of 219 overdue reports,[31] 35 countries have yet to submit their initial reports with three countries having initial reports due as far back 03 September 1982.[32] Predictable is the fact that most of the countries which have not submitted even their initial reports are developing countries, as this reflects prioritisation and commitment at the level of the State.[33] Even when some countries do submit reports, they are of such poor quality that both the tardy submission, as well as the wanting character of the report, is a sad, but true, reflection of the level of commitment of the State involved.[34] In light of the backlog of reports, the Committee has decided to allow States to submit combined reports to encourage submission of reports.[35]

Trinidad and Tobago is, regrettably, one of those delinquent States and only submitted its combined *initial, second and third* periodic report in January 2001,[36] even though it ratified the convention 11 years earlier.[37] Its fourth and fifth periodic reports were due on 17 February 2003 and 2007 respectively but have not yet been submitted.[38] The country stated as its reason for the delay in submitting the 2003 report that "no mechanism existed to deal with reporting under international human rights treaties and insufficient resources had been allocated for that purpose."[39] This problem of insufficient resources is ubiquitous and not limited only to the issue of the submission of reports or to this country or to the national level. Insufficient resources are normally compounded by a lack of political will concerning the implementation of measures designed to promote women's issues. Again, this reflects the level of commitment that the government is willing to give towards honouring its international obligations concerning women's human rights.

The reporting procedures of the Committee take the following simplified format.[40] Countries must submit their written reports which the Committee considers to determine whether it conforms to the guidelines elaborated by the Committee.[41] After having considered the report, a representative of the government of the State whose report is up for discussion is invited to introduce the report. The representative may then field questions or supply additional information or clarification as required by the members. The Committee then supplies its concluding comments on the positive actions taken by governments; the factors and difficulties affecting the implementation of the Convention; notes principle areas of concerns; and makes recommendations.[42] This document drawn up by the Committee is particularly important as it points out priority areas of concern and provides detailed recommendations for action.[43]

While this latter action is commendable, like the CSW, the Committee lacks the institutional weight required to make it as effective as it should be. The budgetary and procedural restrictions placed on the Committee by the General Assembly prevent it from effectively pursuing its mandate.[44] It is also like the CSW, in the sense that it is not empowered to take action with regard to investigating individual cases of violations of women's rights but is only concerned with following general trends and patterns. As stated in Article 21 of CEDAW, the Committee may make suggestions and general recommendations based on their review of the reports and information received to the General Assembly through its parent body, ECOSOC. This means that it is left to the General Assembly to decide whether any particular action can be taken and what that action should constitute.

3.2.4 Gender Mainstreaming and the United Nations

Attention has been given to promoting women's issues over the years, albeit in a piecemeal and largely ineffective fashion. In light of this, the BPFA mandates gender mainstreaming as the main global strategy for promoting gender equality. In each of the twelve critical areas of concern in the BPFA is stated the need for the promotion of "an active and visible policy of mainstreaming a gender perspective into all policies and programmes" which takes into account the effects of such policy on women and men.[45]

ECOSOC, in 1997, defined gender mainstreaming as,

> ...the process of assessing the implications for women and men of any planned action, including legislation, policies or programmes, in all areas and at all levels. It is a strategy for making women's as well as men's concerns and experiences an integral dimension of the design, implementation, monitoring and evaluation of policies and programmes in all political, economic and societal spheres so that women and men benefit equally and inequality is not perpetuated. The ultimate goal is to achieve gender equality.[46]

The International Labour Organization summed up the definition of gender mainstreaming nicely by saying that mainstreaming is "the transformation of unequal social and institutional structures into equal and just structures for both men and women."[47]

Gender mainstreaming is meant to incorporate a gender perspective into all activities at all levels with a view to ensuring that gender equality is placed at the centre of policy decisions, medium-term plans, programme budgets and institutional structures and processes,[48] instead of having separate structures for dealing with women's issues. Initial efforts to achieve gender equality by the UN focussed on separate targeted activities for women, but it was later admitted that this approach did not tackle the structural constraints to gender equality and that an integrative approach would be better suited.[49] Yet, it must be understood that mainstreaming does *not* replace the need for targeted, women-specific policies and programmes, but are complementary strategies, as affirmative action is still required for women's empowerment. Such targeted interventions are necessary where there are "glaring instances of persistent discrimination of women and inequality between women and men."[50]

At the national level, there is debate as to whether the establishment of a single national institution (better known as "national machinery") for the purpose of gender mainstreaming would be more effective than having gender immediately incorporated into the overall governance structure of the State.[51] In 2000, the UN General Assembly held a special session to review the progress made and the obstacles remaining to the implementation of the BPFA.[52] Paragraph 24 recognises that "[n]ational machineries have been instituted or strengthened and recognized as the institutional base acting as "catalysts" for promoting gender equality, gender mainstreaming and monitoring of the implementation of the Platform for Action," but, at the same time, their effectiveness has been hindered largely by "inadequate financial and human resources and a lack of political will and commitment" which have pervasive effects on other related issues.[53] It must also be noted that national machineries have to be sensitive to the socio-political climate of each country and, therefore, are generally not intersubstitutable. Incorporating a gender perspective into the general governance of a State, however, would have the effect of naturalising gender issues by moving them from the margin to the centre, as they would not be treated with by a separate, single national institution; although, national machineries just might prove to be the most feasible starting place for achieving such a goal.

3.3 NON-GOVERNMENTAL ORGANISATIONS

Women's NGOs play an important role both nationally and internationally in the promotion and protection of women's rights and, for this reason, must be included as one of the key institutional players at the international level. Their central role is further enhanced by their very active interface with the UN concerning women's issues the world over. NGOs are certainly not a new phenomenon but today hold greater political influence[54] and have established themselves as important actors in international relations.[55] Women have been organising to effect social change from as early as the mid-1800s, advocating the abolition of slavery and universal female suffrage.[56] Today, the mandates of women's groups may be wide-ranging but their objectives are nevertheless the same: to promote the interests of women at all levels of social, legal, economic, political and cultural development. While environment and development NGOs may be perceived to be of greater effect in promoting social change, perhaps because the results of some of their activities are more readily visible, the importance of women's NGOs should in no way be understated. Their importance as part of the human rights movement is gaining similar popularity in their ability to effect [real] social change, even though such change may be much more muted and difficult to achieve.

Edwards and Hulme state that development NGOs secure small scale successes which tend to be highly localised and fleeting and have little, if any, impact on the distribution of power and resources within and between societies,[57] as their influence has been confined to projects rather than fundamental attitudes and ideology.[58] Women's NGOs, however, with particular reference to the post-Beijing era, hope to achieve much more widespread and permanent successes that necessarily question the status quo privileging men and which ultimately would affect the distribution of power and resources to the benefit of women. Social transformation of this type is a much more lengthy process with much less readily visible results and would explain why the successes of women's NGOs tend to be low-key and difficult to attain.[59]

While many agree that it is difficult to capture the essence of what an NGO is in a simple definition,[60] the term "NGO" consequently has a variety of definitions but "typically are entities that are entirely or largely independent of government and have humanitarian or cooperative rather than commercial objectives."[61] Despite this rather vague and all-encompassing description, Hilhorst denounces such definitional attempts, as she believes that NGOs are many things at the same time, since they are required to present different faces to the various stakeholders (donors, beneficiaries, colleagues) in order to satisfy each.[62] Lewis and Wallace also perceive the term "nongovernmental organisation" as "a virtually meaningless label" precisely because their functions and nature are so diverse.[63] Hilhorst sees NGOs "not as things but as open-ended processes," as they are constituted of people and do not operate in isolation and, consequently, are in a state of constant flux.[64] For her, the question is not what an NGO is, but how "NGO-ing" is *done*.[65] Further, Hilhorst states that NGO definitions and classifications do not question why and how organisations become NGOs or what causes such organisations to adopt the label "NGO." For Hilshorst, the term "NGO" is a *claim-bearing label* imputing a moral component and meaning that the organisation is doing good for the development of others.[66] Women's NGOs certainly seek to do good for the development of women worldwide, providing a forum in which woman are more comfortable to express themselves.

NGOs have created a space for themselves within civil society, both nationally and globally. According to Marchand and Runyan, "civil society is one of the most familiar grounds for feminist activists and women NGOs."[67] They go on to state that "[s]trengthening civil society is often seen as an important tool and objective in the struggle for democracy and in the fight to improve women's/human rights."[68] Within this space, NGOs provide alternative decision-making structures which claim to allow for "greater participation and broader democracy than other top-down institutional forms."[69] It is important, however, not to equate NGOs with civil society, as NGOs are just one of the many actors within civil society and play an important role in its development.[70] According to Grzybowski, "NGOs are a minute fraction of the organisational and active universe that constitute[s] civil societies. To confuse [NGOs] with civil society itself is to ascribe to them capacities and a legitimacy that they do not possess…."[71]

3.3.1 NGOs at the International Level: The UN

At the level of the UN, NGOs do not hold any powers of negotiation or decision making; they are allowed consultative status.[72] The use of the term "consultative status" was deliberately chosen to indicate their secondary role—they would be able to give advice but not take part in the decision making process; in some fields, such as human rights and sustainable development, however, NGOs have become high status participants at the centre of policymaking.[73] Article 71 of the UN Charter provides for NGOs consultative status within ECOSOC: "The Economic and Social Council may make suitable arrangements for consultation with non-governmental organizations which are concerned with matters within its competence." In 1946, ECOSOC granted consultative status to 41 NGOs.[74] Currently, there are 137 NGOs with general consultative status, 2071 with special consultative status and 967 with roster consultative status with ECOSOC.[75] The table below illustrates the various categories.

Table 3.1. NGOs in Consultative Status with ECOSOC

Status	*Number*
ECOSOC General Consultative Status	137
ECOSOC Special Consultative Status	2071
A1—ECOSOC Roster Consultative Status	424
A2—ECOSOC Roster Consultative Status	97
B—ECOSOC Roster Consultative Status	31
C—ECOSOC Roster Consultative Status	415
TOTAL	3175

In 1968, ECOSOC Resolution 1296 (XLIV) defined the rights of NGOs conferred with consultative status[76] and, up until 1996, only international NGOs were so privileged. ECOSOC resolved in 1996 that the process be widened to include the participation of national, sub-regional and regional NGOs as well.[77] In view of such an achievement, if women's NGOs have no decision making powers, what is the purpose of such consultative status? Such status is meant to facilitate advice and information gathering[78] by ECOSOC or any of its bodies and to allow NGOs that represent important elements of public opinion to express their views.[79] The benefit to NGOs of having consultative status is that they are able to lobby governments and have successfully done so, even though such successes may be fairly limited. This forum is important in allowing local women's NGOs to represent themselves and increasing the diversity of voices at the UN.[80]

Gaer makes the point that "[s]trategic, technical and organisational leadership in the UN human rights programming has always come from the NGO sector."[81] Women's movements at the UN provide similar skills in promoting women's rights. The World Conference on Human Rights, held in Vienna, is said to have marked a turning point in women's participation in the UN as a forum in which to advance women's rights.[82] Women in all regions formed an active and effective lobby presence in the preparatory meetings for the conference, participating directly in defining NGO positions and lobbying on women's issues. Since then, women's NGOs have refined their approach and developed key strategies to participate effectively in UN conferences, whether gender specific or not.[83] They:

- Mount global campaigns. In order to exert pressure on official policy makers, women's NGOs mount global campaigns calling for dialogue and action at the local level; for lobbying at the national, regional and international levels; for gathering empirical data; and attending meetings at all levels.
- Build coalitions and consensus. In order to build coalitions and consensus, women's NGOs network and hold meetings with women's NGOs from around the world at all levels.
- Prepare policy documents. Women's NGOs draft their own documents (resolutions, treaties, protocols, conventions, platform documents) to present to and influence policy makers. Being prepared makes it much easier to argue points and persuade than simply presenting one's self "on the spot."[84]
- Influence official delegations. Women's NGOs not only gather and disseminate information but discuss, lobby and nominate representatives to be members of official delegations to influence the position of national governments.

- Bridge NGO and official deliberations. Women's NGOs have developed a mechanism known as the women's caucus which facilitates daily meetings between NGOs and official delegates and policy makers to have their voices heard.

With such detailed organisation, NGOs are sometimes, if not most times, better prepared than official delegates. It is argued that the parallel NGO forums are much more productive than the official conferences, if for no other reason than the fact that they are necessarily less formal and can provide feminist alternatives or lay out issues that have not been addressed by the official conference.[85] West observed that NGO forums "brought to life a participatory democracy that generated immeasurable discussion" in what she calls "counterpolitical spaces."[86] This was certainly the case at the parallel NGO forum held in the Beijing suburb of Huairou, despite the difficulties the host government attempted to create to make it difficult for participants to attend. Nevertheless, some activists have questioned the strategy of working through the UN conference process to advance women's rights for fear that participating to influence pre-set agendas and intergovernmental documentation would result in cooptation.[87] Further, working with governments and UN agencies legitimises the frameworks offered by them which do not typically represent women's interests.

In terms of international activity, women's NGOs are seen to be "more effective in changing policy statements" and "able to lobby their own governments to follow UN recommendations."[88] While this may hold true for what is presented on paper, what actually happens in practice would indicate that these are but hollow victories, both internationally and nationally. Stienstra makes the point that even though women's concerns have been integrated into UN deliberations [and national policies], "the incorporation of these issues has followed a pattern of commitment on paper while ensuring marginalization of these issues through inadequate allocation of resources."[89] The emphasis can no longer remain on measuring "success by how many words or phrases [NGOs] were able to have inserted into international agreements," but the goal must ultimately take into account the need to shift emphasis to implementation and monitoring.[90] This may call for NGOs to form strategic alliances with other civil society based organisations to develop the capacity required to make this ideological shift.[91]

Stienstra has identified what she considers to be reasons for the limited achievements of women's groups at the international level.[92] The first is that negative changes in the global political economy, such as war and economic crises, disproportionately affected women, who tend to be the most vulnerable group in society and, therefore, most susceptible to negative change. This was particularly the case in countries which adopted structural adjustment programmes. The second reason lies with the inherent conservatism of social institutions which reflect power relations and resist any changes to the *status quo*, particularly as concerns changes in gender relations favouring women. The third reason, related to the second, is that institutions and, by extension, governments, are simply unwilling to undertake the radical restructuring of economies and societies required to truly facilitate women's requests. The easiest concession is the incorporation of language that supports broad principles of equality, which tends to appease women's groups, despite the poor history of implementation of such clauses.

3.3.2 NGOs at the National Level: The State

At the domestic level, Ackerly identifies six ways NGOs work to promote women's human rights.[93] These include making legal changes such that domestic or international laws better conform with CEDAW and other international agreements which recognise women's human rights (legal change); reinventing local legal practices (training the judiciary and police officers) (support); providing support systems for survivors of violence (support); educating society generally and broadly (in schools, through the media, gender training programs, creative arts [which could include songs, role-playing, theatre and various other non-threatening forms of advocacy tools to promote political awareness especially among the poorly literate])[94] (education); networking and promoting alliances with women's groups and other civil society organisations (networking); and integrating women's human rights efforts with other initiatives for social, economic and political change (integration).

NGOs' most essential role, either at the national level or the international level, or in tandem with each other, is perhaps their role as agents of change.[95] Historically, it has been NGOs and private citizens, rather than States, that have served as prominent conduits of pressure and influence on State activity and policy with regard to human rights and environmental principles.[96] The question now is how can NGOs have true influence on State activity? Apart from the fact that NGOs prioritise single issues to the exclusion of all others and focus all their energies on promoting that issue, theoretically, social constructivism offers a possible answer.[97] Chapter two above introduced the problems of relying on a realist, reified conception of sovereignty for the purposes of understanding the effects and practicality of international human rights law. It is therefore important at this point to revisit the usefulness of a social constructivist approach, as this offers a better understanding of how (better) human rights practices are adopted by States, especially in conjunction with NGO activity.

Risse and Sikkink offer a theory of socialisation[98] that deals with "the process through which principled ideas ("beliefs about right and wrong held by individuals") become norms ("collective [intersubjective] expectation about proper behaviour for a given identity") which in turn influence the behaviour and domestic structure of states."[99] Norms may also be seen as "standards of behaviour defined in terms of rights and obligations."[100] They identify three types of socialisation processes which operate in conjunction with each other and are necessary for enduring change in human rights issues.

- Processes of adaptation and strategic bargaining
- Processes of moral consciousness-raising, "shaming," argumentation, dialogue, and persuasion
- Processes of institutionalisation and habitualization[101]

They define socialisation as "the induction of new members… into the ways of behaviour that are preferred in a society," the goal of which is "for actors to internalise norms, so that external pressure is no longer needed to ensure compliance."[102]

Unfortunately, it is only with pressure from "above and below," ordinarily initiated by NGO action, that any sort of change takes place.[103] The first process concerns the instrumental adaptation by the State to domestic and international pressures. Governments reacting to accusations of human rights violations may make superficial but tactical concessions such as signing international agreements or releasing political prisoners.[104] Such actions are the result of strategic [crude] cost-benefit analyses or, in Checkel's words, rational means-ends logics,[105] based on the forced imposition of norms executed by the State in question with a view to maximising or optimising given interests and preferences, such as having embargoes lifted or ensuring/regaining access to international aid.[106] The second process, usually coupled with material sanctions, deals with the shaming and persuasion of deviant States. Joachim asserts that, when issues are adopted by the UN, it sends a signal to States concerning which actions are considered proper or satisfactory within the international arena. As a result, NGOs can capitalise on this intersubjective understanding of acceptable behaviour to exert pressure on norm-violating states to "follow through on their international commitments or to shame them by pointing out the gap between national practice and international agreements."[107] This use of tactics such as shaming and denunciation is not meant to change State attitudes with logic but by the isolation and/or embarrassment of the target State. Persuasion need not be only trying to reason with the norm-violating State but by applying pressure in the form of sanctions.[108] The application of sanctions, though, may prove fruitless if the State continues to receive military support, as happened in the early years of the Pinochet regime.[109] It is only when human rights norms become internalised in domestic practices and States comply with them, whether or not they believe in their validity, is the third and final stage in the socialisation process achieved.[110]

In effecting change at the domestic level, NGOs see five phases of State responses when applying pressure from above and below with the help of the transnational network of NGOs. These are:

- Repression
- Denial
- Tactical concessions
- Prescriptive status
- Rule-consistent behaviour.

The first stage begins with a repressive situation in a norm-violating state where domestic opposition is too weak and/or oppressed to pose a significant threat to the government.[111] It is during this time that domestic NGOs, depending on the level of government oppression, can activate links with transnational NGOs. The role of domestic NGOs here is information gathering which will be forwarded to the transnational network. When the network has gathered sufficient information it can expose the norm-violating state at the international level, taking it to the second stage.[112]

In raising international awareness of the violations taking place in the target State through the production and dissemination of information, the transnational network can now begin to lobby international human rights organisations and influential governments, reminding the latter of their own human rights standards, thereby using moral persuasion to get them to take condemnatory action against the norm-violating state. The reaction of the target State tends to be denial, where denial means that the government of the norm-violating state refuses to accept the validity of international human rights norms. Denial also includes the government claiming that such criticism is tantamount to intervention in the sovereign affairs of its territory and may even mobilise nationalist sentiment and domestic support. It is interesting that the government does not deny human rights, but frames its denial in terms of the encroachment of its sovereign rights. Risse and Sikkink assert that the fact that the State feels compelled to deny such charges indicates that a process of international socialisation is already in progress. The transition to the third stage depends largely on the strength and mobilisation of the transnational network and the vulnerability of the norm-violating government to international pressures.

Should international pressures continue and escalate, the norm-violating government would now feel obliged to make tactical concessions by instituting cosmetic changes in an attempt to pacify international criticism with the strategic result of lifting sanctions or lessening international isolation.[113] While visible changes will be effected, this does not translate into a stable amelioration of human rights conditions. This stage facilitates social mobilisation in the target country; it is during this time that domestic groups can mobilise and mount its own campaign against the activities of the government. According to Risse and Sikkink, this is the most precarious stage, as it can have the effect of moving the process forward towards lasting change in human rights conditions or it can result in greater governmental oppression of domestic opposition, either ceasing the forward movement or temporarily and indefinitely halting progress.[114] Government can throw the domestic movement off, as, at this stage, it is often relatively small and dependent on a few key leaders. By removing the leader (by whatever means), the movement becomes leaderless and unable to function.[115]

For those countries on the forward moving path, in addition to the mobilisation of domestic pressure groups, norm-violating governments can no longer deny the validity of international human rights norms when they start making tactical concessions. The explanation for this is that in making the minor concessions, governments are unaware of the potent impact this act engenders. Once governments start "talking the human rights talk," they become entrapped by their own rhetoric and are forced to continue in the face of international processes and strong domestic opposition. At this point, the choices available to government are few. It can begin implementation of human rights norms domestically or increase the level of repression, which only strengthens domestic opposition and alienates itself from any remaining international supporters,[116] which in turn results in a regime change. This stage in the socialisation process marks the transition to stage four.

Stage four sees the target country accepting the validity claims of human rights norms, even if the actual behaviour of the State does not improve.[117] The international community becomes satisfied that governments have accepted the validity of human rights norms when the target State ratifies international human rights conventions; incorporates international human rights instruments into domestic law; establishes a human rights violations complaints mechanism; and no longer denounces international criticism as interference in the sovereign affairs of the country. It is also important that the State maintain a consistent discursive stance on human rights despite regime changes and/or the effluxion of time. Governments may, at this time, create institutions for the promotion of human rights and start training public officials on the subject matter.

With continued pressure from above and below, the State can make the transition to stage five, rule-consistent behaviour.[118] Risse and Sikkink correctly note, however, that, at the end of stage four, much of the international community is satisfied that the target country achieved prescriptive status and that there has been a visible reduction in the intensity of human rights violations; as a result, international attention begins to wane and governments may falter.[119] Consistent pressure is required from above and below to bridge rhetoric and reality. Only when this gap is closed can the final stage in the socialisation process be reached. This is where international human rights norms are fully institutionalised domestically and norm compliance becomes a habitual practice of actors and is enforced by the rule of law. When this is achieved, it can be inferred that human rights norms have been internalised.

While this five-stage model applies to highly oppressive and abusive regimes, there is validity in applying parts of the model to more democratic States, such as the country under study here, Trinidad and Tobago.[120] This country has never been under authoritarian rule but, as with other developing countries, it has to prioritise the issues on the national agenda. As such, human rights issues are not quite at the top of the agenda, let alone issues dealing with the promotion of women's rights. In terms of the model proposed by Risse and Sikkink, Trinidad and Tobago skipped the first three stages and is at the fourth stage, where all international human rights conventions and women-specific conventions have been ratified and some have been incorporated into domestic law in one way or another. The problem lies with the lack of political will which translates into inadequate resources for implementation, monitoring and enforcement procedures. While the role of NGOs should in no way be trivialised in the politicisation and promotion of women's human rights issues, the fact remains that governments still play influential roles in promoting human rights domestically.[121] Brysk makes the point that "[i]n a democratic regime, human rights change must be promoted from above, from below, *and from within*."[122] It is, perhaps, only with pressure from above and below that political will can be forced and the gap between rhetoric and reality can be closed but, as a nation without a history of gross and systemic women's human rights abuses, this may prove quite a challenge.

3.4 CONCLUSION

The UN institutional structure for advancement of women's rights is affected by major obstacles that undermine its ability to foster real and meaningful change. The analysis of the UN system points to the lack of enforcement capabilities regarding State compliance with international legal obligations, such as reporting under CEDAW. The lack of enforcement capabilities, coupled with budgetary and procedural restrictions, creates an environment conducive to ineffectiveness. This picture is hardly surprising considering that the UN governance structure is a reflection of the attitude of the majority of its members. The numerical dominance of developing countries, where the greatest levels of abuse of women's rights exist, contributes largely to the somewhat apparent apathetic approach of the UN. Even where a committee of the UN, such as the Committee on the Elimination of Discrimination Against Women, has a majority membership of women, the fact that around 78 percent of its members are from the developing world could account for the relative ineffectiveness of such a committee. These women members are coming from governance structures that are male dominated and are therefore constrained by how far they can proceed in the struggle for the enhancement of women's rights at the international level.

The struggle for women's rights is not limited to inter-governmental organisations such as the UN. In chapter two, it was noted that DEVAW owed its genesis, to a large extent, to the advocacy activities of NGOs. BPFA, which came out of CEDAW, highlighted the growing significance of NGOs as agents of change in the international attitude to women's rights. The unprecedented gathering of over 30,000 NGO representatives in the unofficial NGO Forum provided a powerful voice that resonated throughout the official meeting. The institutional efforts of NGOs reflect the "bottom-up" approach, as it includes grass roots NGOs and NGO networks. The very nature of NGOs, where membership is generally exclusive of States, ensures that issues can be ventilated without the constraining influence of States.

Having assessed the international approach to women's rights both institutionally and legally, and noted inherent limitations in the "top-down" approach, it is worthwhile to examine the behaviour of one country to help understand why the "top-down" approach is of limited effect and why it must be complemented by the "bottom-up" approach.

NOTES

1. See chapter 1 above.
2. See Article 1, paragraph 3 of the Charter of the UN.
3. Association of Baháí Women, "Gender Studies Forum," accessed 30 March 2005, http://www.bci.org/abw/ABW/forum/tahe.html. See also section 2.3.2 in chapter 2 above.
4. United States of America, "Open Letter to the Women of the World," read by Eleanor Roosevelt at the first session of the General Assembly, A/PV.29, 12 February 1946.

5. UN ECOSOC, "Resolution establishing the Commission on Human Rights and the Subcommission on the Status of Women," E/RES/5(1), 16 February 1946.

6. Bodil Begtrup, "Statement made by the Chair of the Subcommission on the Status of Women to ECOSOC recommending that the status of the Subcommission be raised to full Commission," E/PV.4, 28 May 1946.

7. See UN Division for the Advancement of Women, Paragraph 13, "Progress Achieved in the Implementation of the Convention on the Elimination of All Forms of Discrimination Against Women," CEDAW/C/1995/7, 14 November 1994.

8. See UN ECOSOC, "ECOSOC Resolution establishing the Commission on the Status of Women (CSW)," E/RES/2/11, 21 June 1946. This is one of nine functional commissions set up by the UN. See UN Department of Public Information, "Organization Chart of the United Nations," March 2004. Accessed 04 April 2005, http://www.un.org/aboutun/chart.html.

9. See UN Commission on the Status of Women, "Report of the CSW to ECOSOC on the first session of the Commission, held at Lake Success, New York, from 10 to 24 February 1947," E/281/Rev.1, 25 February 1947, Chapter X.

10. See UN ECOSOC, "ECOSOC resolution defining the functions of the CSW and requesting Member States to provide the Commission with data on the legal status and treatment of women in their countries," E/RES/48(IV), 29 March 1947, Paragraph A.6.

11. See, UN ECOSOC, "ECOSOC resolution requesting the Secretary-General to provide the CSW with communications received concerning the status of women," E/RES/76(V), 5 August 1947.

12. UN, *The United Nations and the Advancement of Women*, 14.

13. See Laura Reanda, "The Commission on the Status of Women," in *The United Nations and Human Rights: A Critical Appraisal*, ed. Philip Alston (Oxford: Clarendon Press, 1995), 269. This chapter offers a comprehensive review of the CSW.

14. Ibid., 269–271.

15. See UN ECOSOC, "ECOSOC Resolution adopting the long-term programme of work of the CSW to the year 2000," E/RES/1987/24, 28 May 1987.

16. See UN General Assembly, "Follow-up to the Fourth World Conference on Women and full implementation of the Beijing Declaration and the Platform for Action," A/RES/50/203, 22 December 1995.

17. UN ECOSOC, "Follow-up to the Fourth World Conference on Women," Resolution 1996/6, 22 July 1996.

18. UN, Commission on the Status of Women, "Functions," accessed 28 January 2004, http://www.un.org/womenwatch/daw/csw/index.html#functions.

19. Reanda, "The Commission on the Status of Women," 301.

20. See UN, *The United Nations and the Advancement of Women*, 15.

21. Extracted from Dorothea Gaudart, "Charter-based Activities Regarding Women's Rights in the United Nations and Specialized Agencies," in Benedek et al, *Human Rights of Women*, 60–61.

22. UN, Division for the Advancement of Women, "About DAW: Brief History," accessed 28 January 2004, http://www.un.org/womenwatch/daw/daw/index.html#history.

23. UN, Division for the Advancement of Women, "About DAW: Mission Statement," accessed 28 January 2004, http://www.un.org/womenwatch/daw/daw/index.html#mission.

24. UN Secretary General, "Report to General Assembly on implementation of the outcome of the Fourth World Conference on Women: Action for Equality, Development and Peace," A/50/744, 10 November 1995, Paragraph 62.

25. Andrew Byrnes, "The Convention on the Elimination of All Forms of Discrimination against Women," in Benedek et al, *Human Rights of Women*, 129.

26. See UN, Division for the Advancement of Women, "Committee on the Elimination of Discrimination Against Women," updated 10 February 2005, accessed 04 April 2005, http://www.un.org/womenwatch/daw/cedaw/committee.htm.

27. See UN General Assembly, "Report of the Secretary-General to the General Assembly on the Convention on the Elimination of All Forms of Discrimination against Women, including the text of the proposed amendment to article 20 of the Convention," A/50/346, 11 August 1995.

28. See UN, *The United Nations and the Advancement of Women*, 54–55.

29. See Roberta Jacobson, "The Committee on the Elimination of Discrimination Against Women," in Alston, *The United Nations and Human Rights*, 466–468.

30. See, UN, Division for the Advancement of Women, "Reporting," updated 10 February 2005, accessed 05 April 2005, http://www.un.org/womenwatch/daw/cedaw/reporting.htm.

31. This includes initial to sixth periodic reports.

32. Numbers derived from Annex I of UN, Secretary-General, "Report to the Committee on the Elimination of Discrimination Against Women: Status of submission of Reports by States Parties under Article 18 of the Convention," CEDAW/C/2005/I/2, 03 December 2004, 2–13.

33. This is not to say that developed countries are not just as guilty. See Philip Alston, "Reconceiving the UN Human Rights Regime: Challenges Confronting the New UN Human Rights Council," Center for Human Rights and Global Justice Working Paper No. 4. (New York: New York University School of Law, 2006), 10–11.

34. See Jacobson, "The Committee," 455.

35. See Byrnes, "The Convention," 133.

36. See UN, General Assembly, "Report of the Committee on the Elimination of Discrimination against Women," A/57/38, 14 January–01 February 2002. The status of submissions is unchanged as at 14 July 2011.

37. See UN DAW, "States Parties."

38. See UN, Secretary-General, "Status of submission of Reports by States Parties under Article 18 of the Convention," Annex I, 12. See also UN, General Assembly, "Report of the Committee on the Elimination of Violence against Women, forty-forth session (20 July–7 August 2009), forty-fifth session (18 January–5 February 2010)," A/65/38, 11 May 2010, 90.

39. Paragraph 121, UN General Assembly, "Report."

40. See Jacobson, "The Committee," 455–462 and Byrnes, "The Convention," 135–137 for greater detail.

41. For the guidelines see UN CEDAW, "Compilation of Guidelines on the Form and Content of Reports to be Submitted by States Parties to the International Human Rights Treaties," HRI/GEN/2/Rev.1/Add.2, 5 May 2003.

42. UN General Assembly, "Report."

43. See Byrnes, "The Convention," 137.

44. See Jacobson, "The Committee," 469.

45. See paragraphs 57, 79, 105, 123, 141, 164, 189, 202, 229, 238, 252 and 273 of the BPFA.

46. UN, Economic and Social Council, "Report of the Economic and Social Council for 1997: Gender Mainstreaming," A/52/3, 18 September 1997, Chapter IV, Part I, A.

47. International Labour Organization, "Gender Equality Tool," accessed 13 April 2005, http://www.ilo.org/public/english/bureau/gender/newsite2002/about/defin.htm.

48. UN, Office of the Special Advisor on Gender Issues and Advancement of Women, "Gender Mainstreaming: Strategy for Promoting Gender Equality," updated August 2001, accessed 13 April 2005, http://www.un.org/womenwatch/osagi/pdf/factsheet1.pdf.

49. UN, Office of the Special Advisor on Gender Issues and Advancement of Women, "The Development of the Gender Mainstreaming Strategy," updated August 2001, accessed 13 April 2005, http://www.un.org/womenwatch/osagi/pdf/factsheet3.pdf.

50. UN, Office of the Special Advisor on Gender Issues and Advancement of Women, "Gender Mainstreaming," accessed 13 April 2005, http://www.un.org/womenwatch/osagi/gendermainstreaming.htm.

51. See Shirin Rai, "Institutional Mechanisms for the Advancement of Women: Mainstreaming Gender, Democratizing the State?" in *Mainstreaming Gender, Democratizing the State? Institutional Mechanisms for the Advancement of Women*, ed. Shirin Rai (Manchester: Manchester University Press, 2003) on national machinery for gender mainstreaming and Kathleen Staudt, "Gender Mainstreaming: Conceptual Links to Institutional Machineries," in Rai, *Mainstreaming Gender* on integrating a gender perspective into the general governance structure.

52. Shirin Rai, "Introduction," in Rai, *Mainstreaming Gender*, 4.

53. UN General Assembly, "Report of the Ad Hoc Committee of the Whole of the Twenty-Third Special Session of the General Assembly," A/S-23/10/Rev.1 (New York: United Nations, 2000), paragraphs 24–25.

54. Environment and development non-governmental organisations emerged explosively on the scene in the 1980s, but were in existence long before. See for example, Michael Cernea, *Nongovernmental Organizations and Local Development* [World Bank Discussion Paper No. 40] (Washington, D.C.: The World Bank, 1988), iii, 1–2.

55. Robert Jordan et al, *International Organizations: A Comparative Approach to the Management of Cooperation* (Westport Connecticut: Praeger Publishers, 2001), 243.

56. See chapter 1 above.

57. Michael Edwards and David Hulme, "Scaling-up the developmental impact of NGOs: concepts and experiences," in *Making a Difference: NGOs and Development in a Changing World*, ed. Michael Edwards and David Hulme (London: Earthscan Publications Ltd., 1992), 13.

58. Michael Edwards and David Hulme, "Making a difference? Concluding Comments," in Edwards and Hulme, *Making a Difference*, 212.

59. See Mary Meyer and Elisabeth Prügl, "Gender Politics in Global Governance," in *Gender Politics in Global Governance*, ed. Mary Meyer and Elisabeth Prügl (Lanham, MD: Rowman and Littlefield Publishers Inc., 1999), 16.

60. Some authors prefer the use of the term "civil society organisation" ("CSO") as a more "neutral and politically correct alternative," as they believe the term "NGO" to be a loaded term referring to very structured, bureaucratic organisations. See Marlies Glasius and Mary Kaldor, "The State of Global Civil Society: Before and After September 11," in *Global Civil Society 2002*, ed. Marlies Glasius, Mary Kaldor and Helmut Anheier (Oxford: Oxford University Press, 2002), 5 and the contributions to the volume.

61. Christopher Gibbs, Claudia Fumo and Thomas Kuby, *Nongovernmental Organizations in World Bank-Supported Projects: A Review* (Washington, D.C.: The World Bank, 1999), 1. NGOs, however, span a continuum from those that are purely voluntary groups with no governmental affiliation or support to those that are creations and arms of governments. Moreover, many are highly market-driven or are relations of corporations so that they are, for all practical purposes, profit-making NGOs (the profits of which are generally reaped back into the NGO activity). In addition, NGOs may not just be concerned with singular issues, such as women's issues or development or human rights only for example, but may represent any combination of all. See Thomas Princen and Matthias Finger, "Introduction," in *Environmental NGOs in World Politics: Linking the Local and the Global*, ed. Thomas Princen and Matthias Finger (London: Routledge, 1994), 15–16. The following terms represent some of the ways in which NGOs attempt to define themselves in terms of their organisational and operational frameworks: CBO: Community Based Organisation; DONGO: Donor Organised Non-governmental Organisation; GONGO: Government Organised Non-Governmental Organisation; NGO: Non-Governmental Organisation; NGDO: Non-Governmental Development Organisation; NPO: Non-Profit Organisation; PDO: Private Development Organisation; PSO: Public Service Organisation; PVO: Private Voluntary Organisation; QANGO: Quasi Non-Governmental Organisation; VALG: Voluntary Agency/Organisation; VO: Voluntary Organisation. University of Colorado, "NGOs," created October 2004, accessed 17 June 2005, http://www.colorado.edu/careerservices/pdf/NGOs.pdf. "COME N'GOs" is the term given to fly by night NGOs.

62. Dorothea Hilhorst, *The Real World of NGOs: Discourse, Diversity and Development* (London: Zed Books, 2003), 3–4. Hilhorst provides a rather insightful ethnographic study of a Philippine NGO, illustrating the impacts of the country's history and culture on the NGO and their effects on the relationship between the NGO and international donor institutions.

63. David Lewis and Tina Wallace, "Introduction," in *New Roles and Relevance: Development NGOs and the Challenge of Change*, ed. David Lewis and Tina Wallace (West Hartford, CT: Kumarian Press, 2000), x. Such diversity derives from differences in size, duration, range and scope of activities, ideology, cultural background,

organisational culture, and legal status. Princen and Finger, "Introduction," in Princen and Finger, *Environmental NGOs in World Politics*, 6.

64. Hilhorst, *The Real World of NGOs*, 4–5.

65. Ibid., 5.

66. Ibid., 7.

67. Marianne Marchand and Anne Runyun, "Feminist Sightings of Global Restructuring: Conceptualizations and Reconceptualizations," in *Gender and Global Restructuring: Sightings, Sites and Resistances*, ed. Marianne Marchand and Anne Runyun (London: Routledge, 2000), 20. It should also be noted that this is the same space within which fundamentalist groups, which tend to be anti-feminist, operate.

68. Ibid.

69. Irene Tinker, "Nongovernmental Organizations: An Alternative Power Base for Women?" in Meyer and Prügl, *Gender Politics in Global Governance*, 94–95.

70. Julie Fisher, *Nongovernments: NGOs and the Political Development of the Third World* (West Hartford, CT: Kumarian Press, 1998), 12. Fisher identifies six major ways in which NGOs promote civil society in developing countries: 1) NGOs act as intermediary between citizen and state; 2) NGOs play an important role in promoting sustainable development and viable civil societies; 3) NGOs promote political rights and civil liberties; 4) NGOs focus on bottom-up democratization; 5) NGOs influence other voluntary organisations, and; 6) NGOs form the crux of the relationship between the profit and non-profit sector of society. See pp. 13–17.

71. Cândido Grzybowski, "We NGOs: A Controversial Way of Being and Acting," in *Debating Development: NGOs and the Future*, ed. Deborah Eade and Ernst Ligteringen (Oxford: Oxfam Publishing, 2001), 215.

72. There are three levels of consultation with the ECOSOC. This status allows some direct participation in the intergovernmental process. Below ECOSOC status, there is "association" with the Department of Public Information, which does not allow participation, but does permit access to the UN. The third level deals with accreditation to conferences and other one-time events, which can permit considerable participation and lobbying in informal sessions, but does not allow a continuing relationship with the UN. Global Policy Forum, "NGO Status at the UN," updated December 2000, accessed 08 July 2005, http://www.globalpolicy.org/ngos/ngo-un/info/status.htm. For information on accreditation, see UN, "How to Obtain Consultative Status with ECOSOC," accessed 14 July 2005, http://www.un.org/esa/coordination/ngo/howtoapply.htm.

73. See Peter Willetts, "From "Consultative Arrangements" to "Partnership": The Changing Status of NGOs in Diplomacy at the UN," *Global Governance* 6, no. 2 (Apr–Jun 2000): 191–213. See Willetts also for the relationship between NGOs and the General Assembly.

74. UN, Economic and Social Council, Non-Governmental Organizations, "Consultative Status with ECOSOC," updated 2007, accessed 26 September 2007, http://www.un.org/esa/coordination/ngo/.

75. Figures collated from UN ECOSOC, "List of non-governmental organizations in consultative status with the Economic and Social Council as of 18 September

2008," accessed 14 July 2011, http://www.un.org/esa/coordination/ngo/pdf/INF_List.pdf.

76. See UN ECOSOC Resolution 1296 (XLIV), "Arrangements for Consultation with Non-Governmental Organizations," 23 May 1968, accessed 08 July 2005. Available from Global Policy Forum, "NGO status at the UN."

77. See article four, UN ECOSOC, "Consultative Relationship between the United Nations and Non-Governmental Organizations," Resolution 1996/31, 25 July 1996.

78. NGOs generally have good, if not the best information, on the subject matter that they represent. See William Hopkinson, "Challenges Facing the International System in the 21st Century," in *The Europa Directory of International Organizations 2003* (London: Europa Publications, 2003), 12.

79. See article twenty of ECOSOC Resolution 1996/31.

80. Alice Miller, "Realizing Women's Human Rights: Nongovernmental Organizations and the United Nations Treaty Bodies," in Meyer and Prügl, *Gender Politics in Global Governance*, 164.

81. Felice Gaer, "Reality Check: Human Rights NGOs Confront Governments at the UN," in *NGOs, the UN, and Global Governance*, ed. Thomas Weiss and Leon Gordenker (Boulder, CO: Lynne Rienner Publishers, 1996), 65.

82. Connors, "NGOs and the Human Rights of Women," 171.

83. See Martha Chen, "Engendering World Conferences: The International Women's Movement and the UN," in Weiss and Gordenker, *NGOs, the UN*, 151.

84. Ibid., 143.

85. Lois West, "The United Nations Women's Conferences and Feminist Politics," in Meyer and Prügl, *Gender Politics in Global Governance*, 193.

86. Ibid., 191.

87. Ellen Dorsey, "The Global Women's Movement: Articulating a New Vision of Global Governance," in *The Politics of Global Governance: International Organizations in an Interdependent World*, ed. Paul Diehl (Boulder, CO: Lynne Rienner Publishers, 2001), 456.

88. Tinker, "Nongovernmental Organizations," 101.

89. Deborah Stienstra, *Women's Movements and International Organizations* (London: St. Martin's Press, 1994), 144. See also paragraph above in section 3.2.3 on Trinidad and Tobago.

90. Deborah Stienstra, "Of Roots, Leaves, and Trees: Gender, Social Movements, and Global Governance," in Meyer and Prügl, *Gender Politics in Global Governance*, 265. See also Deborah Stienstra, "Dancing Resistance from Rio to Beijing: Transnational Women's Organizing and United Nations Conferences, 1992–6," in Marchand and Runyan, *Gender and Global Restructuring*, 220–223.

91. Josephina Stubbs, "Gender in Development: A Long Haul—But We're Getting There!" in Eade and Ligteringen, *Debating Development*, 353.

92. See Stienstra, *Women's Movements and International Organizations*, 157.

93. Ackerly, "Women's Human Rights Activists," 316–317.

94. Brooke Ackerly and Bina D'Costa, "Transnational Feminism: Political Strategies and Theoretical Resources," Working paper 2005/1, (Australian National University, Canberra: Department of International Relations, 2005), 12.

95. NGOs also act as agents of change in the corporate world. See for example Jonathon Doh, "Nongovernmental Organizations, Corporate Strategy and Public Policy: NGOs as Agents of Change," in *Globalization and NGOs: Transforming Business, Government, and Society*, ed. Jonathon Doh and Hildy Teegen (Westport, Connecticut: Praeger Publishers, 2003), 1–18.

96. Ann Marie Clark, "Non-Governmental Organizations and their Influence on International Society," *Journal of International Affairs* 48, no. 2 (Winter 1995): 512.

97. Sikkink states that "[r]ealism offers no convincing explanation for why relatively weak non-state actors [NGOs] could have an impact on state policy or why states would concern themselves with the internal human rights practices of other states...." Sikkink, "Human Rights, Principled Issue-Networks," 437.

98. This is based on case studies of over ten countries with poor human rights records and repressive governments. See Risse et al, *The Power of Human Rights.*

99. Thomas Risse and Kathryn Sikkink, "The Socialization of International Human Rights Norms into Domestic Practices: Introduction," in Risse et al, *The Power of Human Rights*, 7.

100. Andrew Cortell and James Davis, "How do International Institutions Matter? The Domestic Impact of International Rules and Norms," *International Studies Quarterly* 40, no. 4 (December 1996): 452.

101. Risse and Sikkink, "The Socialization of International Human Rights Norms," 11.

102. Ibid.

103. See Alison Brysk, "From Above and Below: Social Movements, the International System, and Human Rights in Argentina," *Comparative Political Studies* 26, no. 3 (October 1993): 259–285.

104. Risse and Sikkink, "The Socialization of International Human Rights Norms," 12.

105. Jeffrey Checkel, "International Norms and Domestic Politics: Bridging the Rationalist-Constructivist Divide," *European Journal of International Relations* 3, no. 4 (1997): 475.

106. See Thomas Risse, "International Norms and Domestic Change: Arguing and Communicative Behaviour in the Human Rights Area," *Politics and Society* 27, no. 4 (December 1999): 530.

107. Jutta Joachim, "Framing Issues and Seizing Opportunities: The UN, NGOs, and Women's Rights," *International Studies Quarterly* 47 (2003): 250.

108. Risse and Sikkink, "The Socialization of International Human Rights Norms," 14.

109. See Darren Hawkins, "Domestic Responses to International Pressure: Human Rights in Authoritarian Chile," *European Journal of International Relations* 3, no. 4 (1997): 411–412.

110. Risse and Sikkink, "The Socialization of International Human Rights Norms," 16–17.

111. Ibid., 22.

112. Ibid., 22–24.

113. Ibid., 25–28.

114. See for example the case of Tunisia in Sieglinde Gränzer, "Changing Discourse: Transnational Advocacy Networks in Tunisia and Morocco," in Risse et al, *The Power of Human Rights*.

115. See for example the case of Guatemala in Stephen Ropp and Kathryn Sikkink, "International Norms and Domestic Politics in Chile and Guatemala," in Risse et al, *The Power of Human Rights*.

116. See for example the case of the Philippines in Anja Jetschke, "Linking the Unlinkable? International Norms and Nationalism in Indonesia and the Philippines," in Risse et al, *The Power of Human Rights*.

117. Risse and Sikkink, "The Socialization of International Human Rights Norms," 29–31.

118. Ibid., 31–35.

119. Political change from authoritarianism to democracy can provoke a similar response. See the case of Argentina in Brysk, "From Above and Below," 280.

120. To be developed in the following chapters.

121. See Bas Arts, "The Global-Local Nexus: NGOs and the Articulation of Scale," *Tijdschrift voor Economische en Sociale Geografie* 95, no. 5 (2004): 498–510.

122. Brysk, "From Above and Below," 280. Emphasis added.

Chapter Four

Trinidad and Tobago's Domestic Gender Policy—The Legislative Response

4.1 INTRODUCTION

An examination of the international legal and institutional response to the promotion of women's rights illustrated the relative lack of effectiveness of the response. This raises the question of the efficacy of using the "top-down" approach to resolving the issue of women's rights. Given that the international community is really a society of individual States, it is useful at this point to focus on the attitude of the individual State to women's rights. The domestic legal and institutional response of Trinidad and Tobago, with respect to the promotion of women's rights, forms the basis of the discussions in chapters four to seven. This chapter establishes the legal background of Trinidad and Tobago and discusses how the country's colonial legacy is relevant to understanding the manner in which particular kinds of elitism and male privilege have become an inherent aspect of its legal system with continuing consequences for the promotion of gender equality using this legislative medium.

At the domestic level, the legislature is enshrined in Parliament which is responsible for making such laws as it determines necessary for the peace, order and good governance of the land; the executive has an administrative role in controlling the affairs of the nation; and, the judiciary is necessary for dispensing justice fairly in the hierarchy of Courts.[1] Trinidad and Tobago emerged from the colonial past with a system of governance that, throughout its post-colonial history, has been dominated by the male elite. By 2006, or almost forty-four years after the end of colonialism in 1962, the participation of women in the structures of power and decision making appears abysmal as appears in Table 4.1.

In the realm of the Parliament, which is the highest institution of power, the dominance of the male elite is quite apparent. The House of Representatives has some nineteen percent of its membership being female while the Senate,

Table 4.1. Participation of Women in the Structures of Power and Decision-Making

Type	*Male*	*Female*	*Total*	*Percent Total*
House of Representatives	29	7	36	19.4
Senate	20	11	31	35.4
Mayors	5	0	5	0
Councillors and Aldermen	107	49	156	31.4

Table reproduced from Gender Affairs Division, Ministry of Community Development, Culture and Gender Affairs, "National Report of the Republic of Trinidad and Tobago for the Presentation at the XXXIII Assembly of Delegates of the Inter-American Commission of Women (CIM)," November 2006, El Salvador. CIM/doc.32/06, 4.

which comprises representatives of the Government, the Opposition and Independent Senators, shows a slightly different picture. Sixteen percent of the Opposition senators is female; thirty-one percent of the Government senators is female; while fifty-five percent of the Independent senators is female. It would appear that women fare better when the selection process is ostensibly not based on political imperatives.

There was an election in May 2010 which heralded the first ever female Prime Minister in the political history of Trinidad and Tobago. Under her governance, female representation has changed and not necessarily for the better. Thirty-three percent of the Opposition Senators is female; eighteen percent of the Government Senators is female; while twenty percent of the Independent Senators is female. The House of Representatives has twenty-eight percent of its membership held by women, with twenty percent held by Government Members of Parliament.[2] Accordingly, there can be no doubt that governance in post-colonial Trinidad and Tobago ("TT") is entrenched in a male elite. Within the context of a dominant male elite, the domestic legal response of TT to gender issues and gender equality will be examined as the domestic behaviour is most likely to be mirrored in the international attitude.

4.2 THE LEGAL TRADITION OF TRINIDAD AND TOBAGO

4.2.1 Background to Governance

Trinidad's colonial history began in 1498 with the rediscovery of the country by Christopher Columbus which he claimed for the Spanish Crown.[3] In 1797, the island was surrendered to the British. Tobago has had a much more colourful history than most other Caribbean islands in that the island changed hands more than 22 times between the French, Dutch, British and even Latvians during the colonial period. Eventually, in 1814, Tobago was ceded to

Britain and TT became a single political entity on 01 January 1889 by virtue of the Orders made pursuant to the *Trinidad and Tobago Act*, 1887.

The twin island entity gained independence in 1962 and became a Republic in 1976, finally freeing itself of monarchal administration. This is not to say, however, that the vestiges of the colonial period are completely gone. The influences of British rule are still evident in the country's current legal practices.

It is often said that TT is a proud heir to that stock of constitutions drawn on the Westminster model. Noted local political analyst and constitutional expert, Hamid Ghany, states, however, that the model followed in this twin island republic should more correctly be referred to as the Whitehall model, as it was the civil servants in Whitehall who were intimately involved in the process of drafting independence constitutions for the Commonwealth Caribbean.[4] The major and most important difference between the two models is that, while the "original Westminster formula emphasises parliamentary sovereignty, the Whitehall variant enshrines the supremacy of the written

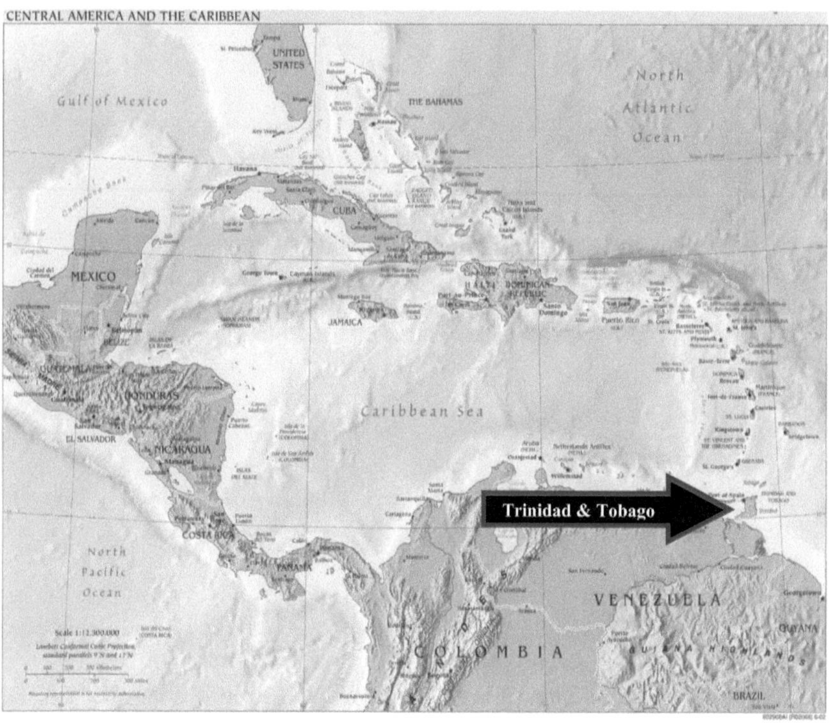

Figure 4.1. Map of Central America and the Caribbean. University of Texas Libraries, "Perry-Castañeda Library Map Collection, Map of Central America and the Caribbean," accessed 27 April 2005, http://www.lib.utexas.edu/maps/americas/central_america_ref02.jpg. Courtesy of the University Libraries, The University of Texas at Austin.

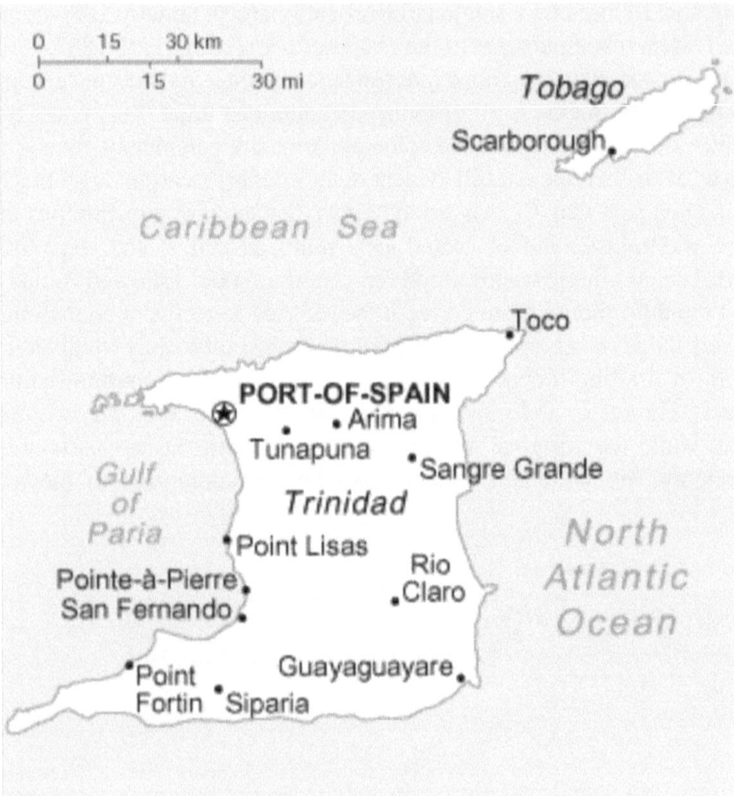

Figure 4.2. Map of Trinidad and Tobago. University of Texas Libraries, "Perry-Castañeda Library Map Collection, Map of Trinidad and Tobago," accessed 27 April 2005, http://www.lib.utexas.edu/maps/cia04/trinidad_tobago_sm04.gif. Courtesy of the University Libraries, The University of Texas at Austin.

constitution,"[5] England being the only member of the Commonwealth with an unwritten constitution.[6]

Ghany identifies five basic tenets of the Whitehall model which distinguish it from the Westminster model:

1. A Bill of Rights in the constitution that diminishes the legislative supremacy of Parliament
2. A bicameral system with a Senate that is unique
3. A definitive enforcement of the Separation of Powers among the Legislature, the Executive and the Judiciary
4. Constitutional conventions that are written and not left to interpretation as obtains under the Westminster model

5. The entrenchment of constitutional articles that further diminishes the legislative supremacy of Parliament.[7]

The issue of the practice of the doctrine of separation of powers is questionable. Some believe in the independence of the judiciary, given its supposed immunity from the executive [read: political pressure] through the buffer provided by the Judicial and Legal Service Commission.[8] Illustrative at this point is an examination of how the various appointments are made.

Figure 4.3 very simply traces the appointments made to the Judicial and Legal Service Commission ("the JLSC"). As the members of the JLSC are all appointed by the President, it is important to examine how the President is appointed. At the very top of Figure 4.3 is a box showing the Electoral College. It is this unit that is responsible for appointing the President. What constitutes the Electoral College? According to Section 28(1) of the *Constitution* of the Republic of Trinidad and Tobago, Chap. 1:01 ("the *Constitution*"), the Electoral College is a unicameral body consisting of all the members of both Houses of Parliament: 31 Senators in the Upper House and 41 Members of Parliament in the Lower House. The President appoints all 31 Senators;[9] however, 16 are appointed on the Prime Minister's recommendations, 6 are appointed on the advice of the Leader of the Opposition, and 9 "Independent Senators" are appointed at the President's discretion. As for the Members of

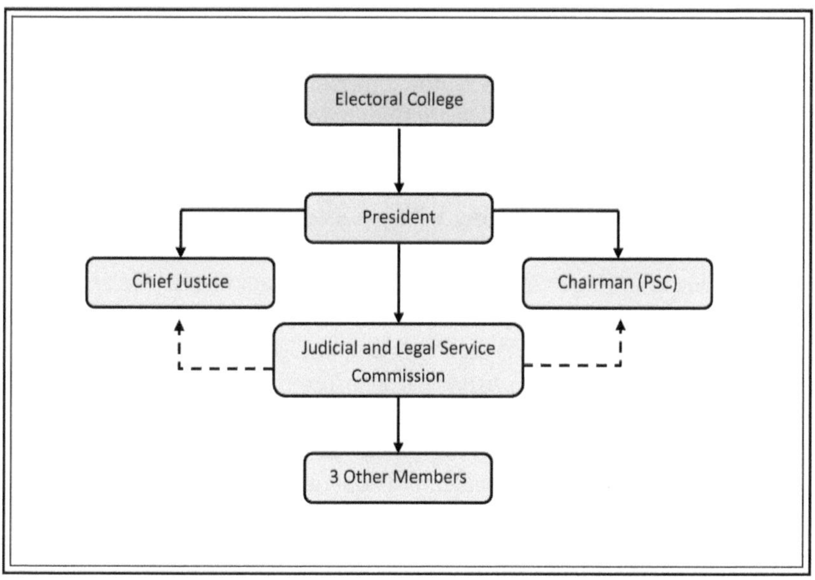

Figure 4.3. Appointments to the Judicial and Legal Service Commission.

Parliament, it is generally the ruling party that has more members.[10] In any event, it is clear that the majority of the Members of Parliament are affiliated with the ruling party and it is these Members that make up the Electoral College which appoints the President. Further, both the Prime Minister and the Leader of the Opposition make recommendations for presidential nominees; needless to say, throughout the history of Independent TT, the recommendation of the latter has never successfully prevailed in the Electoral College. It also goes without saying that the post of Prime Minister is incontrovertibly political. It should be clear from this that the appointment of President is, in fact, a political appointment and that any appointments made by the President will necessarily also be political.[11]

As mentioned above, all members of the JLSC are appointed by the President (Section 110). The Chief Justice and the Chairman of the Public Service Commission ("the PSC") are appointed directly by the President, after consultation with the leaders of both parties.[12] The three other members are appointed through the JLSC in the same manner, with the Chief Justice who acts as Chairman and the Chairman of the PSC who were previously appointed as the core members. Effectively, therefore, the Executive is ever present in these appointments, causing the notion of a separation of powers to be more cosmetic than actual.

4.2.2 Sources of Law

4.2.2.1 The Constitution

Returning to the *Constitution*, it is not surprising that it is the supreme law of the land. Section 2 of the *Constitution* states, "This Constitution is the supreme law of Trinidad and Tobago, and any other law that is inconsistent with this Constitution is void to the extent of that inconsistency."[13] It is from this supreme law that laws dealing with the establishment, composition and functions of Parliament are derived. (There is no such document for the Westminster model.) Ramlogan and Persadie succinctly summarise the objectives of the *Constitution*.[14] The *Constitution* of TT establishes the highest political office of the land, the office of the President, and governs his behaviour and his election to office. The *Constitution* also provides for the regulation of electoral activities. It governs the executive powers to be exercised by all Ministers of Cabinet, as well as the functions, appointment and behaviour of other public officers. Financial provisions are an important part of the *Constitution*, as it provides for the establishment and use of the Consolidated Fund which comprises monies to be used for Government expenditure. The legal basis for the establishment and functioning of the judicature is also to be found in the *Constitution*. The *Constitution* is, therefore, an important source of law with respect to the establishment and regulation of government.

4.2.2.2 Common Law

Another item of inheritance resulting from the colonial experience is the common law legal tradition. Common law was born at the end of the Norman Conquest in 1066 A.D.[15] With common law's origination in England, it is not surprising that it found its way to the former conquered territories of the Commonwealth, such as TT. As Lord Diplock noted in *Kodeeswaran v. Attorney-General of Ceylon*, [1970] A.C. 1111 at page 1116: "In the case of most former British colonies which were acquired by conquest or cession, the English common law is incorporated as part of the domestic law of the now independent State because it was imposed upon the colony…," but this was to be done "subject to such qualifications as local circumstances render necessary."[16] In the case of TT, Section 12 of the *Supreme Court of Judicature Act*, Ch. 4:01, provides for the reception[17] of English law into the local legislation,

> Subject to the provisions of any written law in operation on 1st March 1848, and to any written law passed after that date, the Common Law, Doctrines of Equity, and Statutes of general application in the Parliament of the United Kingdom that were in force in England on that date shall be deemed to have been enacted and to have been in force in Trinidad as from that date and in Tobago as from 1st January 1889.

This means that TT adopted the laws of England on these dates as its own, although not by choice; such laws are amended, repealed and replaced by the Legislature as it sees fit.

Characteristic of the common law tradition is its reliance on precedents and judge-made law, distinct from civil law where legal principles and ideas are officially recorded in the form of a code. Judicial discretion finds expression in common law countries where new law emerges frequently to deal with changing times and needs.[18]

4.2.2.3 Statutory Law

Complementing common law is statute law, which is created by Parliament in the form of legislation.[19] In the Commonwealth, legal systems are based on common law and courts are quite important in interpreting statutes; nevertheless, legislation has become the principal means of law making.[20]

4.3 ASSESSING GENDER LAWS IN THE FRAMEWORK OF THE COLONIAL EXPERIENCE

The analysis that follows will show that the laws made relating to gender in the post-colonial era are very much shaped by what obtained in the colonial period. The colonial legal system was characterised by attributes that seemed to favour the ruling elite and exhibited elements of control, benevolence, inequality, and equality. In the post-colonial era, this characterisation continues to apply, the only difference being that the class elitism of the colonial period is replaced by gender elitism. The post-colonial legal response is largely a reflection of the colonial structure, where the issues of gender and the position of women in society are closer to that of the non-whites / non-elites during colonialism, with men replacing the colonial elite who continue to exercise control.

4.3.1 The Shaping of the Law: The Role of Colonialism

Colonialism has, in fact, left quite an impression on the legal landscape of TT and continues to do so. As Sharma, JA, as he then was, stated,

> …even after independence, our courts have continued to develop law very much in accordance with English jurisprudence…. The inherent danger and pitfall to this approach is that, since independence our society has developed differently from the English and now requires a robust examination in order to render our constitution and common law more meaningful.[21]

Even though many call for legal reform to reflect the uniqueness of this post-colonial society, Meighoo makes the point that society in TT is in a continual state of flux[22] and, as such, a more suitable form of governance would be difficult to model.

Important, too, is not just the form of legal governance imposed by the imperialists, but also the *type* of laws enacted under the guise of attempting to maintain social order. Many authors are of the view that the historical function of law in Caribbean society was to legitimise the exploitative nature of plantation society.[23] While law is meant to be an instrument of social control and public order, it was used very specifically in colonial societies, such as TT, by a dominant elite minority to shape and enact certain laws and use them to serve its own ends, ostensibly with the interest of the public at heart. Knafla and Binnie state, "English law was developed partly to further the interests of an elite white settler minority drawn to the island by the lure of profits from sugar cultivation."[24]

The colonial legal system was characterised by attributes that seemed to favour the ruling elite. The laws exhibited elements of:

- Control (laws granting dominance by elite over non-elite group),
- Benevolence,[25] (laws designed to show the non-elite group that the law-making elite are considerate and conscious of their condition and can be entrusted to ensure their well-being),

- Inequality, which can be further sub-categorised into positive and negative
  - Positive: laws that vested rights in the elite, but not to the non-elite;
  - Negative: laws that create liabilities applicable only to the non-elite group,
- Equality, which can be further sub-categorised into false, inverse and restorative
  - False: laws giving the appearance of equality but, on further examination, are elitist;
  - Inverse: laws conveying rights to the non-elite that are not enjoyed by the elite;
  - Restorative: laws conveying rights to achieve neutrality between the elite and non-elite.

4.3.1.1 Control

After the abolition of slavery, East Indians were brought as indentured workers to labour on sugar plantations and laws were enacted to discourage any possible social cohesion between the different ethnic groups. Divide and conquer seemed to be the ideology at work. Haraksingh makes the point that in post-emancipation Trinidad

> [t]he force of the general law was directed in the first place at maintaining control: the strategy was to prevent the two major groups at the bottom of the social and economic system—the descendents of black ex-slaves and of Indian indentured workers—from establishing any common front.[26]

This was a largely successful enterprise and continues to apply today, although the current socioeconomic and political climate offers new mitigating circumstances.

Control by the elite extended as well to other aspects of life. A significant characteristic of colonial legislation was the presence of laws that promoted the ruling elite. It is acknowledged that religion is a critical tool in controlling a non-ruling majority. Armed with this knowledge, the colonial masters ensured that their elitist control over religious indoctrination was well-entrenched in the law. The *Alien Missionaries and Teachers Ordinance*, No. 22 of 1917, created a statutory preference for the elite, giving only to them free rein to engage in religious or educational work—important tools of social control—in the Colony without written permission from the Governor. This was clearly elitist, as non-natural born or naturalised British subjects were required to obtain prior written permission before engaging in such activities. In prohibiting non-sanctioned religious or educational work, this Ordinance at the same time created negative unequal rights by establishing clear liability for the non-British found in breach.

4.3.1.2 Benevolence

The British colonialists recognised that a system founded on control and repression would have continuously created conditions of dissonance with the ever–present threat of civil unrest from the colonised. It was, therefore, important for the ruling elite to appear to govern with a sense of benevolence that would accomplish the critical objective of demonstrating that they cared and could be entrusted to seek the interest of the colonised. This attitude was exemplified in the laws dealing with education at the secondary school level. The *Secondary Education Ordinance*, No. 13 of 1909 provided for the granting of three exhibitions (scholarships) per year to students who were successful in the secondary school entrance examination and were placed at the Queen's Royal College. While this seems benevolent enough, the hypocrisy of this piece of legislation reveals itself in following section.

4.3.1.3 Inequality

Positive inequality benefited the elite, as it ensured that certain rights were well entrenched in the laws to perpetuate their well-being and future control through their children. The public service in colonial times was largely the domain of the white settlers and non-white residents of TT that were supportive of the white settlers. The son or sons of any deceased public servant could have been lawfully granted admission to the Queen's Royal College without writing the same examination pursuant to the *Secondary Education Ordinance*. Moreover, not only were they eligible for entry, but their fees were paid out of the general revenues. These privileges could possibly have been justified on the basis that, as a public servant, the parent contributed to the building of the nation; therefore, it was only fair that the son's education be paid out of the public coffers.

In continuing to vest rights in the elite, laws were passed that ensured that the non-elite were placed at a distinct disadvantage in the power structure of the colony. Even when democracy was being ostensibly promoted for the colony, the legal requirements in 1925, according to the *Legislative Council (Elections) Ordinance*, Ch. 2 No. 2, to become a member of the Legislative Council ensured that only members of the elite would qualify.[27] These requirements included the ability to read and write English in a society where a large segment of the population comprised East Indian indentures who were, in the main part, English illiterates. In addition, there was an ownership of real estate stipulation, in the district in which one sought to be elected, to qualify as a candidate for election as a member of the Legislative Council. There was the added obstacle of having to ensure that the real estate owned in the electoral district in which one sought election produced a minimum level of clear annual income. The net result of this type of legislation ensured that the majority of the non-elites were kept out of the governing political structure of the society.

The colonial period was also characterised by laws that created liabilities in the non-elite by creating instances of negative inequality. Williams states that, as the black slave population grew, "the resident planters, apprehensive of the growing disproportion between whites and blacks, passed Deficiency Laws to compel absentees, under penalty of fines, to keep white servants."[28] In the immediate post-emancipation era, laws such as the *Tenancy Act* and *Vagrancy Act*, imported from England, sought to force "idle," jobless ex-slaves, devoid of land, money or opportunity, back to the plantations.[29] The *Vagrancy Act* entered the statute books as the *Habitual Idlers Ordinance*, No. 7 of 1918 and defined a habitual idler as "any male person who has no visible means of subsistence, and who, being able to work, habitually abstains from work," and who "has not worked for a period of four hours during each of three days or for a period of 14 hours during such period of 7 days" of the week before his arrest.[30] Haraksingh sardonically notes that "[i]t was not clear what constituted visible means or the ability to work, or even what magic lay in the four-hour stipulation."[31] In any event, Section 5 dealt with the issue of the burden of proof which unfairly lay on the "idler" (non-elite) to prove that he was not, in fact, a habitual idler. Inferred in section 9 of the Ordinance is the fact that "detention in settlement" effectively led the "idler" back to a plantation as part of his punishment. It is clear that the liabilities created by the *Habitual Idlers Ordinance* had as its primary target the non-elite.

4.3.1.4 Equality

Additionally, the colonial elite were very good at promoting legislation that, *prima facie*, would appear to offer equality to all but which, on closer examination, actually worked against the interests of the non-elite while favouring the elite, creating false equality. The part of the *Education Ordinance*, Ch. 14 No. 1 of 1935 dealing with religion in schools seemed to try to accommodate the cosmopolitan nature of the society. At first glance, the provision in question appeared to show appreciation for the need to remain secular in such a society by stating very clearly, "Religious teaching shall not form part of the instruction required to be given at any Government school by any teacher;" yet, it simultaneously gives authority to any Minister of religion to provide "religious instruction to the children of the religious denomination to which the Minister belongs, at such times and places as may be agreed upon between him and the Director." The Director would presumably have been one of the elite who would have practiced Christianity and who would only have known Ministers (Christian) who were of the same class. This necessarily and immediately reduced the possibility of the Minister being of a religion other than that of what the Director practised or believed in, thereby nullifying the ostensible attempt of accommodating and respecting the religious beliefs of all.

Laws that conferred rights on the non-elite that are not enjoyed by the elite are referred to as conferring "inverse equality," as it is presumed here that rights enjoyed by the elite are the standard by which enjoyment of equality of rights will be measured and any rights conferred on the non-elite only will be necessarily inverse. These are, of course, rare; however, the *Truck Ordinance*, No. 34 of 1918 provided that labourers be paid only in money (as they were known to be paid sometimes partially in kind) and created offences for employers attempting to compensate labourers by other means. According to Haraksingh, though, this measure was meant to divert the labour supply from small contractors and emerging middlemen with limited cash to large planters who were able to manage a money payroll,[32] again ensuring a labour supply to the elite-owned plantations.

Laws seeming to remove class differences exhibit the characteristic of restorative equality. One such ordinance was the *Hindu Marriage Ordinance*, No. 13 of 1945. Even though Indians lived in TT for some one hundred years, it took that long for some of their cultural practices to be legally recognised. Section 5(1) of this Ordinance conferred on the Governor the right to authorise Hindu priests to officiate marriage ceremonies, while Section 9(d) allowed the Hindu priest to do so under Hindu rites. This must have represented a major cultural victory, as British practices were always imposed on the various immigrant groups.

4.3.2 Law, Colonialism and Gender in the Post-Colonial Era

There are just about 150 laws, inclusive of the *Constitution* and constitutionally–derived legislation, which deal with gender issues either directly or indirectly in a significant manner.[33] There are two main categories: the *Constitution* and constitutionally–derived subsidiary legislation and general statutes and subsidiary instruments. The *Constitution* referred to here is the one drawn up when TT became a Republic in 1976. The second category consists of acts (post–1962) and ordinances (pre–1962), some of which continued to have effect even after TT gained independence in 1962 and began writing its own laws.

The elements that existed as part of the colonial legal system would appear to have been replicated in the subsequent post-colonial system, where the colonial elite were replaced by the local male elite and the population of former slaves and indentures by women. This means, therefore, that elitism and sexism amount to one and the same. The analysis which follows below will show that the post-colonial legal response is largely a reflection of the colonial structure where the issues of gender and the position of women in society are closer to that of the non-whites / non-elites during colonialism with men replacing the colonial elite who continue to exercise control.

Of all these laws, there are only two pieces of legislation that make specific reference to gender equality with respect to discrimination on the basis of gender. Having reviewed the constitutional and statutory provisions as they relate to gender, it is generally possible to categorise the legal provisions into the same broad categories as were provided above for the analysis of the colonial legal system.

Just as the colonial legal system was characterised by attributes that seemed to favour the ruling elite, so, too, is the post-colonial legal system. In addition to exhibiting elements of control, benevolence, inequality, and equality, there are in fact areas which seem to favour the non-elite. In the post-colonial era, this latter category of equality assumed two different characteristics. While it retains the sub-category of restorative equality, the meaning of it here refers to laws creating rights for women where they were previously non-existent [such as maternity benefits], and conveying rights to achieve gender sameness [such as formalising the rights of the common law wife] or non-gender distinctiveness [such as illustrated by the *Domestic Violence Act*, Chap. 45:56]. Moreover, this period saw the enactment of a constitution which was not part of the colonial legislative framework. Being the supreme law of the land, it guarantees equal rights to all.

4.3.2.1 Control

Unlike law under the colonial system, there are not that many pieces of legislation in the post-colonial period that attempt to exert control over the non-elite. The *Jury Act*, Chap. 6:53 and the *Post Office Savings Bank Act*, Chap. 79:04, however, are two pieces that blatantly control women's behaviour. Under the *Jury Act*, a person is only qualified to be a juror if he is over eighteen years of age, is a resident of TT for at least two years or is born in TT,

Table 4.2. Categories of Colonial and Post-Colonial Law

Main Categories	*Sub-Categories*
Control	None
Benevolence	None
Inequality	Positive Inequality; Negative Inequality
Equality	False Equality; Inverse Equality; Restorative Equality, Constitutional Equality

is English literate, and other conditions relating to the ownership of land and minimum clear annual net income. A married woman, notwithstanding these qualification requirements, shall be eligible to be a juror first if her husband is qualified to be one and then if she is over eighteen and English literate. The husband is not subject to these restrictions: he qualifies on his own merit. The intent and rationale behind this piece of legislation is not quite clear but is certainly prejudiced. Why is her capacity dependent upon her husband's?

The *Post Office Savings Bank Act* provides for the passing of regulations geared towards regulating deposits and withdrawals by minors and married women. Again, there is no such restriction on men, married or unmarried. It is important to note at this point the similar classification of minors and women. This occurs in many pieces of legislation and also lumps into this category those of sub-normal mental capacity, bringing into question the capacity of women to act as full adults.

4.3.2.2 Benevolence

Laws falling into this category seem to seek to protect women's sexual and physical integrity and maternity rights or ensure that they are provided for financially in the event of the death or physical incapacitation of the male breadwinner. The *Offences Against the Person Act*, Chap. 11:08 and the *Sexual Offences Act*, Chap. 11:28 are both meant to protect the sexual integrity of women and young girls. The first seeks to protect against the carnal knowledge of a minor, incest, prostitution, rape (including marital rape), and wilful miscarriage. In addition to dealing with rape, incest and prostitution, the *Sexual Offences Act* is of particular interest, as it attempts to criminalise sex with minors outside of a marital relationship as opposed to simply referring to it as unlawful carnal knowledge as is done under the *Offences Against the Person Act*.

Some laws ensure that where a female must physically interact with another that that other will be female. The *Customs Act*, Chap. 78:01 and the *Military Training (Prohibition) Act*, Chap. 15:04 both state that a female shall not be searched except by a female. The *Police Service Regulations, Police Service Act*, Chap. 15:01 make special provisions for female prisoners—they are only to be entrusted into the custody of a Police Matron, kept in women-only cells, and searched by the Police Matron or a woman police officer.

Labour laws tend to be quite protective of women and pay special attention to maternity issues. The *Maternity Protection Act*, Chap. 45:57 was passed in 1998 to deal with employers' abuses of pregnant employees. It specifically provides in Section 7 that, subject to certain conditions, an employee is entitled to (a) leave of absence for the purpose of maternity leave; (b) pay while on maternity leave; (c) resume work after such leave on terms no less favourable than were enjoyed by her immediately prior to her leave. Certain State bodies, such as the Civil Service (*Civil Service Regulations, Civil Service Act*, Chap. 23:01), teaching service (*Education (Teaching Service) Regulations, Education Act*, Chap. 39:01), fire service (*Fire Service (Terms and Conditions of Employment) Regulations, Fire Service Act*, Chap. 35:50), and police service (*Police Service Regulations, Police Service Act*, Chap. 15:01), provide for maternity issues. The government also decided to protect the maternity rights of certain minimum wage earners through industry specific legislation: *Minimum Wages (Catering Industry) Order, Minimum Wages Act*, Chap. 88:04, *Minimum Wages (Household Assistants) Order, Minimum Wages Act*, Chap. 88:04, *Minimum Wages (Security Industry Employees) Order, Minimum Wages Act*, Chap. 88:04, and *Minimum Wages (Shop Assistants) Order, Minimum Wages Act*, Chap. 88:04.

The *Occupational Safety and Health Act*, Chap. 88:08 ensures that pregnant women do not expose their unborn children to any unnecessary harm at the workplace. The Act also ensures a pregnant woman's employer shall offer her suitable, alternative employment on terms and conditions that are no less favourable than her ordinary terms and conditions of work where she is required to perform work that poses a danger to her safety or health or that of her child. Employers are also required to establish separate washing facilities, sanitary conveniences and locker rooms for both sexes. The *Shop (Hours of Opening and Employment) Act*, Chap. 84:02 ensures that female shop assistants are provided with seats. The *Workmen's Compensation Act*, Chap. 88:05 makes financial provisions for any dependant female, married or unmarried, in the event of her husband's incapacitation or death. The *Private Hospitals Regulations, Private Hospitals Act*, Chap. 29:03 state that where male and female patients are accommodated on the same floor of the hospital, there shall be separate water closets and wash basins for both sexes.

There are many pieces of legislation that seek to ensure that women are well taken care of in the event of her husband's incapacitation or death. The *Airports Authority Act*, Chap. 49:02, *Chaguaramas Development Authority Act*, Chap. 35:02, *Management Development Centre Act,* Chap. 85:51, *National Carnival Commission of Trinidad and Tobago Act*, Chap. 42:01 all state that pension schemes will "grant gratuities, pensions or superannuation allowances to, or to the widows, families or dependants" of its officers and employees. The *Pensions Act*, Chap. 23:52, *Teachers' Pensions Act*, Chap. 39:02, *Police Service Act*, Chap. 15:01, *Fire Service Act*, Chap. 35:50 all make pension provisions for widows on condition that she is "unmarried and of good character." This is important to note as there are no pension provisions for widowers, as it would appear that he was assumed to be the provider in any event. While the *Interpretation Act*, Chap. 3:01 states that references to persons or male persons include references to male and female persons, it is not clear that these pieces of legislation necessarily or primarily catered for adult male dependants. Given the historical evolution of society, it would be easy to infer that such legislative clauses were meant to ensure that female dependants and families would be taken care of in the event of the untimely passing of the male income earner. This is further and specifically exemplified by the *Widows' and Orphans' Pensions Act*, Chap. 23:54. Provisions are made for women and children but there is no corresponding act for *widowers* and orphans, as it is understood that men can provide for themselves and their dependants. This, of course, also reflects the way that society evolved, where women tended to be the homemaker and the husbands the breadwinners. While this situation does not apply as strictly today, there is no corresponding evolution of or amendments to the laws in force.

The *Supplemental Police Regulations, Supplemental Police Act*, Chap. 15:02, made pursuant to Section 12 of the *Supplemental Police Act* states that "[f]emales, lunatics and young children shall never be handcuffed." As mentioned in section 4.3.2.1, this brings into question the ability of women to act in their full capacity as adults. While is it all well and good that women are not perceived as enough of a threat to have to be handcuffed and can, therefore, be treated with greater leniency than men, this certainly is an undesirable way of classifying women.

4.3.2.3 Inequality

Laws reflecting positive inequality vest rights in the elite. Issues of paternity are covered by this category. The *Births and Deaths Registration Act*, Chap. 44:01 vests the right in a father of a child born out of wedlock not to have his name entered as the father unless he so desires. The *Industrial Training Act*, Chap. 39:54 vests a preferential right in fathers over mothers to decide whether their child between the ages of thirteen and eighteen may be taken in as an apprentice. Paternity leave has now been legislated by two State bodies: the fire service (*Fire Service (Terms and Conditions of Employment) Regulations, Fire Service Act*, Chap. 35:50), and the police service (*Police Service Regulations*, Chap. 15:01). If the officer can prove that the child was born to him, he will be allowed three days paternity leave.

The *Deceased Wife's Sister's Marriage Act*, Chap. 45:54 and the *Matrimonial Proceedings and Property Act*, Chap. 45:51 provide other examples of the elitist nature of some of the laws. The first law validates the marriage between a man and his sister-in-law but there is no corresponding provision or separate law to validate the marriage between a woman and her brother-in-law. Why this law was necessary in the first instance is unclear, as the degrees of familial separation are delineated by blood relationships. The second law renders a marriage voidable, where at the time of the marriage, the respondent was pregnant by someone other than the petitioner. Again, there is no corresponding provision or separate law making marriage voidable on the part of a woman where her husband has had children in previous relationships or is having a child with another.

Legislation in the category of negative equality creates liabilities in the non-elite. There are three pieces of legislation which legalise earlier ages at which members of the respective faiths shall be capable of contracting marriage. Under the *Hindu Marriage Act*, Chap. 45:03, the girl can be fourteen and the boy eighteen; under the *Muslim Marriage and Divorce Act*, Chap. 45:02, the girl can be as young as twelve and the boy sixteen; and the Orisas, under the *Orisa Marriage Act*, Chap. 45:04, allow girls of sixteen and boys of eighteen to marry. This means that young girls may be taken out of school and generally be disallowed to fully mature before entering into a marriage, while boys are allowed to finish school.

Women risk having their appointments terminated in cases where they are married and their family obligations are deemed to be affecting their performance at work pursuant to the *Public Service Commission Regulations* and the *Police Service Commission Regulations*. It is important to note here that these regulations are made pursuant to the *Constitution* which, while conferring equal rights on all,[34] seems, at the same time, to place a disproportionate burden on women to perform at work and in the home. It would, therefore, appear unseemly that the supreme law of the land should create unequal rights between the sexes for whatever reason. The *Statutory Authorities' Service Commission Regulations, Statutory Authorities Act*, Chap. 24:01, though not a constitutional derivative, also contain a similar provision.

4.3.2.4 *Equality*

False equality is a characteristic of legislation that appears to confer equality on both sexes but, on closer examination, is elitist. The *Socially Displaced Persons Act*, No. 59 of 2000 is one such act. This Act is meant to provide for the assessment, care and rehabilitation of socially displaced persons, specifically through the establishment of a Socially Displaced Persons Unit. While this is commendable in itself, the Act does not take into account the specific social and security needs of women. Lumping women together with men in this instance can have the potential of not only creating unsafe situations but providing inappropriate or ill-equipped facilities for women. Moreover, Section 8 provides for the establishment of a Social Displacement Board of 12 members but there is no requirement that any of these members be female. It is questionable whether a board comprising only men would be sensitive to the needs of the socially displaced woman.

Laws that confer rights on the non-elite that are not enjoyed by the elite have been termed "inverse equality." It is presumed here that rights enjoyed by men are the standard by which enjoyment of equality of rights will be measured and any rights conferred on women only will be necessarily inverse. Admittedly, these are few, but deserving of mention. The *Criminal Law Act*, Chap. 10:04, for example, allows women to claim as a defence for any offence, apart from treason and murder, that she committed said offence in the presence of and under the coercion of her husband. Similarly, under the *Criminal Procedure Act*, Chap. 12:02, a woman can claim diminished capacity where she wilfully causes the death of her child under twelve months old. She will be found guilty of the lesser charge of infanticide and not murder. Under the *Matrimonial Proceedings and Property Act*, Chap. 45:51, the Court may order costs against the wife only if she owns separate property. These are not rights similarly enjoyed by men.

Restorative equality creates equal rights for men and women through three main means. Such laws create rights for women where women did not previously enjoy such rights or have such rights conferred on them (maternity benefits); they convey rights to achieve gender neutrality (such as seen in the *Cohabitational Relationships Act*, Chap. 45:55); and non-gender distinctiveness (*Domestic Violence Act*).

Before examining these three categorisations, it is useful to review what legislative measures currently exist to promote general equality. The *Registration of Clubs Act*, Chap. 21:02 and the *Theatres and Dance Halls Act*, Chap. 23:02 both specifically prohibit, *inter alia*, gender discrimination on the premises by the owner or occupier and are the only two pieces of legislation to do so. The *Equal Opportunity Act*, Chap. 22:03 deals with discrimination in employment but makes distinctions with respect to the physical biological differences between men and women. Very importantly, though, it does not seem to construe rights associated with childbirth to be differential rights or ones for which men should be accorded any special reciprocal rights. As per Section 20, "It is not a contravention of this Act for a person to grant to a woman rights or privileges in connection with pregnancy or childbirth."

Other pieces of legislation retain in married women their capacity as equal legal individuals to execute deeds (*Conveyancing and Law of Property Act*, Chap. 56:01 and *Real Property Act*, Chap. 56:02); to determine settlement issues (*Income Tax Act*, Chap. 75:01); to enter into contracts, own and sell property, sue and be sued and be subject to the law relating to bankruptcy and to the enforcement of judgments and orders (*Married Persons Act*, Chap. 45:50); and to have their property used as collateral against them (*Remedies of Creditors Act*, Chap. 8:09), as would any man.

Under the first categorisation of restorative equality, which addresses newly conferred rights, maternity benefits have been legislated to ensure that pregnant women and new mothers are not taken advantage of by their employers. As with the *Equal Opportunity Act*, Chap. 22:03, conferring maternity benefits should not be seen as a right to be reciprocated to men as the physical biological/reproductive differences between men and women are real. The importance of legislating maternity benefits should not be trivialised through attempting to confer a reciprocal right on men, basic paternity benefits aside.

Gender neutrality, the second category of restorative equality, deals not only with inter-gender equality but also *intra*-gender equality. Intra-gender equality implies that there is inequality *between* women. Many couples in TT have not formally legalised their relationships and live in "common–law marriages." This meant that women who practiced this type of relationship had no recourse in law when her significant other died or the relationship ended, as rights to property and maintenance required that there be a legal relationship instituted between them. It was only a married woman who could successfully (and legally) claim title to her husband's property. The enactment of the *Cohabitational Relationships Act* changed this, where a cohabitational relationship means "the relationship between cohabitants, who not being married to each other are living or have lived together as husband and wife on a *bona fide* domestic basis." While a woman in a cohabitational relationship may make a claim with regard to property, this right was fettered by the right, title, interest or claim of a legal spouse. This Act now gives women in cohabitational relationships entitlement to estate and the right to contest wills.[35]

Some laws written or amended in the last fifteen to twenty years tend towards the use of gender neutral terms such as "spouse" and in defining "relative" include husband and wife. The *Judges Salaries and Pensions Act*, Chap. 6:02, *Prime Minister's Pension Act*, Chap. 2:51, and *President's Emoluments Act*, Chap. 2:50 are the only three acts that make very clear that any reference to "widow" includes a reference to "widower," thereby ensuring that men receive financial entitlements as well. The *Administration of Estates Act*, Chap. 9:01 makes provision for either spouse to inherit property from his/her deceased spouse. The *National Insurance Act*, Chap. 32:01 and *National Insurance (Benefits) Regulations* both make provisions for either spouse. These are in direct opposition to the various pension acts discussed in section 4.3.2.2 above, where only women were the intended beneficiaries.

Laws such as the *Caribbean Aviation Training Institute Act*, Chap. 39:52, *Caribbean Community Act*, Chap. 81:11, and *Immigration (Caribbean Community Skilled Nationals) Act*, Chap. 18:03 confer diplomatic privileges on its employees and, by extension, spouses and families of such employees during travel and work abroad.

Some pieces of legislation deal with the collection of information through surveys. One such act is the *Counting Unremunerated Work Act*, Chap. 19:09 which is meant to provide for the execution of surveys of people performing unremunerated work. Housework and childcare, *inter alia*, are generally unremunerated and it is primarily women who have the responsibility for providing these services. The *Statistics (Surveys of Industrial or Business Undertakings) Regulations, Statistics Act*, Chap. 19:02 requires that persons engaged in business or industrial undertakings record information such as wages and salaries paid, distinguishing amounts paid to males and females separately.

The third category of restorative equality deals with non-gender distinctiveness. The *Domestic Violence Act*, which was passed in 1999, recognised the grave social problems facing couples and families and added a new component to regulating male-female and parent-child relationships. The various facets of domestic violence are covered by the Act and include not only physical abuse, but also emotional or psychological abuse, financial abuse and sexual abuse. The objects of this Act are to provide immediate injunctive relief to victims of domestic violence; and ensure a prompt and just legal remedy for victims of domestic violence. In addition, this Act seems to have taken on a gender neutral character, which does not take into account the fact that many of the victims are actually women. This is not to say that men are not victims as well, but the majority of victims are women and this Act was perhaps intended to address the abuse suffered by women. In writing the Act in this way, it perhaps detracts from the original intent of the Act.

Constitutional equality must necessarily be dealt with as the *Constitution* is the supreme law. The *Constitution* introduces a new sub-category under equality, as there was no constitution during the colonial era. It is interesting to note what obtains internationally, as Constitutions and Bills of Rights confer equality and a variety of special rights to women in various permutations. Figure 4.5 shows eight different categories of rights that affect women either directly or indirectly.[36] Of just over 190 instruments reviewed, 155 guaranteed women equality before the law while 154 offered gender equality, creating two separate categories of equality. The former recognises men and women as equal legal subjects before the law while the latter specifically states that women shall have equal rights with men (using men as the standard) or that men and women shall have equal rights. Women have the constitutional right to equality at work in 38 countries and equal pay for equal work in 67. Maternity rights are constitutionally guaranteed in 44 countries and women have the right to be considered for promotion in 6. In just 13 countries, women are

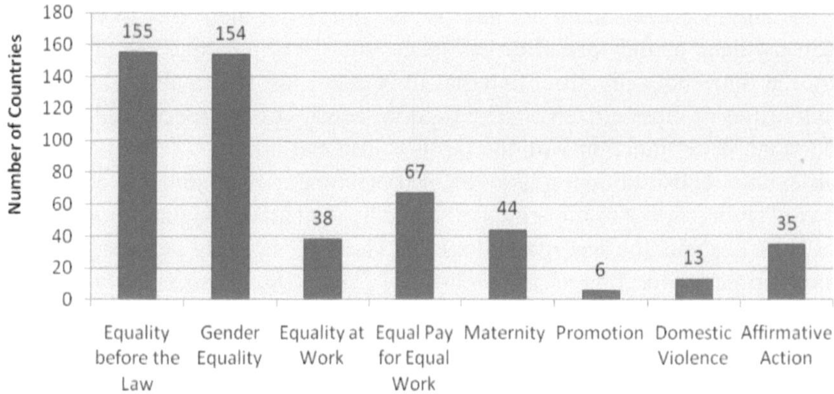

Figure 4.4. International Constitutional/Bill of Rights Provisions relating to Equality and Specific Women's Rights. See Persadie, "A Critical Analysis," Appendix B, 344-351, which provides a full table showing the rights that various countries confer on women.

afforded the protection of the constitution against domestic violence, while 35 instruments provide for affirmative action.

The *Constitution* of TT is one of the 155 that confers on women the right to equality before the law—it is the only one of the eight constitutional rights mentioned that it confers. It enshrines the notion of sexual equality with regard to the four fundamental rights it confers on the citizenry of TT. Section 4(a), in particular, guarantees the right of the individual to life, liberty and security of the person, while Sections 4(b) and (d) ensure the right of the individual to equality before the law and equality of treatment from any public authority in the exercise of its functions in such a capacity. It is interesting to note that these stated rights to equality do not guarantee *general* sexual equality, such as equality between men and women at the workplace. Implying general gender equality from the *Constitution* may prove tricky, given the specifics of Section 4.

It should follow, therefore, that, even though sexual equality at the workplace is not specifically guaranteed by the *Constitution*, women will be treated fairly, in terms of being considered for managerial positions and paid the same salary as male counterparts who are similarly qualified. This is certainly not what obtains in TT, as professional women in industry face patent discrimination with regard to both promotions and salaries. There has been no response from the State in this regard, but this may also be partly due to the fact that these women tend to remain quiet about this discrimination for fear of further discrimination in an already hostile and male-dominated environment.

Equally, women should not have to live in fear for their lives of their violent partners, as they are afforded the constitutional guarantee of protection by the State not only from external threats but also from abuse by public authorities or other citizens.[37] The right to security of person can only be understood in conjunction with the rights to life and liberty. TT does not offer an explicit constitutional guarantee of protection against domestic violence; however, according to the argument made by the Human Rights Commission of New Zealand, the scourge of domestic violence is clearly unconstitutional, as the right to life, liberty and security of person should necessarily encompass domestic violence. Domestic violence deprives women of their right to security of person and life when they are battered and killed. Section 4(a) is clearly breached on a regular basis largely by unconstrained violent male partners with little or no real response from the State. The State, in fact, recognises the apathy that is met by victims of domestic violence who attempt to seek help from those with the legal responsibility to do so. Unfortunately, many of these cases end in the gruesome death of the female partner and in the presence of their children. There are also instances where women react violently and take the life of the abuser.

During the period May 2006—January 2007, three women, all victims of sustained domestic violence, were found guilty of the manslaughter of their husbands. Hillary Narine (03 May 2006), Cecilia Brown-Bedeau (05 May 2006), and Stephanie Bailey (17 January 2007) were all found to be suffering from Battered Woman Syndrome, the Court thereby recognising the scourge of domestic violence and the fact that it seems to be worsening with women taking matters into their own hands. It is interesting to note that all these cases were heard before the same judge, Anthony Carmona, who in each instance made the statement that while "women are under siege in T&T,"[38] "violent behaviour should not be an avenue open to women…to empower themselves."[39] He also recognised the institutional deficiencies through their officials who acted as abettors to the crime. He admitted that the Police Service sometimes ignores women's calls for help when they are abused and said, "The police are far too laid back and this could lead to mayhem in the home."[40]

4.3.3 Case Law and Gender in the Post-Colonial Era

While this chapter deals largely with the bias found in statutory law, it is instructive to note what obtains in case law. Decisions seem generally to be taken on the basis of the facts presented before the Court and, therefore, there appears to be little or no bias as decisions vary according to the peculiar circumstances surrounding each case. A review of relevant cases from 1983 to 2007 revealed six major cases in which women committed the offence of murder and attempted to enter the specific plea of diminished responsibility due to "Battered Woman Syndrome" as a defence. In 1999, in the landmark case of *Indravani Ramjattan v The State*, CrA. No. 59 of 1995, the Appellant, Indravani Ramjattan, was able to successfully claim Battered Woman Syndrome as a defence for having arranged to have her common-law husband killed, reflecting the characteristic of inverse equality as discussed above given that men cannot claim this. Battered Woman Syndrome was only five years prior classified as a mental disease in England (and as many as nine years in Canada), although it was recognised as early as the early seventies as a possible effect of prolonged physical abuse in the context of domestic killings.[41] It would appear that Indravani was a victim of physical abuse from childhood and was forced into a marriage at age seventeen with a man eighteen years her senior who began abusing her three years into the relationship when he discovered that she visited her mother against his will. The abuse became increasingly worse with threats to her life and those of her children. She eventually left to live with another man but was forcibly taken back home where she was beaten unconscious. It was this other man and his friend who eventually carried out the killing of her husband.

In the cases of *Angela Ramdeen v The State*, CrA. No. 33 of 1997 and *Kenrick London and Chandrouti London v The State*, Cr. App. Nos. 31 & 32 of 2002, both women, accused of murder, attempted to enter the plea of diminished responsibility due to Battered Woman Syndrome. While they both failed, each woman had her death sentence commuted to one of life imprisonment due to a Privy Council ruling in *Charles Matthew v The State*, Privy Council Appeal No. 12 of 2004 which ordered that "the sentence of death imposed on those persons awaiting execution pending the determination of *Matthew* be set aside and, in its place, their Lordships directed that a sentence of life imprisonment be imposed on such persons."[42] In *Giselle Stafford and Dave Carter v The State*, Cr. App. No. 88 & 91 of 1996, both Appellants were guilty of murder and sentenced to death. There was no claim of diminished responsibility and in this case Stafford was sentenced in the same manner as Carter.

Men seem to have it much easier than women in claiming diminished responsibility for the murder of their significant female other. It would appear that the defence of diminished responsibility in the form of "provocation" is less difficult to prove than Battered Woman Syndrome. There are many instances of men found guilty of the murder of their wives/common-law wives and were able to successfully claim provocation and receive a more lenient sentence. In *Junior Colin Nicome v The State*, CrA. No. 83 of 1999, *Ashton Lee v The State*, CrA. No. 73 of 2001, *Foster Serrette v The State*, CrA. No 40 of 2001 and *Ramnath Harrilal v The State*, CrA. No. 46 of 1996, all four men were found guilty of the murder of their common-law wives, the first three claiming provocation and the last one claiming diminished responsibility as a defence. In the provocation cases, all men were jilted (in their minds, perhaps, cuckolded) lovers and appeared to react in this fatal manner. Important here is the fact that, in TT, many men have multiple female partners while it is less common for women to behave in the same way. In any event, women tend to be accepting of this state of affairs and accommodate men's behaviour. Men, on the other hand, seem to always jealously safeguard their women and seem unable to exercise restraint on rejection and, perhaps, as an issue of pride, react violently.[43] This is in no way meant to justify their behaviour, regardless of the provocation claimed, but remains a sad reality of the socio-cultural evolution of this society. The judges make it very clear that this type of behaviour is unacceptable;[44] yet, still take into account the extenuating circumstances and allow the plea of diminished responsibility. Unfortunately, while it is expected that men would behave in this atrocious manner, women are expected to be tolerant. Why this seeming leniency? Is it that the elite are privy to positive inequality features even in case law?

An interesting development in case law deals with the issue of the common-law wife. While the *Cohabitational Relationships Act* formally vests the right in a woman to make a claim for maintenance or with regard to a man's estate on his death, it would appear that, prior to the passing of this Act, judges have recognised the legal plight of the common-law wife and saw it fit to recognise that they, too, have rights. Sharma J., as he then was, recognised the common-law relationship as "a voluntary union for life of one man and one woman to the exclusion of all others" and, in so doing, acknowledged "the role of the common law wife in society" and the fact that "she too, like the married woman also has rights,"[45] thereby conferring intra-gender equality on the two classes of women. This point was taken up in *Marjorie Gould v Lenore Bridgelal*, H.C.A. No. S-142 of 1982, where the Defendant attempted to claim her right as the common-law wife against the rights of the lawful wife. Although edifying in his explanations, the judge found that, according to the facts, the Defendant did not meet the criteria of being a common-law wife but that of a mistress and, therefore, not entitled to her claims.

There are many cases of the common-law wife seeking money and property from her husband and, in many cases, it was found that, again, decisions were based on the facts presented, eligibility requirements depending on the statute(s) used to seek redress, and any perceived intention to build a life together / jointly own property in question. Women were generally the petitioner, as they were generally financially dependent on their husbands, and awards were generally made based on the impecunious state of the women and the fact of her contribution to home-making and/or any financial contributions she may have made.[46] In cases where the facts of the case indicate that there was no intention to share property or that contributions on the part of the petitioner were inadequate, her claim would be unsuccessful.[47]

Much like murder charges, claims for maintenance between legally married couples abound. Yet, again, the decisions taken appear to be based on the facts presented, truthfulness of the accounts presented, statutory eligibility requirements, quality of life to which the spouses are accustomed, and contributions by both parties to the life shared.[48] The awards seem to be fair and also take into account periods of pre-marital cohabitation.[49]

In what must be another landmark case, *Josine Johnson and Yuclan Balwant v The Attorney General of Trinidad and Tobago*, H.C.A. No. S-2142 of 2004, the Appellants attempted to argue that the regulations dealing with married women, their family obligations and the effect of these on their performance at work in both the *Police Service Commission Regulations* (made pursuant to the Constitution) and the *Statutory Authorities' Service Commission Regulations* are not only unconstitutional in their discrimination against women but also "failed to give equal treatment in law of against married and unmarried female public servants."[50] This case brings into question the issue of intra-gender equality, as these regulations obviously do not take into consideration the common-law wife with family obligations. Unfortunately, the action failed and the Appellants were unable to make their claim of constitutional discrimination against women.

4.4 DOMESTIC LEGISLATION: A SIMPLE CASE OF REPLACEMENT OF THE ELITE?

The statutory legal framework for gender seems very much to reflect an elitist attitude on the part of those responsible for creating and enacting the various pieces of legislation. This is certainly in keeping with what obtained during the colonial period where laws were enacted to serve the interest of the elite in one way or another. Some 150 pieces of legislation have been cited as having some significant reference to gender; yet, when analysed, they do not lend themselves to the creation of a legal framework that accommodates gender equality in a real manner. This is directly attributable to the fact that the male elite responsible for enacting legislation does not take into account the particular needs of women. Even specific attempts to create equality in law seem to work against women, as laws written with gender neutrality in mind, such as the *Domestic Violence Act*, seem to detract from the importance of the scourge it is attempting to prevent. One important and positive effect, however, was the creation of legislation to protect women's maternity rights. Moreover, conferring maternity rights has not appeared to create a desire by men to have an equal and reciprocal right, which, if done, would perhaps trivialise the importance of biological and reproductive differences between men and women.

In order to fully appreciate the place of gender in national legislation in Trinidad and Tobago, it is necessary to identify a specific area of gender concern and review its treatment within the analytical framework of feminist legal theory. Chapter five will examine domestic violence and its specific treatment in statutory law as a case study to illustrate TT's domestic commitment towards promoting women's human rights, namely the right of a woman to equal protection of the law and security of person.

NOTES

1. See Ramlogan and Persadie, *Commonwealth Caribbean Business Law*, 30–31. This is dealt with further later in this chapter.

2. See Parliament of the Republic of Trindad and Tobago, "Current Members of Parliament," accessed 16 July 2011, http://www.ttparliament.org/members.php?mid=25.

3. For a brief history of Trinidad and Tobago, see NationMaster, "Encyclopedia: History of Trinidad and Tobago" accessed 12 September 2005, http://www.nationmaster.com/encyclopedia/History-of-Trinidad-and-Tobago. Trinidad and Tobago's history is generally taught from an Anglophone perspective. An interesting non-Anglophone account from a country laying claim to Trinidad during the colonial period is provided in Jesse Noel, *Trinidad, Provincia de Venezuela: Historia de la Administración Española de Trinidad* (Caracas: Academia Nacional de la Historia, 1972). Figure 4.1 illustrates Trinidad and Tobago's geographical position within the Caribbean (at the very south of the archipelago) and the Americas (at the north eastern tip of Venezuela), while figure 4.2 shows a more detailed map.

4. Hamid Ghany, "Parliament in Trinidad and Tobago 1962–1987: The Whitehall Model at Work," in *Trinidad and Tobago: The Independence Experience 1962–1987*, ed. Selwyn Ryan (St. Augustine, Trinidad: Institute of Social and Economic Research, UWI, 1988), 175.

5. Selwyn Ryan, *Winner Takes All: The Westminster Experience in the Anglophone Caribbean* (St. Augustine, Trinidad: Institute of Social and Economic Research, UWI, 1999), 8.

6. The British Constitution is drawn from statutes, conventions, case law, custom and common law and authoritative legal writings, but not compiled into a single document. See Richard Mosley, *Westminster Workshop: A Student's Guide to the British Constitution* (Oxford: Pergamon Press, 1967), 4–5.

7. Ghany, "Parliament in Trinidad and Tobago 1962–1987," 175–176.

8. See for example Selwyn Ryan, *The Judiciary and Governance in the Caribbean* (St. Augustine, Trinidad: Sir Arthur Lewis Institute of Social and Economic Studies, UWI, 2001), 7–11 and Ghany, "Parliament in Trinidad and Tobago 1962–1987," 183.

9. See Section 40 of the Constitution.

10. Except in cases of deadlock, where the President has the discretion to choose which party shall govern.

11. In *Director of Personnel Administration and the Police Service Commission v Eusebio Cooper and Others*, Civ. App. No. 10 of 2004 (TT), Chief Justice Sharma also outlined the relationship between the Executive, Legislature and the Judiciary asking, "What can be more political than that?" at paragraph 34, stating at the same time, however, that there must be a presumed integrity of holders of high office or the *Constitution* would be rendered unworkable. See paragraphs 33–39. In Kangaloo JA's judgment of the same case, he admits at paragraph 20 that "the potential for interference must exist once there is the overlap of powers" but emphasises that the real issue is the *degree of influence or interference that is permissible* in any given situation. Conversely, in the Dominican case of *The Constituency Boundaries Commission and the Attorney-General of the Commonwealth of Dominica v Urban Baron*, Civil Appeal No. 12 of 1998 (DM), Singh JA believes that Commissions borne from the *Constitution* "will lean more towards political loyalty than constitutional integrity" due to the same political relationship existing among the three bodies.

12. See Sections 102 and 120 of the *Constitution* respectively.

13. Section 2, The *Constitution* of the Republic of Trinidad and Tobago, Ch. 1:01 (Revised Laws of Trinidad and Tobago, 2009).

14. See Ramlogan and Persadie, *Commonwealth Caribbean Business Law*, 9.

15. John Merryman, *The Civil Law Tradition: An Introduction to the Legal Systems of Western Europe and Latin America* (Stanford: Stanford University Press, 1985), 3.

16. Emphasis added. See Lord Denning's judgement in *Nyali Ld. v Attorney-General*, [1956] 1 Q.B. 1 at 16–17. The imposition of foreign laws without regard to the needs of the population also occurred in colonial Africa. See Terri Nderitu, "Balancing Pill and Patients: Intellectual Property and the HIV/AIDS Crisis," paragraphs 27–32. Accessed 12 January 2007, http://www.murdoch.edu.au/elaw/issues/v8n3/nderitu83nf.html.

17. On the "reception of laws" doctrine, see Rose-Marie Belle Antoine, *Commonwealth Caribbean Law and Legal Systems* (London: Cavendish Publishing Limited, 1999), 57–69.

18. See Ramlogan and Persadie, *Commonwealth Caribbean Business Law*, 4.

19. Gary Slapper and David Kelly, *The English Legal System* (London: Cavendish Publishing Limited, 2000), 5.

20. For more on the actual legislative process, see ibid., 35–44.

21. *Boodram v Attorney General of Trinidad and Tobago*, (1994) 47 WIR 459 at 470, paragraphs e–f.

22. Kirk Meighoo, *Politics in a 'Half-Made Society': Trinidad and Tobago, 1925–2001* (Kingston: Ian Randle Publishers, 2003), xxiii.

23. Antoine, *Commonwealth Caribbean*, 12.

24. Louis Knafla and Susan Binnie, "Beyond the State: Law and Legal Pluralism in the Making of Modern Societies," in *Law, Society and the State: Essays in Modern Legal History*, ed. Louis Knafla and Susan Binnie (Toronto: Toronto University Press, 1995), 14.

25. "Benevolent" here makes reference to the idea of the "benevolent autocrat."

26. Kusha Haraksingh, "Law-Making and Social Change in Colonial Trinidad, 1900–1950," in Knafla and Binnie, *Law, Society and the State*, 130.

27. Singh states that "[t]he sugar planters enjoyed a dominant influence in the Legislative Council through their near monopoly of the nominated seats…," confirming that the elites were the ones who sat on this Council. Kelvin Singh, *Race and Class Struggles in a Colonial State: Trinidad 1917–1945* (Calgary: University of Calgary Press, 1994), 2.

28. Eric Williams, *Capitalism and Slavery* (Kingston: Ian Randle Publishers, 2005), 24–25. The law did not, however, have the desired effect.

29. Antoine, *Commonwealth Caribbean Law*, 14.

30. Section 2 of the *Habitual Idlers Ordinance*, No. 7 of 1918.

31. Haraksingh, "Law-Making and Social Change, 1900–1950," 134.

32. See ibid., 134.

33. The author examined all the laws (ordinances, statutes) of TT to determine which laws were relevant. This information is correct as at 31 December 2006. For the relevant text of each law, see Natalie Persadie, "A Critical Analysis Of The Efficacy Of Law As A Tool To Achieve Gender Equality And To Address The Problem Of Domestic Violence: The Case Of Trinidad And Tobago" (PhD Thesis, University of Birmingham, 2007), Appendix A, 280–343.

34. See more below in section 4.3.2.4 on the Constitution.

35. See Rohandra John, "How common-law wives came into their own," *Sunday Express*, 22 January 2006. Accessed 21 August 2006, http://www.trinidadexpress.com/index.pl/article_news?id=130196924.

36. The author examined all existing constitutions and bills of rights of all countries to determine what types of rights are conferred on women around the world. This information is correct as at March 2006.

37. Human Rights Commission, "Human Rights in New Zealand Today," accessed 12 February 2006, http://www.hrc.co.nz/report/chapters/chapter07/life01.html.

38. Reshma Ragoonath, "Husband killer to serve four years," *Trinidad Guardian*, 06 May 2006, accessed 22 January 2007, http://www.guardian.co.tt/archives/2006-05-06/news3.html.

39. Jade Loutoo, "Toco woman put on $30,000 bond," *Trinidad Guardian*, 04 May 2006, accessed 22 January 2007, http://www.guardian.co.tt/archives/2006-05-04/news1.html.

40. Indarjit Seuraj, "Carmona: Women under siege in this country," *Trinidad Guardian*, 18 January 2007, accessed 22 January 2007, http://www.guardian.co.tt/archives/2007-01-18/news3.html.

41. See Warner J.A., *Indravani Ramjattan vs The State*, CrA. No. 59 of 1995 at 4.

42. R. Hamel-Smith, J.A., *Kenrick London and Chandrouti London v The State*, Cr. App. Nos. 31 & 32 of 2002 at p. 21. In *Matthew*, the majority judgement as delivered by Lord Hoffman stated that "the law imposing the mandatory death penalty for murder in Trinidad and Tobago remains valid" and that "their Lordships will allow the appeal, set aside the sentence of death and impose a sentence of life imprisonment," *Charles Matthew v The State*, Privy Council Appeal No. 12 of 2004, 4, 10 respectively. The *Matthew* judgement overruled the previous case of *Balkissoon*

Roodal v The State, Privy Council Appeal No. 18 of 2003, which stated that the penalty of death for murder is not a fixed penalty but the maximum penalty which can be imposed by discretion, the obvious alternative to which is imprisonment. See Lord Steyn, *Roodal*, 15. Convicted murderers awaiting judgement between *Roodal* and *Matthew* were therefore entitled to the benefit of the decision of the former and had their death sentences commuted to life imprisonment. See also judgement of Sharma, C.J., *The Attorney General of Trinidad and Tobago (Appellant) v Angela Ramdeen (Respondent)*, Cv.A. No. 6 of 2004, 6–7, para 17.

43. It would appear that the other "choice" is suicide: see for example Radhica Sookraj, "Cop drinks poison after domestic row," *Trinidad Guardian*, 23 February 2006, accessed 29 January 2007, http://www.guardian.co.tt/archives/2006-02-23/news3.html and Carol Kissoon, "Cop ties self to tree, drinks weedicide," *Trinidad Express*, 23 February 2006, accessed 29 January 2007, http://www.trinidadexpress.com/index.pl/article_news?id=138085395. Murder-suicide presents yet another option: see for example Geisha Kowlessar, "Stormy relationship ends in murder-suicide in Valencia," *Trinidad Guardian*, 03 August 2004, accessed 29 January 2007, http://www.guardian.co.tt/archives/2004-08-03/news1.html and Earl Manmohan, "Tobagonian chops Italian lover to death…kills himself," *Trinidad Express*, 26 January 2007, accessed 29 January 2007, http://www.trinidadexpress.com/index.pl/article?id=161090340.

44. See Jones, J.A., *Ashton Lee v The State*, CrA. No. 73 of 2001 at 10–11.

45. See Sharma, J. (as he then was), *Ramratie Harrinarine v Rasheed Aziz & Kadar Aziz*, H.C.A. No. S-1992 of 1982, 21–23.

46. See for example, *Ann Charles v Peter McMillan*, H.C.A. No. 141 of 1981; *Violet Bruce v David Chance*, H.C.A. No. 4873 of 1989; *Jasmine Albert v Irwin Mohammed*, H.C.A. No. 1651 of 2003.

47. See for example *Irma Richards v Hamilton Riviears*, H.C.A. No. 2045 of 1992.

48. See for example, *Deokee Beharry v Anthony Beharry*, H.C.A. M-313 of 1998, *Marine Munroe v Gregory Munroe*, H.C.A. 20 of 2000, *Sherma Harrington v Ermath Harrington*, H.C.A. M-1020 of 2002, *Brian Nicholson v Elizabeth Nicholson*, H.C.A. No. FH00712 of 2004.

49. See *Peter O'Neil v Pearly O'Neil*, H.C.A. M-985 of 2002.

50. Best, J., *Josine Johnson and Yuclan Balwant v The Attorney General of Trinidad and Tobago*, H.C.A. No. S-2142 of 2004, 4.

Chapter Five

Trinidad and Tobago and Domestic Violence— The Specific Legislative Response

5.1 INTRODUCTION

Prevention of domestic violence is, in fact, specifically legislated in TT by the *Domestic Violence Act*. As part of the empirical analysis of gender bias in the law, chapter four examined generally the place of gender and gender equality in the legal regime of Trinidad and Tobago. The findings of chapter four suggest that in contemporary TT the bias in favour of the colonial elite has now been replaced by a male elite where women constitute the prejudiced portion of the population. It is necessary to examine this principle against the backdrop of a specific area of gender concern, that is, domestic violence.

Domestic violence is the area chosen for an examination of gender bias in TT, thus the case study starts with a review of the primary piece of legislation that underpins the legal regime for addressing domestic violence, namely the *Domestic Violence Act* ("*Domestic Violence Act*").

5.2 EFFECTIVENESS OF THE *DOMESTIC VIOLENCE ACT*

Hailed by many as a comprehensive piece of legislation, the *Domestic Violence Act* appears to work better in theory than in practice and seems to have many gaps that hinder its effectiveness as a mechanism for safeguarding women from domestic violence. This analysis takes the format of an excerpt from the *Domestic Violence Act* followed by a commentary.

> Preamble: "Whereas incidents of domestic violence continue to occur with alarming frequency and deadly consequences"

The *Domestic Violence Act* starts with a clear recognition by the Government of TT that domestic violence is a major social ill. The preamble of the *Domestic Violence Act* fully illustrates the perception of the State as to the seriousness of domestic violence.

5.2.1 The Prompt and Equitable Response

> Preamble: "And Whereas the Government is of the view that one way to achieve these goals is to strengthen legislation to ensure a prompt and equitable legal remedy for victims of domestic violence..."
>
> 2. The objects of the Act are inter alia to—
>   (a) provide immediate injunctive relief to victims of domestic violence; and
>   (b) ensure a prompt and just legal remedy for victims of domestic violence.

With respect to the "promptness" of the legal remedy, while women[1] can, in fact, obtain immediate injunctive relief in the form of a protection order, this piece of paper cannot, in reality, stop the abuser from abusing. A protection order can even further inflame the situation and, unless the woman has somewhere she can seek refuge, her life may be in imminent danger. There needs to be some sort of State response to provide shelter to these women and their children as many of the shelters that do provide a haven for victims of domestic violence have restrictions on the age and sex of children that can stay, as described in chapter six.

The "equitableness" of the legal remedy creates another issue. While the *Domestic Violence Act* is meant to protect the abused, caution must be exercised in terms of the remedies offered against the abuser. The *Domestic Violence Act* fails to address the psychological fallout of the protection orders on the psyche of the fragile male ego, which probably led to the situation in the first place. He may feel emasculated and seek to intentionally hurt or kill the one who is meant to be protected.

5.2.2 The *Domestic Violence Act* and Women's Constitutional Right

> 1.(2) "The Act shall have effect even though inconsistent with sections 4 and 5 of the Constitution."

Section 4(c) of the Constitution recognises the right of the individual to respect for his private and family life, while section 5 deals with the abrogation, abridgment or infringement by any other law of any rights and freedoms guaranteed by the Constitution. The right to respect for private and family life forms the crux of the public/private divide and, as seen here, even forms part of the supreme law of the land. In the case of male violence against women, does this mean therefore that the State reserves the right to ignore what takes place in private simply because it occurs in private? This cannot be, as section 4(a) of the Constitution confers upon an individual the right to "life, liberty and security of the person." Women facing domestic violence in the home do not appear to enjoy the benefit of this right nor do they seem to have this right enforced. Why, therefore, should the *Domestic Violence Act* be seen as inconsistent with section 4 of the Constitution? Why should it be seen to "abrogate, abridge or infringe" the rights and freedoms guaranteed by the *Constitution* of those (abusers) who take the liberty to adversely affect the Constitutional rights of others (abused)? The *Domestic Violence Act*, of necessity, enters the realm of the private. Is it that section 4(c) is seen to take precedence over section 4(a)? Such an interpretation would be ludicrous and unacceptable. Women, as individuals under the *Constitution*, should be entitled to feel safe in their homes and have the protection of the State where their homes (metaphorically speaking, as domestic violence takes place in public as well) become the site of violence against them. Protection against domestic violence should, therefore, be an implied constitutional guarantee for individuals so threatened, as they are, in fact, guaranteed the right to "life, liberty and security of the person" by the State.

5.2.3 Responsibility of Independent Parties to Seek Protection Orders On Behalf of Victims

> 4. (4) A police officer, probation officer or approved social worker may apply for a Protection Order on behalf of—
> (a) any person referred to in subsection (2); or
> (b) a person or child who is in a residential institution.

In many instances, the victims themselves are unwilling to take the matter any further and, according to the construction of this section, there is no obligation on the police officer, probation officer or social worker to apply for the order, as the *Domestic Violence Act* employs discretionary language with respect to Section 4(4). While the section was not meant to be interpreted this way, but simply to add to the list of people eligible to apply for a protection order, *should* there, in fact, be an obligation on the part of someone in such a position to do so, especially in a case of clear and present danger? While they can refer the victim to a shelter as a temporary safety measure, is that enough? Should proactivity dictate that more be done? There is nothing in section four as a whole that suggests that orders must always be voluntary on the part of the victim. Allowance should be made of involuntary orders as well.

5.2.4 Legislative Discretion to Grant Protection Orders

5. (1) Where, on an application made by a person described in section 4, the Court determines, on a balance of probabilities, that domestic violence has occurred, it may issue a Protection Order containing any or all of the prohibitions or directions referred to in section 6.
(2) The Court shall grant a Protection Order where it is satisfied that the respondent—
(a) is engaging in or has engaged in domestic violence against the applicant; or
(b) is likely to engage in conduct that would constitute domestic violence,
and in either case, having regard to all the circumstances, the Order is necessary for the protection of the applicant.

Sub-section 1 suggests that the Court need not issue a protection order even where it determines that domestic violence has occurred, but why should it not? The Court should adopt a pre-emptive approach to domestic violence given the recognition above of the "alarming frequency and deadly consequences" with which domestic violence occurs. Moreover, there appears to be a conflict between this section and subsection (2)(b) as they both seem to point to the need to prevent the abusive situation and should not be dealt with separately and neither should one be based on discretion. To avoid uncertainty in the exercise of any judicial discretion, the *Domestic Violence Act* should have clearly stated the circumstances under which domestic violence can be established on a balance of probabilities and yet no Protection Order is granted by the Court.

5.2.5 Counselling under the *Domestic Violence Act*

6. (1) A Protection Order may—
(c) direct that the respondent—
(iv) immediately vacate any place or residence for a specified period, whether or not the residence is jointly owned or leased by the respondent and the applicant, or solely owned or leased by the respondent or the applicant;
See above on equitableness of legal remedy.

(viii) or applicant or both, receive professional counselling or therapy from any person or agency or from a programme which is approved by the Minister in writing.
25. (3) Where a bond of good behaviour has been entered into under subsection (2) the Court may prescribe such additional conditions as follows:
(a) that the parties receive professional counselling, including family counseling…

Where Section 6(1)(viii) of the *Domestic Violence Act* says "applicant or both," does this refer to individual sessions, or joint marriage counselling-type sessions? In TT, professional therapy is mainly provided by the private sector and this is usually a paid service. Most victims of domestic violence who seek redress under the *Domestic Violence Act* cannot afford this service and the *Domestic Violence Act* fails to provide a mechanism for facilitating such access. The *Domestic Violence Act* does provide for access to programmes for counselling approved by the Government, but these programmes are usually staffed by specialists who are trained generally in social work and/or psychology.

> (4) Where the Court makes an Order which, inter alia, directs the payment of compensation under subsection (1)(c)(ii), such compensation shall include, but not be limited to—
> (b) medical and dental expenses…

Where professional counselling or therapy is required, medical expenses here could be expanded to include this so that the respondent will be required to pay this cost.

5.2.6 Duration of Protection Orders

> (9) A Protection Order may be made for such period as the Court considers necessary but shall not exceed three years.

What happens after three years or whatever timeframe the Magistrate sees fit? Is it that the abuser is supposed to have been rehabilitated during this time? If the abuser was ordered to immediately vacate the place, will the abuser now be allowed to return to his home after all this time? If counselling is not ordered for the respondent and/or the applicant, the psychological fallout could serve to nullify the original effect and intent of the protection order.

> (10) Where the Order contains any prohibitions or directions, the Court may specify different periods, none of which shall exceed three years as the period for which each prohibition or direction shall remain in force.

Can the abuser then recommence the formerly prohibited action after the period is ended? Does the process then recommence, that is, applying for a protection order and obtaining a new order? The *Domestic Violence Act* should have provided for the seamless extension of a Protection Order beyond the initial three year period where it can be established on a balance of probabilities that the acts of domestic violence have continued or are likely to continue after the expiration of the Protection Order.

> 9. (1) In proceedings under this Act the Court may at any time before the taking of evidence, accept an Undertaking from the respondent given under oath, that the respondent shall not engage in conduct specified in the application or any other conduct that constitutes domestic violence.

> (4) An Undertaking remains in force for the period stated in the Undertaking, but shall not exceed three years.

Related to the duration of Protection Orders is the duration of Undertakings which is based on the three year principle without any indication as to the appropriate course of action after the expiration of the three year period.

5.2.7 Hardship under the *Domestic Violence Act*

> 7. In determining whether or not to impose one or more of the prohibitions or directions specified under section 6, the Court shall have regard to the following:
> (e) the hardship that may be caused as a result of making of the Order;

What hardship, and for whom? The *Domestic Violence Act* identifies hardship as a factor to be considered in the making of a Protection Order but fails to define how this factor ought to operate. Conceivably, the hardship to the abuser may be considered in terms of exclusion from the family home which may be the place of abuse. Such consideration is perverse, as that hardship cannot be a factor in the making of a Protection Order to safeguard the lives of those at risk. Another manifestation of the hardship argument is that a woman could be forced into accepting a Protection Order that is limited in scope because her financial hardship precludes a full Protection Order.

5.2.8 The Preservation and Protection of the Institution of Marriage and Other Relationships

> (g) the need to preserve and protect the institution of marriage and other relationships whilst affording protection and assistance to the family as a unit;

How can the need to preserve and protect the institution of marriage and other relationships outweigh the need to protect people from domestic violence? If the domestic violence continues and escalates to a fatal end, there will be no marriage to protect or preserve!

5.2.9 *In Camera* Proceedings

> 10. Proceedings in respect of an application for a Protection Order shall be held in camera unless the Court directs otherwise.

In what instances would it be permissible to hear proceedings for a Protection Order other than *in camera*? There is a need for guidelines to determine under what circumstances this will be allowed.

5.2.10 Date of Hearing of Application for Protection Orders

> 11. The Clerk shall fix a date for the hearing of the application which shall be no more than seven days after the date on which the application is filed.

While there is no provision for hearing life-threatening matters immediately, the clerk has the discretion to list the matter for hearing on the same day that the application is filed. This discretion is not always exercised and women who have complained of being in fear for their lives still have to wait seven days before the matter is heard. It would have been of greater benefit if the *Domestic Violence Act* had provided for immediate access to an Interim Protection Order on a 24-hour basis.

5.2.11 Non-Service of Summons

> (6) Where the hearing of an application is adjourned because the application and the notice of proceedings have not been served on the respondent, the time and place fixed by the Court for the adjourned hearing, shall be the date, time and place stated in the new notice of proceedings.

Service of the application, deemed also to be a summons by subsection (4), seems to be an issue. Pursuant to Section 43(1) of the *Summary Courts Act*, Chap. 4:20, notice of proceedings for a Protection Order is deemed to be a summons and summonses are to be served by police officers. One applicant attended Court on the set date with police escort only to learn that the respondent was absent because he never received the summons. This was not because he could not be found, but simply because the person to serve it never did so and had no reason for not having served it. Moreover, when such a case is adjourned, the new date is usually two weeks from the original date, showing little regard for the welfare of the applicant. There should be a punitive clause to deal with such acts of negligence by those in whose hands women's hope rest.

5.2.12 Dismissal of Application for Protection Order due to Non-Appearance of Applicant

> 14. If, on the date of the hearing of an application for a Protection Order, the respondent appears in Court, but neither the applicant nor the person on whose behalf the application is made appears either in person or represented by his attorney-at-law, the Court may:
> (b) having received a reasonable excuse for the non-appearance of the applicant or other person, adjourn the hearing upon such terms as it deems just;

The nature of domestic violence is such that it may not be possible for the applicant to send notice of her reasonable excuse for non-appearance. What happens in the event that, on presentation of the summons, the applicant is beaten so severely that she has to be hospitalised and no one is aware of the situation? She will be unable to attend Court or give notice of her absence. The right to dismiss a matter for non-appearance should have been more carefully circumscribed to cater for situations that are natural to cases of domestic violence.

5.2.13 Time of Effect of Protection Order

> 15. Where the Court proposes to make a Protection Order or an Interim Order, and the respondent is before the Court, the Court shall explain to the respondent—
> (a) the purpose, terms and effect of the Order;
> (b) the consequences of failing to comply with the Order; and
> (c) the means by which the Order may be varied or revoked.

It should be clearly stated that, upon explanation of the order to the respondent, it takes immediate effect. There is no section that deals with the time of effect of the order and it cannot be that the order is only of effect when served on the respondent in hard copy.

> 16. Where a Protection Order or Interim Order is made or varied by the Court—
> (b) the Court shall cause a copy of the Order to be served on—
> (i) the respondent;
> (ii) any other person to whom the Order is to apply whether or not the person is a party to the proceedings; and
> (iii) the police officer in charge of the station located nearest to the area where the respondent or applicant resides.

When the Magistrate actually hears the matter, the order of the court is stated in the presence of both parties and then reduced to writing. Accordingly, the time of effect of the Protection Order can be deemed to be when stated to the parties; however, the situation is rendered somewhat complicated when it is an Interim Protection Order that is being sought. It would appear that the Interim Protection Order can only be effected at the time of service on the respondent. Failure to serve the order on the respondent renders the order unenforceable. Moreover, in the event of a breach of the order, the police will have no power to arrest the offender.

> 17. (1) Where, the Court has not been able to serve notice of proceedings or the Order, as the case may be, upon the respondent personally, it may make an Order for substituted service of the notice of proceedings or Order, as the case may be.
> (2) For the purpose of subsection (1)(b) "substituted service" means—

(c) service by advertisement in two daily newspapers which service is deemed to have been effected at midnight on the date of the later advertisement, the cost to be borne by the applicant...

By virtue of section 17, the Court has wide powers to have substituted service which can be as simple as leaving it at the last address of the Respondent. Under these circumstances, the time of effect of the order is not when personally received by the Respondent but when service has been made in such manner as deemed appropriate by the Court.

18. A respondent shall not be bound by a Protection Order or Interim Order—
(a) where he was not present at the time of the making of the Order; or
(b) where the Order has not been served on him personally or in accordance with section 17 (deals with substituted service).

It would appear that Section 18 contradicts Section 8(2) and Section 17 in as much as it would appear to only provide for an order to be effective when personally served or when a respondent was present at the time of the making of the order. What, then, is the purpose of section 8(2), which allows the Court to make an Interim Order in the respondent's absence, or section 8(5) which allows the Court to extend the period of the Interim Order or substitute such an Order with a Protection Order in the respondent's absence? Moreover, what is the purpose of section 13(a) which allows the Court to "proceed to hear and determine the matter in the respondent's absence"? In this last instance, however, he must have been served with the summons before the Court can proceed. It is certainly expected that the respondent will be served with the Order, but, given the difficulty with service, it perhaps makes more sense to have the respondent present in Court when this decision is being made. There is the possibility that the respondent could never be properly served but this must not lead to a defeat of the intent of the Act. There must be some way of ensuring the respondent's presence or proper service on him. This appears to be covered by section 17 dealing with substituted service, which does not require personal service. Fault can, therefore, actually rest with the Court for unenforceability of an order due to not having served the order or having made an order for substituted notice. What remedies exist in the event that an applicant wishes to take action against the Court for negligence?

5.2.14 Variation or Revocation of Orders

19. (1) Where an Order is in force, a party to the proceedings in respect of whom the Order was made may apply to Court on the Form described as "Form 5" in the Second Schedule, for an Order varying or revoking the original Order.

(2) On an application under subsection (1), the Court may, by Order, vary or revoke the Order.
(3) A copy of an application under this section shall be served on each person who was a party to the proceedings in respect of which the original Order was made.
(4) In determining whether to vary or revoke an Order the Court shall have regard to the matters specified in section 7.

There are no guidelines as to the procedure for this. Should it be implied that the procedure for applying for an order will apply to variation, duration and revocation of orders?

5.2.15 Fines and Penalties

20. (1) Subject to subsection (2) a person against whom an Order has been made and who—
(a) has had notice of the Order; and
(b) contravenes any provision of the Order or fails to comply with any direction of the Court, commits an offence and is liable—
(i) on a first conviction to a fine not exceeding nine thousand dollars or imprisonment for a period not exceeding three months;
(ii) on a second conviction to a fine not exceeding fifteen thousand dollars or imprisonment for a period not exceeding twenty-four months or both;
(iii) on any subsequent conviction to a period of imprisonment not exceeding five years.

Would/do these fines/penalties have the desired effect of curbing the unwanted behaviour? In addition, there should not be standard fines applicable to all offences. Someone liable for not paying maintenance as a first or even recurring offence should not necessarily face the same fine as someone causing damage to the applicant's property. There should be a schedule depending on the severity of the offence with a tiered fine and imprisonment system.

5.2.16 Police Intervention

22. Where a Magistrate is satisfied, by information on oath, that—
(a) there are reasonable grounds to suspect that a person on premises has suffered or is in imminent danger of physical injury at the hands of another person in a situation amounting to domestic violence and needs assistance to deal with or prevent the injury; and
(b) a police officer has been refused permission to enter the premises for the purpose of giving assistance to the first mentioned person in paragraph (a),
the Magistrate may issue a warrant in writing authorising a police officer to enter the premises specified in the warrant at any time within twenty-four hours

after the issue of the warrant and subject to any conditions specified in the warrant, to take such action as is necessary to prevent the commission or repetition of the offence or a breach of the peace or to protect life or property.

23. (1) For the avoidance of doubt, a police officer may act in accordance with the provisions of the Criminal Law Act where he has reasonable cause to believe that a person is engaging in or attempting to engage in conduct which amounts to physical violence and failure to act immediately may result in serious physical injury or death.
(3) Where a police officer exercises a power of entry under subsection (1) he shall immediately submit a written report to the Commissioner of Police, through the Head of the Division where the incident occurred, such report to contain the following information:
(a) the reasons for entering the premises without a warrant;
(b) the offence being committed or about to be committed; and
(c) the manner in which the investigation was conducted and the measures taken to ensure the protection and safety of the person at risk.
(4) The report referred to in subsection (3) shall be submitted to the Director of Public Prosecutions by the Commissioner of Police within seven days of receiving the report.
(5) Where a complaint is made against a police officer by a person resident in premises alleging that the officer's entry onto the premises under subsection (1) was unwarranted, the Police Complaints Authority shall investigate the complaint and submit a copy of its report to the Commissioner of Police and the Director of Public Prosecutions within fourteen days of the complaint having been made.
(6) Where the investigation of the Police Complaints Authority finds that the entry under subsection (1) was unwarranted, the Police Complaints Authority shall also submit the report to the Police Service Commission and such report may form the basis of disciplinary action against the police officer.

24. Where an Order is in force and a police officer believes on reasonable grounds that a person has committed or is committing a breach of the Order he may detain and arrest that person without a warrant.

While it is understandable that the time lag in getting the warrant could possibly lead to death of the complainant if she does not seek shelter elsewhere, this provision could possibly lead to abuse of power despite the series of post-entry protocols that could ultimately lead to disciplinary action against the police officer if his actions were found to be unwarranted. The *Domestic Violence Act* provides an excess of checks and balances to police intervention where there is the breach of a Protection Order and this may weigh against the police officer exercising discretion to enter premises to protect someone in the absence of a warrant.

5.2.17 Conditions of Bail

> 27. (2) Notwithstanding the Bail Act, the Court in granting bail, may order that the recognisance be subject to such of the following conditions as the Court considers appropriate:
> (d) where the defendant continues to reside with the victim that the defendant not enter or remain in the place or residence while under the influence of alcohol or a drug.

This section is of particular interest, as many situations involving domestic violence are fuelled or enflamed by alcohol and drug use. This is evidenced by the increase in attendance at the various shelters across the country during the festive seasons of Christmas and Carnival (generally the period between November/December to February/March) when drinking to enhance merriment and celebrate the seasons is at its greatest. However, while the aims of the section may have been commendable, it may prove difficult to implement. There are issues such as the level of influence of alcohol which triggers the exclusion from the house. Is it that the respondent must become a teetotaller to be allowed to remain in the house? What about the use of prescriptive and non-prescriptive drugs that can modify behaviour?

5.3 CONCLUSION

Gender equality and domestic violence are unwitting partners, as women cannot achieve the former without first addressing the latter. With this in mind, domestic violence is dealt with as a subset of gender and its treatment in the law provides an indication as to how seriously it is taken. In TT, domestic violence is largely dominated by the abuse of women. Although data with respect to domestic violence is not sex disaggregated, anecdotal evidence and interviews (see chapter six) indicated that the vast majority of orders sought pursuant to the *Domestic Violence Act* are by women. Legislating a system to deal with domestic violence, therefore, should necessarily take these facts into consideration to provide real and effective relief for those whom the act was intended to serve.

The *Domestic Violence Act* was passed with much fanfare. Heralded as a potent weapon to combat abuse of women, it has not quite lived up to such lofty expectations. The *Domestic Violence Act* contains many deficiencies that undermine its effectiveness. Looking at the *Domestic Violence Act* through gender lenses, it is clear that TT has created a relatively ineffective statutory scheme to combat domestic violence. Perhaps understandably so, considering that the Parliament agenda is controlled by the male governing elite.

Having reviewed the defects in the statutory regime for protection of women from acts of domestic violence, it is necessary to examine the institutional framework that also serves as an equally important and complementary mechanism for protecting women from abuse.

NOTE

1. It must be remembered that the focus here is violence against women even though the Act applies to men, women and children.

Chapter Six

Trinidad and Tobago and Domestic Violence— The Institutional Response

6.1 INTRODUCTION

Legislatively, there appear to be numerous provisions for women and women's issues generally, although there is the overarching issue of the elitist character of the laws favouring men and the fact that laws are not always designed to take into account gender-specific needs. Chapter five explored the specific piece of legislation dealing with domestic violence which constitutes the area of concern for the case study on gender and the law in TT.

Despite inadequacies in the legal regime for dealing with domestic violence, the overall treatment of the problem of domestic violence at the national level cannot be assessed without also understanding the institutional framework within which it must operate. This chapter examines this institutional framework, governmental and non-governmental, focussing on the executive and State authorities which illustrate government's commitment to dealing with domestic violence, as a reflection of the more general treatment of the gender agenda.

6.2 STATE COMMITMENT

The commitment of the State to any issue can be measured in terms of budgetary allocations, policy formulation, and ministerial responsibilities. This section illustrates government's commitment to domestic violence using these measures.

6.2.1 Financial Investment in Dealing with Domestic Violence

The Public Sector Investment Programme ("PSIP") is an integral part of the government's major policy documents illustrating its intentions with respect to resource allocation to achieve strategic national goals and objectives aimed at stimulating further economic growth, promoting sustainable development, and enhancing the quality of life for all citizens.[1] It is a comprehensive instrument of government policy, representing its public investment thrust across sectors and is meant to deal with high priority investment projects. Government's financial investment under the PSIP targets areas deemed to be of critical concern.[2] If this is indeed the case, then reviewing the thrust of government's financial investment would be of interest to help illustrate its commitment to dealing with domestic violence.

As a preliminary point, there is no separate itemisation of Government spending under the rubric domestic violence. Government expenditure on addressing domestic violence is generally lumped into expenditure dedicated to community development and social, cultural and recreational activities. Again, it must be noted that, even when lumped into expenditure dedicated to community development and social, cultural and recreational activities, this is done within the broader category of gender. This situation has arisen because of the fact that gender issues are dealt with by a ministry whose portfolio does not deal solely with gender. The following shows government's commitment to gender through its PSIP for the period 1998–2006.

In 1998–1999, a total of USD$13.4 million, representing 7.7% of total sectoral allocations, was allocated to the Ministries of Social Development and Community Development, Culture and Women's Affairs out of a total of USD$62.6 million allocated to the development of social infrastructure.[3] Expenditure here was dedicated to community centres, halfway houses and rehabilitation centres, refurbishment of cultural centres, and upgrading of library services. There is no gender-specific expenditure, save for projected expenditure of USD$121,000 to complete training and outreach programmes in gender affairs and to purchase equipment, furniture, and promotional materials. This was a four-year programme and only USD$75,000 for the whole programme was financed by the government of Trinidad and Tobago, while external funding in the sum of USD$400,000 was sourced.[4]

For 1999–2000, out of USD$113.7 million allocated to the development of social infrastructure, the Ministry of Culture and Gender Affairs was allocated USD$2.9 million, a mere 1% of total sectoral allocations, half of which was dedicated to the upgrade of library services.[5] The remaining money was dedicated to the establishment and continuation of refurbishment of cultural centres, training for museum staff, and the establishment of a Domestic Violence Unit. The government provided USD$167,000 for a Non Traditional

Training programme for women, with an extra USD$357,000 coming from external sources.[6]

The 2001 PSIP states that a total of USD$2.7 million was allocated to the Ministry of Culture and Gender Affairs, which was dedicated to the renovation and upgrade of several cultural facilities.[7] The Non Traditional Training for Women project was allocated USD$158,730 for its continuation, representing less than 0.1% of total sectoral allocations for the year on gender-related expenditure.

In 2002, the Non Traditional Training for Women project received USD$190,000 for its continuation "[i]n keeping with government's commitment to gender equality and the development/empowerment of women in society."[8] In this year, USD$47,619 was allocated to the establishment of a centre for the empowerment of young women at risk.[9] This expenditure amounted to slightly over 0.1% of total sectoral allocations and 0.2% of money allocated to the development of social infrastructure.

"The 2003 PSIP has been designed to reflect Government's effort at initiating the process of transforming Trinidad and Tobago into a developed country by 2020."[10] Whether gender figures into this development thrust continues to be of interest. It would appear that the trend remains the same. The Non Traditional Training for Women project was continued, but a dollar amount was not specified and was placed under the Community Development Fund Programme. The Ministry of Community Development and Gender Affairs received an allocation of USD$634,920 to focus on its programme of construction and refurbishment of community centres.[11]

The Non Traditional Training for Women project was continued in 2004, but, again, a dollar amount was not specified.[12] The Ministry of Community Development and Gender Affairs was allocated USD$2.22 million for the construction and refurbishment of community centres across the country. Tobago saw the dedication of resources for the construction of a facility for the Women's Federation Headquarters building, but a dollar amount was not specified.[13]

For 2005, the Ministry of Community Development, Culture and Gender Affairs was allocated USD$2.2 million for the preservation of the "national cultural heritage."[14] No specific allocations were made for gender-related activities. USD$285,000 was provided for the reconstruction of a children's home and renovation of the Salvation Army Hostel-Josephine Shaw House for women.[15] It should be noted, however, that, under the Community Development Fund, projects are implemented under the NGO and CBO Grants Window Programme which focus on women, youth, skills training, employment creation and persons with disabilities.[16] The specified focus including women dates back to 2002. Projects and programmes recommended for priority funding (not funded under core PSIP) for 2005 included major energy industry-related projects, industrial development, electricity, and housing.[17]

> As the Government continues its efforts towards the attainment of developed country status by the year 2020, significant resources of USD$51.1 million ha[ve] been provided to continue the upgrade of recreational, community, sport and youth facilities, enhancement of social services delivery, and the promotion and conservation of our national culture.[18]

This notwithstanding, there is no expenditure on gender affairs apart from the Community Development Programme project for 2006. The *Social Sector Investment Programme 2007*, used to gauge the overall annual performance of social sector ministries against the benchmark of the Millennium Development Goals since 2003, however, states that USD$317,460 was allocated to the Women in Harmony/Domestic Violence Programme, where more than USD$129.7 million in total was dedicated to developmental programmes.[19]

Skipping forward a bit, the author thought it would be interesting to examine how expenditure under the new government, and first-ever elected female Prime Minister, is allocated to gender. The PSIP 2011 seems to follow the trends of the other PSIP documents reviewed. Very little is said about gender issues, save that the government intends to prepare a population policy, which will place "specific emphasis on the needs of the poor, and other social, gender and regional disparity issues."[20] There is also an IDB-assisted Citizen Security Programme, which began in 2010 and continues into 2011, which involves the "strengthening of CACs [Community Action Councils] in the areas of domestic violence prevention, crime prevention, communications, advocacy skills and community leadership."[21] This project has been allocated USD$1.59 million.

Having reviewed these PSIPs, it is seen that expenditure is heavily focussed on education, health, roads and bridges, and administration. Expenditure in these areas generally accounts for more than 50% of total allocations:

1998/99—48.3%;
1999/00—52.8%;
2001—57.3%;
2002—57.6%;
2003—56.2%;
2004—59.8%;
2005—48.4%;
2006—46.7%.

For 2011, expenditure in thsese areas has been projected at 43.1%, but, if expenditure on the development of economic infrastructure is included, it rises to 61.8%.

While the focus on health and education is welcome, a well-balanced population requires emphasis on gender differentials as well. Even where government dedicates resources to gender-specific activities, such as the Non Traditional Training Programme for Women, it would appear that the project would not have unfolded without the assistance of external funding. This particular project was funded 31.9% by government and 68.1% by an IDB Grant.

It is clear that the government expenditure in the area of gender remains miniscule and, from the spending pattern, expenditure on domestic violence is a small percentage of the already small percentage spent on gender. It is, therefore, hardly surprising that NGOs, as seen later in this chapter, have highlighted the paucity of State funding as a serious obstacle to dealing with domestic violence, especially with respect to the establishment of the support network to facilitate women who may have availed themselves of legislative protection. Further, chapter five identified the absence of adequate legal provisions in the *Domestic Violence Act* to ensure effective and quality psychological assistance to both victims and perpetrators of domestic violence, and this, no doubt, has to do with the lack of financial commitment by the State to fund the proper response to incidents of domestic violence.

6.2.2 Gender Policy

The Draft National Gender Policy and Action Plan ("the draft policy") was the "culmination of three decades of planning."[22] The draft policy sought to "promote gender equity, equality, social justice and sustainable human development" through improving the quality of life at all levels of society, improving relations between the sexes, and facilitating social and domestic peace, and reducing levels of violence in society.[23] It also sought to transform inequitable gender relations in order to improve women's status relative to that of men, by identifying strategies to facilitate new and equitable relations between men and women. The draft policy was meant to provide written commitment by government to guarantee equality of status between the sexes. It looked specifically at prevention and protection in situations of domestic violence, by examining briefly the passage and use of the 1991 *Domestic Violence Act*, and the situation of shelters. It also briefly looked at the relationship between domestic violence and the judicial process and women's reluctance to avail themselves of it.[24] Additionally, the draft policy visited the issue of other gender-based violence, such as rape/other sexual offences and incest/child abuse.[25] Generally, the draft policy highlighted the issue of gender equity, equality, social justice and the reduction of violence in society, which certainly contemplates domestic violence.

In 2003, the Minister in the Ministry of Community Development, Culture and Gender Affairs recognised the importance of formulating a policy on gender. She recognised the issue of discrimination and stated that, in line with long-term national development, there is a "need to harness all the resources and…give each person an equal chance and, therefore, the national gender policy is…extremely important."[26] The then Honourable Eulalie James also recognised the importance of the gender policy as a "major instrument for managing gender relations."[27]

This policy was never approved by government, even though it figured very prominently in government's *Draft National Strategic Plan* under Gender and Development.[28] It has proven to be a contentious document, due to its recommendation to "review all issues (for example legal, medical, religious and/or cultural) relating to the termination of pregnancy" and its recognition of people who subscribe to relationships which "appear antithetical to proscribed rules of religion and culture."[29] Notwithstanding the apparent favourable position of the then ruling People's National Movement on the draft policy, the matter culminated in a major pronouncement by the Prime Minister as part of his budget presentation in 2005 that effectively dismissed the draft policy. To quote:

> The Government recognises the need to develop a Gender Policy. The draft Gender Policy Document currently being circulated was not issued by the Government and does not reflect Government policy. In fact, *there are certain recommendations in the document to which the Government does not and will not subscribe*. The Government is therefore requesting that the document which purports to be official Government policy be withdrawn from circulation.[30]

The position of the draft policy fully exemplifies the attitude of the male elite that has dominated the governance of TT from the colonial period through to the post-independence era. The government has effectively dismantled a policy developed by the Centre for Gender and Development Studies at the Unversity of the West Indies, with the input of all the major stakeholders and with extensive public consultations, because of the personal disapprobation of the Prime Minister to the deliberate termination of pregnancies and same-sex relationships.

With consideration given to these difficulties, the National Policy on Gender and Development, as it was re-named, was revised in 2009 by the Gender Affairs Division of the Ministry of Community Development, Culture and Gender Affairs in draft form for public comment.[31] The policy document makes very clear that it "does not provide measures dealing with or relating to the issues of termination of pregnancy, same-sex unions, homosexuality or sexual orientation," but does recognise that "[g]ender based violence is an obstacle to national development."[32] While the revised document still addresses gender—based violence by calling for "an expanded, coordinated national approach"[33] to the problem and identifies measures to be implemented,[34] how can matters of reproductive and sexual rights, central to women's rights, be excised so unceremoniously? While one may hold strong opinions on an issue, such opinions are not necessarily reflective of daily, lived realities.

6.2.3 Ministry of Community Development, Culture and Gender Affairs

At the Ministerial level, gender issues fall under the purview of the Gender Affairs Division of the Ministry of Community Development, Culture and Gender Affairs (now re-named the Ministry of Gender, Youth Affairs and Child Development subsequent to a Cabinet re-shuffle, after having been part of the Ministry of Planning, Economic and Social Restructuring and Gender Affairs[35] from May 2010–June 2011). It would appear that this division "has been subject to significant shifts in approach and priorities with changes in ministerial location and political administration."[36] The division saw its beginnings in 1974 when a National Commission on the Status of Women was appointed.[37] In 1986, the Commission was replaced by the assignment of ministerial responsibility for Women's Affairs.[38] Later, a Women's Bureau within the then Ministry of Community Development, Culture and Women's Affairs was also established. The Government signed and ratified the Convention on the Elimination of All Forms of Discrimination Against Women in 1991, which mandated the Government to develop a National Gender Policy.[39] A national focal point for Gender and Development, the Women's Affairs Division (now the Gender Affairs Division) was established in 1991 and institutionally strengthened between 1994–1997, with the help of the Inter-American Development Bank. Government sought, during this period, to expand the Policy Statement on Women to a National Gender Policy.

In the post-Beijing period, the name of the division was changed. In many ways, this change reflected a heightened emphasis on relational aspects of gender, in addition to its original focus on women. Although its activities expanded and entered new areas, the quest to mainstream gender within government programming and policy and to develop a clear framework for the national intervention did not materialise.

Cabinet agreed in 2000 and a Committee was appointed to develop a National Gender Policy, which could not have beeen done in the face of limited time and resources. In 2002, with the support of the United Nations Development Programme ("UNDP") and the Canadian International Development Agency ("CIDA"), the Government agreed to the development of a National Gender Policy and Plan of Action and to execute the strategies identified therein.

The now Gender Affairs Division is meant "to effectively promote gender equity and gender equality through the process of gender mainstreaming in all government policies, programmes and projects."[40] The division's strategic objectives are to:

- Advance the status and rights of women and men.
- Develop policies, projects and programmes relevant to gender and development issues including the elimination of all forms of violence against women and the elimination of poverty.
- Research and disseminate information on gender and development issues.
- Change gender discriminatory social consciousness and traditions.
- Assist in the strengthening of local communities and families.
- Foster participation of women and men in policy formulating processes.

The Gender Affairs Division has ten main programmes and initiatives designed to address key issues:[41]

- The Male Support Programme
- Defining Masculine Excellence Programme
- Domestic Violence Unit
- Domestic Violence Hotline (800-SAVE)
- Drop In Centres
- Maloney Resource Drop In Centre
- Non-Traditional Skills Training Programme For Women
- Women In Harmony Programme
- Vision 2020 Through A Gender Lens
- National Gender Policy and Action Plan Brief

Some recently added programmes include:[42]

- Food Preparation/Fine Dining and Home Management for Men and Boys
- Men's Health Caravan
- Alternative Education

It is necessary now to examine how some of the individual programmes specifically treat with domestic violence.

6.2.3.1 The Male Support Programme

Although the preamble of the 1999 *Domestic Violence Act* recognised the scourge of domestic violence, it was only in 2004 that the Male Support Programme was expanded to address the high incidence of domestic violence, including family disputes, incest, behavioural problems and other acts of violence against men, women and children.

The Male Programme is critically important to any gender thrust, as it engages men in the process of creating gender respect and the reduction of domestic violence. It is not clear from the information reviewed whether this programme still exists.

6.2.3.2 Defining Masculine Excellence Programme

Many men in society have come to equate masculinity with violence, irresponsibility, and underachievement, as well as physical and emotional absence from the home. Some men, unfortunately, seem to have made masculinity synonymous with deviance, violence and abuse of alcohol and drugs; others are often paralyzed by the fear of not measuring up to mainstream perceptions of masculinity.

The Defining Masculine Excellence Programme was developed as a means of stemming the tide of the societal problems associated with the concept and perceptions of masculinity. The Programme sought to train a cadre of men to support a wider initiative that would involve the establishment of support groups for men and the promotion of other initiatives, which would be used to address the issues previously identified.

The Gender Affairs Division has recognised the need to enhance the strategies to retrain and re-educate men through society and to help them to explore the effects that initialised definitions of masculinity have had on their emotional and spiritual well-being and the ways in which this has impacted the roles they play within the workplace and in their social situations.

6.2.3.3 Domestic Violence Unit

The Unit was established in May 1997. Programmes offered by this Unit include counselling to victims of domestic violence, including victims of rape and incest. It also provides information and referral services to persons who require assistance to deal with other personal and family issues, such as drug abuse, anger management, conflict management and teenage pregnancy. In addition, outreach programmes are conducted as a means of preventing violence and encouraging the establishment of support groups within the communities.

In conjunction with the domestic violence hotline and the drop-in centres, these programmes are meant to:

- Reduce the levels of gender-based violence in Trinidad and Tobago.
- Provide a 24-hour toll-free Hotline Listening and Referral Service for victims/perpetrators of Domestic Violence.
- Provide community-based facilities where men, women and children can access help in situations of domestic violence.

- Reduce gender-based violence through the promotion of non-violent forms of conflict resolution and active public awareness campaigns.
- Provide extensive and on-going training for the staff of the Unit, safe-houses, shelters, the police, community and church organisations.
- Actively collect and analyse data and monitor trends in domestic violence.

6.2.3.4 Domestic Violence Hotline (800-SAVE)

In August 1996, in response to the escalating incidence of domestic violence, the Government of Trinidad and Tobago established the National Domestic Violence Hotline. This service is a twenty-four (24) hour toll-free hotline service available to persons experiencing or affected by domestic violence. The line operates seven days per week and can be accessed by phoning the number 800-SAVE (7283). The services provided by the hotline include safe and confidential listening; crisis intervention/counselling; referral to appropriate agencies, such as the police, shelters; and advocacy.

Data for the period 01 October 2005 to 30 September 2006 revealed that a total of 1,867 clients benefited from the national domestic violence hotline, of which 1503 were female and 364 were male.[43] A review of the available updated data in Table 6.1 shows the number of reported calls made between 2005–2008. It is instructive to note that, for each year, women made up over 75% of the callers.

6.2.3.5 Drop In Centres

The Drop-in Centre programme offers counselling to victims of domestic violence, including victims of rape and incest. The programme also provides information and referral services to persons who require assistance to deal with other personal and family issues, such as drug abuse, anger management, conflict management and teenage pregnancy. Outreach programmes are also conducted as a means of preventing violence and encouraging the establishment of support groups within the communities.

Table 6.1. Domestic Violence Hotline Data: Cases Reported

Year	*Total Number of Calls Made*	*Male Callers*	*%*	*Female Callers*	*%*
2005	1993	463	23	1530	77
2006	1949	395	20	1554	80
2007	2654	642	24	2012	76
2008	2565	576	22	1989	78

Ministry of Community Development, Culture and Gender Affairs, "Domestic Violence Hotline Data: Cases Reported," accessed 18 July 2011, http://genderaffairs-tt.net/pdf_docs/DomesticViolenceData.pdf. The data is further disaggregated into the age range of the callers.

The drop-in Centres are primarily located in Community Centres and Complexes. Each Centre is staffed by a trained social worker (contracted through the Domestic Violence Unit) who works as part of a service delivery team. In addition to Secretary/Warden or Manager of the Community Centre or Complex, a police officer, a representative from the Ministry of Community Development, Culture and Gender Affairs, and volunteers from within the community are also members of the team.

6.2.3.6 Food Preparation/Fine Dining and Home Management for Men and Boys

This recently introduced initiative is meant to give men and boys a greater appreciation of women's domestic responsibilities. More specifically, the intiative is supposed to foster an understanding of gender, as well as improve gender relations between men and women and, in so doing, reduce the incidence of domestic and other forms of violence. It is also meant to improve the notion of shared family responsibility and allow men the space to share their concerns and feelings openly and non-violently.

6.2.3.7 Men's Health Caravan

This initiative is geared at raising awareness of male health issues and positively affecting patterns of behaviour associated with masculinity. One such pattern identified for awareness-raising is the cycle of violence and addiction that afflict so many men.

The above description of the work of the Gender Affairs Division in integrating domestic violence in most of its programmes may lead to a perception that domestic violence is receiving priority treatment. This would appear to be far from the reality that currently exists, as field research paints a different picture. For example, the NGOs openly scoff at the Drop-In centres, claiming that they are largely non-functional. Further, the impressive description of Drop-In centres with the high level of skilled staffing only applies to one Drop-In centre in Maloney in north Trinidad. Finally, the abysmal level of funding identified in the section on government funding above for community development, social, recreational and cultural matters is further exacerbated by the fact that gender is but a small subset of these larger components. For example, based on the *Social Sector Investment Programme 2007*, only 0.2% of monies were allocated for social sector programmes and were dedicated to the Women in Harmony/Domestic Violence Programme. Moreover, the 0.2% expenditure is divided between two programmes, of which domestic violence is one.

6.2.4 Ministry of Social Services

While gender issues are dealt with specifically by the Ministry of Community Development, Culture and Gender Affairs, family and other social issues fall under the purview of the Ministry of Social Development. This ministry is responsible for disbursing funds among NGOs that deal with women's issues, as well as subventions to women's halfway houses and shelters. Two other very important services offered by the Ministry of Social Development are provided by the National Family Services Division and the Probation Department.

6.2.4.1 National Family Services Division

Services related to domestic violence are only one aspect of the services available through the ten regional offices of the National Family Services Division.[44] It also addresses abuse/incest, marital problems, depression, parenting, family life, foster care, drug abuse, and life crises.[45] The division was established in 1991 and its mission is to promote healthy family functioning through the provision of preventative, developmental and remedial programmes and services. It realises its mandate through counselling, advice, rehabilitation, consultation, networking, mediation, advocacy, research, lectures/workshops, and placement. Victims and offenders in domestic violence situations access the services of this department mainly through court referrals. A Magistrate, during court proceedings, may request an interim report based on a recommendation of counselling for the parties involved. Friends or other agencies usually refer walk-in and telephone clients to the department. Clients that telephone are asked to visit the office and/or, if necessary, they are referred to another department or are visited at home.

Data is collected by the use of intake forms to record the type of case and the categories of abuse for walk-in and court referrals. Recording of data is difficult since confidentiality is important to the client and the department. Poor recording, as well as the need for confidentiality, sometimes leads to the duplication of service, since two officers may end up managing the same client.

6.2.4.2 The Probation Department

The Probation Department has its head office in Port of Spain and nine district offices located throughout the country.[46] The department and its officers are mandated to promote the rehabilitation of clients through counselling and education, and to promote a healthy lifestyle through proactive intervention. The official system of data collection on domestic violence began with the enactment of the *Domestic Violence Act*, 1991. Under this Act, the Probation

Department is one of two agencies identified for intervention in such cases. Clients are referred to the department by the court and other agencies, such as the Community Policing Unit, 800-SAVE, Justices of the Peace, and walk-ins.

Data are collected and recorded through several methods. During the confidential interview, the probation officers use registration forms for each specific case that give demographic information, as well as descriptions of the issues and incidents of domestic violence against the client. The officers also maintain a domestic violence register in which official requests by the court for reports are recorded. This register contains basic data on the complainant and respondent involved in the court proceeding. The officers collate their domestic violence case data from the register and send them to the head office for submission and inclusion in the *Monthly Returns*. Special registers are created in specific regions where there is a high incidence of abuse.

The Ministry of Social Development has a major role in information dissemination on domestic violence; yet, it is difficult to even directly obtain information in person on the ministry. Moreover, a review of the budgetary allocations for the social and community services, which fall under the Ministry of Social Development, suggests that provisions are not made for either of the National Family Services Division or the Probation Department, of which assistance to victims of domestic violence forms an important component. For 2006, while expenditure on social and community services accounted for 8.5% of total budgetary allocations, most of this was dedicated to the upgrade or construction of recreational, cultural, sporting and even cemetery/cremation facilities with no mention of these two important services.[47] A similar scenario exists in 2011, where social and community services have been allocated 8.8% of total budgetary allocations. This money is dedicated to the establishment of centres, poverty alleviation, improvements and refurbishments to community facilties and community centres,[48] again with no mention of services. This continued low level of funding seriously undermines an effort on the part of the Ministry of Social Development to project itself as an important and effective player in the national effort to address domestic violence.

6.2.5 Gender Department, Tobago House of Assembly

In 1999, a Gender Affairs Unit was established within the Health and Social Services Division of the Tobago House of Assembly.[49] With limited human and social resources, the unit established a 24-hour Tobago Crisis hotline; an information and resource centre; and provided counselling services to survivors and perpetrators of gender-based violence, as well as to persons who were suicidal, addicted, homeless and abandoned and subject to other forms of abuse.

The framework for the formulation and implementation of a Tobago Gender Policy is expressly stated in the Tobago Development Plan Report No. 4. The Plan identified the following gender-specific activities for implementation in the period 1998–2013:

- To support and participate in the development of a national gender policy
- To increase the sensitising of the population to gender issues
- To combat domestic violence in all forms, including rape and incest.

Despite the impressive sounding agenda of the Gender Department of the Tobago House of Assembly, anecdotal evidence from an interview with a member of staff suggested that the department was effectively non-functional because of a change in directorship.[50]

6.3 STATE AUTHORITIES

6.3.1 Magistracy

Applications made under the *Domestic Violence Act* are to be made specifically to a "Court of Summary Jurisdiction"; the Magistrate's Court is such a court.[51] The Magistracy plays an important role in supporting the battle against domestic violence in its implementing capacity of the *Domestic Violence Act*. The Magistracy exercises original jurisdiction in relation to summary criminal matters.[52] The Magistrate's Courts also facilitate preliminary inquiries in serious criminal matters to determine whether a *prima facie* case has been established against an accused person before he/she can be indicted for trial at the High Court. TT is divided into thirteen magisterial districts, with some districts having more than one Magistrate's court.[53] The Magistracy is comprised of a Chief Magistrate, a Deputy Chief Magistrate, twelve senior Magistrates, twenty-nine Magistrates and six temporary Magistrates.

Statistics on the various matters heard in the Magistrate's Courts are made available to the Statistical Office of the Judiciary and are compiled according to district and year for its annual report. Figure 6.1 and table 6.2 illustrate and compile data for domestic violence over the period 1998–2009, with the exception of 2007, for which no data is available.[54]

The statistics in the graph and the table show what appears to be proportional distribution in the number of cases across the districts according to population density. St. George West and San Fernando are both heavily populated areas; conversely, Mayaro and Rio Claro are sparsely populated areas and the numbers of applications filed under the *Domestic Violence Act* reflect this demographic distribution.

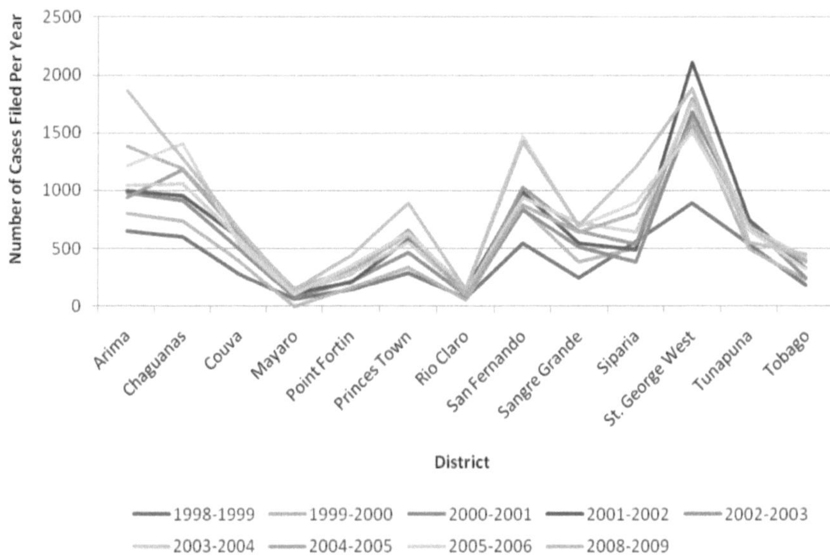

Figure 6.1. Domestic Violence Statistics collected by the Magistrate's Courts for the Period 1998–2009.

While the number of applications under the *Domestic Violence Act* to the Magistrate's Courts would appear to be high, any optimism that the legislation is being well employed must be tempered by the fact that there are no credible statistics on the actual number of incidents of domestic violence in TT. Moreover, it should be noted that many cases are disposed of without even being heard. While yearly totals for disposals are available, the information is not disaggregated into reasons for disposal of cases. Anecdotal evidence would suggest that many cases are disposed of at various stages and, generally, before having been brought to completion.

It is important to assess the role of the Magistracy in the implementation of the *Domestic Violence Act*. In chapter five, a review of the *Domestic Violence Act* demonstrated promptness as a requirement of the legislation. Yet, interviews with stakeholders would suggest that the relief provided is anything but summary. Matters tend to drag on too long and are constantly adjourned. Adjournments can be due to the Magistrate not having time to hear the matter (on any given day, criminal matters are heard first, then followed by family matters), or the absence of the served party. While the Magistrate has the power to issue a warrant for the (absent) respondent's arrest, this is rarely done; a notice with a new date of hearing is served. This process can be repeated until the order is discharged or the applicant becomes weary by the process and ceases to follow up.

Table 6.2. Domestic Violence Statistics Collected by the Magistrate's Courts for the Period 1998–2009

	YEAR								
DISTRICT	*1998–99*	*1999–00*	*2000–01*	*2001–02*	*2002–03*	*2003–04*	*2004–05*	*2005–06*	*2008–09*
Arima	647	804	979	998	942	1041	1378	1215	1867
Chaguanas	601	736	911	951	1178	1059	1187	1404	1280
Couva	277	389	493	594	618	581	652	539	665
Mayaro	61	0	75	109	122	128	152	105	139
Point Fortin	144	161	214	202	276	289	319	347	440
Princes Town	290	337	467	576	659	552	616	635	889
Rio Claro	69	54	91	139	79	120	91	159	142
San Fernando	540	840	834	986	1024	941	874	1469	1422
Sangre Grande	249	386	512	542	649	723	643	690	698
Siparia	559	500	381	491	534	639	801	900	1202
St. George West	890	1626	1677	2105	1791	1768	1566	1512	1883
Tunapuna	537	494	715	744	673	677	665	653	553
Tobago	178	227	246	327	390	422	386	322	449
TOTAL	5042	6554	7595	8764	8935	8940	9330	9950	11629

Statistics obtained from the Annual Reports of the Judiciary of Trinidad and Tobago for the period 1998–2009; there does not appear to be a report for the period 2007–2008.

Simple administrative blunders also frustrate the process. In one instance, an applicant, fearing for her safety, who already had an Interim Order in effect, went to the Magistrate's Court to request an expedited hearing before the Magistrate for the final Protection Order. It can take two weeks before the matter is listed to be heard. The Clerk gave the applicant the (expedited) date and, after having shown up and waited on said date, the applicant was told that there was no record of her application for a hearing. As mentioned above, family matters are heard only after all the criminal matters are heard, but the applicants and respondents are required to be in Court from 9:00 a.m. until such time as the matter is called. In this instance, she waited from 8:30 a.m. to 3:30 p.m. *in the company of* the respondent. Ordinarily, all the listed matters are read at the beginning of the day's proceedings; it is not clear whether this occurred. Moreover, she had to apply for a day off work to attend Court. This does not take into account the time she had to take off work to file the application.

Another failing by the Magistracy has been a lack of strictness in dealing with court attendance for hearings under the *Domestic Violence Act*. The Court can proceed to hear a domestic violence matter in the absence of a respondent that has been served or the Court can issue a warrant for the respondent's arrest. From various interviews conducted by the author, it would appear that these options are hardly ever used, as Magistrates tend simply to schedule a new date, even though this option only applies to respondents who have not actually received summons. The constant rescheduling, without using the provisions of this section, can frustrate the applicant and cause her to drop the case. In other instances, due to the time limits set in the Act, the case is discharged without even being heard.

In some cases, Magistrates have shown an eagerness to dismiss matters when the applicant is believed to be absent from the Court. Applicants have complained that cases have been dismissed even though they are present. Because of the noise level in the courthouse, it is sometimes difficult to hear when the case is called and it can be dismissed as easily as that due to the large volume of cases to be heard on any given day. Further, the absence of the applicant may be justifiable and the summary dismissal of the case is harsh where no excuse has been proffered by the applicant. The nature of domestic violence is such that it may not be possible for the applicant to send notice of her reasonable excuse for non-appearance. What happens in the event that, on presentation of the summons, the applicant is beaten so severely that she has to be hospitalised and no one is aware of the situation? She will be unable to attend court or give notice of her absence.

In the case of one woman, she was taken to a shelter out of fear for her life, after repeated death threats by her husband, and applied for a protection order. When the respondent was finally served with the notice of proceedings (he was not served in time for the first hearing), he appeared at the hearing with a counter-summons stating that the applicant was, in fact, the dangerous one, threatening to kill her children and him. The matter then had to be investigated before any relief could be given. This matter is still ongoing.[55] It is quite possible that the respondent can file proceedings against the applicant in her absence, causing a protection order to be taken out against her, creating a veritable perversion of justice.

It would appear that "the law fell victim to patriarchal "cultural habits" present everywhere in Trinidad and Tobago, including the courtrooms and the clerk offices. As a result, "the vast majority of applications for protection orders do not result in restraining orders."[56] This is compounded by the fact that the institutional support from the Magistracy, required to make the piece of legislation effective, seems to defeat the purpose of the *Domestic Violence Act* which was meant to provide summary relief. The magisterial process seems to preserve and promote gender hierarchies, disempowers complainants, and has even been described as punishment.[57] According to the statistics, women tend to prefer the magisterial route to the police service; however, the magisterial process leaves much to be desired, as matters tend to drag on too long and are constantly adjourned.

6.3.2 Family Court

The Family Court of Trinidad and Tobago hears a variety of family issues and domestic violence as it relates to them but does not hear domestic violence matters as a primary issue.[58] It is a pilot project that commenced operations in May 2004 and is of interest due to the scope of services it offers. In addition to adjudicating family matters, the Family Court offers Children Services, to look after and occupy children while parents deal with legal issues; Probation Services, where specially trained social workers monitor and assist families with respect to compliance orders, resolution of issues and investigation of family problems; Mediation Services, where mediators help couples discuss issues and come to an agreement; and Counselling Services, where both family and individual counselling is available.[59]

This post-order service is what is missing from the magisterial process, where couples are required to deal with the psychological fallout of orders of the court on their own. The process of the Magistrate's Court does not take into account the psychological fallout of the protection orders on the psyche of the fragile male ego, which probably led to the situation in the first place (or on the applicant or children). He may feel emasculated and seek to intentionally hurt or kill the one who is meant to be protected. The Family

Court offers a different type of process, where the abused and the victim can be taken for immediate counselling, which is available on the premises if so ordered. The Family Court assists couples in dealing with the emotional distress resulting from its decision, helping them to sort through the pain of family disintegration or assist in maintaining the family unit where possible. In addition to counselling, the Family Court offers an intake service, children's services, probation services, mediation services, and judicial services. It provides a one-stop shop for all family needs. This may be an approach to dealing with the post-order problems that may arise.

A key goal of the pilot was to continuously test the effectiveness and efficiency of the various innovations and approaches used.[60] The project has been deemed a success, based on annual client ratings,[61] and will therefore be continued and expanded. There is currently only one such Court, but it is intended to expand to five other areas in the country.

6.3.3 Police Service

The Trinidad and Tobago Police Service ("TTPS") is a division of the Ministry of National Security. Prior to 1996, there was a Welfare Section of the TTPS which dealt not only with the welfare of police officers but also of the community.[62] Based on information received from foreign training, the Commissioner of Police in 1996, Noor Mohammed, established the Community Policing Section. There was a perception that police officers were alienated from the clients that they served and this was evidenced by client complaints of unwarranted police hostility. With respect to domestic violence reporting, there was a perception that police officers do not treat with such reports with the necessary degree of seriousness. The establishment of the Community Policing Section, therefore, was meant to deal with this distance and bridge the gap, helping the officers to become more socially aware. The Community Policing Section saw "[t]he police and the community working together to help solve mutually defined problems through deliberate effort aimed at reducing crime, violence, fear, insecurity and community decay."[63]

Police officers from mainstream policing, previously engaged in the Welfare Section, were selected to be a part of this section and trained. Officers from the Community Policing Section would visit communities forging alliances and relationships. These alliances were strategically used to gain information on criminal activity. This section was responsible for the creation of neighbourhood watches; police youth clubs that infused discipline among young people; consultative groups; and carrying out lectures in schools with respect to crime awareness, drug abuse awareness and other topics of that nature. The section also engaged in networking with other agencies, such as joint police-NGO activities. Some people were trained in counselling with respect to domestic violence situations and assisted in referrals to NGOs that could provide the necessary interventions.

In 2000, the Trinidad and Tobago National Quality Council commissioned a report on the effectiveness of the Community Policing Section, which had the effect of "disbanding" the section, as reservations were raised about the creation of a parallel police service that seemed to create a different ethos between the two entities.[64] There was the issue of which service should respond to which matter, with the adverse consequence of undue delays. It was suggested that the Community Policing Section be reintegrated into the main police service even though "[t]his integration within the service should not mean that the sustained focus on community policing will or should be lost or absorbed beyond recognition."[65] This was, however, the ultimate effect. The public perception is that the Community Policing Section has been disbanded although they are not sure when or why, despite the fact that the Trinidad and Tobago Police Service website indicates that the Community Policing Secretariat is one of its departments.[66] It was suggested that all police officers be "equally and properly trained in both tracks of public service,"[67] even though the requisite training was not forthcoming to make this transition.

Domestic violence matters are now, therefore, dealt with by mainstream policing, although it should properly be dealt with by the Community Policing Secretariat. It is, therefore, not surprising that there is continuing strong denunciation of the attitude of the police to domestic violence complaints. In a series of recent judgements on the defence of "Battered Women Syndrome," Justice Carmona endorsed the widely held view of the unresponsiveness of the police to domestic violence complaints.[68]

The police service plays a critical role in the legal regime for dealing with domestic violence. Section 21 of the *Domestic Violence Act* requires the police to respond to complaints and maintain reports on domestic violence, which are to be contained in a National Domestic Violence Register. The Modus Operandi and Records Bureau of the TTPS collects and collates this data from all police stations across the country. Anecdotal evidence gleaned from interviews suggests that domestic violence recording and reporting are not done faithfully. Figure 6.2 and table 6.3 illustrate and compile data for domestic violence over the period 1997–2006.

When the number of complaints filed with the Police is compared to the number of applications made for Protection Orders at the Magistrates' Court, a great disparity is quite apparent. In 2006, for example, 9950 persons sought orders under the *Domestic Violence Act* but only 304 complaints were registered with the police. The number of complaints on domestic violence would suggest that the police are either not recording all the complaints made with

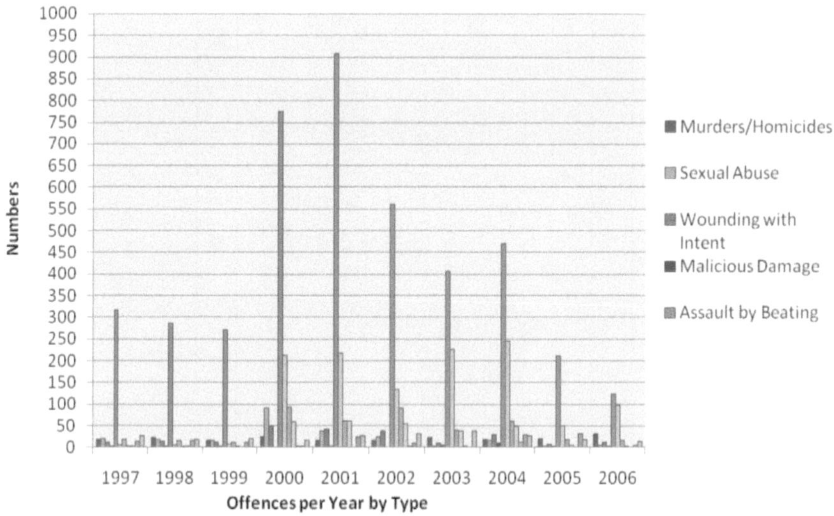

Figure 6.2. Domestic Violence Statistics collected by the Trinidad and Tobago Police Service for the Period 1997–2006.

respect to domestic violence or persons are, in fact, not availing themselves of the services of the police in light of the historically poor attitude of the police to domestic violence complaints. Perhaps the truth lies between both assumptions.

Police officers generally have a duty to deal with domestic violence as part of its mandate to protect and serve; this general duty is specifically contemplated by Section 21(1) of the *Domestic Violence Act*. Perceptions of police response have been mixed, with some stating that the police respond positively and quickly while others state that they dismiss the matter nonchalantly saying that that is an issue between husband and wife and should be sorted out at home. In some cases, the police officers seem apathetic. A possible explanation for this apathy stems from the fact that, in many instances, where they do respond to a complaint, the complainant eventually wants to return to the abuser. The complainant would file a report, be escorted to a shelter, and either run away from the shelter, disclose her location to the abuser, or beg to be allowed to go back to the abuser.[69] This is a regular occurrence and frustrates not only police officers, but shelter management as well. Police officers seem indifferent and even wary/weary of domestic violence reports. Yes, wary as women seeking assistance seem to return to the situation once the crisis point is passed and, consequently, weary because of this. This should not, however, have the effect of diminishing the police officers' responsibility to respond, or numbing their response.

Table 6.3. Domestic Violence Statistics collected by the Trinidad and Tobago Police Service for the Period 1997–2006

	YEAR									
OFFENCE	*1997*	*1998*	*1999*	*2000*	*2001*	*2002*	*2003*	*2004*	*2005*	*2006*
Murders/Homicides	18	23	15	24	17	17	22	18	21	30
Sexual Abuse	21	19	17	92	37	24	3	15	4	5
Wounding with Intent	12	14	11	48	42	37	9	29	7	12
Malicious Damage	2	1	2	0	2	0	5	10	1	1
Assault by Beating	317	287	271	775	907	560	406	470	211	123
Threats	6	5	7	214	217	133	227	245	50	98
Verbal Abuse	18	15	11	94	60	91	40	60	18	15
Emotional / Psychological Abuse	3	1	1	59	61	55	37	49	5	2
Financial Abuse	1	2	0	4	0	1	4	12	0	0
Child Abuse & Abandonment	13	17	12	4	25	9	0	28	31	5
Breach of Protection Order	26	19	21	16	26	30	38	26	19	13
TOTAL	437	403	368	1330	1394	957	791	962	367	304

Statistics obtained from the Modus Operandi and Records Bureau in 2007.

The police, by their conduct, also create circumstances that render the victim of domestic violence fearful of using their services. There was one instance where the victim, whose life was not under immediate threat, had a police escort her to her home so that she could retrieve some personal items. There was a male and a female officer present and, out of earshot of the female police officer, the male police officer started making unsolicited advances on the woman. Even though she was scared and had no one else whom she could trust, she did not give in to his advances and he immediately and henceforth became particularly hostile towards her. The complainant was extremely grateful for the presence of the female officer and was safely delivered to a shelter.

Additionally, the role of the police in the effective implementation of the *Domestic Violence Act* extends to their attitude towards service of documents pertaining to applications for protection orders. Section 12(5) of the *Domestic Violence Act* provides for service of documents by the applicant or the applicant's agent. The primary method of service under the *Domestic Violence Act* is by the police, as noted in Section 12(4). The common practice, however, is for the applicant to be encouraged to effect service directly rather than depend on the police. This practice has emerged because of the perception by the Clerk of the Courts that the police tend to be dilatory in the service of summons as issued under the *Domestic Violence Act*. It is unacceptable that it should even be contemplated that the applicant can serve notice on the respondent. Service should be *strictly* effected by the police or court marshals, as service by the applicant can create a situation of further abuse and even death.

One applicant had the experience of having to serve the summons herself. She went to the Court to make the initial application and was given all the paperwork to serve on the respondent and deliver one copy to the police station in her area. Out of fear of a violent reaction, she served the summons by leaving it on the dresser where the respondent would see it the morning before the actual date and spent that night with her daughter at a friend's. At the courthouse, the clerk advised her to serve it herself, as the general trend is that the police station does not make the necessary arrangements for service and the matter would have to be constantly adjourned until, perhaps, finally discharged. The copy she took to the police station was misplaced; so when she went to make a report of breach of the Interim Order, they had nothing on file to corroborate her complaint. Moreover, on the date for obtaining a final Order, she was told that there was no record of her application and the Interim Order had lapsed. Frustrated, she simply never bothered to follow up and now there is no order against the perpetrator.

The police play a critical role in dealing directly with incidents of domestic violence. Pursuant to Section 22 of the *Domestic Violence Act*, the police can act by means of a warrant to deal with situations of domestic violence; under Section 23 of the *Domestic Violence Act*, the police can act in the absence of a warrant. The power to act without a warrant is an important one, as very often the acts giving rise to the need to act without a warrant can lead to physical harm or death. Yet, the power to so act is heavily regulated such that it has created disincentives for the police to move without a warrant to prevent domestic violence.

It must, nevertheless, be borne in mind that the rules governing the actions of the police to act without warrant in situations involving domestic violence has arisen because of the conduct of the police. Many interviewees stated that police officers abuse their positions of authority and trust and prey on victims of domestic violence. In one particular case, a woman reported an incident of domestic violence against her husband and she and the officer eventually entered into a relationship. A Protection Order was taken out against the husband, after which the police officer falsely reported a breach of the Order and the respondent was jailed. Fortunately, the matter was investigated and the man was released.

6.3.4 Legal Aid and Advisory Authority

The Legal Aid and Advisory Authority was established some thirty-one years ago as a division of the Ministry of Legal Affairs and has nine branches throughout the country.[70] It is meant to provide affordable legal advice and assistance in a variety of matters to members of the public who are of small or moderate means. Applicants for legal aid must not possess disposal capital exceeding a maximum of USD$794.00 nor must their net disposable income exceed USD$1,111.00 per year.[71] Victims of domestic violence seek assistance from Legal Aid generally to get advice on obtaining a protection or an exclusion order. Others come in just to have a confidential discussion, even though the legal officers are not trained as counsellors. As many as one hundred such people can visit a single office in a day.

The process for applying for legal aid involves filling out a form and the legal aid officer instructing the Justice of the Peace at the relevant court. This form is then left with the Magistrate to determine eligibility of the applicant for legal aid. Once the applicant is eligible, the Magistrate grants aid and refers the matter back to the Legal Aid and Advisory Authority for assignment of counsel. Once the matter is complete, the Legal Aid and Advisory Authority pays all legal expenses, which are generally nominal. In cases where it is determined that the applicant is in imminent danger, the Justice of the Peace or Clerk can list the matter to be heard by the Magistrate on the same day. The Magistrate then takes evidence *ex parte* and grants an interim protection order, not to exceed twenty-one days, advising that counsel be present at the hearing. Under section 16A of the *Legal Aid and Advice Act*, Chap. 7:07, the

Legal Aid and Advisory Authority can also prepare an emergency certificate in support of the applicant, in relation to the *Domestic Violence Act* without reference to the Court or the Legal Aid and Advisory Authority, to be forwarded to the Court and an attorney will be provided forthwith.

It would seem, from interviews, that obtaining legal aid has not been problematic with the defining issues being the post-legal aid scenarios as discussed in Sections 6.3.1 and 6.3.3 dealing with the magistracy and the police respectively.

6.4 NON-GOVERNMENTAL ORGANISATIONS

NGOs are integral to the process of change. As discussed in chapter three, NGOs perhaps provide the impetus for action and, depending on the nature of the work undertaken by the organisation, can bring real and immediate relief to those who need it most. This section divides the NGOs that deal with domestic violence in TT into three types: Research and Advocacy, Support Services, and Shelters.[72] While this section is as exhaustive as possible, there are a couple that are not noted here as interviews were not possible and information was not otherwise available.[73]

6.4.1 Research and Advocacy Groups

There are five main groups that engage in advocacy and research on domestic violence issues. These are the Trinidad and Tobago Coalition Against Domestic Violence ("the Coalition"); the Centre for Gender and Development Studies (part of the University of the West Indies, St. Augustine Campus), which also has a Women Development Studies Group; Caribbean Association for Feminist Research and Action ("CAFRA"); Network of NGOs of Trinidad and Tobago for the Advancement of Women; and Women Working for Social Progress.

These groups have lobbied for legislative change, such as seen with the amended *Domestic Violence Act* and *Sexual Offences Act*, and the introduction of legislation with particular reference to children's issues. Major changes to the *Domestic Violence Act* included:

- the introduction of definitions of the various types of abuse that can be suffered (emotional/psychological, financial, physical, sexual) (section 3);
- a change to only prohibitions being placed in a protection order to now include directions concerning interim compensation for monetary loss incurred, monetary relief, relinquishment of firearms, and making or continuation of rent or mortgage payments (section 6(c));

- the need to preserve the family unit (section 7(g));
- the ability of any member of the household to apply for an order (section 4(b));
- admissibility of views expressed by a child or dependent on whose behalf the application for an order is made having regard to the child's age and maturity (section 10(5));
- the introduction of the legal duty of police officers to respond to every complaint or report alleging domestic violence (section 21(1)), to file a report (section 21(3)), and to assist victims when power of entry is used (section 23A);
- the admissibility of a recorded statement where the complainant refuses to be sworn as a witness or gives oral evidence inconsistent or contradictory to the statement forming part of the police record (section 26);
- the introduction of a greater range of offences (First Schedule);
- an increase in the duration of an interim order from 14 days to 21 days (section 8(3));
- an increase in the duration of a protection order from a maximum of one year to a maximum of three years (section 6(a)); and
- an increase in fines for breaches of orders from USD$794/imprisonment not exceeding six months to a tiered system: first conviction USD$1429/ imprisonment not exceeding three months; second conviction USD$2381/ imprisonment not exceeding 24 months; any subsequent conviction would result in imprisonment not exceeding five years.

These latter two changes, meant to truly keep the offender in check, were lauded as the greatest achievements in lobbying for legislative amendments for this particular Act by these NGOs; Justice Carmona, however, has noted that "the sentencing regime employed by the courts appears not to be having the desired impact. The killing goes on callously and unabated."[74] Even lawyers representing murder clients recognise that "these offences are far too common in society today."[75] The *Sexual Offences Act* of 1986 was amended to have marital rape included as an offence, which was finally done in 2000, after much opposition by the government.[76] The original act only acknowledged sexual offences against a wife if the husband had intercourse with her without her consent, or by force of fear where there was some degree of legal separation, or an order by the court for the husband not to molest his wife. Moreover, proceedings for an offence under this section could only have been instituted by or with the consent of the Director of Public Prosecutions.

Research and advocacy NGOs also partake in training sessions, seminars, and workshops (usually by invitation), such as training for members of the police service to apprise them of legal changes, as with the amendment to the

Domestic Violence Act and their role under the Act, as well as sensitisation sessions on domestic and gender-based violence, and treating victims who report such instances. A major training workshop was held in 2004 by the Coalition for members of the judiciary on dealing with domestic violence matters. While research, training and legislative lobbying are high on the agenda of these types of organisations, some also provide drop-in and scheduled counselling services to both victims and perpetrators of domestic violence. As the foremost organisation in TT that deals with domestic violence, the Coalition also provides legal advice, through its legal clinic, to victims of domestic violence.

6.4.2 Support Service Groups

There are a variety of groups that provides varying degrees of support services to victims of domestic violence. These include Lifeline, Families In Action, Rape Crisis Society of Trinidad and Tobago, Flaming Word Ministry (while it is recognised that all religious organisations would be required to provide this type of support if necessary, this one was included as it is a member of the Coalition), Men Against Violence Against Women ("MAVAW"), and Women Against Abuse and Violent Encounters (Women's Support Group) ("WAAVE").

Support groups provide services ranging from listening (where the person is not allowed to counsel or offer advice), counselling, outreach (usually by invitation), referrals to other organisations such as shelters or the domestic violence hotline, skills training to assist women in achieving financial security, and sensitisation programmes. The skills training programmes are designed to provide women with a marketable skill, such as in agro-processing. Sensitisation programmes and outreach range from publications (pamphlets, brochures, posters, booklets) to giving talks at various venues.

There are two organisations in this group of particular interest. MAVAW, the only male group specifically engaged in domestic violence, offers a long-term approach to dealing with the problem, as opposed to the various short-term solutions currently used, such as overnighting at a shelter and obtaining a protection order. MAVAW's philosophical approach allows it to view domestic violence as resulting from dysfunctional relationships and does not believe in terms such as "abuser" and "victim." Its "BSD Syndrome Concept" focuses on identifying belief, behavioural, and biological "deficits," with a view to developing them appropriately, such as the belief that men are superior or the behaviour that allows hitting to be acceptable. The concept also includes a "baggage system dependency" which requires the individual to completely resolve previous relationships before entering another. The concept is meant to scientifically place the violence-in-relationship issue into a medium that takes away the stigma and gender polarisation previously associated with it, at the same time recognising the social roots of the problem. MAVAW anticipates resistance to the concept by some women, "primarily because every statistic, which lists one person being hurt, will also have to list the other person causing pain, as being hurt too."[77]

The other group of interest is WAAVE, a unique support group started by actual victims of domestic violence. They came together to provide support to one another that no organisation, shelter, or counselling session could provide. In speaking with various members of this group, as well as other battered women, it becomes clear that even though women's shelters are run by women, these latter still have little understanding or empathy for those seeking refuge. Some matrons complain that the women who come to the shelters are lazy; while this may be the case for some, it must be that others simply need a resting period before embarking on the rostered tasks at a shelter. These women come to the shelters battered and afraid, should they all be expected to immediately commence chores? Should a small, but reasonable, recovery period not be allowed? While it is certain that a recovery period is allowed, perhaps discretion would dictate whether a longer period can be granted, depending on the individual. There have been instances, however, where women simply refuse to do anything and the reasons for this remain unclear.

6.4.3 Shelters

There are some ten shelters or halfway houses in TT that take in women victims of domestic violence. Shelters, located all around the country, include The Shelter, MIZPEH Halfway House, the Business and Professional Women's Club Halfway House, Goshen Halfway House for Battered Wives and Teenage Pregnancies, Vision of Hope Halfway House, Madinah House, Hope Shelter for Battered Women and Children, National Home for Family Reconciliation, Our Lady of the Wayside Shelter, and Tobago Women's Enterprise for Empowerment and Rehabilitation Towards Self-Sufficiency.

All shelters provide meals, clothing, toiletries, and bedding, as most women who seek refuge at shelters have with them only what they wore to get there. Counselling services are provided by most shelters as an integral part of the emergency services offered. Duration of stay and number and sex of children allowed differ from shelter to shelter. The timeframe seems to be flexible depending on the nature of individual cases. What is clear is that all shelters have restrictions on entry of boys of various ages into the shelter. This means that the mother must either decide to seek refuge elsewhere, be faced with the decision to split her family further during a time of crisis, or remain at home with the abuser. The women of WAAVE have recognised this problem and hope one day to run a shelter with facilities to accommodate boys. All the shelters have cited reasons of uncontrollability and curiosity of the female sex, whether innocent or not, as reasons for restricting entry of older boys into the shelters. While the need to preserve feminine modesty is foremost, what about the integrity of the family unit? Even this need is legislated (see the *Domestic Violence Act*). Surely splitting the family will have further adverse effects on the psyches of all involved and requires extensive reconsideration.

Most of the shelters offer skills training programmes aimed at empowering women to be self-sufficient. Programmes and courses in etiquette, crafts, sewing, needlework, gardening, animal husbandry, food preparation, pastry-making, flower-making, childcare, parenting, housekeeping, hairdressing, lay counselling, adult literacy, computer literacy, and nursing are among the many to which women have access while at the shelters. In some cases, where the shelter does not actually provide the programmes or courses, they may locate venues where they are offered and pay for the women to attend once money is available.

Most of the shelters interviewed receive no government assistance but rely on corporate and individual contributions to meet their expenses. These funds are supplemented by various fund-raising activities. Shelters which do receive a government subvention complain that it is very little and certainly not enough to run the homes. While this is the case, all the homes visited had quite a bit of spare capacity at the time, so that expenses should be less during such times. This also raises the question as to why women are not using the facilities available to them. Not wanting to split the family, hoping the abuser would eventually change, the fact that the children are clothed and fed at home, socialised to believe that violence against women is part of family life may all be reasons why women do not use the facilities offered by the shelters.

Women are referred to shelters either by the police, Court, or the domestic violence hotline. There are few walk-in victims. Shelters prefer referrals so as to have official records of the women's presence there. Many shelters report having positive relationships with the area police station but often complain that their response time to situations is too long. There was one shelter, in particular, that stated that when they call the area police station they do not receive full cooperation and are told that they cannot help. They have to rely on a police station many miles away to provide assistance. In some cases, the police officers disclose the women's locations (the location of the shelters is generally unknown), thereby destroying the confidence and security of the victim.

Several trends were observed at the various shelters and can be said to be generally applicable to women victims of domestic violence. Women:

- Stay one week to one month
- Are generally of East Indian or African descent
- Are young mothers up to age forty
- Are of all religious backgrounds
- Bring at least two children
- Are in a common-law relationship
- Are unemployed and/or unskilled
- Have a history of abuse

There also tend to be more women seeking shelter between November and February. This increase is directly related to the seasons of Christmas and Carnival when excessive alcoholic intake and expenditure take place.

6.5 CONCLUSION

The level of financing for gender issues generally, and domestic violence specifically, reflects the failure of the State to treat meaningfully with women's rights. The poor level of funding is exacerbated by the fact of government's recognition of the problem of domestic violence. State institutions meant to support the battle against domestic violence can be accused of not being sufficiently sensitive to the issue. While, to some extent, the magistracy is hindered by legislation that reflects the bias of the male elite that was responsible for its passage in Parliament, much more can be done to make the existing legal regime more workable.

The police service, the other major State institution, is also male dominated and the attitude of the police exemplifies the male bias. Police officers are known to abuse their spouses as well. It is difficult for such a victim to make a report, as the matter tends to be immediately reported to the abuser which translates into more abuse for her. How, then, should she seek assistance? In other instances, the police response tends to be poor, as they feel that the women waste their time. This is largely due to the fact that the majority of women eventually plead on the men's behalf to have them released or they leave the shelters to which they were police-escorted to return to the men. When women come to the station, the police officers repeatedly ask whether they are sure they want to file the report for fear of what they feel would be the inevitable response from the complainant which would result in a waste of time and effort. There was one anomalous instance of an upper-class woman who filed a report at the police station and when her father found out, he "had the file destroyed" by a friend at the station.

Another problem is the fact that police officers seem to take advantage of female victims of domestic violence. Some people interviewed stated that women get involved with the officers to expedite matters. In one particular case, a battered woman, after going to the police station, was escorted home by two officers to collect some personal belongings and the male police officer made unsolicited advances towards her. With no one else to turn to, this put the woman in a very difficult situation. She was able to keep him at bay but he became very hostile towards her.

That aside, the apathy and hesitancy on the part of police officers point to something serious—not simply dismissal of domestic violence as between husband and wife. The women themselves appear to be confused. They flee for their lives and then beg for the men not to be harmed and to be released. It is understandable why the officers would take the approach that they do, but certainly does not justify it. They have a duty to serve and to protect and should take that seriously.

The non-State actors, namely the NGOs, have also suffered, due to their reliance on the State for driving the forces necessary to address domestic violence. There remains very little evidence of these groups seeking to take control of the domestic violence agenda to ensure meaningful change in society with respect to how the issue is addressed. The dominant role played by research and advocacy groups remains the effort towards legislative reform. Having regard to the fact that the legislative agenda is controlled by the male elite, it is hardly surprising that the legal regime for addressing domestic violence is of limited effect. Chapter five discussed many of the deficiencies in the *Domestic Violence Act* and discussions on the magistracy and the police contained in Sections 6.3.1 and 6.3.3 respectively of this chapter further illustrate the problems inherent in the legal regime for addressing domestic violence.

It has been noted that many of the women who seek help, in fact, fall within the lower socioeconomic bracket. Domestic violence, however, knows no class or race boundaries. Anecdotal evidence suggests that even up to the ministerial level and in affluent neighbourhoods abuse occurs. This information is, therefore, quite telling. Moreover, there are male victims of domestic violence, but the reported numbers are few. One interviewee observed that male battering appears to be a new trend, but shame and pride prevent reports from being made. The NGOs that provide support services are limited by the availability of financial resources. These NGOs, by and large, depend on external sources for financial resources and the male-dominated State governance apparatus has not shown any great inclination to treat domestic violence with the seriousness it deserves, as illustrated in Section 6.2 of this chapter by the level of funding directed to gender issues generally and domestic violence specifically. One issue that illustrates the limitations of support services provided by NGOs pertains to the provision of counselling. It was raised several times in interviews that many of the counsellors available at the various NGOs are not properly trained in the field of counselling. They are trained in psychology and/or social work and are allowed to provide "counselling" services to the abused. This is not to diminish in any way the services they provide, as social work provides a different but equally important form of assistance. Counselling specifically requires special training and skills which are not necessarily provided by the courses taken in psychology or social work. There are, in fact, some professional therapists that volunteer their time to some of the NGOs once to twice a week. There are many professionals in private practice who are eminently qualified in counselling, but this is a paid service and not readily accessed. The male elite driven State has not seen it fit (yet) to place some of these counsellors on a retainer to counsel a certain number of victims per month who are unable to pay for the service but need it.

It would appear that leaving an abuser is not as easy as deciding to leave after the first instance of abuse. Some stay for the benefit of the children who are clothed and fed; others stay because they believe that abuse in a relationship is acceptable; while yet others stay because they were there during the tough times and helped make him a success and do not wish for someone else to benefit from that sacrifice. Some interviewees cited the "male dependency syndrome," where women believe that they need a man to define them or simply feel that they cannot live without him. Apart from emotional dependency, there is financial dependency either because she is unskilled and cannot find employment or, surprisingly, because she is lazy and does not *wish* to work and desires to maintain a certain lifestyle. One woman from an affluent home decided to take the abuse because, if she left, she would no longer be able to drive the Mercedes Benz her abusive husband bought for her. These tough choices…

The fact remains that the NGOs that provide shelters are in need of proper funding, not just to house persons that are the victims of domestic violence but also entire families. Moreover, women who elect to leave situations of domestic violence need expert psychological assistance and job training to develop the means to be independent of the abuser. For a shelter to fulfil these needs, they either turn to the State where funding is derisory, or to private corporate citizens that are also managed by the male elite. In both instances, the true needs of the victims are not met and this is perhaps why the available shelters would appear to be underutilised. In addition, an important point was made that, when women seek shelter, they sometimes have nowhere to go when they leave, mostly due to financial problems. This issue of post-shelter housing and a support system to help monitor women's progress, or simply provide assistance along the way, seems to be lacking.

The emerging picture of an institutional framework for addressing domestic violence in TT is not pretty. The State institutions are poorly equipped and funded to deal with domestic violence; this is a mere reflection of TT's lack of concern with the "softer" issues, such as protection of women. Further, the reliance of the non-state institutions on State *largesse* to achieve their objectives of protection of women from domestic violence would appear to be misguided. The situation in TT necessarily points to the need for women to seek to understand their peculiar role in protecting their vulnerable sisters from domestic violence and to seek to find the solutions from within their sphere of power, rather than rely on a post-colonial male elite.

Having examined the domestic attitude of TT to domestic violence, both legally and institutionally, it is important to review the behaviour of TT at the international and regional levels with respect to the issue of domestic violence, so as to ascertain whether there is consistency of behaviour or whether TT expounds one set of principles at the international stage but practices another at the domestic level.

NOTES

1. See Republic of Trinidad and Tobago, *Public Sector Investment Programme 2005* (Port of Spain, Trinidad: Ministry of Planning and Development and Ministry of Finance, 2004), 1.
2. Republic of Trinidad and Tobago, *Public Sector Investment Programme 2002* (Port of Spain, Trinidad: Ministry of Finance, 2001), 3.
3. Republic of Trinidad and Tobago, *Public Sector Investment Programme 1998/1999* (Port of Spain, Trinidad: Ministry of Finance, 1998), 33 and 74. US$1.00 = TT$6.30.
4. See ibid., 53.
5. Republic of Trinidad and Tobago, *Public Sector Investment Programme 1999/2000* (Port of Spain, Trinidad: Ministry of Finance, 1999), 39.
6. Ibid., 57.
7. Republic of Trinidad and Tobago, *Public Sector Investment Programme 2001* (Port of Spain, Trinidad: Ministry of Finance, 2000), 40.
8. Republic of Trinidad and Tobago, *PSIP 2002*, 41.
9. It is not clear "at risk" of what.
10. Republic of Trinidad and Tobago, *Public Sector Investment Programme 2003* (Port of Spain, Trinidad: Ministry of Planning and Development, 2002), 1.
11. Ibid., 43.

12. Republic of Trinidad and Tobago, *Public Sector Investment Programme 2004* (Port of Spain, Trinidad: Ministry of Planning and Development, 2003), 54–55.

13. Republic of Trinidad and Tobago, *Public Sector Investment Programme—Tobago 2004* (Port of Spain, Trinidad: Ministry of Planning and Development, 2003), 19.

14. Republic of Trinidad and Tobago, *PSIP 2005*, 73.

15. Ibid., 71.

16. Ibid., 74.

17. Ibid., 152–159.

18. Republic of Trinidad and Tobago, *Public Sector Investment Programme 2006* (Port of Spain, Trinidad: Ministry of Planning and Development and Ministry of Finance, 2005), 73.

19. Republic of Trinidad and Tobago, *Social Sector Investment Programme 2007* (Port of Spain, Trinidad: Government of the Republic of Trinidad and Tobago, 2006), 9 and 67.

20. Republic of Trinidad and Tobago, *Public Sector Investment Programme 2011* (Port of Spain, Trinidad: Ministry of Finance, 2010), 120.

21. Ibid., 106.

22. Senator The Honourable Joan Yuille-Williams, *Appropriation Bill (Budget)*, Senate, Friday October 14, 2005, 435.

23. Ministry of Community Development, Culture and Gender Affairs, *Draft National Gender Policy and Action Plan* (Port of Spain, Trinidad: Ministry of Community Development, Culture and Gender Affairs, 2005), 4.

24. See ibid., 69–71 and 71–72.

25. See ibid., 76–78.

26. Senator The Honourable Joan Yuille-Williams, *Appropriation Bill (Budget)*, Senate, Thursday October 23, 2003, 334.

27. The Honourable Eulalie James, *Appropriation Bill (Budget)*, Senate, Friday October 15, 2004, 582.

28. See Government of the Republic of Trinidad and Tobago, *Vision 2020: Draft National Strategic Plan*, 168–172.

29. Ministry of Community Development, *Draft National Gender Policy*, 94, 81.

30. The Honourable Prime Minister Patrick Manning, *Budget Presentation 2006*, Wednesday 28 September 2005, 25. Emphasis added.

31. Republic of Trinidad and Tobago, *Social Sector Investment Programme 2011* (Port of Spain, Trinidad: Government of the Republic of Trinidad and Tobago, 2010), 45. Its current status, at the date of publication of this text, remains unchanged.

32. Ministry of Community Development, Culture and Gender Affairs, *Draft National Policy on Gender and Development of the Republic of Trinidad and Tobago* (Port of Spain, Trinidad: Ministry of Community Development, Culture and Gender Affairs, 2009), 5 and 34. Emphasis in the original.

33. Ibid., 34.

34. Ibid., 35–36.

35. The purpose of including gender in this Ministry was to ensure gender mainstreaming in the general planning process.

36. Ministry of Community Development, *Draft National Gender Policy*, 21.

37. Ministry of the Attorney General and Legal Affairs, *Initial, Second and Third Periodic Report of the Republic of Trinidad and Tobago* (Port of Spain, Trinidad: Ministry of the Attorney General and Legal Affairs, 2000), CEDAW/C/TTO/1–3, 25.

38. Brief history of the Division taken from Ministry of Community Development, *Draft National Gender Policy*, 17–18.

39. Ministry of Community Development, Culture and Gender Affairs, "National Gender Policy and Action Plan," 2006, accessed 02 April 2007, http://www.cdcga.gov.tt/progs/genderpolicy.php.

40. Ministry of Community Development, Culture and Gender Affairs, "About the Gender Affairs Division," 2006, accessed 02 April 2007, http://www.cdcga.gov.tt/ga/aboutgender.php. Revised objectives are taken from Gender Affairs Division, Ministry of Planning, Economic and Social Restructuring and Gender Affairs, "Overview of the Gender Affairs Division," 2009, accessed 18 July 2011, http://genderaffairs-tt.net/.

41. All taken from Ministry of Community Development, Culture and Gender Affairs, "Programmes and Initiatives," 2006, accessed 02 April 2007, http://www.cdcga.gov.tt/ga/genderprog.php. Information on the descriptions of the selected programmes below is also from this source.

42. Revised objectives are taken from Gender Affairs Division, Ministry of Planning, Economic and Social Restructuring and Gender Affairs, "Overview of the Gender Affairs Division." 2009. Information on the descriptions of the selected programmes below is also from this source.

43. Ministry of Community Development, Culture and Gender Affairs, "National Domestic Violence Hotline: Report for the period 01.10.05 to 30.09.06." (Port of Spain: Ministry of Development, Culture and Gender Affairs, 2006).

44. Taken from Domestic Violence Unit, Division of Gender Affairs, Ministry of Community Development, Culture and Gender Affairs, *Report on Policy Round Table on Domestic Violence in Trinidad and Tobago*, 26 February 1999, 5; Ministry of Social Development, *A Guide to Social Programmes and Services* (Port of Spain, Trinidad: Ministry of Social Development, 2005), 66. Attempts to arrange interviews were repeatedly cancelled, so dated information was all that was available and the links on the ministry's website returned error pages. This information is correct at July 2007.

45. Information taken from a brochure prepared by the Ministry of Social Development about the National Family Services Division.

46. Taken from Domestic Violence Unit, *Report on Policy Round Table*, 6–7; Ministry of Social Development, *A Guide to Social Programmes and Services*, 68.

47. Republic of Trinidad and Tobago, *PSIP 2006*, Appendix III, 132.

48. Republic of Trinidad and Tobago, *PSIP 2011*, 97–99.

49. Taken from Ministry of Community Development, *Draft National Gender Policy*, 22. It is now known as the Gender Department. See Ministry of Community Development, *Draft National Policy on Gender and Development*, 58.

50. Correct as at March 2007.

51. According to section 2 of the *Summary Courts Act* (Chap. 4:20), a "“Court" or "Summary Court," or "Court of summary jurisdiction," unless the same is expressly or by implication qualified, means any Magistrate or Justice when sitting in open Court to hear and determine any matters within his power and jurisdiction, either under this Act or any other written law, and such Magistrate or Justice when so sitting aforesaid shall be and be deemed a "Court" or "Summary Court" or "Court of summary jurisdiction" within the meaning of this Act."

52. Judiciary of the Republic of Trinidad and Tobago, *Annual Report 2005–2006* (Port of Spain, Trinidad: Judiciary of the Republic of Trinidad and Tobago, 2006), 4.

53. Ibid., 5.

54. See Judiciary of the Republic of Trinidad and Tobago, *Annual Report 2006–2007* (Port of Spain, Trinidad: Judiciary of the Republic of Trinidad and Tobago, 2007).

55. Correct as at March 2007.

56. Michèle Alexandre, "Dance Halls, Masquerades, Body Protest and the Law: The Female Body as a Redemptive Tool against Trinidad's Gender-Biased Laws," *Duke Journal of Gender Law and Policy* 13 (2006): 192.

57. See Mindie Lazarus-Black, "The Rite of Domination: Tales from Domestic Violence Court," Working Paper No. 7, (Centre for Gender and Development Studies, The University of the West Indies: St. Augustine, Trinidad, 2002).

58. Judiciary of the Republic of Trinidad and Tobago, *Annual Report 2004–2005* (Port of Spain, Trinidad: Judiciary of the Republic of Trinidad and Tobago, 2005), 12–13. There have been three versions of a Family Court Bill in 2001, 2007 and 2009, each of which lapsed and, therefore, the intended act has never been enacted. See Parliament of the Republic of Trinidad and Tobago, "Bills," accessed 19 July 2011, http://www.ttparliament.org/publications.php?mid=28. This act would have given full jurisdiction to the Family Court over matters concerning the *Domestic Violence Act*.

59. Information taken from a brochure prepared by the Family Court of Trinidad and Tobago.

60. Family Court of Trinidad and Tobago, *Family Court Evaluation: First Year Report* (Port of Spain, Trinidad: Family Court of Trinidad and Tobago, 2005), 1.

61. Judiciary of the Republic of Trinidad and Tobago, *Annual Report 08–09* (Port of Spain, Trinidad: Judiciary of the Republic of Trinidad and Tobago, 2009), 125.

62. Inspector Glen Hackett, *Interview with author*, Port of Spain, Trinidad, 16 March 2007.

63. Ramesh Deosaran, *The Dynamics of Community Policing: Theory, Practice and Evaluation* (St. Augustine, Trinidad: Centre for Criminology and Criminal Justice, 2000), 32.

64. See ibid., 117, 204.

65. Ibid., 204.

66. Trinidad and Tobago Police Service, "Departments," updated 2009, accessed 19 July 2011, http://www.ttps.gov.tt/AboutTTPS/Departments/tabid/65/Default.aspx.

67. Deosaran, *The Dynamics of Community Policing*, 204.

68. See Seuraj, "Carmona: Women under siege in this country."

69. See for example, Keino Swamber, "Wife pleads but husband lands in jail." *Saturday Express*, 04 February 2006, accessed 11 April 2007, http://www.trinidadexpress.com/index.pl/article_news?id=133510992. "A woman's pleas to a High Court Judge to spare her common-law husband a jail term failed on Thursday after she said the man was physically and verbally abusive to her during their seven-year relationship."

70. Natalie Diop, Legal Officer, *Interview with author*, Port of Spain, Trinidad, 12 February 2007. Further information also available from pamphlet prepared by the Ministry of Legal Affairs on the Legal Aid and Advisory Authority. Currently (2007), at the Tobago office, domestic violence matters are without Legal Aid representation as Attorneys at Law are refusing to accept legal aid matters.

71. These figures are slightly higher than what is found in the *Legal Aid and Advice Act* (Chap. 7:07) where both the disposable capital and income are not to exceed USD$714.00. The definition of disposable income was amended by the *Legal Aid and Advice (Amendment) Act*, No. 18 of 1999 but does not offer a ceiling under which disposable income must stay for eligibility.

72. Detailed descriptions of each NGO discussed in section 6.4 are available in Persadie, "A Critical Analysis," Appendix C, 352–377.

73. This is due to non-response from unwillingness to be interviewed so the information used is dated (true in the case of one NGO) and where literature on the organisation was not available and, therefore, not included at all (true in the case of one NGO). This information is correct as at July 2007.

74. Imran Ali, "San Juan man gets 12 years for killing wife," *Saturday Express*, 12 November 2005, accessed 28 March 2007, http://www.trinidadexpress.com/index.pl/article_news?id=115329965.

75. Keino Swamber, "Guilty of killing wife: sentencing today," *Trinidad Express*, 17 November 2005, accessed 28 March 2007, http://www.trinidadexpress.com/index.pl/article_news?id=116629552.

76. See section 5 of the *Sexual Offences Act*, No. 27 of 1986—now repealed.

77. Email communication between Donald Berment and Bert Hoff, 15 October 2003.

Chapter Seven

Trinidad and Tobago and Domestic Violence— The International Response

7.1 INTRODUCTION: INTERNATIONAL CONTEXT

Trinidad and Tobago has illustrated some degree of commitment in dealing with the issue of violence against women, especially with respect to the passage and amendment of legislation and discussions on accepting a national policy on gender (and development). Nevertheless, these legislative changes seemed only to come about after extensive and unwavering lobbying by various interest groups and the policy remains a working, yet-to-be finalised document reflecting the true intent of those in authority. Furthermore, the financial commitment seems to be sorely lacking on the part of government and is reflective of the priority given to the issue at hand. This chapter will examine what TT has committed to internationally and regionally, with respect to dealing with domestic violence, to gauge the consistency of its international attitude with its domestic agenda.

7.2 INTERNATIONAL LEGAL INSTRUMENTS

7.2.1 Convention on the Elimination of All Forms of Discrimination Against Women

One of the most important international conventions on women's issues was the Convention on the Elimination of All Forms of Discrimination Against Women ("CEDAW"), held in 1979. TT signed the convention in 1985 and ratified it in 1990. As a party to the convention, TT was expected to submit to the Secretary-General of the UN, within one year after the entry into force for

TT, pursuant to Article 18, "a report on the legislative, judicial, administrative or other measures" adopted to give effect to the provisions of the convention. Particular reference is made by the Committee to the inclusion of information and data on violence against women. As mentioned in chapter three above, TT is, regrettably, one of those delinquent States and only submitted its combined *initial, second and third* periodic report in January 2001,[1] even though it ratified the convention 11 years earlier.[2] Its fourth and fifth periodic reports were due on 17 February 2003 and 2007 respectively but have not yet been submitted.[3] The government representative stated as the reason for the delay in submitting the 2003 report that "no mechanism existed to deal with reporting under international human rights treaties and insufficient resources had been allocated for that purpose."[4] Insufficient resources result in inaction at many levels on many issues and are certainly reflective of government's position with respect to violence against women. Important, however, was one of the Committee's many concerns that "despite innovative legislation, policies and programmes, violence against women remains a serious reality that is being perpetuated by deeply rooted traditional patriarchal attitudes, apparently tolerated by society" and also that these "constitute obstacles to the full implementation of the Convention."[5]

Admittedly, CEDAW does not once mention the word "violence" in the text of the document. Nevertheless, at its eleventh session in 1992, the Committee made clear the connection between discrimination against women and gender-based violence, recognising that the former can only be eliminated in tandem with eradication of the latter, as the definition of discrimination implicitly includes gender-based violence.[6] The Committee also recognised that "family violence is one of the most insidious forms of violence against women."[7] With this in mind, the Committee urged TT in its report

> to place a high priority on measures to address violence against women in the family and in society in accordance with the Committee's general recommendation 19 and the Declaration on the Elimination of Violence against Women. The Committee recommends that the State party introduce further measures to raise public awareness about violence against women and urges the State party to strengthen its activities and programmes to focus on sexual violence, incest and prostitution.[8]

The Gender Affairs Division is currently[9] working on the combined fourth and fifth periodic report for submission to the Committee which were due on 17 February 2003 and 17 February 2007 respectively.

With respect to the Optional Protocol, TT indicated that it was not considering accession to it.[10]

7.2.2 Declaration on the Elimination of Violence Against Women

As stated in chapter three, the Declaration on the Elimination of Violence Against Women ("DEVAW") was adopted by the General Assembly on 20 December 1993. According to the draft Gender Policy, TT signed/adopted the declaration in 1994. There is very little in the way of national policy, legal or administrative action to suggest that TT has done anything major in line with this declaration. Steps were taken to amend the *Domestic Violence Act* and the *Sexual Offences Act* to afford greater power to women, but this was not accompanied by the necessary institutional capacity building to make them effective enough. Selected members of the police service and the judiciary received training to increase their awareness of the issue but this, too, did not seem to have had the desired effect, as chapter six above clearly illustrated. Moreover, it would appear that it was the local NGO movement that made these advances possible and was not necessarily directly attributable to the declaration.

7.2.3 The Beijing Declaration and Platform for Action

In 1995, the Women Affairs Division, as it was then, prepared a report for the Fourth World Conference on Women. It again recognised the problem of domestic violence and reported that steps were being taken to address the issue, such as the increase in the number of support services for both victims and perpetrators, and the commencement of male outreach programmes.[11] The report recognised the need for increased research on the relationship between gender-based violence and male dominance in the national context; sensitisation of the judiciary, police, health and other professionals with whom victims of domestic violence have contact; and greater and strengthened support services and outreach programmes specifically targeting men and boys.[12] It also noted that domestic violence has the tacit acceptance of society as a part of life.[13] Legislative changes did not seem to have the intended effect of curbing the problem and support services, even though increasing in number, were still insufficient.[14]

The Beijing Declaration and Platform for Action was adopted unanimously by all countries that took part, TT included. In June 2000, the then Minister of Culture and Gender Affairs, Senator the Honourable Daphne Phillips, presented a progress report on TT's actions and initiatives post-Beijing.[15] She reported on ten areas in which action was taken, one of them being violence against women. She spoke of amendments to legislation, the establishment of the Domestic Violence Unit, and other work undertaken by the Gender Affairs Division. She ended the statement by speaking of the challenges involved in realising the goals of the Beijing Platform for Action, which included inadequate human and financial resources. In TT's response to a questionnaire on the implementation of the Beijing Platform for Action, more specific constraints included:[16]

- Financial resources: the budgetary allocation of the Gender Affairs Division is inadequate to ideally implement and execute projects and programmes.
- Human resources: extra technical and administrative staff is needed to ideally carry out the increased work load of the division.
- Limited information sharing: in terms of intra-agency information.
- Lack of disaggregated data: data from most sectors are not disaggregated.
- The absence of a fully operationalised Inter-Ministerial Committee: the current membership is positioned at varying levels of authority in their respective ministries and this affects their ability to influence policy.
- Ineffective ways of collaboration: there is a need to develop more effective ways of collaboration with NGOs intersectorally.

7.3 REGIONAL LEGAL INSTRUMENTS

7.3.1 Inter-American Convention on the Prevention, Punishment, and Eradication of Violence Against Women

The Inter-American Convention on the Prevention, Punishment, and Eradication of Violence Against Women (Convention of Belém do Pará) was adopted in June 1994 and signed and ratified by TT in November 1995 and January 1996 respectively. This was an initiative of the Inter-American Commission of Women ("CIM"), a specialised organisation of the Organization of American States, which is the principal forum for generating hemispheric policy to advance women's rights and gender equality.[17] Established in 1928 at the Sixth International Conference of American States (Havana, Cuba), the CIM was the first official intergovernmental agency in the world created expressly to ensure recognition of the civil and political rights of women. As such, it has played a crucial role in making the participation and support of women a legitimate and indispensable part of governance and international consensus-building in the Americas.

In 1986, the CIM began an analysis of violence against women, which was followed by the 1990 Inter-American Consultation on Women and Violence, at which it thoroughly examined the topic of violence against women and the feasibility of drafting an inter-American convention on the subject.[18] Emerging from this was the 1994 Convention of Belém do Pará, the first ever treaty instrument dealing with violence against women, and a subsequent strategic plan of action presented at Beijing, which dealt with violence against women as one of ten major areas.

In 2001, the CIM commissioned a report on violence in the Americas, which examined national programs of ten Caribbean countries designed to deal with implementation of the convention. With respect to TT, it mentioned government initiatives taken since ratification of the convention. This included the strengthening of the National Domestic Violence Unit, support services and legislative provisions, as well as data collection (including the commencement of gender-disaggregated data) and sensitisation training for those in direct contact with victims of domestic violence.[19] The report questioned the institutional capacity to properly support legislative changes, such as the ability of the court to enforce protection orders.[20] This is a problem which continues today. The authors of the report note quite correctly that

> the implementation of the Convention of Belém do Pará has progressed very slowly in all of the Caribbean countries reviewed. Efforts to prevent, punish and eradicate violence against women in the Caribbean have concentrated on piecemeal legal reform, initiatives to raise public awareness of the issue, and initiatives to sensitise and train local officials. The provision of emergency services to victims of domestic violence, such as a hotline or some form of crisis intervention, and the establishment of shelters for women threatened by domestic violence were responsibilities largely left to the private and volunteer sectors.... Some emphasis has been placed on offering training and education to the officials and professionals on whom victims of gender-based violence must rely for protection, help, information, financial assistance, and redress. These initiatives, unfortunately, were rarely sustained....
>
> Social attitudes and cultural practices have also created powerful obstacles that have tended to be ignored at least as often as they were confronted. Governments have relied very heavily on nongovernmental organizations and women's groups to offer the most basic level of support and assistance to women victims of violence. However, they have done so in ways that often ignore the fact that these organizations are themselves relying totally on their limited ability to raise their own funding and to recruit volunteers.[21]

As a member of the Organization of American States, TT submitted its third national biennial report to the Inter-American Commission of Women in August 2006 dealing with seven areas of relevance, one of which dealt with violence against women. This section mentioned the establishment of the domestic violence unit, the 24-hour hotline and the development of a systematic format for domestic violence data collection.[22] Unfortunately, the above analysis of the status of the implementation of the Convention of Belém do Pará remains true still.

7.3.2 Charter of Civil Society for the Caribbean Community

At a Conference of Heads of Government of the Caribbean Community at their Special Meeting in Port-of-Spain, Trinidad and Tobago, in October 1992, the various governments adopted the recommendation of the West Indian Commission that a Charter of Civil Society for the Caribbean Community be subscribed to by Member States of the Community.[23] This "oft-forgotten Regional instrument"[24] was adopted on 19 February 1997[25] by member countries of Caricom, Trinidad and Tobago included, and seeks "to ensure continuing respect for internationally recognised civil, political, economic, social and cultural rights," as well as to "respect the fundamental human rights and freedoms of the individual without distinction as to age, colour, creed, disability, ethnicity, gender, language, place of birth or origin, political opinion, race, religion or social class." Article XII, in particular, deals with the "promotion of policies and measures aimed at strengthening gender equality" and states categorically that "all women have equal rights with men in the political, civil, economic, social and cultural spheres." Sub-article (d) provides for "legal protection including just and effective remedies against domestic violence, sexual abuse and sexual harassment."

While specific mention is made of the right of women to legal protection and effective remedies against domestic violence, it would appear that the existence of the Charter is not well known, therefore, application of the principles by signatory countries is unlikely. Moreover, there is no documentation to suggest that it has been taken into account.

7.4 CONCLUSION

Several observations can be made about the conduct of TT at the international level, three of which are important here. TT takes a long time to officially accept international law addressing gender issues, such as reflected in its eleven-year delay to ratify CEDAW, which is the primary international legal instrument seeking to address gender issues. It must be noted, however, that TT showed a greater sense of alacrity in ratifying the Convention of Belém do Pará and adopting the Charter of Civil Society for the Caribbean Community. After accepting its international obligations by ratification of the international instrument, it lags behind in its reporting duties, as again illustrated by its conduct towards the implementation of CEDAW. The first report was due in 1991 and was submitted in 2002 as a combined initial, second and third report, while the fourth and fifth reports were originally due in 1995 and 1999. No further reports have yet been submitted by TT. At the national level, no real attempt has been made to enact the international obligations contained in CEDAW in domestic law, thereby denying women the benefit of having those provisions enacted. CEDAW remains of no legal effect as it must be incorporated into national statutory law. It is a fair conclusion that the malaise displayed by TT at the domestic level is certainly mirrored in its international behaviour and *vice versa*.

NOTES

1. See UN, General Assembly, "Report of the Committee on the Elimination of Discrimination against Women."
2. See UN DAW, "States Parties."
3. See UN, Secretary-General, "Status of submission of Reports," Annex I, 12. See also UN, General Assembly, "Report of the Committee," A/65/38, 90.
4. General Assembly, "Report," Paragraph 121.
5. Ibid., Paragraphs 145 and 135 respectively.
6. The Committee, *General Recommendation No. 19*, (11th session, 1992), paras 4 and 6.
7. Ibid., para. 23.
8. General Assembly, Paragraph 146, "Report."
9. May 2007.
10. See UN, Committee on the Elimination of Discrimination Against Women, *Committee on the Elimination of Discrimination Against Women Concludes Consideration of Trinidad and Tobago Report*, (Press Release) WOM/1316, 26th Session, 547th Meeting, 29 January 2002.
11. Ministry of Community Development, Culture and Women's Affairs, "National Report on Status of Women in Trinidad and Tobago," August 1995, presented at the Fourth World Conference on Women, Beijing, China, September 1995, 4.
12. Ibid., 7–8.
13. Ibid., 32.
14. Ibid., 60–61.
15. Senator the Honourable Dr. Daphne Phillips, Minister of Culture and Gender Affairs (as she then was), "Statement to the Twenty-Third Special Session of the General Assembly entitled "Women 2000: gender equality, development and peace for the twenty-first century,"" at the United Nations General Assembly, New York, 6 June 2000, accessed 30 April 2007, http://www.un.org/womenwatch/daw/followup/beijing+5stat/statments/trinidad6.htm.
16. UN, Division for the Advancement of Women, "Replies to Questionnaire on the Implementation of the Beijing Platform for Action: Trinidad and Tobago," 02 June 1999, accessed 30 April 2007, http://www.un.org/womenwatch/daw/followup/responses/trinidad.html.
17. Organisation of American States, Inter-American Commission of Women, "Who we are," 2000, accessed 02 May 2007, http://www.oas.org/cim/English/About.htm.

18. Organisation of American States, Inter-American Commission of Women, "Strategic Plan of Action of the Inter-American Commission of Women," 2000, accessed 02 May 2007, http://www.oas.org/cim/English/Strategic Plan.htm.

19. Vivienne Chin and Yvon Dandurand, *Violence in the Americas: A Regional Analysis. National Programs to Prevent, Punish and Eradicate Violence Against Women in Ten Caribbean Countries* (San Jose: ILANUD, 2001), 11–12.

20. Ibid., 31.

21. Ibid., 61.

22. Gender Affairs Division, "National Report… Inter-American Commission of Women."

23. Caribbean Community (CARICOM) Secretariat, "Charter of Civil Society for the Caribbean Community," updated 2006, accessed 24 August 2007, http://www.caricom.org/jsp/secretariat/legal_instruments/chartercivilsocietyresolution.jsp?menu=secretariat.

24. Désirée Bernard, "Advances made on Gender Equality and Women's Human Rights in the Caribbean Region," 50th Anniversary Commemoration of the United Nations Commission on the Status of Women, United Nations Headquarters, New York, 10 November 2006, 14. Also available from http://www.caribbeancourtofjustice.org/papers_addresses.html.

25. Caribbean Community (CARICOM) Secretariat, "Charter of Civil Society Resolution, 1997," updated 2006. Accessed 24 August 2007, http://www.caricom.org/jsp/secretariat/legal_instruments/chartercivilsociety.jsp.

Chapter Eight

Conclusion

This study sought to examine the effectiveness of law as a tool to achieve gender equality and address the problem of domestic violence in TT. Research has shown that passing legislation alone is clearly not enough, but must be complemented by an effective institutional framework and well-trained human resource component to make implementation and enforcement of the law workable. In the absence of government commitment to provide a comprehensive framework for achieving gender equality and protection of women against domestic violence, there would appear to be very little else that can forge lasting and substantive positive change.

8.1 GENDER EQUALITY AND THE LAW IN TT

The legislative framework of TT ostensibly provides for gender equality. The supreme law, the *Constitution*, provides women a circumscribed right to equality. As mentioned in chapter four, sections 4(b) and (d) ensure the right of the individual to equality before the law and equality of treatment from any public authority in the exercise of its functions in such a capacity. These rights to equality are with specific reference to treatment of individuals by the State and its representatives, but do not guarantee *general* sexual equality, such as equality between men and women at the workplace. Attempting to infer general gender equality from the *Constitution* may prove tricky, given the specifics of Section 4. *Constitution* aside, the general legal framework seems controlling and patronising and lacks the ability to promote gender equality on a broad level. The statutory legal framework for gender seems very much to reflect an elitist attitude on the part of those responsible for creating and enacting the various pieces of legislation. This mirrors what obtained during the colonial period, when laws were enacted to serve the interest of the elite in one way or another. Even current attempts to create equality in law seem to work against women, as laws written with gender neutrality in mind, such as the *Domestic Violence Act*, seem to detract from the importance of the scourge it is attempting to prevent.

8.2 THE ROLE OF NGOS IN TT

The challenges of the legal framework notwithstanding, the role of NGOs in providing assistance to and promoting the protection of women against domestic violence must be recognised. NGOs in TT consist of three major types. The support service groups provide emotional support for dealing with post-violence experiences, although the quality of the support provided has been brought into question. This is certainly not to decry the support that is provided, but, perhaps, with assistance from the State, it could be improved. The second group consists of NGOs that provide shelter to those in fear of their lives from domestic violence. This is an essential facility which, in TT, is largely funded by private individuals. Proper funding from the State would assist in many ways, one of which is housing not only persons who are the victims of domestic violence but also entire families, if necessary. Moreover, many women who elect to leave situations of domestic violence need expert psychological assistance and job training to develop the means to be independent of the abuser. While shelters do provide these, it may not be enough. For a shelter to fulfil these needs, they either turn to the State, where funding is derisory, or to private corporations. In both instances, the true needs of the victims are not met and this is, perhaps, why the available shelters would appear to be underutilised. In addition, when women seek shelter, it would appear that they sometimes have no where to go when they leave, mostly due to financial problems. This issue of post-shelter housing and a support system to help monitor women's progress, or simply provide assistance along the way, seem to be lacking.

The research and advocacy groups have had some success in raising awareness of the problem of domestic violence among the population and in effecting legislative changes in favour of women. These changes were viewed as real victories because they went to the root of male-female relationships to have marital rape and domestic violence officially recognised as problems by the legislature, thereby traversing the public-private divide into the previously-protected realm of the family. In chapter seven, it was noted that TT indicated that it was not considering accession to the Optional Protocol to CEDAW. Perhaps the research and advocacy groups could lobby the TT government to accede to the Protocol. However, would accession to the Protocol assist women in their struggle against gender inequality and domestic violence? It most likely would not, given the government's general response to CEDAW itself. TT is a signatory but has taken no positive steps towards implementing the convention or incorporating it into domestic law. Why would it then take steps to implement the Protocol which provides for specificity with respect to the main convention? Government commitment with respect to women's issues seems to be severely lacking.

It has become obvious that, where the State falls short with respect to promoting women's interests, such as seen with the protection of women against domestic violence, NGOs have featured prominently in filling in these gaps. A study by Alvarez, on several Latin American countries, revealed a trend by States of "sub-contracting" their responsibilities to NGOs, from policy assessment to service delivery.[1] This points to an effective abdication of State responsibility, but the claim of limited or even no resources has given rise to this development. Nevertheless, in TT, NGOs are not even sub-contracted for the roles they play. It simply falls to the NGOs to effect service delivery without recompense. While this has its advantages (such as not being seen as a State pawn and allowing NGOs to be more effective political actors), it means that NGOs perform these services with limited resources, and more specifically, without State support.

8.3 THE COLONIAL LEGACY OF LEGAL ELITISM

The actual national legal and institutional response reflects this lack of commitment, despite the government rhetoric espoused at various forums. Legislative changes at the national level, in favour of women's rights, seemed only to have come about due to the unwavering efforts of support and advocacy groups. Moreover, the general statutory legal framework for gender seems very much to reflect an elitist attitude on the part of those responsible for creating and enacting the various pieces of legislation. This is due, in large part, to TT's colonial legal heritage that witnessed the enactment of laws during the colonial period that served the interest of the ruling elite in one way or another. This elitism has been perpetuated in the post-independence era by replacing class elitism of the former era with gender elitism in the current one. As mentioned earlier, current attempts to create equality in law seem to trivialise issues affecting women, as laws written with gender neutrality in mind, such as the *Domestic Violence Act*, seem to detract from the importance of the scourge it is attempting to prevent. Even though the *Domestic Violence Act* was passed with much fanfare and heralded as a potent weapon to combat abuse of women, it has not quite lived up to such lofty expectations, as it contains many deficiencies that undermine its effectiveness. In addition, the concomitant institutional framework to render the law effective has not been put in place. TT seems to have created a relatively ineffective statutory scheme to combat domestic violence.

8.4 THE INSTITUTIONAL RESPONSE

Institutionally, as mentioned previously, the response seems equally poor. State institutions, such as the Magistracy and the Police Service, are poorly equipped and funded to deal with domestic violence; this is a mere reflection of TT's lack of concern with the "softer" issues, such as protection of women. Government's alleged commitment to dealing with domestic violence is not reflected in the amount of funding made available to State institutions to address the problem in a real way. The necessary human resource training for those who deal directly with women victims of domestic violence has been sporadic at best, causing women to appear to prefer the least possible personally interactive route to protection—applying for a protection order. Insensitivity and apathy on the part of government officials have been general responses; however, this would appear to be due to their experience in dealing with family situations. Unfortunately, women are partially at fault with respect to the institutional response, as they have been known to suffer changes of heart when sentencing and/or jail time comes around for the abuser. While this should in no way negatively affect the institutional response to victims of domestic violence, it certainly presents a real complication. With respect to NGOs, as mentioned earlier, they provide an array of services designed to assist women; however, they, too, are poorly funded and sometimes insensitive to the abused who seek their help. Their reliance on State *largesse*, to achieve their objectives of protection of women from domestic violence, would appear to be misguided. The situation in TT necessarily points to the need for women to seek to understand their peculiar role in protecting their vulnerable sisters from domestic violence and to seek to find the solutions from within their sphere of power, rather than rely on a post-colonial male elite.

These issues appear to permeate all levels. The international legal and institutional response is similar, if not worse than what obtains nationally, given the very nature of the international system of governance. Law created at this level is not binding in the strict sense and implementation and enforcement present their own difficulties. Even gaining consensus on articles for inclusion in treaties is complicated, as participating countries bring their own prejudices to the table. As noted with CEDAW, it has the largest number of reservations entered for an international convention, reflecting States Parties' unwillingness to accept the full scope of obligations contained in the instrument. How, therefore, can international law be deemed a serious means of promoting change at the national level?

Once again, it would appear that, even at the international level, NGOs are largely responsible for the "legal successes" in international law-making with respect to the advancement of women's concerns. In chapter two, it was noted that DEVAW owed its genesis chiefly to the advocacy activities of NGOs. BPFA, a successor to CEDAW, highlighted the growing significance of NGOs as agents of change in the international attitude to women's rights. The unprecedented gathering of over 30,000 NGO representatives, in the unofficial NGO Forum, provided a powerful voice that resonated throughout the official meeting. The institutional efforts of NGOs reflect the "bottom-up" approach, as it includes grass roots NGOs and NGO networks. The very nature of NGOs, where membership is generally exclusive of States, ensures that issues can be ventilated without the constraining influence of States.

While NGOs do have the power to effect change at the international and national levels, the individual domestic context can significantly contribute to or impede the success of such efforts. Risse and Sikkink's model of socialisation, dealt with in chapter three above, seems to offer a possible way around the inherent ineffectiveness of international law, with respect to human rights abuses and issues at the national level. Global civil society has been known to effectively play the naming and shaming game to provoke positive responses at the level of the State. It is important to note, however, that this model applies to highly oppressive and abusive regimes and may not, therefore, be applicable to countries under democratic rule.

TT seems to be one of those countries which will be left unaffected, as it has never been under authoritarian rule. As a developing country, it prioritises the issues placed on the national agenda and human rights / women's rights certainly do not fare well in this regard. Measures have, in fact, been taken to sign and ratify human rights conventions and women-specific conventions and some have even been incorporated into domestic law in one way or another. The problem lies with the lack of political will, which translates into inadequate resources for implementation, monitoring and enforcement procedures. Current political and economic events in TT may be conspiring to work against the fortification of this political will to deal with "softer" legal issues, although, this could be said to be true of TT throughout its post-independence history. TT has a hydrocarbon-based economy and is at this time one of the countries benefiting from record oil prices and the economy is booming. Government attention is, and has always been, therefore, on developing the hydrocarbon sector, as well as the upstream and downstream industries and associated economic growth, with little focus on issues that do not have adverse effects on such growth. Women's rights and domestic violence are not seen as directly relevant to TT's current growth spurt and will therefore continue to be marginalised as a policy issue. Having a female Prime Minister has not changed the *status quo* in any way. These reasons all contribute to the inefficacy of international law, and even domestic law, to forge positive and sustained changes in women's quest for equal treatment and protection against domestic violence.

8.5 CHALLENGES AT THE LEVEL OF THE UN

The actual UN institutional structure for advancement of women's rights is affected by major obstacles that undermine its ability to foster real and meaningful change. The analysis of the UN system points to the lack of enforcement capabilities regarding State compliance with international legal obligations, such as reporting under CEDAW. Inability to enforce, coupled with budgetary and procedural restrictions, severely fetters UN bodies' capacity for effectiveness. In the absence of the UN's ability to perform enforcement and monitoring functions, however, NGOs have an extremely important role to play here, as they can remind States of their obligations under international law and continue to "persuade" them to give effect to these obligations at the national level. As noted in chapter three, this has been done with positive effects in many States.

8.6 TT'S RESPONSE TO ITS INTERNATIONAL LAW COMMITMENTS

TT's response to international law instruments and its commitment to adhering to such instruments are telling. TT takes a long time to officially accept international law instruments addressing gender issues, such as evidenced by the eleven-year delay in ratifying CEDAW, which is the primary international legal instrument seeking to address gender issues. It seemed, however, to show a greater sense of alacrity in ratifying and adopting regional instruments, such as the Convention of Belém do Pará and the Charter of Civil Society for the Caribbean Community, although nothing came of these either. Even when TT accepted its international obligations by ratifying CEDAW, it showed little real commitment in its reporting duties. The first report was due in 1991 and was submitted in 2002 as a combined initial, second and third report, while the fourth and fifth reports would have been due in 1995 and 1999 respectively. No further reports have yet been submitted by TT. At the national level, no real attempt has been made to enact the international obligations contained in CEDAW in domestic law, thereby denying women the benefit of having those provisions enacted. CEDAW continues to remain of no legal effect, as it must first be incorporated into national statutory law. It is a fair conclusion to make that the malaise displayed by TT at the domestic level is certainly mirrored in its international behaviour and *vice versa*.

8.7 LIMITATIONS OF INTERNATIONAL LAW TO EFFECT CHANGE AT THE NATIONAL LEVEL: THE PROBLEM OF MALE BIAS

The analysis of the international legal and institutional response to women's rights shows limited success. The "top-down" approach, which promotes the use of international law as a mechanism for influencing national behaviour, would appear to find little support for revolutionising the women's rights agenda. The weaknesses of the "top-down" approach must be properly understood if the international community is going to play a meaningful role in promoting and facilitating women's rights.

These poor legal and institutional responses are exacerbated by the fact that an examination of the systems of governance, at the international and national levels, illustrate that they are both inherently masculine in nature. Naturally, legislative frameworks created from within such systems reflect this bias and would also account for the lack of political will in promoting women's issues. While international human rights conventions have evolved over time and, are indeed becoming increasingly inclusive, human rights are not necessarily synonymous with women's rights and have not included the notion of gender; human rights would seem to be the human rights of men. At the international level, this is, perhaps, because early international law was predicated on Western theological notions in which the role of women was accorded little or no significance. That notwithstanding, the situation did not change perceptibly in the Renaissance period when international law assumed a more secular character. This period emphasised the notion of sovereignty and rights, but rights as applicable to men. Continued bias at the level of the State in international law has circumscribed the inclusion of women's rights as part of general human rights discussions. At the national level in TT, such male bias seems to be a direct result of its colonial legal heritage, which bestowed on the legal system an entrenched sense of elitism with gender representing the new category for discrimination.

Within this peculiar post-colonial context, the male elite emerges as the defining influence in the development of the national legal system. The relationship between political representation, power and lack of political will has been borne out by the research conducted. Women in TT are poorly represented in the power structure and limited support is derived from the State in women's attempt to deal with gender issues. This is despite the fact that Trinidad and Tobago currently has a female Prime Minister; her presence at the top of the political power structure has had no effect on women's issues.

In the specific study of domestic violence in TT, as a breach of women's fundamental right and ability to achieve equal treatment before the law, the male bias infuses the legal and institutional regime for addressing this aspect of women's fundamental rights and is translated into the system's inefficient and inadequate nature. It would appear, however, that when women occupy a meaningful place in governance structure, they can certainly strike significant blows against gender inequality.[2] This, however, may not necessarily be the case when women have power in the context of such power being based on strong male support. Indira Gandhi ruled India for many years but did little for promoting the equality of women in India. This is due largely to the fact that she understood the religious and social forces that underlay her power and she was unwilling to threaten such bases, as it would have resulted in her political demise.[3] Perhaps this is the dilemma facing TT's Prime Minister, Mrs Kamla Persad-Bissessar.

8.8 EFFICACY OF LAW AS AN AGENT OF CHANGE

Law, as an agent of change, has not proven quite effective in promoting gender equality or in protecting women against domestic violence in TT, either from efforts at the level of the State or from the regional and international levels. While legislation seems to have been passed and amended, largely through the unwavering efforts of NGOs, the concomitant institutional capacity building and/or strengthening was not forthcoming, thereby nullifying the positive potential of the law; nevertheless, the role of NGOs in effecting change and in providing support should in no way be understated, despite the constraints they face. TT's colonial heritage, however, further exacerbated the problem, as it bequeathed a legal legacy of entrenched class elitism, which provided a ready framework in the post-independence era for the perpetuation of this elitism, this time with a gender slant, where laws tend to be written by and for the elite, with little real reference to a gender perspective. This reflects unequal power relationships at various levels and has translated into a patent lack of political will, creating even more obstacles in women's struggle for gender equality and protection against domestic violence.

The statutory legal framework for gender in TT seems very much to reflect an elitist attitude on the part of those responsible for creating and enacting the various pieces of legislation. This is certainly in keeping with what obtained during the colonial period, when laws were enacted to serve the interest of the elite in one way or another. Some 150 pieces of legislation in the post-colonial era have been cited as having some significant reference to gender; yet, when analysed, they do not lend themselves to the creation of a legal framework that accommodates gender equality in a real manner. This is directly attributable to the fact that the male elite, responsible for enacting legislation, does not take into account the particular needs of women. Feminist legal theory and feminist critical theory were used to expose the masculine nature of law and practice, which create inherent difficulties in trying to achieve gender equality, especially in the absence of legal and institutional reform, as well as offer possible ways of addressing the situation.

More specifically, domestic violence was dealt with as a subset of gender and its treatment in the law provided an important indicator. In TT, domestic violence is largely dominated by the abuse of women. Although data with respect to domestic violence is not sex disaggregated,[4] anecdotal evidence and interviews indicated that the vast majority of orders sought pursuant to the *Domestic Violence Act* are by women. Legislating a system to deal with domestic violence, therefore, should necessarily take these facts into consideration to provide real and effective relief for those whom the act was intended to serve.

Various NGOs were quick to highlight the problems arising from male elitism and male domination. They invariably cited the insensitivity of State personnel who interacted with victims of domestic violence and their inability to be more accommodating. One NGO, in particular, formed support groups to accompany victims to court, as the administration of justice in domestic violence cases seems to have the effect of preserving and promoting gender hierarchies, disempowering complainants, and has even been described as punishment.[5] The Magistrate's Court process is very user-unfriendly to women victims of domestic violence. The Family Court, however, offers a service that might prove much less traumatic, if the court were enabled to allow hearings on domestic violence as a primary matter and not as incidental to family relations.

Nevertheless, the politics of emancipation depends on a legal framework geared towards gender equality, supported by the inclusion of women's voices from within the governance structure. Activists play an equally important, if not greater, role from without, in realising the true emancipatory potential of law. Once activists are able to use their power of "persuasion" and Keck and Sikkink's "accountability politics"[6] to effect legislative change at the national level, they can be said to have partially realised the emancipatory potential of law. Partially, since legislative change requires an effective concomitant institutional framework to give proper effect to the new legal provisions.

8.9 EFFECTING CHANGE

The effectiveness of international law depends on understanding the dynamics of the issue which is the subject of international law. To ensure an international law regime that can deal with a specific problem, it is necessary to understand the elements that may undermine its effectiveness. The attitude of TT, with particular reference to its lack of political will, coloured by patent male bias and its focus on the hydrocarbon sector to the detriment of "softer" (non-economic [read: gender]) issues, amply illustrates why international law may not always have the desired effect at the national level. In understanding such a domestic contextual background, international law makers can anticipate and, possibly, address obstacles to effect successful international law regimes. Moreover, this study also illustrated the very inherently gendered nature of both international relations and international (and domestic) law, which compounds the ability of the international community and domestic governments to even recognise the problem before they can possibly attempt to deal with it.

In light of the government's unwillingness to take up the cause on behalf of women, it stands to reason, therefore, that gender equality and protection against domestic violence, as fundamental human rights, must flow, in no small part, from the struggle of women. Women, particularly from the developing world, must be wary of the "top-down" approach in relying on the international community to provide the necessary impetus for the achievement of gender equality. International conventions have proven to be somewhat myopic. These legal instruments have remained rather restrained in their ability to improve, or even affect, the condition of women and are criticised as representing little more than statements of good intentions on behalf of the parties to the international conventions.[7] Yet, the international trends are predictable, as the majority of nations are developing countries and the real power structure is held, in most cases, by the male elite, even where there are female Heads of State.[8] Trinidad and Tobago is certainly a case in point. Women cannot wholly depend on the international community to gain gender equality; the analysis of the international legal regime and the UN readily demonstrates how limited such reliance can be. Even at the level of the State in developing countries, reliance on the "top-down" approach disappoints. The executive may well enact certain legislative provisions, but if the State does not provide the necessary resources and institutional capacity to implement the law, then it may as well not have enacted the law in the first place.

There must be no fear of dealing with the issue of gender, even where it may delve into the realm of the personal relations between men and women. The difficulty of interfering in an area which has traditionally been outside the scope of State intervention must be overcome. States must take responsibility domestically and internationally for the actions and human rights abuses of private citizens within this private realm.[9] Failing to do so would sanction an approach to gender relations that perpetuates violence towards women, as illustrated by domestic violence.

The situation is admittedly bleak. How to break the cycle of gender inequality and domestic violence? Important to the process are education, from a very early age, to change traditional and (often) discriminatory attitudes; training; legal literacy; adequate gender representation in top policy-making positions; and the provision of resources, financial and otherwise, which, if provided, would indicate political will at the level of the State. This political will can be forced through the application of pressure from above and below. The role of NGOs, again, comes to the fore here, as they have an important role in fostering change and making sure that it is sustainable.

NOTES

1. Sonia Alvarez, "Advocating Feminism: The Latin American NGO Boom," accessed 14 October 2007, http://www.antenna.nl/~waterman/alvarez2.html.
2. See the case of Finland, for example. See Parliament of Finland, "Women Members of Finland's Parliament," 08 March 2006, accessed 25 May 2007, http://www.parliament.fi/efakta/opas/tiedotus/naisede.htm.
3. See for example also Amrita Basu, "Introduction," in *The Challenge of Local Feminisms: Women's Movements in Global Perspectives*, ed. Amrita Basu (Boulder, CO.: Westview Press, 1995), 15, where she states that politicians make platform promises, but ultimately bow to pressures from conservative and religious groups.
4. This does not apply to all data, as data collected by the National Domestic Violence Hotline has been disaggregated into many categories. See, for example, Gender Affairs Division, Ministry of Planning, Economic and Social Restructuring and Gender Affairs, "National Domestic Violence Hotline: Summary Report for period 01.01.08 to 31.12.08," accessed 20 July 2011, http://genderaffairs-tt.net/pdf_docs/2008%20Year-end%20Report.pdf.
5. See Lazarus-Black, "The Rite of Domination," 4, 13, 27.
6. See Keck and Sikkink, *Activists Beyond Borders*, 24–25.
7. Reanda, "Human Rights and Women's Rights," 21.
8. Steans, *Gender and International Relations*, 5.
9. Deutz, "Gender and International Human Rights," 36.

Bibliography

PUBLISHED WORKS

Chapters, Books

Adams, Kirstine, and Andrew Byrnes, ed. *Gender Equality and the Judiciary: Using International Human Rights Standards to Promote the Human Rights of Women and the Girl-child at the National Level.* London: Commonwealth Secretariat, 1999.

Alcoff, Linda. "Cultural Feminism versus Post-Structuralism: The Identity Crisis in Feminist Theory." In Malson, *Feminist Theory in Practice and Process*, 295–326.

Alston, Philip, ed. *The United Nations and Human Rights: A Critical Appraisal*. Oxford: Clarendon Press, 1995.

Antoine, Rose Marie. *Commonwealth Caribbean Law and Legal Systems.* London: Cavendish Publishing Limited, 1999.

Aristotle. *Politics.* Translated by Benjamin Jowett. Whitefish, MT: Kessinger Publishing, 2004.

Arneil, B. *Politics and Feminism.* Malden, MA.: Blackwell, 1999.

Ashworth, Georgina. "The Silencing of Women." In Dunne and Wheeler, *Human Rights in Global Politics*, 259–276.

Assiter, Alison. *Enlightened Women: Modernist Feminism in a Postmodern Age.* London: Routledge, 1996.

Atherton, Margaret. "Feminist Critiques of Cartesianism." In Code, *Encyclopedia of Feminist Theories*, 72.

Barrow, Christine. "Introduction: Defining "woman" in the Law." In Leo-Rhynie, *Gender: A Caribbean Multi-Disciplinary Perspective*, 78–83.

———. "Men, Women and Family in the Caribbean: A Review." In Mohammed, *Gender in Caribbean Development*, 149–163.

Bartlett, Katharine, and Rosanne Kennedy, ed. *Feminist Legal Theory: Readings in Law and Gender.* Boulder, CO.: Westview Press, 1991.

Bartlett, Katharine, and Rosanne Kennedy. "Introduction." In Bartlett, *Feminist Legal Theory*, 1–14.

Basu, Amrita. "Globalizing Local Women's Movements." In *Localizing Knowledge in a Globalizing World: Recasting the Area Studies Debate*, edited by Ali Mirsepassi, Amrita Basu and Frederick Weaver, 82–100. Syracuse, NY: Syracuse University Press, 2003.

Basu, Amrita. "Introduction." In *The Challenge of Local Feminisms: Women's Movements in Global Perspectives*, edited by Amrita Basu, 1–21. Boulder, CO.: Westview Press, 1995.

Baylis, John, and Steve Smith, ed. *The Globalization of World Politics: An Introduction to International Relations*. New York: Oxford University Press, 1997.

de Beauvoir, Simone. *The Second Sex*. Translated and edited by H. M. Parshley. London: Vintage, 1997.

Beckles, Hilary. "Taking liberties: enslaved women and anti-slavery in the Caribbean." In Midgley, *Gender and Imperialism*, 137–157.

Bell, Christine. "Women's rights as Human Rights: Old Agenda in New Guises." In Hegarty, *Human Rights*, 139–154.

Benedek, Wolfgang, Esther Kisaakye and Gerd Oberleitner, ed. *Human Rights of Women: International Instruments and African Experiences.* London: Zed Books, 2002.

Benhabib, Seyla. "Feminism and the Question of Postmodernism." In *Situating the Self*, 203–241.

———. *Situating the Self: Gender, Community and Postmodernism in Contemporary Ethics.* Oxford: Polity Press, 1992.

———. "The Generalized and the Concrete Other." In *Situating the Self*, 148–177.

Beveridge, Fiona, and Siobhan Mullally. "International Human Rights and Body Politics." In *Law and Body Politics: Regulating the Female Body*, edited by Jo Bridgeman and Susan Millns, 240–272. Aldershot: Dartmouth, 1995.

Bhandar, Davina. "Citizenship." In Code, *Encyclopedia of Feminist Theories*, 88–89.

Birnie, Patricia, and Alan Boyle. *International Law and the Environment*. Oxford: Clarendon Press, 1992.

Blumenfeld-Kosinski, Renate, ed. *The Selected Writings of Christine de Pizan.* Translated by Renate Blumenfeld-Kosinski and Kevin Brownlee. New York: W.W. Norton & Company, 1997.

Booth, Ken. "Three Tyrannies." In Dunne and Wheeler, *Human Rights in Global Politics*, 31–70.

Bordo, Susan. "Feminism, Postmodernism, and Gender-Scepticism." In Nicholson, *Feminism/Postmodernism*, 133–156.

Bottomley, Anne, ed. *Feminist Perspectives on the Foundational Subjects of Law.* London: Cavendish Publishing Limited, 1996.

Boxill, Eileen. "The Reform of Family Law as it affects Women." In Leo-Rhynie, *Gender: A Caribbean Multi-Disciplinary Perspective*, 91–105.

Brautigam, Christine. "International Human Rights Law: The Relevance of Gender." In Wolfgang, *Human Rights of Women*, 3–29.

Brennan, Teresa, and Carole Pateman. "'Mere Auxiliaries to the Commonwealth': Women and the Origins of Liberalism." In Phillips, *Feminism and Politics*, 93–115.

Brereton, Bridget. "General Problems and Issues in Studying the History of Women." In Mohammed, *Gender in Caribbean Development*, 119–135.

Bridgeman, Jo, and Susan Millns. *Feminist Perspectives on Law: Law's Engagement with the Female Body.* London: Sweet and Maxwell, 1998.

Brown, Beverly. "Contracting Out/Contracting In: Some Feminist Considerations." In Bottomley, *Feminist Perspectives*, 5–16.

Brown, Chris. "Universal Human Rights: A Critique." In Dunne and Wheeler, *Human Rights in Global Politics*, 103–127.

Brown, Chris, Terry Nardin and Nicholas Rengger, ed. *International Relations in Political Thought: Texts from the Ancient Greeks to the First World War*. Cambridge: Cambridge University Press, 2002.

Brownlie, Ian. *Basic Documents in International Law.* Oxford: Oxford University Press, 1995.

———. *Principles of Public International Law.* Oxford: Clarendon Press, 1996.

Bryson, Valerie. *Feminist Political Theory: An Introduction.* Basingstoke, Hampshire: Palgrave MacMillan, 2003.

Bull, Hedley. *The Anarchical Society: A Study of Order in World Politics.* New York: Columbia University Press, 1977.

Bunch, Charlotte. "Organizing for Women's Human Rights Globally." In Kerr, *Ours By Right*, 141–149.

———. "Transforming Human Rights from a Feminist Perspective." In Peters and Wolper, *Women's Rights, Human Rights*, 11–17.

Burchill, Scott, Richard Devetak, Andrew Linklater, Matthew Paterson, Christian Reus-Smit, and Jacqui True, ed. *Theories of International Relations*. Hampshire: Palgrave, 2001.

Burrows, Noreen. "International Law and Human Rights: the Case of Women's Rights." In *Human Rights: From Rhetoric to Reality*, edited by Tom Campbell, David Goldberg, Sheila Mclean and Tom Mullen, 80–98. Oxford: Basil Blackwell, 1986.

Bustelo, Mara. "The Committee on the Elimination of Discrimination against Women at the crossroads." In *The Future of UN Human Rights Treaty Monitoring*, edited by Philip Alston and James Crawford, 79–112. Cambridge: Cambridge University Press, 2000.

Butler, Judith. *Gender Trouble: Feminism and the Subversion of Identity.* New York: Routledge, 1999.

Byrnes, Andrew. "The Convention on the Elimination of All Forms of Discrimination against Women." In Wolfgang, *Human Rights of Women*, 119–172.

Byrnes, Andrew. "Using Gender-specific Human Rights Instruments in Domestic Litigation: the Convention on the Elimination of all Forms of Discrimination against Women." In Adams and Byrnes, *Gender Equality and the Judiciary*, 51–84.

Byron, Dennis. "Equality Jurisprudence under Commonwealth Caribbean Constitutions and Legislation relating to the Human Rights of Women: The Eastern Caribbean." In Adams and Byrnes, *Gender Equality and the Judiciary*, 189–200.

Cain, Patricia. "Feminist Jurisprudence: Grounding the Theories." In Bartlett, *Feminist Legal Theory*, 263–280.

Capra, Fritjof. *The Turning Point: Science, Society and the Rising Culture*. London: Flamingo, 1983.

Chapman, Jenny. "The Feminist Perspective." In *Theory and Methods in Political Science*, edited by David Marsh and Gerry Stoker, 94–114. Basingstoke, Hampshire: Palgrave MacMillan, 1995.

Charlesworth, Hilary. "Human Rights as Men's Rights." In Peters and Wolper, *Women's Rights, Human Rights*, 103–113.

———. "Taking the Gender of Rights Seriously." In *Rethinking Human Rights*, edited by Brian Galligan and Charles Sampford, 31–49. Sydney: The Federation Press, 1997.

———. "What are "Women's International Human Rights"?" In Cook, *Human Rights of Women*, 58–84.

Charlesworth, Hilary and Christine Chinkin. *The boundaries of international law: A feminist analysis*. Manchester: Manchester University Press, 2000.

Chen, Martha. "Engendering World Conferences: The International Women's Movement and the UN." In *NGOs, the UN, and Global Governance*, edited by Thomas Weiss and Leon Gordenker, 139–158. Boulder, CO: Lynne Rienner Publishers, 1996.

Chinkin, Christine. "Cultural Relativism and International Law." In Howland, *Religious Fundamentalisms*, 55–66.

———. "Gender Inequality and International Human Rights Law." In *Inequality, Globalization, and World Politics*, edited by Andrew Hurrell and Ngaire Woods, 95–121. Oxford: Oxford University Press, 2000.

Code, Lorraine. "Introduction." In Code, *Encyclopedia of Feminist Theories*, xv–xxvi.

———, ed. *Encyclopedia of Feminist Thought.* London: Routledge, 2003.

———. "Feminist Epistemology." In Code, *Encyclopedia of Feminist Theories*, 170–173.

———. "Patriarchy." In Code, *Encyclopedia of Feminist Theories*, 378–379.

———. "Power." In Code, *Encyclopedia of Feminist Theories*, 399–400.

Colebrook, Claire. *Gender.* Basingstoke, Hampshire: Palgrave MacMillan, 2004.

Connell, Robert. *Masculinities.* Cambridge: Polity Press, 1995.

Connelly, Alpha. "Ireland and the European Convention." In *Human Rights and the European Convention: The Effects of the Convention on the United Kingdom and Ireland*, edited by Brice Dickson, 185–210. London: Sweet and Maxwell, 1997.

Conaghan, Joanne. "Tort Law and the Feminist Critique of Reason." In Bottomley, *Feminist Perspectives*, 47–68.

Connors, Jane. "NGOs and the Human Rights of Women at the United Nations." In Willetts, *"The Conscience of the World,"* 147–180.

Cook, Rebecca, ed. *Human Rights of Women: National and International Perspectives*. Philadelphia: University of Pennsylvania Press, 1994.

———. "State Accountability Under the Convention on the Elimination of All Forms of Discrimination Against Women." In Cook, *Human Rights of Women*, 228–256.

———. "Women's International Human Rights Law: The Way Forward." In Cook, *Human Rights of Women*, 3–36.

Coomaraswamy, Radhika. "Different but Free: Cultural Relativism and Women's Rights as Human Rights." In Howland, *Religious Fundamentalisms*, 79–92.

———. *Reinventing International Law: Women's Rights as Human Rights in the International Community*. Massachusetts: Harvard Law School Human Rights Program, 1997.

———. "To Bellow like a Cow: Women, Ethnicity, and the Discourse of Rights." In Cook, *Human Rights of Women*, 39–57.

Crawford, Charmaine. *The Intensification of Violence Against Women in Trinidad and Tobago During the Period of Structural Adjustment.* Toronto: York University, 1996.

Crawford, James. "The UN human rights treaty system: A system in crisis?" In *The Future of UN Human Rights Treaty Monitoring*, edited by Philip Alston and James Crawford, 1–14. Cambridge: Cambridge University Press, 2000.

Creque, Merri. *A Study of the Incidence of Domestic Violence in Trinidad and Tobago from 1991 to 1993.* Port of Spain, Trinidad: Trinidad and Tobago Coalition Against Domestic Violence, 1995.

Cumper, Peter. "Human Rights: History, Development and Classification." In Hegarty, *Human Rights*, 1–14.

Denzin, Norman. "Postmodernism and Deconstructionism." In *Postmodernism and Social Inquiry*, edited by David Dickens and Andrea Fontana, 182–202. London: University College of London Press, 1994.

Deosaran, Ramesh. *The Dynamics of Community Policing: Theory, Practice and Evaluation.* St. Augustine, Trinidad: Centre for Criminology and Criminal Justice, 2000.

Desai, Manisha. "From Vienna to Beijing: Women's Human Rights Activism and the Human Rights Community." In *Debating Human Rights: Critical Essays from the United States and Asia*, edited by Peter Van Ness, 184–196. London: Routledge, 1999.

Devetak, Richard. "Critical Theory." In Burchill et al, *Theories of International Relations*, 155–180.

Di Stephano, Christine. "Dilemmas of Difference: Feminism, Modernity, and Postmodernism." In Nicholson, *Feminism/Postmodernism*, 63–82.

Doh, Jonathan. "Nongovernmental Organizations, Corporate Strategy and Public Policy: NGOs as Agents of Change." In *Globalization and NGOs: Transforming Business, Government, and Society*, edited by Jonathan Doh and Hildy Teegen, 1–18. Westport, CT: Praeger Publishers, 2003.

Donnelly, Jack. "The Social Construction of International Human Rights." In Dunne and Wheeler, *Human Rights in Global Politics*, 71–102.

Dorsey, Ellen. "The Global Women's Movement: Articulating a New Vision of Global Governance." In *The Politics of Global Governance: International Organizations in an Interdependent World*, edited by Paul Diehl, 335–359. Boulder, CO: Lynne Rienner Publishers, 2001.

Duncan, Sheila. "The Mirror Tells its Tale: Constructions of Gender in Criminal Law." In Bottomley, *Feminist Perspectives*, 173–190.

Dunne, Timothy. "Realism." In Baylis and Smith, *The Globalization of World Politics*, 109–124.

Dunne, Timothy and Nicholas Wheeler, ed. *Human Rights in Global Politics*. Cambridge: Cambridge University Press, 1999.

———. "Introduction: Human Rights and the Fifty Years' Crisis." In Dunne and Wheeler, *Human Rights in Global Politics*, 1–28.

Edwards, Michael and David Hulme. "Making a Difference? Concluding Comments." In Edwards and Hulme, *Making a Difference*, 211–216.

———, eds. *Making a Difference: NGOs and Development in a Changing World.* London: Earthscan Publications Ltd., 1992.

———. "Scaling-up the Developmental Impact of NGOs: Concepts and Experiences." In Edwards and Hulme, *Making a Difference*, 13–27.

Eisenstein, Zillah. *The Radical Future of Liberal Feminism*. New York: Longman, 1981.

Elshtain, Jean Bethke. *Public Man, Private Woman: Women in Social and Political Thought.* Oxford: Princeton University Press, 1981.

Enloe, Cynthia. *Bananas, Beaches and Bases: Making Feminist Sense of International Politics.* Berkeley: University of California Press, 2000.

———. "Margins, Silences and Bottom Rungs: How to Overcome the Underestimation of Power in the Study of International Relations." In Smith et al, *International Theory*, 186–202.

Ehrenreich, Barbara. "Life Without Father: Reconsidering Socialist-Feminist Theory." In Tuana and Tong, *Feminism and Philosophy*, 265–271.

Evans, Judith. *Feminist Theory Today: An Introduction to Second-Wave Feminism.* London: Sage Publications, 1995.

Farganis, Sondra. "Postmodernism and Feminism." In *Postmodernism and Social Inquiry*, edited by David Dickens and Andrea Fontana, 101–126. London: University College London, 1994.

Ffolkes, Suzanne. "Violence against Women: Some Legal Responses." In Leo-Rhynie, *Gender: A Caribbean Multi-Disciplinary Perspective*, 118–129.

Fisher, Julie. *Nongovernments: NGOs and the Political Development of the Third World.* West Hartford, CT: Kumarian Press, 1998.

Flanz, Gisbert H., and Albert P. Blaustein, ed. *Constitutions of the Countries of the World: a Series of Updated texts, Constitutional Chronologies and Annotated Bibliographies*. Dobbs Ferry, NY: Oceana Publications, 1971–.

Flax, Jane. "Postmodernism and Gender Relations in Feminist Theory." In Nicholson, *Feminism/Postmodernism*, 39–62.

Fleming, Marie. "Feminism and Critical Theory." In Code, *Encyclopedia of Feminist Theories*, 110–111.

Forsythe, David. *Human Rights in International Relations.* Cambridge: Cambridge University Press, 2000.

Foucault, Michel. *The Archaeology of Knowledge.* London: Routledge, 2002.

Fraser, Nancy. "What's Critical About Critical Theory? The Case of Habermas and Gender." In Tuana and Tong, *Feminism and Philosophy*, 272–298.

Fraser, Nancy and Linda Nicholson. "Social Criticism without Philosophy: An Encounter between Feminism and Postmodernism." In Nicholson, *Feminism/Postmodernism*, 19–38.

Freeman, Marsha. "Women, Development and Justice: Using the International Convention on Women's Rights." In Kerr, *Ours By Right*, 93–105.

Friedman, Elisabeth. "Women's Human Rights: The Emergence of a Movement." In Peters and Wolper, *Women's Rights, Human Rights*, 18–35.

Frye, Marilyn. "Feminism." In Code, *Encyclopedia of Feminist Theories*, 195–197.

Gaer, Felice. "Reality Check: Human Rights NGOs Confront Governments at the UN." In *NGOs, the UN, and Global Governance*, edited by Thomas Weiss and Leon Gordenker, 51–66. Boulder, CO: Lynne Rienner Publishers, 1996.

Galey, Margaret. "Forerunners in Women's Quest for Partnership." In *Women, Politics and the United Nations*, edited by Anne Winslow, 1–10. Westport, Connecticut: Greenwood Press, 1995.

Gaudart, Dorothea. "Charter-based Activities Regarding Women's Rights in the United Nations and Specialized Agencies." In Wolfgang, *Human Rights of Women*, 50–104.

Gandhi, Nandita, and Nandita Shah. "Organizations and Autonomy." In Menon, *Gender and Politics in India*, 299–341.

Ghandhi, P. R. *Blackstone's International Human Rights Documents*. New York: Oxford University Press, Inc., 2002.

Ghany, Hamid. "Parliament in Trinidad and Tobago 1962–1987: The Whitehall Model at Work." In *Trinidad and Tobago: The Independence Experience 1962–1987*, edited by Selwyn Ryan, 175–192. St. Augustine, Trinidad: Institute of Social and Economic Research, UWI, 1988.

Gibbs, Christopher, Claudia Fumo and Thomas Kuby. *Nongovernmental Organizations in World Bank-Supported Projects: A Review.* Washington, D.C.: The World Bank, 1999.

Gierycz, Dorota. "Human Rights of Women at the Fiftieth Anniversary of the United Nations." In Wolfgang, *Human Rights of Women*, 30–49.

Gilligan, Carol. *In a Different Voice: Psychological Theory and Women's Development.* Cambridge, MA: Harvard University Press, 1982.

Glasius, Marlies, and Mary Kaldor. "The State of Global Civil Society: Before and After September 11." In *Global Civil Society 2002*, edited by Marlies Glasius, Mary Kaldor and Helmut Anheier, 3–34. Oxford: Oxford University Press, 2002.

Glasius, Marlies, Mary Kaldor and Helmut Anheier, ed. *Global Civil Society 2002.* Oxford: Oxford University Press, 2002.

Glover, David, and Cora Kaplan. *Genders.* London: Routledge, 2000.

Gopaul, Roanna, Paula Morgan, and Rhoda Reddock, ed. *Women, Family and Family Violence in the Caribbean: the Historical and Contemporary Experience, with special reference to Trinidad and Tobago.* St. Augustine, Trinidad: Center for Gender and Development Studies, UWI, 1996.

Goodrich, Peter. "Gender and Contracts." In Bottomley, *Feminist Perspectives*, 17–46.

Gränzer, Sieglinde. "Changing Discourse: Transnational Advocacy Networks in Tunisia and Morocco." In Risse et al, *The Power of Human Rights*, 109–133.

Graycar, Reg. "Feminist Legal Theory." In Code, *Encyclopedia of Feminist Theories*, 198–200.

Green, Joyce. "Public/Private." In Code, *Encyclopedia of Feminist Theories*, 412.

Groom, A.J.R. "Introduction: The Past as Prelude." In *Contemporary International Relations: A Guide to Theory*, edited by A.J.R. Groom and Margot Light, 1–6. London: Pinter Publishers Ltd., 1994.

Grzybowski, Cândido. "We NGOs: A Controversial Way of Being and Acting." In *Debating Development: NGOs and the Future*, edited by Deborah Eade and Ernst Ligteringen, 209–221. Oxford: Oxfam Publishing, 2001.

Gunning, Isabelle R. "Uneasy Alliances and Solid Sisterhood: A Response to Professor Obiora's "Bridges and Barricades."" In *Global Critical Race Feminism: An International Reader*, edited by Adrien Wing, 275–284. New York: New York University Press, 2000.

Habermas, Jürgen. *Knowledge and Human Interests*. Translated by Jeremy Shapiro. London: Heinemann, 1972.

Halliday, Fred. *Rethinking International Relations*. Basingstoke, Hampshire: MacMillan Press, 1994.

Haraksingh, Kusha. "Law-Making and Social Change in Colonial Trinidad, 1900–1950." In *Law, Society and the State: Essays in Modern Legal History*, edited by Louis Knafla and Susan Binnie, 130–144. Toronto: Toronto University Press, 1995.

Harding. Sandra. "The Instability of the Analytical Categories of Feminist Theories." In Malson, *Feminist Theory in Practice and Process*, 15–34.

Harris, David J. *Cases and Materials on International Law*. London: Sweet & Maxwell, 1998.

Harris, Sonia. "Review of Institutional Mechanisms for the Advancement of Women and for Achieving Gender Equality." In Nain and Bailey, *Gender Equality in the Caribbean*, 178–200. Kingston, Jamaica: Ian Randle Publishers, 2003.

Harstock, Nancy. "Foucault on Power." In Nicholson, *Feminism/Postmodernism*, 157–175.

Hawkesworth, Mary. "Knowers, Knowing, Known: Feminist Theory and Claims of Truth." In Malson, *Feminist Theory in Practice and Process*, 327–352.

Hay, Colin. *Political Analysis: A Critical Introduction*. Basingstoke, Hampshire: Palgrave MacMillan, 2002.

Hegarty, Angela, and Siobhan Leonard, ed. *Human Rights: An Agenda for the 21st Century*. London: Cavendish Publishing Limited, 1999.

Held, David. *Introduction to Critical Theory: Horkheimer to Habermas*. Berkeley: University of California Press, 1980.

Hilhorst, Dorothea. *The Real World of NGOs: Discourse, Diversity and Development*. London: Zed Books, 2003.

Hollis, Martin. "The last post." In Smith et al, *International Theory*, 301–308.

———. *The Philosophy of Social Science: An Introduction*. Cambridge: Cambridge University Press, 2002.

Hong, Zhu. "The Testimony of Women Writers: The Situation of Women in China Today." In Peters and Wolper, *Women's Rights, Human Rights*, 96–102.

Hopkinson, William. "Challenges Facing the International System in the 21st Century." In *The Europa Directory of International Organizations 2003*. London: Europa Publications, 2003.

hooks, bell. "Black Women: Shaping Feminist Theory." In *The Black Feminist Reader*, edited by Joy James and T. Denean Sharpley-Whiting, 131–145. Malden, MA: Blackwell Publishers Limited, 2000.

Howland, Courtney. "Introduction." In Howland, *Religious Fundamentalisms*, xi–xxv.

———, ed. *Religious Fundamentalisms and the Human Rights of Women*. New York: Palgrave, 1999.

———. "Safeguarding Women's Political Freedoms under the International Covenant on Civil and Political Rights in the Face of Religious Fundamentalism." In Howland, *Religious Fundamentalisms*, 93–104.

Jacobson, Roberta. "The Committee on the Elimination of Discrimination Against Women." In Alston, *The United Nations and Human Rights*, 444–472.

Jaising, Indira. "Violence against Women: The Indian Perspective." In Peters and Wolper, *Women's Rights, Human Rights*, 51–56.

James, Susan and Stephanie Palmer, ed. *Visible Women: Essays on Feminist Legal Theory and Political Philosophy*. Oxford: Hart Publishing, 2002.

Jayawickrama, Nihal. *The Judicial Application of Human Rights Law: National, Regional and International Jurisprudence*. Cambridge: Cambridge University Press, 2002.

Jetschke, Anja. "Linking the Unlinkable? International Norms and Nationalism in Indonesia and the Philippines." In Risse et al, *The Power of Human Rights*, 134–171.

Johnson-Odim, Cheryl. "Common Themes, Different Contexts: Third World Women and Feminism." In *Third World Women and the Politics of Feminism*, edited by Chandra T. Mohanty, Ann Russo and Lourdes Torres, 314–327. Bloomington: Indiana University Press, 1991.

Jordan, Robert, Clive Archer, Gregory Granger, and Kerry Ordes. *International Organizations: A Comparative Approach to the Management of Cooperation*. Westport Connecticut: Praeger Publishers, 2001.

Kaufman, Natalie, and Stephanie Lindquist. "Critiquing Gender-Neutral Treaty Language: The Convention on the Elimination of All Forms of Discrimination Against Women." In Peters and Wolper, *Women's Rights, Human Rights*, 114–125.

Keck, Margaret, and Kathryn Sikkink. *Activists Beyond Borders: Advocacy Networks in International Politics*. New York: Cornell University Press, 1998.

Kerr, Joanna, ed. *Ours By Right: Women's Right as Human Rights*. London: Zed Books, 1993.

———. "The Context and the Goal." In Kerr, *Ours By Right*, 3–9.

Kingdom, Elizabeth. *What's Wrong With Rights? Problems for Feminist Politics of Law*. Edinburgh: Edinburgh University Press, 1991.

Knafla, Louis and Susan Binnie. "Beyond the State: Law and Legal Pluralism in the Making of Modern Societies." In *Law, Society and the State: Essays in Modern*

Legal History, edited by Louis Knafla and Susan Binnie, 3–33. Toronto: Toronto University Press, 1995.

Knop, Karen. "Why Rethinking the Sovereign State is Important for Women's International Human Rights Law." In Cook, *Human Rights of Women*, 153–164.

Kramnick, Miriam. Introduction to *Vindication of the Rights of Woman*, by Mary Wollstonecraft. Harmondsworth: Pelican Books, 1975.

Krause, Jill. "Gender Inequalities and Feminist Politics in a Global Perspective." In *Globalization: Theory and Practice*, edited by Eleonore Kofman and Gillian Youngs, 225–237. London: Pinter, 1996.

Kuhn, Thomas. *The Structure of Scientific Revolutions*. Chicago: The University of Chicago Press, 1996.

Lacey, Nicola. "An Introduction to the Essays." In *Unspeakable Subjects*, 1–18. Oxford: Hart Publishing, 1998.

———. "Closure and Critique in Feminist Jurisprudence: Transcending the Dichotomy or a Foot in Both Camps?" In *Unspeakable Subjects*, 167–187. Oxford: Hart Publishing, 1998.

———. "Theories of Justice and the Welfare State: A Feminist Critique." In *Unspeakable Subjects*, 46–70. Oxford: Hart Publishing, 1998.

———. "Violence, Ethics and Law: Feminist Reflections in a Familiar Dilemma." In James and Palmer, *Visible Women*, 117–136.

———. *Unspeakable Subjects: Feminist Essays in Legal and Social Theory*. Oxford: Hart Publishing, 1998.

Lazarus-Black, Mindie. "Domestic Violence in Trinidad and Tobago." In *Encyclopedia of Domestic Violence*, edited by Nicky Jackson, 712. New York: Routledge, 2007.

Leng, Kwok. "Difference." In Code, *Encyclopedia of Feminist Theories*, 135–136.

Leo-Rhynie, Elsa, Barbara Bailey, and Christine Barrow, ed. *Gender: A Caribbean Multi-Disciplinary Perspective*. Kingston, Jamaica: Ian Randle Publishers, 1997.

Lerner, Gerda. *The Creation of Feminist Consciousness: From the Middle Ages to Eighteen-seventy*. New York: Oxford University Press, 1993.

Lewis, David and Tina Wallace. "Introduction." In *New Roles and Relevance: Development NGOs and the Challenge of Change*, ed. David Lewis and Tina Wallace, ix–xvii. West Hartford, CT: Kumarian Press, 2000.

———, eds. *New Roles and Relevance: Development NGOs and the Challenge of Change*. West Hartford, CT: Kumarian Press, 2000.

Lewis, Reina and Sara Mills. "Introduction." In *Feminist Postcolonial Theory: A Reader*, edited by Reina Lewis and Sara Mills, 1–24. Edinburgh: Edinburgh University Press, 2003.

Linklater, Andrew. "The Achievements of Critical Theory." In Smith et al, *International Theory*, 279–300.

Lloyd, Genevieve. *The Man of Reason: 'Male' & 'Female' in Western Philosophy*. London: Routledge, 1993.

Locke, John. "Second Treatise on Civil Government: An Essay Concerning the True Original, Extent and End of Civil Government." In *Social Contract: Essays by Locke, Hume and Rousseau*, edited by Ernest Barker. London: Oxford University Press, 1947.

Logue, Margaret. "The Practice of Equality." In Hegarty, *Human Rights*, 155–168.

MacKinnon, Catharine A. "Difference and Dominance: On Sex Discrimination." In *Feminism Unmodified*, 32–45.

———. *Feminism Unmodified: Discourses on Life and Law.* Cambridge, MA: Harvard University Press, 1987.

———. "Introduction: The Art of the Impossible." In *Feminism Unmodified*, 1–20.

———. "Privacy v. Equality: Beyond Roe v. Wade." In *Feminism Unmodified*, 93–102.

———. "The Liberal State." In *Toward A Feminist Theory of the State*, 157–170. Cambridge, MA: Harvard University Press, 1991.

———. *Toward A Feminist Theory of the State.* Cambridge, MA: Harvard University Press, 1991.

Mahoney, Kathleen. "Gender and the Judiciary: Confronting Gender Bias." In Adams and Byrnes, *Gender Equality and the Judiciary*, 85–111.

Majury, Diana. "Strategizing in Equality." In *At the Boundaries of Law, Feminism and Legal Theory*, edited by Martha A. Fineman and Nancy S. Thomadsen, 320–338. London: Routledge, 1991.

Malson, Micheline, Jean O'Barr, Sarah Westphal-Wihl, and Mary Wyer, ed. *Feminist Theory in Practice and Process*. Chicago: University of Chicago Press, 1989.

Marchand, Marriane, and Jane Parpart. "Exploding the Canon: An Introduction/Conclusion." In *Feminism/Postmodernism/Development*, edited by Marriane Marchand and Jane Parpart, 1–22. London: Routledge, 1999.

Marchand, Marriane, and Anne Sisson Runyun. "Feminist Sightings of Global Restructuring: Conceptualizations and Reconceptualizations." In *Gender and Global Restructuring: Sightings, Sites and Resistances*, ed. Marriane Marchand and Anne Sisson Runyun, 1–22. London: Routledge, 2000.

Mayer, Ann. "Cultural Particularism as a Bar to Women's Rights: Reflections on the Middle Eastern Experience." In Peters and Wolper, *Women's Rights, Human Rights*, 176–188.

———. "Religious Reservations to the Convention on the Elimination of All Forms of Discrimination against Women: What Do They Really Mean?" In Howland, *Religious Fundamentalisms*, 105–116.

McPherson, Kathryn. "First-Wave/Second-Wave Feminism." In Code, *Encyclopedia of Feminist Theories*, 208–210.

Mehta, Brinda. "Postcolonial Feminism." In Code, *Encyclopedia of Feminist Theories*, 395–397.

Meighoo, Kirk. *Politics in a 'Half-Made Society': Trinidad and Tobago, 1925–2001.* Kingston: Ian Randle Publishers, 2003.

Menon, Nivedita, ed. *Gender and Politics in India.* New Delhi: Oxford University Press, 1999.

———. "Introduction." In Menon, *Gender and Politics in India*, 1–36.

Merryman, John. *The Civil Law Tradition: An Introduction to the Legal Systems of Western Europe and Latin America.* Stanford: Stanford University Press, 1985.

Meyer, Mary, and Elisabeth Prügl, ed. *Gender Politics in Global Governance.* Lanham, MD: Rowman and Littlefield Publishers Inc., 1999.

Midgley, Claire. "Anti-slavery and the roots of 'imperial feminism.'" In Midgley, *Gender and Imperialism*, 161–179.

———. ed. *Gender and Imperialism.* Manchester: Manchester University Press, 1998.

———. "Gender and imperialism: mapping the connections." In Midgley, *Gender and Imperialism*, 1–18.

Mill, John Stuart. *The Subjection of Women*. New York: Prometheus Books, 1986.

Miller, Alice. "Realizing Women's Human Rights: Nongovernmental Organizations and the United Nations Treaty Bodies." In Meyer and Prügl, *Gender Politics in Global Governance*, 161–178.

Millett, Kate. *Sexual Politics.* Champaign, IL: First Illinois Paperback, 2000.

Mirhosseini, Akram. "After the Revolution: Violations of Women's Human Rights in Iran." In Peters and Wolper, *Women's Rights, Human Rights*, 72–77.

Mohammed, Patricia, and Catherine Shepherd, ed. In *Gender in Caribbean Development*. Kingston, Jamaica: Canoe Press, 1999.

Mohanty, Chandra T. "Introduction – Cartographies of Struggle: Third World Women and the Politics of Feminism." In *Third World Women and the Politics of Feminism*, edited by Chandra T. Mohanty, Ann Russo and Lourdes Torres, 1–50. Bloomington: Indiana University Press, 1991.

———. *Feminism Without Borders: Decolonizing Theory, Practicing Solidarity.* London: Duke University Press, 2003.

———. "Under Western Eyes: Feminist Scholarship and Colonial Discourses." In *Feminist Postcolonial Theory: A Reader*, edited by Reina Lewis and Sara Mills, 49–74. Edinburgh: Edinburgh University Press, 2003.

van der Molen, Gesina. *Alberico Gentili and the Development of International Law: His Life Work and Times*. Leyden: A. W. Sijthoff Uitgeversmaatschappi, 1968.

Mosley, Richard. *Westminster Workshop: A Student's Guide to the British Constitution.* Oxford: Pergamon Press, 1967.

Mumisa, Michael. *Islamic Law: Theory and Interpretation.* Maryland: Amana Publications, 2002.

Naffine, Ngaire. "Can Women be Legal Persons?" In James and Palmer, *Visible Women*, 69–90.

Nain, Gemma T., and Barbara Bailey, ed. *Gender Equality in the Caribbean: Reality or Illusion.* Kingston, Jamaica: Ian Randle Publishers, 2003.

Naples, Nancy. "Changing the Terms: Community Activism, Globalization, and the Dilemmas of Transnational Feminist Praxis." In *Women's Activism and Globalization: Linking Local Struggles and Transnational Politics*, edited by Nancy Naples and Manisha Desai, 3–14. New York: Routledge, 2002.

———. "The Challenges and Possibilities of Transnational Feminist Praxis." In *Women's Activism and Globalization: Linking Local Struggles and Transnational Politics*, edited by Nancy Naples and Manisha Desai, 267–282. New York: Routledge, 2002.

Nash, Kate. *Contemporary Political Sociology: Globalization, Politics, and Power.* Malden: Blackwell Publishers Limited, 2000.

———. "Equality and Difference." In Code, *Encyclopedia of Feminist Theories*, 174–176.

———. "Liberal Feminism." In Code, *Encyclopedia of Feminist Theories*, 303–305.

Nicholson, Linda, ed. *Feminism/Postmodernism.* New York: Routledge, 1990.

———. "Introduction." In Nicholson, *Feminism/Postmodernism*, 1–18.

Noel, Jesse. *Trinidad, Provincia de Venezuela: Historia de la Administración Española de Trinidad.* Caracas: Academia Nacional de la Historia, 1972.

Noonan, Sheila. "Battered Woman Syndrome: Shifting the Parameters of Criminal Law Defences (or (Re)Inscribing the Familiar?)." In Bottomley, *Feminist Perspectives*, 191–222.

O'Donovan, Katherine. "A New Settlement Between the Sexes? Constitutional Law and the Citizenship of Women." In Bottomley, *Feminist Perspectives*, 243–260.

Okin, Susan. "Gender, the Public, and the Private." In Phillips, *Feminism and Politics*, 116–141.

Palmer, Stephanie. "Critical Perspectives on Women's Rights: The European Convention on Human Rights and Fundamental Freedoms." In Bottomley, *Feminist Perspectives*, 223–242.

Palmer, Stephanie. "Feminism and the Promise of Human Rights: Possibilities and Paradoxes." In James and Palmer, *Visible Women*, 91–116.

Parekh, Bhikhu. "Non-Ethnocentric Universalism." In Dunne and Wheeler, *Human Rights in Global Politics*, 128–159.

Pargass, Gaietry, and Roberta Clarke. "Violence Against Women: A Human Rights Issue. Post Beijing Five Year Review." In Nain and Bailey, *Gender Equality in the Caribbean*, 39–72.

Peppin, Patricia. "A Feminist Challenge to Tort Law." In Bottomley, *Feminist Perspectives*, 69–86.

Persadie, Natalie. "A Critical Analysis Of The Efficacy Of Law As A Tool To Achieve Gender Equality And To Address The Problem Of Domestic Violence: The Case Of Trinidad And Tobago." PhD Thesis, University of Birmingham, 2007.

Peters, Julie and Andrea Wolper, ed. *Women's Rights, Human Rights: International Feminist Perspectives*. London: Routledge, 1995.

Peterson, V. Spike, ed. *Gendered States: Feminist (Re)Visions of International Relations Theory*. Boulder, Co.: Lynne Rienner Publishers, 1992.

———. "Introduction." In Peterson, *Gendered States*, 1–30.

———. "Security and Sovereign States: What Is at Stake in Taking Feminism Seriously?" In Peterson, *Gendered States*, 31–64.

Peterson, V. Spike, and Laura Parisi. "Are Women Human? It's Not an Academic Question." In *Human Rights Fifty Years On: A Reappraisal*, edited by Tony Evans, 132–160. Manchester: Manchester University Press, 1998.

Pettman, Jan. "Gender Issues." In Baylis and Smith, *The Globalization of World Politics*, 483–497.

Phillips, Anne, ed. *Feminism and Politics*, Oxford: Oxford University Press, 1998.

———. "Introduction." In Phillips, *Feminism and Politics*, 1–22.

———. "Feminism and the Politics of Difference. Or, Where Have All the Women Gone?" In James and Palmer, *Visible Women*, 11–28.

Pietilä, Hilkka and Jeanne Vickers. *Making Women Matter: The Role of the United Nations.* London: Zed Books, 1994.

Plato. *Republic*. Translated by Paul Shorey. Cambridge, MA: Harvard University Press, 1969.

Popper, Karl. *The Logic of Scientific Discovery*. London: Routledge, 2002.

Poullain de la Barre, François. *De L'Egalité des Deux Sexes: Discours Physique et Moral (Où l'on voit l'importance de se défaire des Préjugez)*. Paris: Jean Du Puis, 1673.

Princen, Thomas and Matthias Finger. "Introduction." In *Environmental NGOs in World Politics: Linking the Local and the Global*, edited by Thomas Princen and Matthias Finger, 1–28. London: Routledge, 1994.

Prügl, Elisabeth, and Mary Meyer. "Gender Politics in Global Governance." In Meyer and Prügl, *Gender Politics in Global Governance*, 3–18.

Raday, Frances. "Religion and Patriarchal Politics: The Israeli Experience." In Howland, *Religious Fundamentalisms*, 155–166.

Rahim, Jennifer. "Trinidad and Tobago Women's Writing, 1929–69." In Leo-Rhynie, *Gender: A Caribbean Multi-Disciplinary Perspective*, 222–239.

Rai, Shirin. "Institutional Mechanisms for the Advancement of Women: Mainstreaming Gender, Democratizing the State?" In Rai, *Mainstreaming Gender*, 15–39.

———. "Introduction." In Rai, *Mainstreaming Gender*, 1–12.

———, ed. *Mainstreaming Gender, Democratizing the State? Institutional Mechanisms for the Advancement of Women.* Manchester: Manchester University Press, 2003.

Ramlogan, Rajendra. *The Developing World and the Environment: Making the Case for the Effective Protection of the Global Environment.* Lanham, MD: University Press of America, 2004.

Ramlogan, Rajendra and Natalie Persadie. *Commonwealth Caribbean Business Law.* London: Cavendish Publishing Limited, 2004.

———. *Developing Environmental Law and Policy in Trinidad and Tobago.* San Juan, Trinidad: Lexicon, 2004.

Randall, Vicky. "Feminism." In *Theory and Methods in Political Science*, edited by David Marsh and Gerry Stoker, 109–130. Basingstoke, Hampshire: Palgrave MacMillan, 2002.

———. *Women and Politics: An International Perspective.* Basingstoke, Hampshire: MacMillan, 1987.

Rao, Arati. "The Politics of Gender and Culture in International Human Rights Discourse." In Peters and Wolper, *Women's Rights, Human Rights*, 167–175.

Reanda, Laura. "The Commission on the Status of Women." In Alston, *The United Nations and Human Rights*, 265–303.

Reddock, Rhoda. *Women and Family in the Caribbean: Historical and Contemporary considerations, with special reference to Jamaica and Trinidad and Tobago.* Georgetown, Guyana: Caricom, 1999.

———. *Women and the Slave Plantation Economy in the Caribbean (with special reference to Trinidad and Tobago): Theoretical and Methodological Perspectives.* St. Augustine, Trinidad, 1988.

Reus-Smit, Christian. "Constructivism." In Burchill et al, *Theories of International Relations*, 209–230.

Rhode, Deborah L. "Feminist Critical Theories." In Bartlett, *Feminist Legal Theory*, 333–350.

Rishmawi, Mona. "The Developing Approaches of the International Commission of Jurists to Women's Human Rights." In Cook, *Human Rights of Women*, 340–348.

Risse, Thomas, Stephen Ropp and Kathryn Sikkink, ed. In *The Power of Human Rights: International Norms and Domestic Change.* Cambridge: Cambridge University Press, 2002.

Risse, Thomas and Kathryn Sikkink. "The Socialization of International Human Rights Norms into Domestic Practices: Introduction." In Risse et al, *The Power of Human Rights*, 1–38.

Romany, Celina. "State Responsibility Goes Private: A Feminist Critique of the Public/Private Distinction in International Human Rights Law." In Cook, *Human Rights of Women*, 85–115.

Ropp, Stephen and Kathryn Sikkink. "International Norms and Domestic Politics in Chile and Guatemala." In Risse et al, *The Power of Human Rights*, 172–204.

Rosenau, Pauline. *Post-Modernism and the Social Sciences: Insights, Inroads and Intrusions*. Princeton, NJ: Princeton University Press, 1992.

Rosthein, Robert L. "On the costs of realism." In *Perspectives on World Politics: A Reader*, edited by Richard Little and Michael Smith, 388–397. London: Routledge, 1991.

Runyun, Anne. "Women in the Neoliberal "Frame."" In Meyer and Prügl, *Gender Politics in Global Governance*, 210–220.

———. "The "State" of Nature: A Garden Unfit for Women and Other Living Things." In Peterson, *Gendered States*, 123–140.

Ryan, Selwyn. *The Judiciary and Governance in the Caribbean.* St. Augustine, Trinidad: Sir Arthur Lewis Institute of Social and Economic Studies, UWI, 2001.

———. *Winner Takes All: The Westminster Experience in the Anglophone Caribbean.* St. Augustine, Trinidad: Institute of Social and Economic Research, UWI, 1999.

Sankey, John. "Conclusions." In Willetts, *"The Conscience of the World,"* 270–276.

Sapiro, Virginia. "Feminist Studies and Political Science – and Vice Versa." In Phillips, *Feminism and Politics*, 161–192.

Scales, Ann C. "The Emergence of Feminist Jurisprudence: An Essay." In *Feminist Jurisprudence*, edited by Patricia Smith, 94–109. Oxford: Oxford University Press, 1993.

Schneider, Elizabeth. "The Dialectic of Rights and Politics: Perspectives from the Women's Movement." In Bartlett, *Feminist Legal Theory*, 318–332.

Scott, Joan Wallach. *Only Paradoxes to Offer: French Feminists and the Rights of Man.* Cambridge, MA: Harvard University Press, 1996.

Seierstad, Åsne. *The Bookseller of Kabul*. Translated by Ingrid Christopherson. London: Virago, 2004.

Sen, Ilina. "Feminists, Women's Movement, and the Working Class." In Menon, *Gender and Politics in India*, 370–380.

Seth, Vickram. *A Suitable Boy.* London: Phoenix, 2003.

Shalev, Carmel. "Women in Israel: Fighting Tradition." In Peters and Wolper, *Women's Rights, Human Rights*, 89–95.

Shaw, Malcolm. *International Law*. Cambridge: Cambridge University Press, 1997.

Shearer, Ian. *Starke's International Law*. London: Butterworths, 1994.

Singer, Michael. "Relativism, Culture, Religion and Identity." In Howland, *Religious Fundamentalisms*, 45–54.

Singh, Kelvin. *Race and Class Struggles in a Colonial State: Trinidad 1917–1945.* Calgary: University of Calgary Press, 1994.

Sinha, Surya P. *What is Law?: The Differing Theories of Jurisprudence*. New York: Paragon House, 1989.

Slapper, Gary and David Kelly. *The English Legal System.* London: Cavendish Publishing Limited, 2000.

Slater, Don. "Public/Private." In *Core Sociological Dichotomies*, edited by Chris Jenks, 138–150. London: Sage Publications, 1998.

Smart, Carol. *Feminism and the Power of Law.* London: Routledge, 1989.

———. "Gender Issues in Law: A Feminist Perspective." In Leo-Rhynie, *Gender: A Caribbean Multi-Disciplinary Perspective*, 84–90.

Smith, Patricia. "On Equality: Justice, Discrimination, and Equal Treatment." In *Feminist Jurisprudence*, edited by Patricia Smith, 17–47. Oxford: Oxford University Press, 1993.

Smith, Steve, and John Baylis. "Introduction." In Baylis and Smith, *The Globalization of World Politics*, 1–12.

Smith, Steve, Ken Booth and Marysia Zaleweski, ed. *International Theory: Positivism and Beyond.* Cambridge: Cambridge University Press, 2002.

Squires, Judith. *Gender in Political Theory*. Cambridge: Polity Press, 2000.

Stamatopoulou, Elissavet. "Women's Rights and the United Nations." In Peters and Wolper, *Women's Rights, Human Rights*, 36–50.

Stanley, Liz, and Sue Wise. *Breaking Out Again: Feminist ontology and epistemology*. London: Routledge, 2002.

Staudt, Kathleen. "Gender Mainstreaming: Conceptual Links to Institutional Machineries." in Rai, *Mainstreaming Gender, Democratizing the State*, 40–66.

Steans, Jill. *Gender and International Relations: An Introduction.* New Jersey: Rutgers University Press, 1998.

Steans, Jill and Lloyd Pettiford. *International Relations: Perspectives and Themes.* London: Longman, 2001.

Stephenson, Carolyn. "Women's International Nongovernmental Organizations at the United Nations." In *Women, Politics and the United Nations*, edited by Anne Winslow, 135–154. Westport, Connecticut: Greenwood Press, 1995.

Stienstra, Deborah. "Dancing Resistance from Rio to Beijing: Transnational Women's Organizing and United Nations Conferences, 1992–6." In *Gender and Global Restructuring: Sightings, Sites and Resistances*, ed. Marriane Marchand and Anne Sisson Runyun, 209–224. London: Routledge, 2000.

———. "Of Roots, Leaves, and Trees: Gender, Social Movements, and Global Governance." In Meyer and Prügl, *Gender Politics in Global Governance*, 260–272.

———. *Women's Movements and International Organizations.* London: St. Martin's Press, 1994.

Stubbs, Josefina. "Gender in Development: A Long Haul – But We're Getting There!" In *Debating Development: NGOs and the Future*, edited by Deborah Eade and Ernst Ligteringen, 348–358. Oxford: Oxfam Publishing, 2001.

Sullivan, Donna. "The Public/Private Distinction in International Human Rights Law." In Peters and Wolper, *Women's Rights, Human Rights*, 126–134.

Sylvester, Christine. "Feminist and Realists View Autonomy and Obligation in International Relations." In Peterson, *Gendered States*, 155–178.

———. *Feminist International Relations: An Unfinished Journey.* Cambridge: Cambridge University Press, 2002.

———. "Homeless in International Relations? 'Women's' Place in Canonical Texts and Feminist Reimaginings." In Phillips, *Feminism and Politics*, 44–66.

———. "Looking Backwards and Forwards at International Relations around Feminism." In *Feminist International Relations: An Unfinished Journey.* Cambridge: Cambridge University Press, 2002.

———. "The Contributions of Feminist Theory to International Relations." In Smith et al, *International Theory*, 254–278.

Symonides, Janusz and Vladimir Volodin. *A Guide to Human Rights: Institutions, Standards, Procedures.* Paris: United Nations Educational, Scientific and Cultural Organization, 2003.

Taylor, Ewart. "Women in School Administration: Exclusion and Isolation." In Leo-Rhynie, *Gender: A Caribbean Multi-Disciplinary Perspective*, 183–199.

The Holy Bible: New International Version. Lutterworth: The Gideons International, 1981.

Tickner, J. Ann. *Gender in International Relations: Feminist Perspectives on Achieving Global Security.* New York: Columbia University Press, 1992.

Tinker, Irene. "Nongovernmental Organizations: An Alternative Power Base for Women?" In Meyer and Prügl, *Gender Politics in Global Governance*, 88–106.

Tong, Rosemarie. *Feminist Thought: A More Comprehensive Introduction.* Boulder, CO: Westview Press, 1998.

———. "Radical Feminism." In Code, *Encyclopedia of Feminist Theories*, 419–421.

True, Jacqui. "Feminism." In Burchill et al, *Theories of International Relations*, 231–276.

Tuana, Nancy and Rosemarie Tong, ed. *Feminism and Philosophy: Essential Reading in Theory, Reinterpretation, and Application.* Colorado: Westview Press, 1995.

———. "Liberal Feminist Perspectives." In Tuana and Tong, *Feminism and Philosophy*, 5–9.

Vassell, Linnette. "Women, Power and Decision-Making in CARICOM Countries: Moving Forward From a Post-Beijing Assessment." In Nain and Bailey, *Gender Equality in the Caribbean*, 1–18.

de Vattel, Emmerich. *The Law of Nations or Principles of the Law of Nature, Applied to the Conduct and Affairs of Nations and Sovereigns*. Translated and edited by Joseph Chitty. London: Law Booksellers and Publishers, 1834.

Vincent, R. John. *Human Rights and International Relations*. Cambridge: Cambridge University Press, 1986.

Walker, Robert B.J. "Gender and Critique in the Theory of International Relations." In Peterson, *Gendered States*, 179–202.

Wallace, Rebecca, and Kenneth Dale-Risk. *International Human Rights: Texts and Materials.* London: Sweet and Maxwell, 2001.

Watterson, Bill. *There's Treasure Everywhere.* London: Time Warner Paperbacks, 2002.

Weber, Cynthia. *International Relations Theory: A Critical Introduction.* London: Routledge, 2001.

Weedon, Chris. "Poststructuralism/Postmodernism." In Code, *Encyclopedia of Feminist Theories*, 397–399.

Weiss, Thomas, David Forsythe and Roger Coate. *The United Nations and Changing World Politics*. Boulder, CO: Westview Press, 2001.

West, Lois. "The United Nations Women's Conferences and Feminist Politics." In Meyer and Prügl, *Gender Politics in Global Governance*, 177–198.

West, Robin. "Jurisprudence and Gender." In Bartlett, *Feminist Legal Theory*, 201–234.

Whelehan, Imelda. *Modern Feminist Thought: From the Second Wave to 'Post-Feminism.'* Edinburgh: Edinburgh University Press, 1995.

Whitworth, Sandra. *Feminism and International Relations: Towards a Political Economy of Gender in Interstate and Non-Governmental Institutions.* Basingstoke, Hampshire: Palgrave MacMillan, 1997.

Willetts, Peter. "Consultative Status for NGOs at the United Nations." In Willetts, *"The Conscience of the World,"* 31–62.

———. "Introduction." In Willetts, *"The Conscience of the World,"* 1–14.

———, ed. *"The Conscience of the World": The Influence of Non-Governmental Organisations in the U.N. System*. London: Hurst & Company, 1996.

Williams, Eric. *Capitalism and Slavery.* Kingston: Ian Randle Publishers, 2005.

Williams, Patricia. "On Being the Object of Property." In Bartlett, *Feminist Legal Theory*, 165–180.

Williams, Wendy W. "The Equality Crisis: Some Reflections on Culture, Courts, and Feminism." In Bartlett, *Feminist Legal Theory*, 15–34.

Wiltshire-Brodber, Rosina. "Gender, Race and Class in the Caribbean." In Mohammed, *Gender in Caribbean Development*, 136–148.

Wollstonecraft, Mary. *Vindication of the Rights of Woman*. Edited by Miriam Kramnick. Harmondsworth: Pelican Books, 1975.

Young, Iris. "Polity and Group Difference: Critique of the Ideal of Universal Citizenship." In Phillips, *Feminism and Politics*, 401–429.

Zemer, Moshe. *Evolving Halakhah: A Progressive Approach to Traditional Jewish Law.* Vermont: Jewish Lights Publishing, 1999.

Zweigert, Konrad, and Hein Kötz. *An Introduction to Comparative Law*. Translated by Tony Weir. Oxford: Oxford University Press, 1998.

Government Publications (Trinidad and Tobago)

Domestic Violence Unit, Division of Gender Affairs, Ministry of Community Development, Culture and Gender Affairs. *Report on Policy Round Table on Domestic Violence in Trinidad and Tobago.* 26 February 1999.

Family Court of Trinidad and Tobago. *Family Court Evaluation: First Year Report.* Port of Spain, Trinidad: Family Court of Trinidad and Tobago, 2005.

Gender Affairs Division, Ministry of Planning, Economic and Social Restructuring and Gender Affairs. "National Domestic Violence Hotline: Summary Report for period 01.01.08 to 31.12.08." Accessed 20 July 2011, http://genderaffairs-tt.net/pdf_docs/2008%20Year-end%20Report.pdf.

———. "Overview of the Gender Affairs Division," 2009. Accessed 18 July 2011, http://genderaffairs-tt.net/.

James, Eulalie. *Appropriation Bill (Budget).* Senate, Friday October 15, 2004.

Judiciary of the Republic of Trinidad and Tobago. *Annual Report 2008–2009.* Port of Spain, Trinidad: Judiciary of the Republic of Trinidad and Tobago, 2009.

———. *Annual Report 2006–2007.* Port of Spain, Trinidad: Judiciary of the Republic of Trinidad and Tobago, 2007.

———. *Annual Report 2005–2006.* Port of Spain, Trinidad: Judiciary of the Republic of Trinidad and Tobago, 2006.

———. *Annual Report 2004–2005.* Port of Spain, Trinidad: Judiciary of the Republic of Trinidad and Tobago, 2005.

———. *Annual Report 2003–2004.* Port of Spain, Trinidad: Judiciary of the Republic of Trinidad and Tobago, 2004.

———. *Annual Report 2002–2003.* Port of Spain, Trinidad: Judiciary of the Republic of Trinidad and Tobago, 2003.

———. *Annual Report 2001–2002.* Port of Spain, Trinidad: Judiciary of the Republic of Trinidad and Tobago, 2002.

———. *Annual Report 2000–2001.* Port of Spain, Trinidad: Judiciary of the Republic of Trinidad and Tobago, 2001.

———. *Annual Report 1999–2000.* Port of Spain, Trinidad: Judiciary of the Republic of Trinidad and Tobago, 2000.

———. *Annual Report 1998–1999.* Port of Spain, Trinidad: Judiciary of the Republic of Trinidad and Tobago, 1999.

Manning, Patrick. *Budget Presentation 2006.* Wednesday 28 September 2005.

Ministry of Community Development, Culture and Gender Affairs. "About the Gender Affairs Division," 2006. Accessed 02 April 2007, http://www.cdcga.gov.tt/ga/aboutgender.php.

——— "Domestic Violence Hotline Data: Cases Reported." Accessed 18 July 2011, http://genderaffairs-tt.net/pdf_docs/DomesticViolenceData.pdf.

———. *Draft National Gender Policy and Action Plan.* Port of Spain, Trinidad: Ministry of Community Development, Culture and Gender Affairs, 2005.

———. *Draft National Policy on Gender and Development of the Republic of Trinidad and Tobago.* Port of Spain, Trinidad: Ministry of Community Development, Culture and Gender Affairs, 2009.

———. "National Domestic Violence Hotline: Report for the period 01.10.05 to 30.09.06." Port of Spain: Ministry of Development, Culture and Gender Affairs, 2006.

———. "National Gender Policy and Action Plan," 2006. Accessed 02 April 2007, http://www.cdcga.gov.tt/progs/genderpolicy.php.

———. "National Report of the Republic of Trinidad and Tobago for the Presentation at the XXXIII Assembly of Delegates of the Inter-American Commission of Women (CIM)." November 2006, El Salvador. CIM/doc.32/06.

———. "Programmes and Initiatives," 2006. Accessed 02 April 2007, http://www.cdcga.gov.tt/ga/genderprog.php.

Ministry of Community Development, Culture and Women's Affairs. "National Report on Status of Women in Trinidad and Tobago." August 1995. Presented at the Fourth World Conference on Women, Beijing, China, September 1995.

Ministry of Culture and Gender Affairs. "Updating the report on the Status of Women in Caricom States." Presented at the Meeting of Directors/Coordinators of Women's Bureaux, Basseterre, St. Kitts and Nevis, 22–23 April 1999. Rep. 99/1/59 W/BUR(DC).

Ministry of Social Development. *A Guide to Social Programmes and Services.* Port of Spain, Trinidad: Ministry of Social Development, 2005.

Ministry of the Attorney General and Legal Affairs. *Initial, Second and Third Periodic Report of the Republic of Trinidad and Tobago.* CEDAW/C/TTO/1-3. Port of Spain, Trinidad: Ministry of the Attorney General and Legal Affairs, 2000.

Parliament of the Republic of Trinidad and Tobago. "Bills." Accessed 19 July 2011, http://www.ttparliament.org/publications.php?mid=28.

Republic of Trinidad and Tobago. *Public Sector Investment Programme 2011.* Port of Spain, Trinidad: Ministry of Finance, 2010.

———. *Public Sector Investment Programme 2006.* Port of Spain, Trinidad: Ministry of Planning and Development and Ministry of Finance, 2005.

———. *Public Sector Investment Programme 2005.* Port of Spain, Trinidad: Ministry of Planning and Development and Ministry of Finance, 2004.

———. *Public Sector Investment Programme 2004.* Port of Spain, Trinidad: Ministry of Planning and Development, 2003.

———. *Public Sector Investment Programme 2003.* Port of Spain, Trinidad: Ministry of Planning and Development, 2002.

———. *Public Sector Investment Programme 2002*. Port of Spain, Trinidad: Ministry of Finance, 2001.

———. *Public Sector Investment Programme 2001.* Port of Spain, Trinidad: Ministry of Finance, 2000.

———. *Public Sector Investment Programme 1999/2000.* Port of Spain, Trinidad: Ministry of Finance, 1999.

———. *Public Sector Investment Programme 1998/1999.* Port of Spain, Trinidad: Ministry of Finance, 1998.

———. *Public Sector Investment Programme – Tobago 2004.* Port of Spain, Trinidad: Ministry of Planning and Development, 2003.

———. *Social Sector Investment Programme 2011.* Port of Spain, Trinidad: Government of the Republic of Trinidad and Tobago, 2010.

———. *Social Sector Investment Programme 2007.* Port of Spain, Trinidad: Government of the Republic of Trinidad and Tobago, 2006.

Trinidad and Tobago Police Service. "Departments," 2009. Accessed 19 July 2011, http://www.ttps.gov.tt/AboutTTPS/Departments/tabid/65/Default.aspx.

Yuille-Williams, Joan. *Appropriation Bill (Budget)*. Senate, Thursday October 23, 2003.

———. *Appropriation Bill (Budget)*. Senate, Friday October 14, 2005.

Journal Articles, Conference Proceedings, Discussion Papers

AAWORD/AFARD Seminar Participants. "The Dakar Declaration on Another Development with Women." *Development Dialogue* 1–2 (1982): 11–16.

Abbott, Kenneth W., and Duncan Snidal. "Hard and Soft Law in International Governance." *International Organization* Summer 54, no. 3 (2000): 421–456.

Ackerly, Brooke. "Women's Human Rights Activists as Cross Cultural Theorists." *International Feminist Journal of Politics* 3, no. 3 (Autumn 2001): 311–346.

Afshar, Haleh. "Women and the Politics of Fundamentalism in Iran." *Political Studies Association*, Conference Proceedings, University of Wales (1994): 452–463.

Akashi, Kinji. "Hobbes' Relevance to the Modern Law of Nations." *Journal of the History of International Law* 2 (2000): 199–216.

Alexandre, Michèle. "Dance Halls, Masquerades, Body Protest and the Law: The Female Body as a Redemptive Tool against Trinidad's Gender-Biased Laws." *Duke Journal of Gender Law and Policy* 13 (2006): 177–202.

Ali, Akleema, and Hari D. Maharajh. "Social Predictors of Suicidal Behaviour in Adolescents in Trinidad and Tobago." *Social Psychiatry & Psychiatric Epidemiology* 40, no. 3 (March 2005): 186–191.

Alston, Philip. "Richard Lillich Memorial Lecture: Promoting the Accountability of Members of the New UN Human Rights Council." *Journal of Transnational Law and Policy* 15, no. 1 (2006): 49–96.

Alvarez, Sonia, Elisabeth Jay Friedman, Ericka Beckman, Maylei Blackwell, Norma Chinchilla, Nathalie Lebon, Marysa Navarro, and Marcela Ríos Tobar. "Encountering Latin American and Caribbean Feminisms." *Journal of Women in Culture and Society* 28, no. 2 (2002): 537–579.

Ames, Roger T. "Continuing the Conversation on Chinese Human Rights." *Ethics and International Affairs* 11 (1997): 177–205.

Arts, Bas. "The Global-Local Nexus: NGOs and the Articulation of Scale." *Tijdschrift voor Economische en Sociale Geografie* 95, no. 5 (2004): 498–510.

Ashenden, Samantha. "At the Boundaries of the Political: Feminist Beyond Identity Politics?" *Political Studies Association*, Conference Proceedings, University of Glasgow (1996): 1853–1862.

Ashley, Richard, and Robert B.J. Walker. "Introduction: Speaking the Language of Exile: Dissident Thought in International Studies." *International Studies Quarterly* 34, no. 3 (September 1990): 259–268.

Assing-Murray, Ewa. "The Feminization of HIV/AIDS: An Analysis of its Impact on Women in Trinidad and Tobago." *Dissertation Abstracts International, A: The Humanities and Social Sciences* 67, no. 3 (September 2006): 1108.

Babwah, Feaz, Soraiya Baksh, Leandra Blake, Janine Cupid-Thuesday, Ian Hosein, Anneela Sookhai, Celia Poon-King, Gerard Hutchinson. "The Role of Gender in Compliance and Attendance at an Outpatient Clinic for Type 2 Diabetes Mellitus in Trinidad." *Pan American Journal of Public Health* 19, no. 2 (February 2006): 79–84.

Barriteau, Eudine. "Theorizing Gender Systems and the Project of Modernity in the Twentieth-Century Caribbean." *Feminist Review* 59 (1998): 186–210.

Beaulac, Stéphane. "The Westphalian Legal Orthodoxy – Myth or Reality?" *Journal of the History of International Law* 2 (2000): 148–177.

Binion, Gayle. "Human Rights: A Feminist Perspective." *Human Rights Quarterly* 17, no. 3 (1995): 509–526.

Bissessar, Ann Marie. "Determinants of Gender Mobility in the Public Service of Trinidad and Tobago." *Public Personnel Management* 28, no. 3 (Fall 1999): 409–422.

———. "Policy Transfer and Implementation Failure: A Review of the Policy of Domestic Violence in Trinidad and Tobago." *Caribbean Journal of Criminology and Social Psychology* 5, nos. 1–2 (January–July 2000): 57–80.

Boon, Foo Kim. "The Rio Declaration and its Influence on International Environmental Law." *Singapore Journal of Legal Studies* (1992): 347–364.

Bretherton, Charlotte. "Ecofeminism: Good News for Women?" *Political Studies Association*, Conference Proceedings, University of York (1995): 642–650.

Broniak, Christopher. "What is Emancipation for Habermas?" *Philosophy Today* 32, no. 3 (Fall 1988): 195–206.

Brown, Sarah. "Feminism, International Theory, and International Relations of Gender Inequality." *Millennium: Journal of International Studies* 17, no. 3 (Winter 1988): 461–475.

Brysk, Alison. "From Above and Below: Social Movements, the International System, and Human Rights in Argentina." *Comparative Political Studies* 26, no. 3 (October 1993): 259–285.

Bubeck, Diemut. "Thin, Thick and Feminist Conceptions of Citizenship." *Political Studies Association*, Conference Proceedings, University of York (1995): 461–473.

Bunch, Charlotte. "Women's Rights as Human Rights: Toward a Re-Vision of Human Rights." *Human Rights Quarterly* 12, no. 4 (November 1990): 486–498.

Bunch, Charlotte, and Susana Fried. "Beijing '95: Moving Women's Human Rights from Margin to Center." *Signs* 22, no. 1 (Autumn 1996): 200–204.

Busia, Abena. "On Cultures of Communication: Reflections from Beijing." *Signs* 22, no. 1 (Autumn 1996): 204–210.

Campbell, Rosie. "Gender, Ideology and Issue Preference: Is There such a Thing as Political Women's Interest in Britain?" *British Journal of Politics and International Relations*, 6 (2004): 20–44.

Carty, Anthony. "Critical International Law: Recent Trends in the Theory of International Law." *European Journal of International Law* 2 (1999): 1–27.

Carver, Terrell, Molly Cochran and Judith Squires. "Gendering Jones: feminisms, IRs, and masculinities." *Review of International Studies* 24 (1998): 283–297.

Charlesworth, Hilary. "Feminist Methods in International Law." *The American Journal of International Law* 93, no. 2 (April 1999): 379–394.

———. "Women as Sherpas: Are Global Summits Useful for Women?" *Feminist Studies* 22, no. 3 (Autumn, 1996): 537–547.

Charlesworth, Hilary, and Christine Chinkin. "Sex, Gender and September 11." *The American Journal of International Law* 96, no. 3 (July 2002): 600–605.

Charlesworth, Hilary, Christine Chinkin and Susan Wright. "Feminist Approaches to International Law." *The American Journal of International Law* 85, no. 4 (October 1991): 613–645.

Checkel, Jeffrey. "International Norms and Domestic Politics: Bridging the Rationalist-Constructivist Divide." *European Journal of International Relations* 3, no. 4 (1997): 473–495.

Childs, Sarah. "A Feminised Style of Politics? Women MPs in the House of Commons." *British Journal of Politics and International Relations* 6 (2004): 3–19.

Chinkin, Christine. "A Critique of the Public/Private Dimension." *European Journal of International Law* 10, no. 2 (1999): 387–395.

———. "Violence Against Women: The International Legal Response." *Gender and Development* 3, no. 2 (June 1995): 23–28.

Chow, Esther. "Making Waves, Moving Mountains: Reflections on Beijing '95 and Beyond." *Signs* 22, no. 1 (Autumn 1996):185–192.

Clark, Ann Marie. "Non-Governmental Organizations and their Influence on International Society." *Journal of International Affairs* 48, no. 2 (Winter 1995): 507–525.

Clark, Belinda. "The Vienna Convention Reservations Regime and the Convention on Discrimination Against Women." *The American Journal of International Law* 85, no. 2 (April 1991): 281–321.

———. "Advancing Gender Equality in the Caribbean: Legislative Approaches to Sex Discrimination." *The Lawyer* 7, no. 3 (February 2003): 21–26.

Collier, Terry. "Women at the Edge of Politics: Past and Present." *Political Studies Association*, Conference Proceedings, University of Nottingham (1999).

Connell, Robert. "The State, Gender and Sexual Politics: Theory and Appraisal." *Theory and Society* 19, no. 5 (October 1990): 507–544.

Coppin, Addington. "A Comparison of Male-Female Earnings Differences across Two Caribbean Economies." *Journal of Developing Areas* 32, no. 3 (Spring 1998): 375–393.

———. "Women's Earnings in Trinidad & Tobago: An Analysis by Household Status and Ethnicity." *Social and Economic Studies* 46, no. 4 (December 1997): 61–82.

Cortell, Andrew, and James Davis. "How do International Institutions Matter? The Domestic Impact of International Rules and Norms." *International Studies Quarterly* 40, no. 4 (December 1996): 451–478.

Cowling, Mark. "Socialism, Feminism and Patriarchy: Does the Concept of Femininities Provide a Useful Link?" *Political Studies Association*, Conference Proceedings [Draft Paper], University of Nottingham (1999): 1–24.

Cox, Robert. "Social forces, state and world orders: beyond international relations theory." *Millennium: Journal of International Studies* 10, no. 2 (1981): 126–155.

Cutler, Clarie. "Critical reflections on the Westphalian assumptions of international law and organization: a crisis of legitimacy." *Review of International Studies* 27 (2001): 133–150.

Dallmayr, Fred. "Critical Theory Criticized: Habermas's *Knowledge and Human Interests* and its Aftermath." *Philosophy of the Social Sciences* 2, no. 3 (Sept 1972): 211–229.

Day, Marcus, and Lisa R. Norman. "An Exploration of Gender Differences in the Initiation of and Attitudes toward Crack Cocaine Use in the English-Speaking Caribbean." *Addiction Research & Theory* 15, no. 3 (2007): 285–297.

Deutz, Andrew. "Gender and International Human Rights." *The Fletcher Forum of World Affairs* 17, no. 2 (Summer 1993): 33–52.

Donnelly, Jack. "International Human Rights: A Regime Analysis." *International Organization*, 40, no. 3 (Summer 1986): 599–642.

Dupuy, Pierre Marie. "Dionisio Anzilotti and the Law of International Responsibility of States." *European Journal of International Law* 3 (1992): 139–148.

Edwards, John. "Two Cultures of Rights." *Netherlands Quarterly of Human Rights* 17, no. 1 (1999): 105–107.

Ehrenreich, Barbara. "Men Hate War Too." *Foreign Affairs* 78, no. 1 (Jan/Feb 1999): 118–122.

Ehrenreich, Barbara, Katha Pollit, R. Brian Ferguson, Lionel Tiger, and Jane Jaquette. "Fukuyama's Follies: So What if Women Ruled the World?" *Foreign Affairs* 78, no. 1 (Jan/Feb 1999): 118–129.

Eid, Elisabeth. "Interaction between International and Domestic Human Rights Law: A Canadian Perspective." *Sino Canadian International Conference on the Ratification and Implementation of Human Rights Covenants*. Beijing, China, October 2001.

Elshtain, Jean Bethke. "Exporting Feminism." *Journal of International Affairs* 48, no. 2 (Winter 1995): 541–558.

———. "Women and War: ten years on." *Review of International Studies* 24 (1998): 447–460.

Ertürk, Yakin. "Considering the role of men in gender agenda setting: Conceptual and policy issues." *Feminist Review* 78 (2004): 3–21.

Evans, Peter. "Fighting Marginalization with Transnational Networks: Counter-Hegemonic Globalization." *Contemporary Sociology* 29, no. 1 (Jan., 2000): 230–241.

Farer, Tom. "Human Rights in Law's Empire: The Jurisprudence War." *The American Journal of International Law* 85, no. 1 (January 1991): 117–127.

Ferguson, Brian. "Perilous Positions." *Foreign Affairs* 78, no. 1 (Jan/Feb 1999): 125–127.

Fukuyama, Francis. "Women and the Evolution of World Politics." *Foreign Affairs* 77, no. 5 (Sept/Oct 1998): 24–40.

Gaer, Felice. "Human Rights at the UN: Women's Rights are Human Rights." *In Brief* No. 14 (November 1999).

Glendon, Mary Ann. "John P. Humphrey and the Drafting of the Universal Declaration of Human Rights." *Journal of the History of International Law* 2 (2000): 250–260.

Goetz, Anne. "Feminism and the Limits of the Claim to Know: Contradictions in the Feminist Approach to Women in Development." *Millennium: Journal of International Studies* 17, no. 3 (Winter 1988): 477–496.

Gopaul, Roanna, and Maureen Cain. "Violence between spouses in Trinidad and Tobago: A research note." *Caribbean Quarterly* 42, nos. 2–3 (June–September 1996): 28–40.

Griffith, Sandy, Charles Negy, and Derek Chadee. "Trinidadian and U.S. Citizens' Attitudes Toward Domestic Violence and their Willingness to Intervene: Does Culture Make a Difference?" *Journal of Cross-Cultural Psychology* 37, no. 6 (November 2006): 761–778.

Hadeed, Linda. "Domestic Violence in Trinidad and Tobago: Why Women Stay in Abusive Relationships." *Dissertation Abstracts International, A: The Humanities and Social Sciences* 64, no. 4 (October 2003): 1407-A.

Hadeed, Linda, and Nabila El-Bassel. "Social Support among Afro-Trinidadian Women Experiencing Intimate Partner Violence." *Violence Against Women* 12, no. 8 (August 2006): 740–760.

Halliday, Fred. "Hidden from International Relations: Women and the International Arena." *Millennium: Journal of International Studies* 17, no. 3 (Winter 1988): 419–428.

Hartigan, Pamela. "La OPS enfoca el problema de la violencia contra la mujer." *Pan American Journal of Public Health* 2, no. 4 (October 1997): 290–294.

Hawkins, Darren. "Domestic Responses to International Pressure: Human Rights in Authoritarian Chile." *European Journal of International Relations* 3, no. 4 (1997): 403–434.

Hevener, Natalie. "An Analysis of Gender Based Treaty Law: Contemporary Developments in Historical Perspective." *Human Rights Quarterly* 8, no. 1 (1986): 70–88.

Hill, Melvyn. "Jürgen Habermas: A Social Science of the Mind." *Philosophy of the Social Sciences* 2, no. 3 (Sept 1972): 247–259.

Hoffman, Mark. "Critical Theory and the Inter-Paradigm Debate." *Millennium: Journal of International Studies* 16, no. 2 (1987): 231–249.

Hoffman, John. "Blind Alley: Defining Feminism." *Politics* 21, no. 3 (2001): 193–199.

———. "What on Earth have Sovereignty and the State to do with the Question of Gender?" *Political Studies Association*, Conference Proceedings, University of Glasgow (1996): 623–633.

Hooper, Charlotte. "Masculinities, IR and the 'Gender Variable': A Cost-Benefit Analysis for (Sympathetic) Gender Sceptics." *Review of International Studies* 25 (1999): 475–491.

Howard, Judith, and Carolyn Allen. "Introduction." *Signs* 22, no. 1 (Autumn 1996): 181–185.

Hughes-Tafen, Denise. "Women, Theatre and Calypso in the English-Speaking Caribbean." *Feminist Review* 84 (2006): 48–66.

Hutchinson, G., C. Ramcharan, and K. Ghany. "Gender and Ethnicity in First Admissions to a Psychiatric Unit in Trinidad." *West Indian Medical Journal* 52, no. 4 (December 2003): 300–3.

Jaquette, Jane. "States Make War." *Foreign Affairs* 78, no. 1 (Jan/Feb 1999): 128–129.

———. "Women in Power: From Tokenism to Critical Mass." *Foreign Policy* (Fall 1997): 23–37.

Joachim, Jutta. "Framing Issues and Seizing Opportunities: The UN, NGOs, and Women's Rights." *International Studies Quarterly* 47 (2003): 247–274.

Jones, Adam. "Does 'Gender' Make the World Go Round? Feminist Critiques of International Relations." *Review of International Studies* 22, no. 4 (1996): 405–429.

———. "Engendering debate." *Review of International Studies* 24 (1998): 299–303.

———. "Individuals, communities and human rights." *Review of International Studies* 26 (2000): 199–215.

Joseph, Janice, Zelma Henriques, Kaylene Richards. "The Legal Response to Domestic Violence in the English-Speaking Caribbean Countries." *Caribbean Journal of Criminology and Social Psychology* 3, nos. 1–2 (January–July 1998): 174–187.

Kennedy, David. "Critical Theory, Structuralism and Contemporary Legal Scholarship." *New England Law Review* 21, no. 2 (1985–1986): 209–289.

———. "The International Human Rights Movement: Part of the Problem?" *Harvard Human Rights Journal* 15 (2002): 101–125.

Keohane, Robert. "Beyond Dichotomy: Conversations Between International Relations and Feminist Theory." *International Studies Quarterly* 42, no. 1 (1998): 193–198.

———. "International Institutions: Two Approaches." *International Studies Quarterly* 34, no. 4 (December 1988): 379–396.

———. "International Relations Theory: Contributions of a Feminine Standpoint." *Millennium: Journal of International Studies* 18, no. 2 (Summer 1989): 245–253.

Korthals, Michiel. "The Philosophical Foundation of the Social Sciences in the Theory of Jürgen Habermas." *Philosophy of the Social Sciences* 18, no. 1 (March 1988): 69–72.

Krause, Jill. "Political Theory, International Politics and the 'Problem' of Gender." *Political Studies Association,* Conference Proceedings, University of Wales (1994): 610–620.

Lacey, Nicola. "Theory into Practice? Pornography and the Public/Private Dichotomy." *Journal of Law and Society* 20, no. 1 (Spring 1993): 93–113.

Langlois, Anthony. "Human rights: the globalisation and fragmentation of moral discourse." *Review of International Studies* 28 (2002): 479–496.

Lapid, Yosef. "The Third Debate: On the Prospects of International Theory in a Post-Positivist Era." *International Studies Quarterly* 33, no. 3 (Sept. 1989): 235–254.

Lawson, Gary. "Feminist Legal Theories." *Harvard Journal of Law and Public Policy* 18, no. 2 (Spring 1995): 325–331.

Lazarus-Black, Mindie. "Law and the pragmatics of inclusion: Governing domestic violence in Trinidad and Tobago." *American Ethnologist* 28, no. 2 (May 2001): 388–416.

———. "The Politics of Place: Practice, Process and Kinship in Domestic Violence Courts." *Human Organization* 65, no. 2 (Summer 2006): 140–155.

———. "The (heterosexual) regendering of a modern state: Criminalizing and implementing domestic violence law in Trinidad." *Law and Social Inquiry – Journal of the American Bar Foundation* 28, no. 4 (Fall 2003): 979–1008.

Legohérel, Henri. "Jean Bodin et l'Europe de son temps." *Journal of the History of International Law* 1 (1999): 38–47.

Legro, Jeffrey. "Which Norms Matter? Revisiting the "Failure" of Internationalism." *International Organization* 51, no. 1 (Winter 1997): 31–63.

Lever, Annabelle. "Must Privacy and Sexual Equality Conflict? A Philosophical Examination of Some Legal Evidence." *Social Research* 67, no. 4 (Winter 2000): 1137–1171.

Littleton, Christine A. "Reconstructing Sexual Equality." *California Law Review* 79 (1987): 1279–1337.

Loenen, Titia. "Women's Human Rights on the Eve of the 21st Century." *Netherlands Quarterly of Human Rights* 17, no. 1 (1999): 3–4.

Lowndes, Vivienne. "Getting On or Getting By? Women, Social Capital and Political Participation." *British Journal of Politics and International Relations* 6 (2004): 45–64.

Luciano, Dinys, Simel Esim, and Nata Duvvury. "How to make the law work? Budgetary implications of domestic violence law in Latin America, Central America, and the Caribbean." *Journal of Women Politics and Policy* 27, no. 1–2 (2005): 123–133.

MacCorquodale, Patricia and Gary Jensen. "Women in the Law: Partners or Tokens?" *Gender and Society* 7, no. 4 (Dec., 1993): 582–593.

MacKay, Fiona. "Gender and Political Representation in the UK: The State of 'Discipline.'" *British Journal of Politics and International Relations* 6 (2004): 99–120.

Maharajh, Hari D., and Akleema Ali. "Social and Cultural Aspects of Gender Differences in Depression among Secondary School Students in Trinidad and Tobago." *Journal of Affective Disorders* 78 (March 2004): 558–559.

Maharajh, Hari D., and Monique Konings. "Cannabis and Suicidal Behaviour among Adolescents: A Pilot Study from Trinidad." *The Scientific World Journal* 5 (August 2005): 576–585.

Maharajh, Hari D., and Petal S. Abdool. "Cultural Aspects of Suicide." *The Scientific World Journal* 5 (September 2005): 736–746.

Maharajh, Hari D., Monique Konings, and Nelleen Baboolal. "Gender and Ethnic Differences in Urban and Rural First-Contact Schizophrenia Outpatients in Trinidad." *Reviews on Environmental Health* 21, no. 1 (Jan–Mar 2006): 69–79.

Malleson, Kate. "Justifying Gender Equality on the Bench: Why Difference Won't Do." *Feminist Legal Studies* 11 (2003): 1–24.

Marchand, Marriane. "Different Communities / Different Realities / Different Encounters: A Reply to J. Ann Tickner." *International Studies Quarterly* 42, no. 1 (1998): 199–204.

Marle, Van Karin. "'The Capabilities Approach,' 'The Imaginary Domain,' and 'Asymmetrical Reciprocity': Feminist Perspectives on Equality and Justice." *Feminist Legal Studies* 11 (2003): 255–278.

Martin, Patricia, John Reynolds, and Shelley Keith. "Gender Bias and Feminist Consciousness among Judges and Attorneys: A Standpoint Theory Analysis." *Signs* 27, no. 3 (Spring, 2002): 665–701.

Modeste, Naomi N., Claudette Francis, and Dumiso Matshazi Francis. "AIDS-Related Knowledge, Attitudes, Beliefs, and Behavioural Intentions of Adolescents in Trinidad: A Pilot Study." *International Quarterly of Community Health Education* 14, no. 3 (1993): 273–281.

Mohammed, Patricia. "Gender as a Primary Signifier in the Construction of Community and State among Indians in Trinidad." *Caribbean Quarterly* 40, nos. 3–4 (September–December 1994): 32–43.

———. "Reflections on the Women's Movement in Trinidad: Calypsos, Changes and Sexual Violence." *Feminist Review* 38 (Summer 1991): 33–47.

———. "Towards Indigenous Feminist Theorizing in the Caribbean." *Feminist Review* 59 (Summer 1998): 6–33.

Murphy, Craig. "Seeing Women, Recognizing Gender, Recasting International Relations." *International Organization* 50, no. 3 (Summer 1996): 513–538.

Murphy, James. "Aristotle, Feminism and Biology: A Response to Larry Arnhart." *International Political Science Review / Revue internationale de science politique* 15, no. 4 (Oct. 1994): 417–426.

Nardin, Terry. "International pluralism and the rule of law." *Review of International Studies* 26 (2000): 95–110.

Nash, Kate. "Beyond Liberalism? Feminist Theories of Democracy." *Political Studies Association*, Conference Proceedings, University of York (1995): 1203–1209.

Norman, Lisa R. "Predictors of Consistent Condom Use: a Hierarchical Analysis of Adults from Kenya, Tanzania and Trinidad." *International Journal of STD & AIDS* 14, no. 9 (September 2003): 584–590.

Olsen, Reid N., and Addington Coppin. "The Determinants of Gender Differentials in Income in Trinidad and Tobago." *Journal of Development Studies* 37, no. 5 (June 2001): 31–56.

Peterson, V. Spike. "Feminisms and International Relations." *Gender and History* 10, no. 3 (November 1998): 581–589.

———. "The Politics of Identity in International Relations." *The Fletcher Forum of World Affairs* 17, no. 2 (Summer 1993): 1–12.

———. "Transgressing Boundaries: Theories of Knowledge, Gender and International Relations." *Millennium: Journal of International Studies* 21, no. 2 (1992): 183–206.

———. "Whose Rights? A Critique of the "Givens" in Human Rights Discourse." *Alternatives* 15 (1990): 303–344.

Phillips, Daphne. "Domestic Violence and Public Policy in Trinidad and Tobago." *Caribbean Journal of Criminology and Social Psychology* 5, nos. 1–2 (January–July 2000): 181–188.

Pollit, Katha. "Father Knows Best." *Foreign Affairs* 78, no. 1 (Jan/Feb 1999): 122–125.

Prokhovnik, Raia. "Hobbes's *Leviathan*: Feminist Interpretation and Feminist Theorising." *Political Studies Association*, Conference Proceedings, University of Glasgow (1996): 1709–1720.

———. "Public and Private Citizenship: From Gender Invisibility to Feminist Inclusiveness." *Feminist Review* 60 (Autumn 1998): 86–104.

Puwar, Nirmal. "Thinking About Making a Difference." *British Journal of Politics and International Relations* 6 (2004): 65–80.

Ramsaran, D. "The Interaction of Race and Gender in Development Policy Implementation: the Case of a Small Developing Third World Society." *International Journal of Contemporary Sociology* 36, no. 1 (April 1999): 32–55.

Randall, Vicky, and Joni Lovenduski. "Gender in Contemporary British Politics." *British Journal of Politics and International Relations* 6 (2004): 1–2.

Rao, Arati. "Home-Word Bound: Women's Place in the Family of International Human Rights." *Global Governance* 2 (1996): 241–260.

Rao, Aruna. "Engendering Institutional Change." *Signs* 22, no. 1 (Autumn 1996): 218–221.

Rawlins, Joan. "Domestic Violence in Trinidad: A Family and Public Health Problem." *Caribbean Journal of Criminology and Social Psychology* 5, nos. 1–2 (January–July 2000): 165–180.

Reanda, Laura. "Human Rights and Women's Rights: The United Nations Approach." *Human Rights Quarterly* 3, no. 2 (1981): 11–31.

Reddock, Rhoda. "Contestations over Culture, Class, Gender and Identity in Trinidad and Tobago: 'The Little Tradition.'" *Caribbean Quarterly* 44, nos. 1–2 (March–June 1998): 62–80.

———. "Women's Organizations and Movements in the Commonwealth Caribbean: The Response to Global Economic Crisis in the 1980s." *Feminist Review* 59 (Summer 1998): 57–73.

Reisman, W. Michael. "Sovereignty and Human Rights in Contemporary International Law." *The American Journal of International Law* 84, no. 4 (October 1990): 866–876.

Reus-Smit, Christian. "Human rights and the social construction of sovereignty." *Review of International Studies* 27 (2001): 519–538.

Ridgeway, Cecilia, and Shelley Correll. "Limiting Inequality through Interaction: The End(s) of Gender." *Contemporary Sociology* 29, no. 1 (January 2000): 110–120.

Risse, Thomas. "International Norms and Domestic Change: Arguing and Communicative Behaviour in the Human Rights Area." *Politics and Society* 27, no. 4 (December 1999): 529–559.

Roach Anleu, Sharyn L. "Critiquing the Law: Themes and Dilemmas in Anglo-American Feminist Legal Theory." *Journal of Law and Society* 19 (Winter 1992): 423–440.

Runyan, Anne Sisson, and V. Spike Peterson. "The Radical Future of Realism: Feminist Subversions of IR Theory." *Alternatives* 16 (1991): 67–106.

Sargisson, Lucy. "Contemporary Feminist Utopianism: The equality/difference dilemma." *Political Studies Association*, Conference Proceedings, University of Ulster (1997): 272–282.

Savage, Michael. "The Juridification of International Law: Sovereignty and International Legal Theory." *Political Studies Association*, Conference Proceedings, University of Nottingham (1999): 1–16.

Seguino, Stephanie. "Why are women in the Caribbean so much more likely than men to be unemployed?" *Social and Economic Studies* 52, no. 4 (December 2003): 83–120.

Sikkink, Kathryn. "Human Rights, Principled Issue-Networks, and Sovereignty in Latin America." *International Organization* 47, no. 3 (Summer 1993): 411–441.

———. "Transnational Politics, International Relations Theory, and Human Rights." *Political Science and Politics* 31, no. 3 (Sept. 1998): 516–523.

Singer, David J. "The Level-of-Analysis Problem in International Relations." *World Politics* 14, no. 1 (October 1961): 77–92.

Smookler, Jennifer. "Feminism, liberal democracy and the politics of inclusion and exclusion." *Political Studies Association*, Conference Proceedings, University of London (2000): 1–13.

Special Edition: "Women in International Relations," *Millennium: Journal of International Studies* 17, no. 3 (Winter 1988).

Spees, Pam. "Women's Advocacy in the Creation of the International Criminal Court: Changing the Landscapes of Justice and Power." *Journal of Women and Culture and Society* 28, no. 4 (2003): 1233–1254.

Squires, Judith and Mark Jones. "New Labour, Gender Mainstreaming and the Women and Equality Unit." *British Journal of Politics and International Relations* 6 (2004): 81–98.

Sohrab, Julia A. "Avoiding the 'Exquisite Trap': A Critical look at the Equal Treatment/Special Treatment Debate in Law." *Feminist Legal Studies* 1 (1993): 141.

Steans, Jill. "Engaging from the Margins: Feminist Encounters with the 'Mainstream' of International Relations." *British Journal of Politics and International Relations* 5, no. 3 (August 2003): 428–454.

Steans, Jill, and Vafa Ahmady. "Negotiating the Politics of Gender and Rights: Some Reflections on the Status of Women's Human Rights at 'Beijing Plus Ten.'" *Global Society* 19, no. 3 (July 2005): 227–245.

Sukhu, Raquel. "Domestic Violence and Power: A War of Words and Fists." *Caribbean Journal of Criminology and Social Psychology*, 5, nos. 1–2 (January–July 2000): 228–236.

Sullivan, Donna. "Women's Human Rights and the 1993 World Conference on Human Rights." *The American Journal of International Law* 88, no. 1 (January 1994): 152–167.

Sylvester, Christine. "Feminist Theory and Gender Studies in International Relations." *International Studies Notes* 16/17, 3/1 (Fall 1991/Winter 1992): 32–38, http://www.isanet.org/sections/ftgs/femir.html.

Tang, Kwong-Leung. "The Leadership Role of International Law in Enforcing Women's Rights." *Gender and Development* 8, no. 3 (November 2000): 65–73.

Tanikella, Leela. "The Politics of Hybridity: Race, Gender, and Nationalism in Trinidad." *Cultural Dynamics* 15, no. 2 (2003): 153–181.

Theodore, Joseph. "Domestic Violence, National Security and Public Policy." *Caribbean Journal of Criminology and Social Psychology* 5, nos. 1–2 (January–July 2000): 189–192.

Thomas, Dorothy, and Michele Beasley. "Domestic Violence as a Human Rights Issue." *Human Rights Quarterly* 15, no. 1 (February 1993): 36–62.

Thomas, Jeremy. "The Intertwining of Law and Theology in the Writings of Grotius." *Journal of the History of International Law* 1 (1999): 61–100.

Tickner, J. Ann. "Continuing the Conversation…." *International Studies Quarterly* 42, no. 1 (1998): 205–210.

———. "Why Women Can't Run the World: International Politics According to Francis Fukuyama." *International Studies Review* 1, no. 3 (1999): 3–11.

———. "You Just Don't Understand: Troubled Engagements Between Feminists and IR Theorists." *International Studies Quarterly* 41 (1997): 611–632.

Tiger, Lionel. "Prehistory Returns." *Foreign Affairs* 78, no. 1 (Jan/Feb 1999): 127–128.

True, Jacqui, and Michael Mintrom. "Transnational Networks and Policy Diffusion: The Case of Gender Mainstreaming." *International Studies Quarterly* 45 (2001): 27–57.

Watson-Brown, Linda, and Graham Dawson. "Misplaced Loyalty: Women and the Politics of Economic Exclusion." *Political Studies Association*, Conference Proceedings, University of Glasgow (1996): 1539–1550.

Walker, Robert B.J. "Security, Sovereignty, and the Challenges of World Politics." *Alternatives* 15 (1990): 3–27.

Wendt, Alexander. "Anarchy is What States Make of It: The Social Construction of Power Politics." *International Organization* 46, no. 2 (Spring 1992): 391–425.

———. "The Agent-Structure Problem in International Relations Theory." *International Organization* 41, no. 3 (Summer 1987): 335–370.

Wharfe, Phyllis. "How Women Manage Their Professional and Personal Lives in a Time of Profound and Rapid Social Change: A Study of Six Trinidadian Women in Midlife." *Dissertation Abstracts International, A: The Humanities and Social Sciences* 65, no. 12 (June 2005): 4723-A.

Whitworth, Sandra. "Gender in the Inter-Paradigm Debate." *Millennium: Journal of International Studies* 18, no. 2 (Summer 1989): 265–272.

Williams, Monica. "Domestic Violence and Family Relationships: Policy Recommendations." *Caribbean Journal of Criminology and Social Psychology* 5, no. 1–2 (January–July 2000): 193–201.

Willetts, Peter. "From "Consultative Arrangements" to "Partnership": The Changing Status of NGOs in Diplomacy at the UN." *Global Governance* 6, no. 2 (Apr–Jun 2000): 191–213.

Windsor, Philip. "Women and International Relations: What's the Problem?" *Millennium: Journal of International Studies* 17, no. 3 (Winter 1988): 451–460.

Zalewski, Marysia. "Well, What is the Feminist Perspective on Bosnia?" *International Affairs* 71, no. 2 (1995): 339–356.

Zellerer, Evelyn. "Domestic Violence in Trinidad and Tobago: Some Comments." *Caribbean Journal of Criminology and Social Psychology* 5, no. 1–2 (January–July 2000): 209–227.

Zheng, Wang. "A Historic Turning Point for the Women's Movement in China." *Signs* 22, no. 1 (Autumn 1996): 192–199.

Newspaper Articles

Ali, Imran. "San Juan man gets 12 years for killing wife." *Saturday Express*, 12 November 2005. Accessed 28 March 2007, http://www.trinidadexpress.com/index.pl/article_news?id=115329965.

Beharry, Prior. "Judge slams 'unholy' draft gender policy: Calls for prayers, protest." *Sunday Express*, 01 May 2005, 3.

Boodan, Adrian. "Kamla: Women's health issues on back burner." *Trinidad Guardian*, 03 September 2007. Accesssed 13 September 2007, http://www.guardian.co.tt/archives/2007-09-03/news9.html.

Booth, Robert. "Woman loses embryos case." *Guardian Unlimited*, 07 March 2006. Accessed 07 March 2006, http://society.guardian.co.uk/health/story/0,,1725427,00.html.

"Domestic violence case training." *Trinidad Express*, 15 September 2004, 22.

Donegan, Lawrence. "The Woman who is taking on Wal-Mart." *The Observer*, 27 June 2004. Accessed 28 June 2004, http://observer.guardian.co.uk/international/story/0,6903,1248204,00.html.

Hassanali, Shaliza. "Legislation planned to help crime victims." *Sunday Guardian*, 13 November 2005. Accessed 29 April 2006, http://www.guardian.co.tt/news10.html.

International Herald Tribune. "Sarkozy names revamped French Cabinet," 18 May 2007. Accessed 25 May 2007, http://www.iht.com/articles/ap/2007/05/18/europe/EU-POL-France-New-Government.php#top.

Jankie, Ariti. "Violence against women rising; Kamla: Govt not doing enough." *Trinidad Express*, 03 September 2007. Accessed 13 September 2007, http://www.trinidadexpress.com/index.pl/article?id=161197866.

John, Rohandra. "Donations rescue Coalition." *Trinidad Express*, 09 March 2006. Accessed 09 March 2006, http://www.trinidadexpress.com/index.pl/article?id=141720535.

———. "How common-law wives came into their own." *Sunday Express*, 22 January 2006. Accessed 21 August 2006, http://www.trinidadexpress.com/index.pl/article_news?id=130196924.

Kissoon, Carol. "Cop ties self to tree, drinks weedicide." *Trinidad Express*, 23 February 2006. Accessed 29 January 2007, http://www.trinidadexpress.com/index.pl/article_news?id=138085395.

Kowlessar, Geisha. "Stormy relationship ends in murder-suicide in Valencia." *Trinidad Guardian*, 03 August 2004. Accessed 29 January 2007, http://www.guardian.co.tt/archives/2004-08-03/news1.html.

Krum, Sharon. "Store Wars." *The Observer*, 02 July 2001. Accessed 28 July 2004, http://www.guardian.co.uk/women/story/0,3604,515455,00.html.

Lord, Richard. "Humanity over sovereignty." *Trinidad Express*, 11 December 2003. Accessed 11 December 2003, http://www.trinidadexpress.com/politics.asp?mylink=2003-12-11%2Fpolitics%2FHumanity%20over%20sovereignty.htm&mydate=2003-12-11&mypage=politics.

Loutoo, Jade. "Toco woman put on $30,000 bond." *Trinidad Guardian*, 04 May 2006. Accessed 22 January 2007, http://www.guardian.co.tt/archives/2006-05-04/news1.html.

Manmohan, Earl. "Tobagonian chops Italian lover to death…kills himself." *Trinidad Express*, 26 January 2007. Accessed 29 January 2007, http://www.trinidadexpress.com/index.pl/article?id=161090340.

Matroo, C. "Gender behaviour changes over time: Yuille-Williams." *Trinidad Guardian*, 22 June 2006, 12.

Meighoo, Kirk. "Leadership and Legitimacy." *Sunday Express*, 24 October 2004. Accessed 03 November 2004, http://www.trinidadexpress.com/index.pl/article_opinion?id=43442127.

Mills, H. "Brown: Support Gender Policy and Action Plan." *Trinidad Express*, 06 March 2006. Accessed 06 March 2006, http://www.trinidadexpress.com/index.pl/article?id=140915241.

Murray, Lucy. "Myanmar's lesson in 'discipline democracy.'" *Asia Times Online*, 17 February 2005. Accessed 27 February 2006, http://www.atimes.com/atimes/Southeast_Asia/GB17Ae01.html.

Paul, A. "A celebration of womanhood." *Trinidad Express*, 09 March 2006. Accessed 09 March 2006, http://www.trinidadexpress.com/index.pl/article?id=141720540.

———. "PM knocked for 'pulling out.'" *Trinidad Express*, 09 March 2006. Accessed 09 March 2006, http://www.trinidadexpress.com/index.pl/article?id=141720543.

Ragoonath, Reshma. "Equality between sexes still and elusive goal." *Sunday Guardian*, 12 September 2004, 13.

———. "Husband killer to serve four years." *Trinidad Guardian*, 06 May 2006. Accessed 22 January 2007, http://www.guardian.co.tt/archives/2006-05-06/news3.html.

———. "Man pleads guilty to strangling wife." *Trinidad Guardian*, 27 May 2005, 8.

Reuters. "Einstein's Theory May Be Relatively Wrong," 08 August 2002. Accessed 13 September 2004, http://edition.cnn.com/2002/WORLD/asiapcf/auspac/08/07/australia.lightspeed/.

Seuraj, Indarjit. "Carmona: Women under siege in this country." *Trinidad Guardian*, 18 January 2007. Accessed 22 January 2007, http://www.guardian.co.tt/archives/2007-01-18/news3.html.

Sookraj, Radhica. "Cop drinks poison after domestic row." *Trinidad Guardian*, 23 February 2006. Accessed 29 January 2007, http://www.guardian.co.tt/archives/2006-02-23/news3.html.

Stapleton, R. "NGOs call for proper accountability systems." *Trinidad Express*, 31 August 2005, http://www.trinidadexpress.com/index.pl/article?id=99102247.

Swamber, Keino. "Guilty of killing wife: sentencing today." *Trinidad Express*, 17 November 2005. Accessed 28 March 2007, http://www.trinidadexpress.com/index.pl/article_news?id=116629552.

———. "Wife pleads but husband lands in jail." *Saturday Express*, 04 February 2006. Accessed 11 April 2007, http://www.trinidadexpress.com/index.pl/article_news?id=133510992.

"When Rape becomes Genocide." *The New York Times*, 05 September 1998. Accessed 16 January 2008, http://query.nytimes.com/gst/fullpage.html?res=990DE3D9163EF936A3575AC0A96E958260.

Wickham, Peter. "Privy Council triumph?" *Trinidad Express*, 23 July 2004, 11.

Online Resources

Alvarez, Sonia. "Advocating Feminism: The Latin American NGO Boom." Accessed 14 October 2007, http://www.antenna.nl/~waterman/alvarez2.html.

Association of Bahái Women. "Gender Studies Forum." Accessed 30 March 2005, http://www.bci.org/abw/ABW/forum/tahe.html.

"Bangalore Principles." Accessed 15 January 2005, http://www.nji.ca/cciawj/Bangalore%20Principles.doc.

Blackstone, William. "Commentaries on the Laws of England (1765–1769)." Accessed 05 February 2008, http://www.lonang.com/exlibris/blackstone/bla-115.htm.

Call, Jeremy. "The Halakhah and its Role in Modern Israeli Law." Accessed 08 April 2005, http://www.law2.byu.edu/lwb/papers/Call-Halakhah_FINAL.PDF.

Caribbean Community (CARICOM) Secretariat. "Charter of Civil Society for the Caribbean Community," updated 2006. Accessed 24 August 2007, http://www.caricom.org/jsp/secretariat/legal_instruments/chartercivilsocietyresolution.jsp?menu=secretariat.

———. "Charter of Civil Society Resolution, 1997," updated 2006. Accessed 24 August 2007, http://www.caricom.org/jsp/secretariat/legal_instruments/chartercivilsociety.jsp.

———. Caricom Secretariat. "Gender and Development Sub-Programme – Elements of the Work Programme 2007/2008," updated 2006. Accessed 10 May 2007, http://www.caricom.org/jsp/community_organs/gender/work_programme.jsp.

Centre for Gender and Development Studies. "About the Centre," 20 March 2007, http://sta.uwi.edu/cgds/aboutus.asp.

———. "Women Development and Studies Group," 20 March 2007, http://sta.uwi.edu/cgds/wdsg.asp.

Centre for Human Rights, University of Pretoria. "African Human Rights Documents," 2005. Accessed February–March 2006, http://www.chr.up.ac.za/hr_docs/docs_country.html.

Center for Women's Global Leadership, the NGO Committee on the Status of Women, and the Women's Environment and Development Organization. "2005 CSW Review of the Beijing Platform for Action (Beijing +10)," April 2004, http://www.peacewomen.org/un/Beijing10%20/NGOCSWBeijing10.html.

Franklin and Eleanor Roosevelt Institute. "Eleanor Roosevelt," 05 August 1998. Accessed 11 October 2007, http://www.udhr.org/history/frbioer.htm.

Global Policy Forum. "NGO Status at the UN," updated December 2000. Accessed 08 July 2005, http://www.globalpolicy.org/ngos/ngo-un/info/status.htm.

Halsall, Paul. "Modern History Sourcebook: The Declaration of Sentiments, Seneca Falls Convention, 1848," November 1998. Accessed 13 June 2004, http://www.fordham.edu/halsall/mod/Senecafalls.html.

Human Rights Commission. "Human Rights in New Zealand Today." Accessed 12 February 2006, http://www.hrc.co.nz/report/chapters/chapter07/life01.html.

Infoplease. "Women Political Leaders – Historical and Current," 2007. Accessed 25 May 2007, http://www.infoplease.com/ipa/A0801534.html.

International Court of Justice. "Statute of the International Court of Justice." Accessed 18 October 2004, http://www.icj-cij.org/icjwww/ibasicdocuments/Basetext/istatute.htm.

International Labour Organization. "Gender Equality Tool." Accessed 13 April 2005, http://www.ilo.org/public/english/bureau/gender/newsite2002/about/defin.htm.

Kirby, Michael. "The Growing Rapprochement Between International and National Law." Essays to honour His Excellency Judge C.J. Weeramantry, 1998. Accessed 15 January 2005, http://www.hcourt.gov.au/speeches/kirbyj/kirbyj_weeram.htm.

Legal Information Institute. "Critical Legal Studies: An Overview." Accessed 08 February 2005, http://www.law.cornell.edu/topics/critical_theory.html.

MAVAW. "MAVAW," 06 April 2006. Accessed 27 February 2007, http://www.mavaw.com/.

Merganthal Jr., Edward R. "Greek & Roman Theatre," 01 December 1998. Accessed 03 November 2004, http://www.geocities.com/Broadway/Balcony/7634/greek_and_roman_theatre.htm.

Naming the Grace. "Early Feminism: Equality, Ethical Theory and Religion." Accessed 13 June 2004, http://www.naminggrace.org/id64.htm.

NationMaster. "Encyclopedia: History of Trinidad and Tobago," 2004. Accessed 12 September 2005, http://www.nationmaster.com/encyclopedia/History-of-Trinidad-and-Tobago.

Nderitu, Terri. "Balancing Pill and Patients: Intellectual Property and the HIV/AIDS Crisis." Accessed 12 January 2007, http://www.murdoch.edu.au/elaw/issues/v8n3/nderitu83nf.html.

Organisation of American States, Inter-American Commission of Women. "Strategic Plan of Action of the Inter-American Commission of Women," 2000. Accessed 02 May 2007, http://www.oas.org/cim/English/Strategic Plan.htm.

Organisation of American States, Inter-American Commission of Women. "Who we are," 2000. Accessed 02 May 2007, http://www.oas.org/cim/English/About.htm.

Parliament of Finland. "Women Members of Finland's Parliament," 08 March 2006. Accessed 25 May 2007, http://www.parliament.fi/efakta/opas/tiedotus/naisede.htm.

Parliament of the Republic of Trindad and Tobago. "Current Members of Parliament." Accessed 16 July 2011, http://www.ttparliament.org/members.php?mid=25.

Phillips, K. "Ancient Greek Theatre." Posted 29 March 2000. Accessed 03 November 2004, http://www.richeast.org/htwm/Greeks/theatre/actors.html.

Schabas, William. "New Perspectives on International Human Rights Law for Administrative Tribunals," 2001, http://www.themis.umontreal.ca/consultation_gratuite/icaj2001/19_schabas.pdf.

Sen, Amartya. "More Than 100 Million Women Are Missing." *New York Review of Books* 37, no. 20 (December 1990), http://ucatlas.ucsc.edu/gender/Sen100M.html.

Sveriges Riksdag. "The Constitution." Accessed 14 April 2006, http://www.riksdagen.se/templates/R_Page____6357.aspx.

The Internet Classics Archive, "Politics by Aristotle." Translated by Benjamin Jowett. Accessed 09 August 2007, http://classics.mit.edu/Aristotle/politics.1.one.html.

Toope, Stephen J. "Inside and Out: The Stories of International Law and Domestic Law." Accessed 15 January 2005, http://www.lawsite.ca/IAWJ/CRToope_e.htm.

Trinidad and Tobago Coalition Against Domestic Violence. "Trinidad and Tobago Coalition Against Domestic Violence." Accessed 25 February 2007, http://www.ttcadv.org/.

University of Colorado. "NGOs," October 2004. Accessed 17 June 2005, http://www.colorado.edu/careerservices/pdf/NGOs.pdf.

University of Richmond, School of Law. "Constitution Finder," 2005. Accessed February–March 2006, http://confinder.richmond.edu.

University of Texas Libraries. "Perry-Castañeda Library Map Collection, Map of Central America and the Caribbean." Accessed 27 April 2005, http://www.lib.utexas.edu/maps/americas/central_america_ref02.jpg.

———. "Perry-Castañeda Library Map Collection, Map of Trinidad and Tobago." Accessed 27 April 2005, http://www.lib.utexas.edu/maps/cia04/trinidad_tobago_sm04.gif.

Reports, Discussion Papers, Lectures, Speeches

Ackerly, Brooke. and B. D'Costa. "Transnational Feminism: Political Strategies and Theoretical Resources." Working paper 2005/1. Australian National University, Canberra: Department of International Relations, 2005.

Alston, Philip. "Reconceiving the UN Human Rights Regime: Challenges Confronting the New UN Human Rights Council." Center for Human Rights and Global Justice Working Paper No. 4. New York: New York University School of Law, 2006.

Amnesty International. "Trinidad and Tobago: Woman sentenced to corporal punishment." March 1996. AMR 49/07/96.

Bernard, Désirée. "Advances made on Gender Equality and Women's Human Rights in the Caribbean Region." 50th Anniversary Commemoration of the United Nations Commission on the Status of Women, United Nations Headquarters, New York, 10 November 2006. Also available from http://www.caribbeancourtofjustice.org/papers_addresses.html.

———. "Confronting Gender-Based Violence in the Caribbean." Fifth Biennial Lucille Mathurin Mair Public Lecture, University of the West Indies, Mona Jamaica, 29 November 2006. Also available from http://www.caribbeancourtofjustice.org/papers_addresses.html.

———. "Employing Strategies to Combat Violence Against Women." Ministry of Community Development, Culture and Gender Affairs Distinguished Lecture and Workshop Series, Queen's Hall, St. Anns, Trinidad, 25 September 2005. Also available from http://www.caribbeancourtofjustice.org/papers_addresses.html.

———. "The Promotion and Enforcement of Women's Human Rights within the Judicial Systems of the Caribbean." Paper presented at the University of the West Indies, Cave Hill, Barbados, 18 November 2005. Also available from http://www.caribbeancourtofjustice.org/papers_addresses.html.

Caribbean Association for Feminist Research and Action. "A Pilot Survey on the Incidences of Violence and Responses to such Violence among 200 randomly selected Women in Trinidad." St. Augustine, Trinidad, 1998.

———. *CAFRA Annual Report 2004*. CAFRA: Tunapuna, Trinidad, 2004.

Centre for Gender and Development Studies. *Research Activity and Output: 1993–2006.* St. Augustine, Trinidad: Centre for Gender and Development Studies, 2006.

Chin, Vivienne, and Yvon Dandurand. *Violence in the Americas: A Regional Analysis. National Programs to Prevent, Punish and Eradicate Violence Against Women in Ten Caribbean Countries*. San Jose: ILANUD, 2001.

Cernea, Michael. *Nongovernmental Organizations and Local Development.* [World Bank Discussion Paper, No. 40]. Washington, D.C.: The World Bank, 1988.

Lazarus-Black, Mindie. "The Rite of Domination: Tales from Domestic Violence Court." Working Paper No. 7. Centre for Gender and Development Studies, The University of the West Indies: St. Augustine, Trinidad, 2002.

Rape Crisis Society of Trinidad and Tobago. *The National Conference on Revisiting Abuse: The Impact on the Individual, Family and National Community.* Rape Crisis Society: Port of Spain, Trinidad, 2005.

United Nations Development Fund for Women/Economic Commission for Latin America and the Caribbean. *Eliminating Gender-Based Violence, Ensuring Equality: UNIFEM/ECLAC Regional Assessment of Actions to End Violence Against Women in the Caribbean.* Christchurch, Barbados: UNIFEM, 2005.

United Nations Development Programme. *National Reports on the Situation of Gender Violence Against Women: National Report – Trinidad and Tobago*. Regional Project RLA/97/014. April 1999.

Women's Environment and Development Organization. *Beijing Betrayed: Women Worldwide Report that Governments have failed to turn the Platform into Action.* New York: Women's Environmental and Development Organization, 2005.

United Nations Documents and Online Resources

Begtrup, Bodil. "Statement made by the Chair of the Subcommission on the Status of Women to ECOSOC recommending that the status of the Subcommission be raised to full Commission." E/PV.4, 28 May 1946.

Phillips, Daphne. "Statement to the Twenty-Third Special Session of the General Assembly entitled "Women 2000: gender equality, development and peace for the twenty-first century."" United Nations General Assembly, New York, 6 June 2000. Accessed 30 April 2007, http://www.un.org/womenwatch/daw/followup/beijing+5stat/statments/trinidad6.htm.

United Nations. "How to Obtain Consultative Status with ECOSOC." Accessed 14 July 2005, http://www.un.org/esa/coordination/ngo/howtoapply.htm.

———. "NGOs in Consultative Status with ECOSOC," 15 March 2005. Accessed 14 July 2005, http://www.un.org/esa/coordination/ngo/pdf/INF_List.pdf.

———. "Report of the Fourth World Conference on Women." A/CONF.177/20, 17 October 1995.

———. "Rwanda International Criminal Tribunal Pronounces Guilty Verdict in Historic Genocide Trial." Press Release AFR/94 L/2895, 02 September 1998. Accessed 16 January 2008, http://www.un.org/News/Press/docs/1998/19980902.afr94.html.

———. *The United Nations and the Advancement of Women 1945–1996.* New York: Department of Public Information, 1996.

———. "United Nations Declaration of Human Rights." Adopted 10 December 1948. In *Basic Documents on Human Rights*, edited by Ian Brownlie. Oxford: Oxford University Press, 1992.

———. "Vienna Declaration and Programme of Action." A/CONF.157/24, 13 October 1993.

United Nations, Commission on the Status of Women. "Functions." Accessed 28 January 2004, http://www.un.org/womenwatch/daw/csw/index.html#functions.

———. "Report of the CSW to ECOSOC on the first session of the Commission, held at Lake Success, New York, from 10 to 24 February 1947." E/281/Rev.1, 25 February 1947.

United Nations, Commission on Human Rights. "Resolution appointing a Special Rapporteur on violence against women." ESCOR, 1994, Suppl. No. 4.

United Nations, Committee on the Elimination of Discrimination Against Women. "Committee on the Elimination of Discrimination Against Women Concludes Consideration of Trinidad and Tobago Report." WOM/1316, 26th Session, 547th Meeting, 29 January 2002.

———. "Compilation of Guidelines on the Form and Content of Reports to be Submitted by States Parties to the International Human Rights Treaties." HRI/GEN/2/Rev.1/Add.2, 5 May 2003.

———. "General Recommendations," 10 February 2005. Accessed 11 April 2005, http://www.un.org/womenwatch/daw/cedaw/recommendations/recomm.htm.

United Nations, Department of Economic and Social Affairs. *The World's Women 2005: Progress in Statistics*. New York: United Nations, 2006.

United Nations, Department of Public Information. "Beijing at Ten: Achieving Gender Equality, Development and Peace." Press Release, DPI/2363F, March 2005.

———. "Focus on Women: UN Action for Women." DPI/1796/Rev.1, May 1996.

———. "Fourth World Conference on Women: Beijing, China, 4–15 September 1995." DPI/1324, February 1993.

———. "From Beijing, a Platform for Action and a clear mandate for women's progress." DPI/1749/WOM, October 1995.

———. "Organization Chart of the United Nations," March 2004. Accessed 04 April 2005, http://www.un.org/aboutun/chart.html.

United Nations, Division for the Advancement of Women. "About DAW: Brief History." Accessed 28 January 2004, http://www.un.org/womenwatch/daw/daw/index.html#history.

———. "About DAW: Mission Statement." Accessed 28 January 2004, http://www.un.org/womenwatch/daw/daw/index.html#mission.

———. "Beijing +5: Process and Beyond." Accessed 28 January 2004, http://www.un.org/womenwatch/daw/followup/bfbeyond.htm.

———. "Committee on the Elimination of Discrimination Against Women," 10 February 2005. Accessed 04 April 2005, http://www.un.org/womenwatch/daw/cedaw/committee.htm.

———. "Declarations, Reservations and Objections to CEDAW," 10 February 2005. Accessed 07 April 2005, http://www.un.org/womenwatch/daw/cedaw/reservations-country.htm.

———. "Optional Protocol to the Convention on the Elimination of All Forms of Discrimination against Women," 10 February 2005. Accessed 11 April 2005, http://www.un.org/womenwatch/daw/cedaw/protocol/.

———. "Optional Protocol to Women's Convention Comes Into Force." Press Release, WOM/1242, 21 December 2000. Accessed 11 April 2005, http://www.un.org/womenwatch/daw/cedaw/protocol/wom1242.htm.

———. "Progress Achieved in the Implementation of the Convention on the Elimination of All Forms of Discrimination Against Women." CEDAW/C/1995/7, 14 November 1994.

———. "Replies to Questionnaire on the Implementation of the Beijing Platform for Action: Trinidad and Tobago," 02 June 1999. Accessed 30 April 2007, http://www.un.org/womenwatch/daw/followup/responses/trinidad.html.

———. "Reporting," 10 February 2005. Accessed 05 April 2005, http://www.un.org/womenwatch/daw/cedaw/reporting.htm.

———. "Reservations to CEDAW," 10 February 2005. Accessed 08 April 2005, http://www.un.org/womenwatch/daw/cedaw/reservations.htm.

———. "Short History of CEDAW Convention," 10 February 2005. Accessed 06 April 2005, http://www.un.org/womenwatch/daw/cedaw/history.htm.

———. "States Parties," 29 March 2005. Accessed 11 April 2005, http://www.un.org/womenwatch/daw/cedaw/states.htm.

———. "What is an Optional Protocol?" 10 February 2005. Accessed 11 April 2005, http://www.un.org/womenwatch/daw/cedaw/protocol/whatis.htm.

———. "Why an Optional Protocol?" 10 February 2005. Accessed 11 April 2005, http://www.un.org/womenwatch/daw/cedaw/protocol/why.htm.

United Nations, Economic and Social Council. "Arrangements for Consultation with Non-Governmental Organizations," 23 May 1968. ECOSOC Resolution 1296 (XLIV). Accessed 08 July 2005, http://www.globalpolicy.org/ngos/ngo-un/info/res-1296.htm.

———. "Consultative Relationship between the United Nations and Non-Governmental Organizations." ECOSOC Resolution 1996/31, 25 July 1996.

———. "Declaration adopted by the Commission on the Status of Women at its forty-ninth session as orally amended." E/CN.6/2005/L.1, 03 March 2005.

———. "ECOSOC Resolution establishing the Commission on the Status of Women (CSW)." E/RES/2/11, 21 June 1946.

———. "ECOSOC resolution requesting the Secretary-General to provide the CSW with communications received concerning the status of women." E/RES/76(V), 5 August 1947.

———. "Follow-up to the Fourth World Conference on Women." Resolution 1996/6, 22 July 1996.

———. "List of non-governmental organizations in consultative status with the Economic and Social Council as of 18 September 2008." E/2008/INF/5. Accessed 14 July 2011, http://www.un.org/esa/coordination/ngo/pdf/INF_List.pdf.

———. "Report of the Economic and Social Council for 1997: Gender Mainstreaming." A/52/3, 18 September 1997.

———. "Resolution adopting the long-term programme of work of the CSW to the year 2000." E/RES/1987/24, 28 May 1987.

———. "Resolution calling for the preparation of a convention on the nationality of a married woman." E/RES/242 C (IX), 1 August 1949.

———. "Resolution calling on Member States to implement the principle of equal pay for work of equal value for men and women workers, irrespective of nationality, race, language or religion." E/RES/121 (VI), 10 March 1948.

———. "Resolution defining the functions of the CSW and requesting Member States to provide the Commission with data on the legal status and treatment of women in their countries." E/RES/48(IV), 29 March 1947.

———. "Resolution establishing the Commission on Human Rights and the Subcommission on the Status of Women." E/RES/5(1), 16 February 1946.

United Nations, Economic and Social Council, Non-Governmental Organizations. "Consultative Status with ECOSOC," 2007. Accessed 26 September 2007, http://www.un.org/esa/coordination/ngo/.

United Nations, Fourth World Conference on Women. "Platform for Action: Critical Areas for Concern." Accessed 28 January 2004, http://www.un.org/womenwatch/daw/beijing/platform/plat1.htm#concern.

———. "Platform for Action: Mission Statement." Accessed 28 January 2004, http://www.un.org/womenwatch/daw/beijing/platform/plat1.htm#statement.

United Nations, General Assembly. "Convention on the Elimination of All Forms of Discrimination Against Women." A/RES/53/118, 05 February 1999.

———. "Declaration on the Elimination of Violence Against Women." A/RES/48/104, 23 February 1994.

———. "Draft Convention and Draft Recommendation on Consent to Marriage, Minimum Age for Marriage and Registration of Marriages." A/RES/1763/ (XVII), 07 November 1962.

———. "Follow-up to the Fourth World Conference on Women and full implementation of the Beijing Declaration and the Platform for Action." A/RES/50/203, 22 December 1995.

———. "Further Actions and Initiatives to Implement the Beijing Declaration and Platform for Action." A/RES/S-23/3, 16 November 2000.

———. "Implementation of the Outcome of the Fourth World Conference on Women: Report of the Secretary General." A/51/322, 03 September 1996. Accessed 08 June 2004, http://www.un.org/documents/ga/docs/51/plenary/a51-322.htm.

———. "Political Declaration." A/RES/S-23/2, 16 November 2000.

———. "Report of the Committee on the Elimination of Discrimination Against Women." A/54/38, 04 May 1999.

———. "Report of the Committee on the Elimination of Discrimination against Women." A/57/38, 14 January-01 February 2002.

———. "Report of the Committee on the Elimination of Violence against Women, forty-forth session (20 July–7 August 2009), forty-fifth session (18 January–5 February 2010)." A/65/38, 11 May 2010.

———. "Report of the Ad Hoc Committee of the Whole of the Twenty-Third Special Session of the General Assembly." A/S-23/10/Rev.1. New York: United Nations, 2000.

———. "Resolution calling on Member States to adopt measures necessary to fulfil the aims of the Charter of the United Nations in granting women the same political rights as men." A/RES/56 (I), 11 December 1946.

———. "Resolution calling on the CSW to complete the draft convention on the elimination of discrimination against women." A/RES/3521 (XXX), 15 December 1975.

———. "Resolution on Implementation of the Nairobi Forward-Looking Strategies and requesting the CSW to complete work on a declaration on the elimination of violence against women." A/RES/47/95, 16 December 1992.

———. "Resolution requesting ECOSOC and the CSW to prepare a draft declaration on the elimination of discrimination against women." A/RES/1921 (XVIII), 05 December 1963.

United Nations, Office of the Special Advisor on Gender Issues and Advancement of Women. "Gender Mainstreaming." Accessed 13 April 2005, http://www.un.org/womenwatch/osagi/gendermainstreaming.htm.

———. "Gender Mainstreaming: Strategy for Promoting Gender Equality," August 2001. Accessed 13 April 2005, http://www.un.org/womenwatch/osagi/pdf/factsheet1.pdf.

———. "The Development of the Gender Mainstreaming Strategy," August 2001. Accessed 13 April 2005, http://www.un.org/womenwatch/osagi/pdf/factsheet3.pdf.

United Nations, Office of the United Nations High Commissioner for Human Rights. "Structure of the United Nations Human Rights Bodies and Mechanisms." Accessed 23 June 2005, http://www.ohchr.org/english/structure_small.htm.

United Nations, Secretary-General. "Report of the Secretary-General to the CSW on the possibility of proposing a convention on the political rights of women." E/CN.6/143, 28 April 1950.

———. "Report to the Committee on the Elimination of Discrimination Against Women: Status of submission of Reports by States Parties under Article 18 of the Convention." CEDAW/C/2005/I/2, 03 December 2004.

———. "Report to the General Assembly on the Convention on the Elimination of All Forms of Discrimination against Women, including the text of the proposed amendment to article 20 of the Convention." A/50/346, 11 August 1995.

———. "Report to the General Assembly on implementation of the outcome of the Fourth World Conference on Women: Action for Equality, Development and Peace." A/50/744, 10 November 1995.

United Nations, Special Rapporteur on Violence. "Preliminary Report to the Commission on Human Rights." E/CN.4/1995/42, 22 November 1994.

United Nations Children's Fund. *The State of the World's Children. Women and Children: The Double Dividend of Gender Equality.* New York: UNICEF, 2006.

United Nations Development Programme. *Human Development Report 2006. Beyond scarcity: Power, poverty and the global water crisis.* New York: UNDP, 2006.

United Nations Development Programme. "Human Development Report 2006: Human Development Indicators. Country Fact Sheets: Trinidad and Tobago." Accessed 06 October 2007, http://hdr.undp.org/hdr2006/statistics/countries/country_fact_sheets/cty_fs_TTO.html.

United Nations Treaty Collection. "Convention on the Elimination of All Forms of Discrimination against Women: Declarations and Reservations," 13 July 2011. Accessed 13 July 2011, http://treaties.un.org/Pages/ViewDetails.aspx?src=TREATY&mtdsg_no=IV-8&chapter=4&lang=en#74.

United States of America. "Open Letter to the Women of the World." Read by Eleanor Roosevelt at the first session of the General Assembly. A/PV.29, 12 February 1946.

UNPUBLISHED WORKS

Interviews

Aird, J.M. *Interview with author*. Curepe, Trinidad, 07 March 2007.
Allen, D. *Interview with author*. Chaguanas, Trinidad, 06 March 2007.
Berment, D. *Interview with author*. St. Augustine, Trinidad, 09 February 2007.
Brathwaite, S. *Interview with author*. St. Augustine, Trinidad, 07 February 2007.
Burgess, J. *Interview with author*. Tunapuna, Trinidad, 24 February 2007.
Clarke, C. *Interview with author*. Port of Spain, Trinidad, 09 February 2007.
Coombs, K. *Interview with author*. Port of Spain, Trinidad, 09 February 2007.
Gibson, I. *Interview with author*. Port of Spain, Trinidad, 26 February 2007.
Gordon, S. *Interview with author*. Scarborough, Tobago, 01 March 2007.
Greyson, J. *Interview with author*. Arima, Trinidad, 12 March 2007.
Hackett, G. *Interview with author*. Port of Spain, Trinidad, 16 March 2007.
Jeelal, V. *Interview with author*. Chaguanas, Trinidad, 22 February 2007.
Joseph, A. *Interview with author*. Scarborough, Tobago, 01 March 2007.
Joseph, G. *Interview with author*. Scarborough, Tobago, 01 March 2007.
Joseph, S. *Interview with author*. Mt. Grace, Tobago, 01 March 2007.
Leith, S. *Interview with author*. Mt. Grace, Tobago, 01 March 2007.
Munroe, A. *Interview with author*. Scarborough, Tobago, 01 March 2007.
Rambachan, B. *Interview with author*. El Socorro, Trinidad, 22 February 2007.
Stewart, B. *Interview with author*. Mt. Grace, Tobago, 01 March 2007.
Talma, J. *Interview with author*. Port of Spain, Trinidad, 07 March 2007.

INTERNATIONAL CONVENTIONS, DECLARATIONS, PROTOCOLS

Charter of Civil Society for the Caribbean Community, October 1992. Available from Internet: http://www.caricom.org/jsp/secretariat/legal_instruments/chartercivilsocietyresolution.jsp?menu=secretariat.
Convention on Consent to Marriage, Minimum Age for Marriage and Registration of Marriages. Adopted 07 November 1962. UN Treaty Series, Vol. 521, No. 7525, 231.
Convention on the Elimination of All Forms of Discrimination Against Women. Adopted 18 December 1979. In *Basic Documents on Human Rights*, edited by Ian Brownlie. Oxford: Oxford University Press, 1992.
Convention on the Nationality of Married Women. Adopted 29 January 1957. UN Treaty Series, Vol. 309, No. 4468, 65.

Convention on the Political Rights of Women. Adopted 20 December 1952. UN Treaty Series, Vol. 193, No. 2613, 135.

Convention for the Suppression of the Traffic in Persons and of the Exploitation of the Prostitution of Others. Adopted 02 December 1949. United Nations Treaty Series, Vol. 96, No. 1342, 271.

Declaration on the Elimination of Discrimination Against Women. A/RES/2263 (XXII), 7 November 1967.

Declaration on the Elimination of Violence Against Women. A/RES/48/104, 20 December 1993.

Inter-American Convention on the Prevention, Punishment, and Eradication of Violence Against Women (Convention of Belém do Pará), 09 June 1994, http://www.oas.org/cim/English/Convention%20Violence%20Against%20Women.htm.

Optional Protocol to the Convention on the Elimination of All Forms of Discrimination against Women. A/RES/54/4, 15 October 1999.

Vienna Convention on the Law of Treaties. Adopted 22 May 1969. Accessed 23 January 2004, http://www.un.org/law/ilc/texts/treaties.htm.

Index

www.ingramcontent.com/pod-product-compliance
Ingram Content Group UK Ltd.
Pitfield, Milton Keynes, MK11 3LW, UK
UKHW041633031026
15587UKWH00001B/253

9 780761 858096